BREAKING THE
CODE OF CHANGE

BREAKING THE CODE OF CHANGE

EDITED BY

Michael Beer
Nitin Nohria

Harvard Business School Press

BOSTON, MASSACHUSETTS

Printed in the United States of America

04   03   02   5   4

Library of Congress Cataloging-in-Publication Data

Breaking the code of change / [edited by] Michael Beer,
Nitin Nohria.
        p. cm.
    Papers from a Summer 1998 conference organized by the
editors and held at the Harvard Business School.
    Includes bibliographical references and index.
    ISBN 1-57851-331-6 (alk. paper)
    1. Organizational   change—Congresses. 2. Leadership—
Congresses. I. Beer, Michael. II. Nohria, Nitin, 1962–

HD58.8 .B735 2000
658.4′06—dc21   00-025425

The editors are contributing their royalties from the sale of this
book to Harvard Business School.

The paper used in this publication meets the requirements of the
American National Standard for Permanence of Paper for Publications and Documents in Libraries and Archives Z39.48-1992.

Contents

SECTION VII

PREFACE AND
ACKNOWLEDGMENTS

T HE DEMANDS of an ever competitive and changing environment are increasing the need for knowledge about how to lead and manage organizational change rapidly, efficiently, and effectively. The management mantra as we enter the twenty-first century is "lead change." The results are not always encouraging, however. The demise of many Fortune 500 companies in the 1980s and 1990s suggests that the leaders of these companies were ineffective in responding to changes in the business environment; they were unable to overcome rigidities in their firms until it was too late. The dramatic reduction in CEO tenure confirms that many leaders do not have the knowledge, the skills, or perhaps the will to transform their companies. Moreover, the rate of failure of many organizational change initiatives—such as Total Quality Management, reengineering, leveraged buyouts, and other efforts to transform organizations and their cultures—suggests that even when the will exists, general managers lack the knowledge to manage change effectively. Efforts to make organizations more efficient and to improve shareholder value do not always result in stronger organizational capability to succeed in the long run. Yet changes in organizational capability and culture are all too often disconnected from the economic and strategic purpose of the firm. Nor are these problems in managing change restricted to large companies undertaking revitalization. Small high-technology companies face severe tests in managing change as they grow and frequently do not survive their first few years of existence.

It is quite understandable that CEOs lack knowledge and skills in managing change. It was not until the 1980s that firms were challenged to globalize, improve shareholder value, increase their quality, speed their response to market changes, or diversify their workforce, for example. It was not until the 1990s that the Internet revolution took hold in full force, giving rise to an unprecedented number of new start-ups. The challenge of change has given rise to a CEO labor market that places a premium on a person's track record in leading change. It has also led to a dramatic increase in the number and variety of consulting firms that advise management on what to change about their business and how to change their organization.

While the need for knowledge about organizational change has risen dramatically, the state of theory, research, and practice is, in our view, relatively undeveloped compared to the enormous need that exists. As we surveyed the state of theory and practice in the field, it seemed to us that underlying the wide array of managerial practice in managing change were dramatically different assumptions about the purpose of and the means for organizational change. If there was a "code" that could unlock our understanding of how change might best be managed, it had not yet been broken. To us breaking the code did not mean finding the one best way to manage change. It meant developing a conceptual framework that would place diverse theories and practices in perspective and help practitioners confront choices among change strategies and types of consultants.

To this end, in the summer of 1998 we organized a research conference at the Harvard Business School called "Breaking the Code of Change." Our purpose was to bring together the best and most experienced scholars and practitioners in organizational change. We wanted them to help us develop a better understanding of what we do know, what we need to know, and how research in this field might proceed. We invited approximately fifty leading scholars from a diverse set of disciplines and countries; twenty-five consultants from leading large and small consulting firms; and six CEOs from different industries and countries, all of whom had led frame-breaking changes in their companies. With the right conference design, we felt, these outstanding minds might enable us to take an important first step in developing an integrative conceptual framework that would inform the question being asked by managers around the world: How do I go about managing change effectively?

The first day was organized around a discussion of three Harvard Business School cases of major and very different organizational change endeavors—Scott Paper, Champion International, and Asda (one of Britain's largest grocery chains). Scott Paper already existed as a case; the other two cases were written specifically for the conference. For each of the cases, the discussion leader asked the question, "Was this change effort successful?" The discussion was lively and very revealing to participants and to us. Dramatically different assumptions about the purpose for and means of organizational change emerged. The CEOs who had led the changes in the cases provided their perspective at the end of each discussion. And at the end of the day, they and the other CEOs present formed a panel that further illuminated the complex choices CEOs face when leading change.

The second day of the conference was devoted to a set of debates about best practice. We chose six key approaches to change that our experience told us were embedded in the three cases and in almost all change efforts. For each practice domain we asked two conference participants to come prepared with arguments and supporting research to defend opposite positions we staked out for them. For example, a debate between Michael Jensen, a leading economist, and Peter Senge, a leading thinker in organizational learning, was about shareholder value as the central purpose and measure of organizational change effectiveness versus organizational learning as the organizing purpose. Warren Bennis and Jay Conger, both scholars and consultants in the area of leadership, debated top-down versus participative change strategies. Economist Karen Wruck and organizational psychologist Gerald Ledford, both experts in compensation, discussed the arguments for monetary incentives used to lead and drive change in behavior versus the arguments for such incentives as a lag and far less central strategy for change. Two noted consultants, Terry Neill from Andersen Consulting and Robert Schaffer from Robert Schaffer & Associates, presented arguments for and against large and small consulting firms' approaches to change management and the very different assumptions about change embedded in their practice. The issues raised by these and other debates were discussed in smaller and larger groups, and a debate moderator put the discussions into perspective.

On the third half day, the conference addressed approaches to researching organizational change. Because organizational change is a field of practice, it seemed to us that a discussion of normal science, the dominant research paradigm of the academy, versus action science, a less pervasive but more action-oriented approach to research in which researcher and management are jointly engaged in inquiry, was warranted. Andrew Van de Ven and Chris Argyris, both noted for their scholarly work in organizational change, debated these positions. The conference ended with a discussion of next steps in research and practice. There was wide agreement that more collaboration between academics on the one hand and practitioners—consultants and CEOs—on the other hand was essential.

The structure of this book reflects the debate structure we created. In the introductory chapter we argue that there are two underlying theories of change reflected in practice today. We call these Theory E (economic value–driven change), and Theory O (organizational capability–driven change). Our formulation of Theories E and O was implicit in the debate structure we created, but was not clearly formulated in advance of the conference. The theories emerged as we listened and reflected on the cases and debates. When we saw leading scholars disagree (sometimes violently) about the relative success or failure of organizational change in a given case and heard them articulate the reasons for their views, our intuition in forming the debates before the conference turned into clear conceptual framework.

The remainder of the book is organized into seven sections, each consisting of two papers by opposing debaters and a chapter by the moderator that presents a synthesis. The book ends with a critique of the conference by Roger Martin and our own epilogue.

The reader should know that we asked each debater to represent a viewpoint with which he or she might not necessarily agree. We wanted to marshal the best arguments and supporting evidence for opposing views and approaches to change. Debaters were not always comfortable with this, but we felt that this structure would lead to more conceptual clarity than does the traditional presentation of participant research papers so often the format at research conferences. We believe, and hope the reader will agree with us, that the result leads to better definition of the paradoxes inherent in choices about how to change organizations.

We chose to call the conference "Breaking the Code of Change" to motivate participants and ourselves to stretch our thinking. We had no illusions that one conference would enable us to achieve the lofty ambition reflected in the conference name. The conference did, however, create a dialogue among academics, consultants, and executives that is all too infrequent and that is needed if the code of change is to be broken. And the diversity of perspectives enabled us to develop the Theory E and Theory O framework, about which we are genuinely excited. This framework will, we hope, aid researchers and practitioners engage the inherent, often unarticulated, tension between enhancing economic value and developing organizational capability as ends and means of change. At the same time we would be pleased if the conference model we developed—case discussion, debates, and substantive discussion by practitioners and academics—offers a new method of inquiry for fields in which theory and practice are tightly intertwined.

Acknowledgments

Many people helped us plan and implement the conference and this volume. To Dexter Dunphy of the University of South Wales and the Center for Corporate Change in Sydney, Australia, goes the credit for motivating the conference in the first place. He organized a conference on organizational change in Sydney in 1995 and saw it as the first in a series. He persisted in motivating us to put on a sequel at the Harvard Business School. Judging by Roger Martin's plan to host "Breaking the Code of Change II" at the University of Toronto in August 2000, Dexter's vision of an ongoing dialogue has become a reality. To Steve Dichter, formerly head of McKinsey & Company's Change Center (no longer in existence), we owe the title of the conference and the book. Steve's experience as a consultant convinced him that efforts to change organizations were both difficult and largely ineffective. He convinced McKinsey that a Change Center at the firm would advance McKinsey's practice. His vision for the center was to break the code—to unravel the mystery of why so many good ideas and methods offered by the best academics and consultants do not "take."

Without the participation of all those who attended the conference, new insights would not have been possible. We thank all who were present for their enthusiastic participation. We owe a special debt to the contributors to this volume, who took the time to develop their views into chapters for the book. Because we wanted to use the conference as a learning vehicle, we did not ask debaters to write chapters in advance, and we had some concerns about obtaining finished chapters. None of our concerns turned out to be merited. Virtually all the authors wrote their chapters well in advance of the deadline, and all received our editorial feedback with an open mind and made revisions accordingly.

Several participants played a special role at the conference. C. K. Prahalad gave a stirring keynote address, highlighting the transformation in organization form that is challenging our assumptions about how to organize and manage business enterprises in the twenty-first century. Stuart Gilson contributed the case on Scott Paper, originally written for a course in finance, and stayed throughout the conference to help us link our interest in organizational change with his interest in financial restructuring. Russell Eisenstat skillfully led one of the case discussions.

We are particularly grateful to the following senior executives who gave us the benefit of their insights. They were: Basil Anderson, executive vice president and CFO, Campbell Soup Company and formerly CFO at Scott Paper; Robert Bauman, former CEO of SmithKline Beecham, who led the SmithKline and Beecham merger and the dramatic organizational changes that followed; Dermot Dunphy, CEO of Sealed Air, who led a very innovative leveraged recapitalization that stimulated a total transformation of the company; Allan Leighton, chief executive at Asda, who played a key role in that company's recovery; Y. Aikin Ongor, president and CEO of Ganantin Bank, a model of organizational innovation and transformation in the Turkish banking industry; Richard Olson, CEO of Champion International, who played a key role in the fundamental transformation of that company's organization and culture over a ten-year period; and Mark Childers, Champion's chief human resources officer, who played an important supporting role. Thanks also to Archie Norman, former chief executive of Asda Group Plc, who, with Allan Leighton, led the remarkable transformation of Asda from near bankruptcy to industry leadership.

He could not be at the conference but supported the conference by giving us time for the development of the Asda case.

Many individuals at the Harvard Business School worked behind the scenes to make the conference and the book possible. Very special thanks go to Jim Weber, our research assistant on this project, who played a key role in helping us with the conference. He wrote the cases we discussed, helped with the organization leading up to the conference, and helped with the introductory chapter. David Ager, Edith Greenblatt, Martine Haas, Misiek Piskorski, Mike Raynor, and Andy Zelleke, doctoral students at the school, helped us extensively by taking notes of the debates and providing excellent summaries. Special thanks to Misiek Piskorski, who devoted a considerable amount of time to developing a Web site where conference participants could post views and continue the debate during and after the conference. Jacqueline Baugher, in executive education, did her usual masterful job in providing the necessary administrative support for a large conference. Finally, without the excellent work of our administrative assistants, Kimberly Sharp, who helped extensively with the conference and the manuscript, and Diana Line and Joan McDonald, who supported us in many other ways, this book would never have come into being.

The Division of Research of the Harvard Business School, led by Dwight Crane at the time we were planning the conference, funded the conference and the editorial work that has gone into this book. We are also grateful to the Harvard Business School Press and in particular to Lindsay Whitman, the editor for this project, for help in making this edited volume possible.

BREAKING THE
CODE OF CHANGE

RESOLVING THE TENSION BETWEEN THEORIES E AND O OF CHANGE

Michael Beer and Nitin Nohria

W E LIVE in a world in which the nature of organizations and the practice of management are being profoundly changed. Most people accept that we are living through a period of great business turmoil. And most managers and organizations have accepted Tom Peter's dictum that they must "change or die." Yet although executives, consultants, financial analysts, and academics all agree that change is a constant in today's world, they have very different views on the process by which underperforming mature companies ought to be changed. An integrated theory or framework for understanding change does not exist. Academics and consultants often give very different and contradictory advice. Economists recommend the use of incentives tied to shareholder value as the motivating force for change, whereas academics in the field of organization behavior recommend high employee involvement to motivate change and develop a high-commitment culture. Large management consulting firms employ legions of bright M.B.A.s to analyze a company and recommend a new strategy and structure, whereas smaller consulting firms believe that the client's management must be involved in analyzing the problem and deciding on what has to change. They aim to help the client through a process that surfaces difficult issues and makes them discussible, not to provide the expertise large management consulting firms see as their distinctive contribution. Not surprisingly, the lack of a widely agreed-upon approach leads to considerable variance in the outcomes of change initiatives. Most such initiatives—be they downsizing, restructuring, the introduction of new technology, or efforts to change the corporate culture—have very low success rates. Research suggests that only a third of these initiatives achieve any success at all.[1]

Given companies' acute need for change and the significant human and economic toll that accompanies any effort to change, we think it is imperative to create some knowledge and understanding that helps us improve the odds of success. If we can find ways to help managers and organizations more effectively manage the process of change, we cannot only enhance firm performance but increase employee well-being and reduce the economic anxiety that has gripped so many societies. In short, there are huge payoffs from producing usable knowledge about the process of change.

The 1998 "Breaking the Code of Change" conference at the Harvard Business School was a first step in an intellectual journey that we hope may ultimately unlock our understanding of organizational change. Our main purpose at the conference was to identify the key considerations in choosing among different change strategies in the transformation of large underperforming companies. This is the change task that many American corporations have confronted in the last decade. While many of these companies must now deal with the consequences of change strategies they have chosen, the pressure to change and the choice of a change strategy faces companies in Europe, Africa, South America, Japan, and the rest of Asia. As these companies struggle to become competitive, should they follow the example of Scott Paper, a company that delivered a rapid turnaround in shareholder value under the leadership of CEO Al Dunlap? Should they follow the change process of Champion International, a paper company in a different segment of the industry, which over a decade dramatically changed its organizational capability and culture? Or should they follow the example of the British grocery chain Asda, which was led by Archie Norman and Allan Leighton through a very successful turnaround?[2]

Although the conference focused principally on the problem of changing large established corporations buffeted by competitive pressures, the conceptual framework that we present in this chapter can also apply to smaller and fast-growing technology and information-age companies. These firms do not face the problem of reversing the erosion of shareholder value. Instead they face the challenges that accompany rapid growth. At the end of this chapter we will discuss how managers of these fast-growing smaller firms might apply our theoretical framework.

Theories E and O of Change

Two dramatically different approaches to organizational change are being employed in the world today, according to our observations, research, and experience. We call these Theory E and Theory O of change. Like all managerial action, these approaches are guided by very different assumptions by corporate leaders about the purpose of and means for change. In effect these two approaches to organizational change represent theories in use by senior executives and the consultants and academics who advise them. By "theory in use" we mean an implicit theory that one can deduce from examining the strategies for change employed.

Theory E has as its purpose the creation of economic value, often expressed as shareholder value. Its focus is on formal structure and systems. It is driven from the top with extensive help from consultants and financial incentives. Change is planned and programmatic.

Theory O has as its purpose the development of the organization's human capability to implement strategy and to learn from actions taken about the effectiveness of changes made. Its focus is on the development of a high-commitment culture. Its means consist of high involvement, and consultants and incentives are relied on far less to drive change. Change is emergent, less planned and programmatic.

Table I-1 summarizes the E and O approaches to organizational change. In the remainder of this chapter we will present Theories E and O in more detail and discuss their benefits and costs. These theories are archetypes. Certain companies, including Scott Paper and Champion International, about which we developed cases, seem to be pure cases of these archetypes. An examination of many other organizations will show a mixture of these strategies, often in uneasy coexistence. We argue that both theories have validity. That is, each of them

Table I-1
Theories E and O of Change

Purpose and Means	Theory E	Theory O
Purpose	Maximize economic value	Develop organizational capabilities
Leadership	Top-down	Participative
Focus	Structure and systems	Culture
Planning	Programmatic	Emergent
Motivation	Incentives lead	Incentives lag
Consultants	Large/knowledge-driven	Small/process-driven

does promote some objectives that management explicitly or implicitly intends to achieve. But each also has costs, often unintended. The problem managers face is resolving the tension between E and O in a way that obtains the benefits of each and minimizes the negative consequences of each. Too often, these theories are mixed without the resolution of the inherent tension between them. This leads, we argue, to maximization of the costs and minimization of the potential benefits of each theory. The objective, we argue, should be to integrate these theories and their strategies in a way that resolves the tension between them. One of our goals in this book is to help academics from different fields frame research questions in a way that will lead to an integrative theory of change. Such a theory would clarify the trade-offs between different approaches to change and would aid in defining choices and consequences. This integration, we argue, is essential if executives want to develop business organizations that satisfy shareholders and yet have the capacity to adapt and survive as viable institutions in the long run.

Theory E

In 1994 Al Dunlap became CEO of troubled Scott Paper. Like Champion International, a comparison company we will discuss as an example of Theory O change, Scott Paper operated in a highly competitive, cyclical, capital-intensive global industry. Like Champion International, it operated in two different segments of the paper industry and had several businesses in markets related to its core consumer package paper business.[3]

Throughout the tenure of Dunlap's predecessor, Phillip Lippincott, Scott had struggled to improve its operational effectiveness at the plant level by working on process improvement and launching an effort to work cooperatively with its union. In the 1980s the company had also initiated layoffs aimed at reducing overhead, and it was planning an additional layoff of 8,300 employees at the time Dunlap took over. At the same time it invested in new paper machines and attempted to consolidate its global position by acquiring several foreign subsidiaries and fashioning a worldwide organization. Despite these efforts and occasional spurts of good financial performance, the company's returns to shareholders remained low and well below the cost of capital. Over an extended period of time, Scott Paper had managed to destroy wealth. This was despite Lippincott's awareness of the need to provide shareholder returns in excess of the cost of capital.

When Dunlap took over the leadership of the company, he immediately announced and implemented a reduction of 11,000 people at both the management and working levels. He fired many members of the existing top management team. Not long after these initial steps, Dunlap sold off several businesses, retaining for the time being the core consumer products business. He moved the head office out of Scott's longtime corporate building and into a much smaller building near his home in Florida.

The executives Dunlap retained and those he brought in to fill the vacancies he had created needed to sign on to his philosophy: that shareholder value was the single objective to which a corporation should dedicate itself. To focus executives single-mindedly on shareholder interests, he used financial incentives, mainly stock options. Dunlap's own compensation package (which ultimately netted him more than $100 million) was also tightly linked to shareholders' interests.

Dunlap's actions restored Scott Paper's profitability. But its long-run viability as an independent business in an industry with significant overcapacity was yet uncertain. Thus, in a last dramatic act, Dunlap sold Scott Paper to Kimberly-Clark, its longtime competitor. Even though Scott Paper ceased to exist as an independent company, the results from a shareholder perspective were stunning. In just fifteen months Dunlap had managed to increase total shareholder return by 200 percent, making rich not only shareholders but numerous employees (including himself and many top managers he fired), whose stock obtained through options increased in value dramatically. The financial community applauded these efforts and saw the Scott Paper story as a good example of what could be done in other companies to improve returns for shareholders.

The story of Scott Paper illustrates the Theory E pattern of organizational changes carried out in many large underperforming corporations in the United States. We argue that the purpose of and means for change that characterized these Theory E companies were the following.

Purpose: A Singular Focus on Economic Value

Much of what happened at Scott Paper and at companies that have employed a similar pattern of change can be explained by the CEO's singular focus on shareholder value. In speeches Dunlap gave he was fond of saying: "Shareholders are the number one constituency. Show me an annual report that lists six or seven constituencies and I'll show you a mismanaged company."

Dunlap echoes economists such as Michael Jensen (see chapter 1), and Milton Friedman before him, who argue that the sole ethically justifiable contribution of corporations to society is to produce profits and economic value. Markets are the best arbiters of the many trade-offs business leaders face—not leaders' own judgments, colored as they may be by personal and political considerations. Moreover, more than one objective function (or constituency, in Al Dunlap's term) distracts executives from achieving the only objective function that ultimately matters. Jensen's research has shown that many top managers have destroyed wealth and that in the long run the many constituencies executives care about are disadvantaged. Phil Lippincott, former CEO of Scott Paper, knew that his firm needed to earn above the cost of capital; but somehow, despite his best intentions, it didn't happen. It is too easy, Jensen argues, to be distracted for political and psychological reasons. Defensive routines can cause managers to rationalize decisions that suboptimize economic return. A single objective function focuses the minds of both top management and lower-level employees. In the end, Jensen argues, markets will punish firms that do not appropriately consider the economic value of commitment from employees, customers, and communities. As a result, managers should be motivated by shareholder value goals to make the appropriate trade-off decisions. There is no need for other goals.

Leadership: Top-Down

Leaders who subscribe to Theory E manage change from the top down. Such leaders set goals based on the expectations of financial markets. They typically do not involve their management team, and certainly not lower employee levels or unions, in discussing and arriving at consensus about goals and means. Dunlap was the clear commander in chief at Scott Paper. Most of the other employees were simply charged with implementing his commands, not with participating in making strategic choices. As an executive engaged in a merger of two global companies driven by economic value said to one of the authors recently, "I have a goal of $176 million this year and there is no time to involve others or develop organizational capability."

Proponents of Theory E argue that a top-down leadership approach makes sense when a firm is in the throes of forces that can destroy it. Employing the military metaphor, Jay Conger (see chapter 4), argues that only generals have a view of the total battlefield. That is, only CEOs can make the kinds of strategic decisions on restructuring, information technology, and reengineering initiatives companies need to survive in a turbulent world. The capital requirements for these initiatives are simply too big and the implications too profound for lower-level managers to make the decisions. And the incremental change decisions lower-level managers can make are simply not enough anymore. Moreover, in many change situations, leaders do not have the time it takes to build consensus through participation. Speed is of the essence, and it is faster for one person—the leader—to make the decisions and for others to implement them.

Focus: Structure and Systems

Leaders in predominantly Theory E–driven change efforts focus first on changing strategies, structures, and systems—the "hardware" of the organization. These are elements that can readily be changed from the top down to yield quick financial results. Virtually all of Dunlap's actions were focused on restructuring in the sense of reducing the size and structure of central headquarters and selling businesses and assets.

Little formal attention was paid to attitudes or behavior—the "software" of the organization.

Jay Galbraith, a noted researcher and scholar in the field of organizational design, supports this initial focus on the hardware of the organization. He argues (see chapter 7) that the strategic shifts firms need to make these days can be accomplished only through the use of powerful managerial levers like structure and systems. For example, reorienting a firm from a functional or country orientation to a customer or market orientation demands a shift in power. Product, customer, or market managers must have the power to allocate resources according to the dictates of the horizontal segment of the business they manage. By starting with structure and systems, leaders can spell out decision rights clearly and quickly.

Planning: Planned and Programmatic

Theory E change strategies tend to be driven by the expectations of the marketplace. It is not surprising, therefore, that financial goals and programs to achieve them dominate the agenda. Capital market expectations force a short and tight schedule for change. It is helpful to communicate to both internal and external constituencies a clear plan of change that sets out the various stages in which restructuring will occur. A well-sequenced, carefully planned change effort facilitates internal coordination and inspires external confidence.

Theory E change strategies are based on the view that a general fighting a battle for survival of the firm is unlikely to succeed without a comprehensive battle plan controlled from the top. Citing their research at General Electric and other companies, Sumantra Ghoshal and Christopher Bartlett (see chapter 10) argue that CEOs who manage an economic turnaround do it by following a clear sequential plan. The first step is shaking up the firm's portfolio of businesses and ensuring that each is doing what it needs to do to survive and prosper. These efforts cannot be allowed to emerge from below according to the timing and objectives of lower-level managers. Indeed, imposing a plan is a way to motivate action and force tough decisions that have not been made in the past. And programs driven by smart staff groups and consultants, who typically support the CEO's turnaround efforts, should be established to equip lower-level managers with the knowledge and solutions they must have lacked, given past failures in performance. The next step in the change plan is to find ways of integrating high-performing individual business units, a process that requires a different set of hardware and software levers than did the first stage. Like other proponents of a Theory E approach, Ghoshal and Bartlett argue that a well-choreographed plan of change is more likely to yield results than are change efforts that are more spontaneous and emergent.

Motivation: Financial Incentives

Theory E changes rely heavily on financial incentives to motivate the singular focus on creating economic value. In the 1990s the percentage of compensation plans employing financial incentives rose sharply.[4] According to agency theory developed by economists such as Michael Jensen and Karen Wruck (see chapters 1 and 13), incentives that align the interests of management and shareholders are essential for change to occur.

These financial incentives have symbolic and motivational value. Getting the incentives right, Wruck argues, is the key to getting managers' attention and focusing them on the right things. Without these incentives, managers are likely to be overtaken by too many distractions and extraneous considerations. Even if other ways can ultimately be found to move managers toward the best economic decisions, financial incentives will ensure that these decisions will not be derailed by personal and political considerations. Moreover, Wruck contends that these incentives are also essential to give top executives the sense that they are being rewarded fairly for a difficult job for which they are often reviled by employees and the larger community.[5] Without substantial executive incentives, why would anyone in his or her right mind take on the job of leading an economic recovery?

Consultants: Large Firms with Superior Knowledge and Solutions

To achieve rapid and extraordinary improvements in economic value, companies often hire large consulting firms in multimillion-dollar engagements to bring in the motivation and knowledge employees are thought to lack. In 1997 AT&T was reported to have spent $200 million on consultants. Armed with the latest analytic methods and a large cadre of very smart people, consulting firms often drive change by infusing the company with new ways to look at their business and new methods for managing it. Consulting firms help new CEOs who are uncertain of employee support and capability, and they offer important political cover to existing CEOs under fire from financial markets for the underperformance of their companies.[6]

The merits of such large-scale interventions are spelled out by Terry Neill, head of Andersen Consulting's worldwide change management practice, in chapter 16. Neill and Mindrum maintain that an organization can substantially improve its performance only by simultaneously changing various facets of a nested social system. Strategy changes must be accompanied by changes in a host of other systems, or the change will fail. Neill also believes that clients can benefit from the substantive expertise and knowledge that consulting firms such as Andersen bring to the table. Most organizations, the argument goes, have a limited view of management research and best practice. This is because companies don't have a natural incentive to accumulate such knowledge, whereas consulting firms have every incentive to do so.

In the 1990s the Theory E perspective became the dominant model of change in the United States. It is also beginning to penetrate management practice in other parts of the world, particularly in Europe. Among the most important reasons are powerful and increasingly efficient capital markets. A global financial system is making the performance of corporations instantly accessible to investors, and investors increasingly are large financial institutions whose fund managers must show good performance. Pressure from financial markets in turn places pressures on firms and their boards for rapid change. Often boards respond to this push for change by changing the leadership of the firm. A clear manifestation is the historically high rate of CEO turnover in recent years.[7]

In the face of pressures for short-term performance improvements, and fearing failure for which they could be fired, CEOs are logically drawn to restructuring and layoffs. The psychological makeup required for this task makes it more likely that CEOs implementing Theory E change will possess the values and skills of the turnaround artist, not the institution builder. Dunlap at Scott Paper, probably the most extreme example of this pattern, illustrates the point. He is a person who enjoys the nature of the E game. Many other CEOs, perhaps not intrinsically so inclined, are drawn into the E style by a complicated process. Forced by circumstance to make tough restructuring decisions, they distance themselves from the organization and its people; it is simply too painful otherwise. Once distant, these new CEOs feel they cannot rely on existing employees, whom they see as part of the problem, to identify problems or propose creative new solutions.

Given this context it is not surprising that new CEOs, or incumbent CEOs who have determined they must do something drastic, see large consulting firms with armies of smart people as essential allies in what they expect will be a struggle with resistant employees. Indeed, consulting firms enable such CEOs to delegate painful and difficult change. This is precisely how Eberhardt von Kerber, the new president of ABB Germany, saw the value added by McKinsey and Andersen Consulting and other consulting firms he hired to help him turn around a company with what he perceived to be highly resistant managers and a combative labor force and union.[8] Moreover, a plethora of new technology and of new management knowledge and practice, touted as the reason for successful turnarounds of competitors, also attracts top management to consulting firms that have knowledge about new practices.

As CEOs distance themselves by these means, they rationalize big incentives as a just reward, particularly as they see the compensation of other CEOs rising. Pressure for performance is also a justification. Financial incentives provide a quick way to establish motivation and alignment among senior managers. The discrepancy that emerges between top management's incentives compensation and the fate of lower-level employee's layoffs and employment further disconnects senior executives from the people in the organization. Becoming disconnected from the people makes it easier for top management increasingly to see the firm as an economic institution only and to ignore its human side and purpose. Developing a partnership with employees and developing organizational and human capability becomes more difficult when one is in E mode. Moreover, CEOs who are attracted to the E role probably tend not to be individuals with the values or skills to lead a change from a Theory O perspective, which calls for a fundamental transformation in the organization and in the commitment of its people.

In summary, we argue that once a CEO defines the singular purpose of change as increasing economic value, a series of forces are typically unleashed that lead the CEO to choose the cluster of strategies we are calling Theory E. Later we will argue that this choice need not be inevitable—indeed, that it may not be the optimum approach; but it is clear that many companies exposed to the powerful pressure of the market for corporate control find themselves following the Theory E path.

The arguments offered by scholars and practitioners of Theory E change strategies are persuasive and are supported by the experience of the 1990s. It may seem hard to argue against the enormous success that American firms have had using Theory E change strategies without appearing somewhat foolish. Nevertheless, what are the arguments and the evidence against Theory E change? These will become clear as we describe Theory O change strategies.

Theory O

In response to poor performance, a decade of adversarial relations with unions, and a prolonged and costly mill strike, CEO Andrew Sigler of Champion International launched an organizational change effort in 1981. It was designed to alter fundamentally the culture and behavior of management, unions, and workers. Sigler gathered his top executives to develop a vision of the new Champion called the Champion Way. "The Champion Way statements described a vision and values for the company and how it would relate to its stakeholders. Key values included involvement of all employees in improving the company, fair treatment of workers, support for the community around its plants, and openness and truthfulness in the company."[9]

Unlike the vision statements of some companies, the Champion Way document did not remain an inert reminder of management's failure to translate its words into action. In the years that followed, Champion's management orchestrated one of the most effective organization development efforts we have seen in several decades. With the help of a few very talented organization development consultants, Champion was able to use a high-involvement method called socio-technical redesign to change its approach to organizing and managing people in all of its plants. The transformation effort started with a few new plants and by the early 1990s included all of Champion's operations.

To support these changes Champion improved its relations with its unions through cooperative mechanisms. It applied the same high-involvement sociotechnical method to redesign the organization and management of all its corporate functions, including research and development. And by the early 1990s the corporation had completely reorganized itself around a market by function matrix structure intended to focus on customers. Compensation systems were aligned with culture change objectives. A skill-based pay system was installed in all production facilities to encourage employees to learn multiple skills. A corporationwide gains-sharing plan was introduced to mold union workers and management into a common community of purpose. Throughout the decade of change, there were no layoffs, although many managers at the plant and corporate level were replaced if their management style did not fit the new philosophy.

By 1997 employee surveys and productivity data clearly showed that Champion had achieved the cultural transformation embodied in the Champion Way. Nevertheless, new CEO Richard Olson was faced with an uncomfortable reality. Though the company had survived a difficult economic period and had improved its performance along several key operational indicators (such as plant yields, quality, etc.), the company's shareholders had not seen a significant increase in the economic value of the firm. Champion's share price had not only failed to keep pace with the S&P 500 index; it had failed to keep pace with companies in its own industry. Return on assets, return on equity, return on sales, and sales per employee were all below those of comparison companies in the paper industry.

Champion International is an archetype of Theory O change. Below we describe the purpose and means of this change theory.

Purpose: Developing Organization Capabilities

The purpose of Theory O change efforts is to develop organizational capabilities, particularly the capability of employees to become involved in identifying and solving work-related problems. The objective is to create a work system in which employees become emotionally committed to improving the performance of the firm. By focusing on the effectiveness and efficiency with which work is carried out at every level, leaders of these change efforts believe, the firm will enhance its economic value.

Theory O proponents such as Peter Senge (see chapter 2) argue that making economic value the singular objective function in managing change is mistaken even though the objective itself is right and appropriate. Using system dynamics theory, Senge argues that organizations are nonlinear dynamic systems in which there are many unintended consequences when direct linear action is taken. By setting economic goals at the top, management may actually prevent the company from discovering the factors that may be critical to its economic health. Serge argues for building organizational capability to learn.

Though they don't place shareholder returns at the top of their agenda, proponents of Theory O change believe that a healthy "learning organization" is the best way to meet shareholder interests in the long run. In their desire to maintain social and psychological contracts, Theory O managers try to avoid the radical restructuring and layoffs we see in E-driven change efforts.

Leadership: Participative

High levels of involvement and collaboration characterize Theory O change. Top teams are jointly involved in drafting value statements. Unions are brought into a dialogue at every level. Employees are involved in identifying problems and solving them. As Warren Bennis argues (see chapter 5), the underlying assumption is that involvement is essential for building the partnership, trust, and commitment thought to be vital for long-term performance improvements.

Participation, rather than top-down change, is key if one assumes that most information is widely held in the organization. Top management is farthest away from customers and operations. Moreover, information about barriers to achieving top management's goals are not likely to be communicated upward in a firm managed strictly from the top down.[10]

Focus: Culture

A focus on values and behavior, as at Champion, is the hallmark of all O-driven change strategies. Top management typically articulates a set of values or principles—such as the Champion Way—that it hopes will inform the corporate culture and guide the behavior of employees.

The emphasis is on values intended to create emotional attachment. Emotional attachment is thought to be critical to commitment. If commitment is developed, then hierarchical control will be unnecessary. Champion banked on commitment to drive performance improvements.

Proponents of Theory O maintain that an emphasis on structure and systems, particularly if imposed from the top, will not achieve fundamental change. The exceptions may be self-imposed and self-designed structures and systems at the unit level. But corporate decisions about structure and systems for local units are unlikely to take into account employees' tacit knowledge about problems in enacting the strategy at the local level. Furthermore, as Larry Hirschhorn points out (see chapter 8), employees invest structure and systems with moral meaning. So the change problem is one of changing culture— belief systems and values that over time have given structure and systems legitimacy. Simply changing structure and systems does not change culture. Cultural change requires management to engage people emotionally in examining why the existing structure and systems are not meeting the new challenges confronting the organization.[11] This examination process, which Hirschhorn calls creating a counter-structure, provides a safe way to mobilize aggression against the current order while at the same time building a new psychological contract between management and employees.

Planning: Nonprogrammatic and Emergent

Champion's change effort spanned well over a decade. There was no master blueprint for it in 1981; in effect, experiences in one plant led to attempts to replicate these changes in other new and old plants and then in corporate functions. There was no single total quality or cultural change program. As a result of this pattern, local leaders took responsibility for change, and top management and corporate staff groups had less power than in typical Theory E change efforts. At Champion it is hard to identify any single individual as the change champion. Unlike Dunlap at Scott Paper, who appeared to be the person behind most changes, Sigler was not the primary driver of change at Champion, despite the fact that he initiated the change process with the creation of the Champion Way.

Proponents of a Theory O approach such as Karl Weick (see chapter 11) suggest that the apparent success of the centrally planned change efforts favored by Theory E may well be illusory. We tend to attribute success in change to high-profile initiatives, but these rarely change the underlying fabric of the organization. Organizations are constantly changing as a result of continuous local experimentation. Why not, therefore, amplify this natural dynamic in organizations by encouraging experimentation and using it effectively to promote learning in the rest of the organization?[12] Again, top management is too distant from the level where employees meet customers and confront the task of creating a profitable enterprise. Executives are best advised, this argument goes, to create a context for local experimentation and to work hard to diffuse innovations by exposing people to what has been learned and by transferring managers from innovative units to lagging units. This more emergent, ground-up process is viewed as being more likely to yield lasting change than a centrally planned programmatic process.

Motivation: Financial Incentives as Lagging, Not Driving, Change

An O strategy of change typically places less emphasis on financial incentives, particularly individual incentives. The assumption is that people are motivated by the way management involves them in the essential questions facing the enterprise (see Roger Martin's discussion in chapter 22). Financial incentives are used as a supplementary mechanism. At Champion, skills-based pay systems were used to support high involvement and teamwork, not to drive it. The driving mechanisms included reorganization of work and changes in management style. The power of Champion's change strategy lay in the company's engaging people at every level in redefining the nature of work, thereby creating commitment to the new arrangements. A gains-sharing plan was used to seal and reinforce the sense of community, not to motivate particular behaviors. Champion did use a corporation-wide financial bonus to motivate the achievement of goals in two separate years, but this occurred very late in the transformation process and played a minor role.

Proponents of a Theory O approach accept that money is important, of course. There is no question that money moves people; but that is not the same as motivating them—as engaging them emotionally. Incentive-driven strategies for change undoubtedly obtain eager compliance, but compliance is not commitment. Moreover, as Gerald Ledford argues (see chapter 14), an incentives-led change strategy requires executives to understand the strategy and behavior they require from managers and workers very early in the process of change. Getting the strategic direction right so early, Ledford contends, is rarely possible. The proper strategy and required behaviors are more often discovered in the process of change. Locking in an incentive scheme early will inevitably lead to a need to change it. But changing incentives once they have been announced may lead employees to feel that a trust has been broken, thereby undermining management's moral authority and rupturing the cultural fabric that Hirschhorn argues must undergird sustained commitment to change. Based on these arguments, Ledford suggests that it is best to use incentives later in a change process, as Sigler did at Champion, to reinforce emergent behavior, rather than to use incentives early, as Al Dunlap did at Scott, to drive behavior.

Consultants: Small, Process-Oriented Firms

Unlike companies that use large consulting firms to assist with Theory E transformations, Champion utilized a handful of organization development consultants who introduced the high-involvement sociotechnical method of change. The consultants helped set up a process by which managers and workers then made their own analysis of the situation and crafted their own solutions. The consultants' role was to facilitate the process and be a resource. Although the consultants came with certain values and ideas about what makes an effective human organization, they did not recommend a corporationwide program by which top management should implement their ideas. They relied on managing a process of discovery and learning.

It is not hard to see why Theory O change requires a different consulting model; namely, the process consulting model seen at Champion rather than the expert consulting model typical of Theory E change. If beliefs and values need to change, if change emerges from employee participation in solving problems, if the objective of change is to create a learning organization, then large consulting firms staffed by smart people delivering elegant packaged solutions will not work. And Robert Schaffer (see chapter 17) argues that such packaged solutions are rarely successful in getting results. Their failure lies not in the quality of the prescribed solution but in the organization's capacity to enact it. Schaffer argues for much smaller projects aimed at obtaining measurable results. Consultants do not bring in the solution. They lead relevant organizational members through a process of analysis, redesign, and change. In this process the commitment and capability needed to enact the solution are developed. That is precisely how a handful of consultants at Champion managed to foster the cultural transformation that Schaffer argues often eludes larger consulting firms, focused as they are on injecting superior knowledge and solutions into the organization.

Theory O change strategies are far less pervasive as pure types than Theory E change strategies, particularly in the United States. The increasingly powerful market for corporate control within which American firms, in particular, operate makes it difficult for many companies to adopt an O strategy. Hard seems to be driving out soft.

Firms that do adopt Theory O strategies are often those that have strong, long-held psychological contracts with their employees. Such firms' management is more likely to see the risks in breaking those contracts. Their leaders also possess different assumptions about the purpose of the firm and the means for change. For example, when Hewlett-Packard's performance flagged during the mid-1980s, the company did not turn to an E strategy. Instead, its management articulated their values and involved their people in the problem of change.[13] They avoided layoffs through extensive relocation efforts. Japanese firms and European firms, with a few recent exceptions, have shown the same reluctance to apply Theory E change. The value they see in employee commitment motivates them to resist the Theory E approach. As Hewlett-Packard's former CEO Lou Platt has said, without people's commitment everything becomes more difficult. Platt regards HP's people and their commitment as a source of competitive advantage.

As with Theory E changes, the various elements of Theory O change strategies seem to cluster together. The assumption that the purpose of the firm is to build shared-destiny relationships with multiple stakeholders rather than to focus on shareholder value alone naturally leads to engagement with employees, unions, suppliers, and customers as well as with shareholders. Because management recognizes that commitment cannot be developed by decree from the top, Theory O firms rely far less on central planning. Local innovation in product and organizational arrangements are allowed to flourish. For the same reason, these firms focus less on top-down changes in structure and systems to drive change. Similarly, they tend to use incentives and consultants to support an emergent process of change, rather than to drive a programmatic plan of change.

But leaders with Theory O inclinations have to be very strong in their convictions to withstand the pressures to move to Theory E change. Consider the case of Hewlett-Packard. For nearly sixty years HP never employed financial incentives to motivate senior executives. No bonus system existed, and all employees were eligible for stock options. But in 1997, for the first time in its history, HP instituted an executive incentive scheme for its top forty or so managers. The reason: the Securities and Exchange Commission's rule that top management compensation above $1 million has to be contingent on firm performance in order to be deductible. That rule stems from the prevailing E theory that economic value can only be wrung out of an organization through variable compensation plans.

Just as the scholars and practitioners at the conference articulated strong arguments for Theory E, so proponents for Theory O change made an equally powerful set of arguments. There is an extensive research literature that supports the notion that organizational capabilities such as coordination, commitment, conflict management, communication, and creativity lead to sustainable competitive advantage.[14] These studies illustrate the connection between organizational capabilities and culture on the one hand and financial performance on the other. They suggest that organizational capability, because it cannot be bought or easily replicated, may be the only source of sustainable competitive advantage.

Resolving the Tension between E and O

The arguments for E and O change are equally persuasive. Theories E and O approach the problem of organizational change from two different but equally legitimate perspectives. Although employing one or the other of these archetypal approaches to change may be the easiest and the most natural, for reasons already discussed, neither achieves all the objectives of management in most cases. Scott Paper under Dunlap delivered dramatic increases in shareholder value. The firm's market capitalization at the time of sale was three times what it was at the time Dunlap took over the firm only a few months earlier. But there is little doubt that the organizational capability to compete in the long run had not been built. Equally ineffective was Champion's pure Theory O strategy: A more effective organization that still does not create economic wealth for its shareholders will not long survive. Indeed, Champion was acquired in early 2000. For 1.5 times its market capitalization when CEO Sigler launched his cultural transformation in 1981.

Where the objective is to enable an institution to adapt, survive, and prosper in the long run, Theory E change must be combined with Theory O. In effect we are arguing for the and/also, for the management of a paradox. It is the way to get rapid improvements in economic value while also building sustainable advantage inherent in building organizational capability.

The and/also is also the hardest approach and thus requires great will, skill, and wisdom. The alternative—an arbitrary and halfhearted mixing of E and O—is extremely confusing and debilitating to an organization. Instead of this halfhearted approach, managers are better off picking a pure model: a clear Theory E approach with its benefits and costs or a pure Theory O approach with its benefits and costs.

How can E and O be integrated? There are only two ways. A company can sequence the two approaches, or it can employ them more or less simultaneously. We will now turn to these two approaches. We argue, based on the case of Asda, a U.K. grocery chain that underwent a successful transformation using Theory E and O strategies simultaneously, that the simultaneous approach is more desirable. It is arguably much more difficult to implement, but it is also likely to be a source of sustainable competitive advantage.

Sequencing E and O

Of the two sequencing strategies possible, leading with E and then following with O makes the most sense. CEO Jack Welch at General

Electric employed this approach with considerable success. Phase I of his change effort was very much driven by a Theory E approach. It began with a demand that every GE business had to achieve a number one or number two position in its industry. Businesses that didn't meet this objective had to be fixed, sold, or closed. This phase included an effort to streamline and simplify the GE bureaucracy through a massive downsizing. Between 1981 and 1985, GE's employment dropped from 412,000 to 299,000 while revenues increased by 19.7 percent and net income increased by 37.8 percent. The number of management levels was reduced from nine to six. Corporate staff, mostly strategic planning and finance staff, was reduced by 60 percent. It was during this phase that Welch began to be called Neutron Jack. Indeed, a climate of fear and intimidation probably accompanied this phase— hardly a climate conducive to Theory O strategies. One severe critic of GE and Welch described him as being, among other things, "cocksure, domineering, boisterous, [and] crude."[15]

Unlike many other CEOs who choose a Theory E strategy for change, however, Welch realized that this approach by itself was not sufficient. He followed the initial E strategy with an O strategy. Between 1985 and the early 1990s, Welch instituted numerous organizational initiatives. He declared that the organization had to become "boundaryless." Workout, an open-forum process in which executives in each business unit learned from their own employees about barriers to organizational effectiveness, became a universal procedure that business unit leaders had to employ. The purpose of Workout was to break down hierarchy and to promote feedback and open communication.[16] Welch also articulated a set of values and made promotion contingent on behaving consistently with those values. As the capabilities of the organization grew, Welch initiated a philosophy of stretch goals. Finally, the company began to develop its global organization.

John Reed, now co-CEO of Citigroup, used the same sequence of E followed by O when he changed what was then Citicorp's backroom office. An overnight change in the backroom process had resulted in operational problems and strained relations with the marketing organization. The answer was Project Paradise, an effort to rebuild relationships with marketing and trust within the backroom office. Management education soon followed.[17]

Does this sequence of E and O work? Certainly, Welch's and

Reed's successes would suggest that it is a viable approach. The rapid, dramatic, and painful changes that may be required to increase a firm's economic value, one can argue, cannot be achieved through a long-term Theory O strategy. Moreover, an O strategy cannot easily be followed by an E strategy that tears at the fabric of the organization. This is a problem that Champion faced after nearly two decades of building trust and commitment among management, employees, and unions. In 1997 Richard Olson, Sigler's successor, declared that increasing shareholder value was now Champion's prime objective. Selling or closing units and the layoffs that accompany the move became a necessity. The acquisition of Champion in 2000 suggests that Olson and his management team were unsuccessful in effecting these moves. Making them would have destroyed the trust and commitment Olson and his team had spent years developing. It is therefore not surprising that they failed to execute the needed E strategy. We therefore argue that when it comes to adopting a sequenced approach, only the E- followed-by-O strategy makes sense.

There are, however, problems and costs to the E-followed-by-O sequence that argue for better integration of E and O. Few CEOs can evolve their thinking and their change strategies the way Jack Welch has. It takes an extraordinary individual to change direction from E to O. Nor do most CEOs enjoy the long tenure that Welch has had. The overwhelming evidence from studies of turnaround managers is that the great majority of these managers are unable to stay beyond the turnaround. They are forced out in part because they are unable to change their style and thinking, and in part because they cannot overcome the perceptions of employees that they are ruthless and cannot be trusted. Indeed, it is questionable if even the best-intentioned effort to rebuild trust, foster commitment, and create a learning organization can overcome a bloody past. Stories of the Guns of August—an uncharacteristic layoff that occurred in the mid-1970s in one large blue-chip company—are still told at that company today. It isn't hard to imagine that subsequent generations of employees will approach emotional commitment to the firm with caution. And emotional commitment is at the heart of extraordinary passion and effort. All this suggests that a sequencing approach may require two CEOs carefully chosen for their complementary styles and philosophies. The good cop must follow the bad cop.

Holding the Tension Simultaneously: Integrating E and O

Although it is difficult, we believe that the simultaneous integration of Theories E and O provides the most effective approach to organizational change. It requires that a single leader—or, more likely, a team of leaders—embody the assumptions and styles of both E and O theories. This happened at Asda plc. Archie Norman, the company's CEO from 1991 to 1997, and Allan Leighton, whom Norman hired shortly after taking over a nearly bankrupt company and who eventually succeeded him, were able to achieve improvements in shareholder value while also developing the organization's effectiveness. And the development of organizational effectiveness has given this major grocery chain sustainable advantage in its industry. Indeed, Asda has reshaped the industry. Since Archie Norman took over in 1991, the company has outperformed its competitors in like-for-like sales. In 1999 Wal-Mart bought Asda for eight times its 1991 value, a large increase in shareholder value. How did Norman and Leighton do this? They did it by integrating E and O approaches to change. Archie Norman's opening speech to the executive team at Asda on a foggy day in December 1991 illustrates how he, from the outset, believed that Theories E and O could be applied simultaneously.[18] After finding the parking lot empty when he arrived at 8:00 A.M., Norman met with the executive team at 9:00 A.M. He had never met any of them before. As he described it later, here is what he said:[19]

> Today is Day Zero in our recovery program. This business is in poor shape and must change sharply in order to survive. Incremental change is not enough. There are no sacred cows and nothing that can't be examined. Our number one objective is to secure value for our shareholders and secure the trading future of the business. I am not coming in with any magical solutions. I intend to spend the next few weeks listening and forming ideas for our precise direction.

Norman continued by listing a number of specifics.

- We need cash. We must look at every possible source in the business for realizing cash.

- Asda stores must be built around the original core values of the Asda brand, and this includes being price competitive.

- We are going to have two experimental store formats up and running within six months.

- We need a culture built around common ideas and goals that include listening, learning, and speed of response, from the stores upwards.

- There will be a management reorganization. My objective is to establish a clear focus on the stores, shorten lines of communication, and build one team.

- I want everyone to be close to the stores. We must love the stores to death; that is our business.

Norman concluded:

> Finally, a few words of warning about me and my management style. First, I am forthright and I like to argue. Secondly, I want to discuss issues as colleagues. I am looking for your advice and your disagreement. I want an organization that is transparent. That means sharing knowledge, plans, and intentions. Lastly, if we can together restore a future for our business, that will be a great achievement. In doing so, I hope we can have some great fun as well. We must not lose sight of the need to make Asda a great place for everyone to work.

A synthesis of E and O theories requires simultaneous and equal emphasis on optimizing shareholder value and developing organizational capabilities. Leaders cannot be emotionally conflicted about demanding both. His opening speech shows quite clearly that Norman embodied both E and O assumptions. His ability to hold the tension between E and O theories of change was reflected in and enhanced by his decision to hire Allan Leighton as a key member of the top team. Though both men shared the E and O values, Leighton, who came from Mars, a company known for its people-oriented culture, was generally perceived to be warmer and more people-oriented than Norman. As one employee told us, "people respect Archie but love Allan."

Below we illustrate how Norman and Leighton, acting in concert, integrated E and O strategies to achieve remarkable improvements in both economic value and organizational effectiveness.

Purpose: Economic Value and Development of Organizational Capability

On the first day Norman embraced the purposes of both E and O theories of change. He articulated the Theory E goal of increasing shareholder value. He enacted it by firing, on the first day, the CFO who had been part of Asda's disastrous financial policies. He also brought in a new CFO to oversee the sale of noncore businesses. He reined in spending by enacting a wage freeze for everyone (management and workers) and laying off excess employees. Yet, on that same first day, he also embraced Theory O of change by articulating values of teamwork, excellence, and openness to debate and new ideas. He bought time for the O strategy, by warning capital markets that financial recovery was three years away. In his initial speech he announced the "renewal strategy" whereby one experimental store, to be followed later by two additional stores, was put into a risk-free zone. A cross-functional task force was appointed to redesign the experimental store's retail proposition and its approach to organizing and managing people. In the three years that followed, while the company's economic recovery was taking place, Norman says he spent 75 percent of his time as the company's human resources director—making the company flatter, more egalitarian, and more transparent. Embedded in all of these actions were Norman's dual purposes: both shareholder value and the development of an effective human organization.

Leadership: Top-Down and Yet Participative

A synthesis of E and O requires that the top leaders mobilize energy for performance improvement, but also that they enable managers throughout the organization to lead a process of innovation and change. Integrating E and O demands more top-down direction than Champion's CEO Sigler exhibited, but far more participation than Al Dunlap utilized at Scott Paper. Leaders who combine E and O stimulate change, yet also learn from it.

There is no question that Norman energized the change process at Asda from the top by setting an overall direction. He did this through his articulation of financial goals and of principles that would guide managerial behavior consistent with his values of listening, transparency, and involvement. However, he also said in his opening speech that he did not have all the answers. He then launched a series of initiatives to involve employees at all levels in surfacing problems and crafting solutions. He visited stores unannounced to obtain the opinions of store managers who had been ignored by previous management. He and Leighton held quarterly regional meetings with store managers to hear their ideas. They launched a variety of means for listening to employees and customers, such as colleague and customer circles and a "Tell Archie" program by which employees could contact Norman directly with ideas and concerns.

A synthesis of E and O change implies both analytic and emotional engagement. Norman and Leighton shared E and O values, but each related with Asda's employees differently—Norman intellectually, with the power of his mind and ideas, and Leighton emotionally, with the power of his personality.

Focus: Changing Organization Design and Culture

All effective and relatively rapid transformations require changes in organizational design. A synthesis of E and O requires, however, that leaders be able to mobilize commitment to the redesign by creating emotional commitment to the changes. Under this synthesis leaders involve key managers in focusing on new economic and strategic goals and in debating and experimenting with new designs. In this way the new arrangements and resultant changes in relationships and understandings acquire legitimacy and moral meaning.

Norman changed Asda's formal organization design almost immediately. He delayered the organization at the top and through the renewal program established a new flatter structure (from five to three levels) at the experimental stores, a structure later replicated in all stores. Additionally, a knowledge management system was created through cross-store best-practice teams. Both Norman and Leighton were, however, keenly aware that their task was to change the hearts and minds of people. Accordingly, both executives also spent an enormous amount of time infusing the company with a new passion and set of values. Leighton in particular served as Norman's cultural emissary. By bringing together key executives in open debates and discussions of problems and what to do about them, Leighton created what Hirschhorn (chapter 8) calls a counterstructure. This enabled him to change relationships and gain emotional commitment to the new Asda. It also caused people to love him, an emotion necessary for passion and commitment to change to be unleashed.

Process: Planned/Programmatic and Emergent

A synthesis of E and O requires that leaders focus on planning the change process, but not on announcing all the solutions to the problems the organization is confronting. In this way they avoid top-down solutions that may not work and to which there is little commitment. They encourage, even demand that lower-level leaders innovate and manage change at their level. Through this process leaders create managers capable of leading change and organizations that are adaptive—the one capability most needed for survival in a fast-changing world.

Asda's recovery plan specified three phases in the change process, each lasting about a year. The plan named no solutions, but it did specify the unit-by-unit experimental change process called the renewal strategy. Innovations in the first few stores would eventually spread to all 200 stores, but the innovations would continue to be modified with each new store that undertook renewal. Changes in organizing and managing people emerged from experimentation and discovery within this framework rather than from brilliant foresight on the part of Norman. As Norman said, he did not have the answers but he wanted debate. The renewal program encouraged debate. All along the way management and employees learned. What emerged was not conceived at the start. For example, management learned that it could not renew a store unless the management team in the store was ready to apply new ideas. This discovery led to an innovation called the "Driving Test." Decisions about which store managers to replace emerged from the Driving Test and implementation of renewal, as opposed to being made in advance. Managers were replaced—and in some cases departed voluntarily—when new demands on their skills revealed shortcomings that they could not overcome. Training programs, total quality programs, and culture programs driven from the top did not play a prominent role in Asda change. Managers at every level were encouraged, indeed required, to lead a change process in their local organization.

Motivation: Financial Incentives in a Supportive but Not Leading Role

A synthesis of E and O recognizes that compensation is a powerful tool that can focus the attention of managers and motivate them, but that financial incentives can also damage the capacity of the organization to develop teamwork, commitment, and learning. There is a recognition that making monetary incentives contingent on accomplishing specific goals can move people to do what is specified by the incentive plan, but that contingent rewards can also prevent managers from seeing and doing the right thing in a changing environment. For that reason, under a synthesis of E and O, incentives are used principally to attract and keep employees. They are used to recognize and reward performance motivated by involvement and commitment rather than to motivate directly. Compensation is seen as a means for ensuring a fair exchange between the firm and individual employees. And compensation plans typically follow rather than lead change.

Compensation plans were part of the change process at Asda. The company used stock options to recruit senior executives. It developed a stock ownership plan for all employees. It used variable compensation (pay based on both corporate and store performance) at the store level to align rewards with performance. But more than incentives, better management was seen as the primary means of motivation. Norman and Leighton clearly stated in an interview that incentives did not play a major role in motivating change at Asda.[20] Indeed, their own compensation was relatively modest when compared with the incentives of many turnaround executives.

Consultants: Consultants That Support but Do Not Drive Change

A synthesis of E and O recognizes the value that outside resources can bring. Consultants can bring specialized expertise, knowledge of best practices, and technical skills that may not be extant in the firm. But an integrative stance also recognizes the potentially deleterious effects of consultant-driven change. Consultants are used to support but not drive change.

At Asda consultants were not hired to define problems and change programs. Senior management did this. Consultants' expertise was used to support Asda's management. Norman used three consulting firms in the early stages of change, when technical support was needed. He employed McKinsey to help with financial analysis at the firm and store level. He hired Crispen Tweddel to consult with the renewal team on store organization. And he engaged a psychologist to do a management assessment of the top thirty or so executives. However, all of these consultants supported top management and task forces in managing the transformation of Asda. Their engagements were clearly delimited and were curtailed over time. Norman clearly understood that his own people had to manage change.

Managing the Paradox of E and O: An Ideal Approach

The discussion above clearly shows that Norman and Leighton continually managed a paradox. They managed to lay off employees, sell businesses, fire ineffective store managers, and delayer the organization, all acts that normally cause executives to distance themselves from their organization and people. At the same time Norman and Leighton invested enormous amounts of time and energy in involving people; they encouraged participating, listening, communicating, relating, debating, and learning. They managed to hold the tension between two approaches to managing change that are rarely combined simultaneously.

We believe that the emotional incongruence of Theories E and O makes it hard to integrate these theories. Yet we also believe integrating E and O is the best change strategy for firms that want to develop a sustained competitive advantage. That sustained advantage can come only from organizational capability both to enact the new direction and to inquire continually into how well the firm is creating economic value. Such capability requires leaders who embrace the and/also.

A CEO who faces a major transformation of his or her company should avoid being drawn into an E *or* O approach without thinking through the ultimate long-term consequences. It is easy to eschew one or the other of these approaches based on ideology; Japanese and European firms, for example, typically find the E approach abhorrent and embrace the pure O, whereas American firms typically embrace the E approach. Half measures are equally ineffective; they are likely to obtain the worst outcomes of both strategies and none of the benefits of either. We believe it is very unusual for a single individual to embody both E and O assumptions and skills, so a team of executives hired and charged by the board of directors to synthesize their E and O approaches may be a solution. The next best alternative is to begin with E and follow with O.

The arguments we have outlined in this paper are most applicable to mature large organizations that must change in order to reverse competitive decline. But we believe they are also important to those who are managing growing entrepreneurial companies. Even in these situations, we tend to observe two types of entrepreneurs. One group subscribes to an ideology akin to Theory E. The primary goal of these entrepreneurs is to prepare their enterprise for a cash-out event such as an IPO or an acquisition by an established player. Maximizing market value prior to this cash-out event is their sole and abiding purpose. In keeping with this purpose, the emphasis is on shaping the firm's strategy, structure, and systems so that it can quickly build a strong presence in the marketplace. Mercurial leaders with a strong top-down style are typically at the helm of such firms. They attract others to join them by using high-powered incentives such as stock options. The lure is the hope of getting rich quick.

In contrast to this purely financially driven group of entrepreneurs are those whose ideology is more akin to Theory O. These entrepreneurs are driven more by the purpose of building an institution. Accumulating wealth is important but is not the primary driving purpose. The focus of these entrepreneurs is often to build a company that is based on a deeply held set of values and has a strong culture. Although such entrepreneurs are certainly charismatic, they are likely to subscribe to an egalitarian style that invites participation and involvement from everyone in their firm. They look to attract others who share their passion about the cause they are pursuing, though they certainly provide them with generous stock options as well. The lure in this case is the hope of making a difference—not just making money.

The contrast between E and O approaches to entrepreneurial start-ups is vividly captured by James Daly, editor in chief of a new Internet magazine, Business 2.0:

> I am waiting for the title that reveals the overriding goal of today's average net startup: exit strategy. No longer are entrepreneurs interested in becoming the next America Online or Yahoo or Microsoft. Instead, they want to be purchased by AOL, or Yahoo, or Microsoft. Usually within two years. For about $100 million. . . . I can't help thinking we are losing something vital, as entrepreneurs morph from dreamers into sellouts. Big plans and big executions—like those that created such companies as Dell Computer and Amazon.com—have given way to short-term strategies. Even when the sell-out plan works, it can still leave the participants feeling queasy. Witness Tripod, a vibrant Net community that sold itself to Lycos in February 1998 for $61.5 million. Founder Bo Peabody must get stomach cramps when he sees the similar Geocities valued at more than $3.4 billion.[21]

Unlike Daly, we are not critics of those entrepreneurs who are driven by a Theory E view of the world. We can think of other entrepreneurs who have destroyed businesses because they were overly wrapped up in the Theory O pursuit of a higher ideal and paid insufficient attention to the pragmatics of the marketplace. Steve Jobs's venture Next comes to mind. Even when the challenge is managing the changes associated with rapid entrepreneurial growth, we believe the most successful approach is one that combines Theories E and O. Leaders who can get past the tyranny of the either/or and embrace the paradox of and/also are most likely to break the code of change—whether they find themselves in a situation of reversing economic decline or in a situation of capitalizing on economic growth.

Notes

1. Gene Hall, Jim Rosenthal, and Judy Wade, "How to Make Reengineering Really Work," *Harvard Business Review*, Nov.–Dec. 1993; Michael Beer, Russell A. Eisenstat, and Bert Spector, *The Critical Path to Corporate Renewal* (Boston: Harvard Business School Press, 1990); and Bert Spector and Michael Beer, "Beyond Total Quality Management Programmes," *Journal of Organizational Change Management* 7, no. 2 (1994).

2. See Stuart C. Gilson and Jeremy Cott, "Scott Paper Company," Case 9-296-048 (Boston: Harvard Business School, 1998); Michael Beer and James Weber, "Champion International," Case 9-499-019 (Boston: Harvard Business School, 1998); and Michael Beer and James Weber, "Asda (A)," Case 9-498-005, "Asda (A-1)," Case 9-498-006, "Asda (B)," Case 9-498-007, and "Asda (C)," Case 9-498-008 (Boston: Harvard Business School, 1998). Additionally, the Champion International story has been documented in Richard Ault, Richard Walton, and Mark Childers, *What Works: A Decade of Change in Champion International* (San Francisco: Jossey Bass, 1998). In mid-1999 Asda was acquired by Wal-Mart.

3. See Gilson and Cott, "Scott Paper Company."

4. J. Pfeffer, *The Human Equation* (Boston: Harvard Business School Press, 1998).

5. Consider the abuse that William Anders, CEO of General Dynamics, and Al Dunlap, CEO of Scott Paper, took for their efforts to wrest economic value from failing institutions. See Kevin J. Murphy and Jay Dial, "General Dynamics: Compensation and Strategy (A)," Case 9-494-048, and "General Dynamics: Compensation and Strategy (B)," Case 9-494-049 (Boston: Harvard Business School, 1994). Also Gilson and Cott, "Scott Paper Company."

6. In a recent personal conversation with one of the authors, a senior executive at a Fortune 500 company acknowledges that his CEO had told him that a large and well-known management consulting firm he had hired was there to reassure capital markets and take pressure off him.

7. See Rakesh Khurana, "The Changing of the Guard: Causes, Process, and Consequences of Chief Executive Turnover" (Ph.D. diss., Harvard University, 1998); and Nitin Nohria, "From the M-Form to the N-Form: Taking Stock of Changes in the Large Industrial Corporation," working paper, 96-054. Harvard Business School, Boston, Mass., 1992.

8. Hugo E. R. Uyterhoeven, "ABB Deutschland (A)," Case 9-393-130, "ABB Deutschland (B)," Case 9-393-131, and "ABB Deutschland (C)," Case 9-393-132 (Boston: Harvard Business School, 1993).

9. Michael Beer and James Weber, "Champion International."

10. See Michael Beer and Russell Eisenstat, "The Silent Killers: Overcoming the Hidden Barriers to Organizational Fitness," working paper 98-064, Harvard Business School, Boston, Mass., 1998.

11. Quay Nguyen Huy finds that interventions that engaged people emotionally were more successful in a firm facing a major economic and strategic crisis. Unfortunately, these were the exception. See Quay Huy, "Emotional Capability, Emotional Intelligence and Radical Change," *Academy of Management Review*, 1999.

12. See Beer, Eisenstat, and Spector, *The Critical Path to Corporate Renewal*.

13. See Michael Beer and Gregory C. Rogers, "Human Resources at Hewlett Packard (A)," Case 9-495-051, and "Human Resources at Hewlett Packard (B)," Case 9-495-052 (Boston: Harvard Business School, 1995).

14. See, among others, James C. Collins and Jerry I. Porras, *Built to Last: Successful Habits of Visionary Companies* (New York: Harper Business, 1994); Jeffrey Pfeffer, *The Human Equation: Building Profits by Putting People First* (Boston: Harvard Business School Press, 1998); John P. Kotter and James L. Heskett, *Corporate Culture and Performance* (New York: Free Press, 1992); Daniel R. Dennison, *Corporate Culture and Organizational Effectiveness* (New York: Wiley,

1990); and Brian E. Becker, Mark A. Huselid, Peter S. Pickus, and Michael F. Spratt, "HR as a Source of Shareholder Value: Research and Recommendations," *Human Resource Management* (spring 1997).

15. See James L. Heskett, "GE: We Bring Good Things to Life (A)," Case 9-899-162, and "GE: We Bring Good Things to Life (B)," Case 9-899-163 (Boston: Harvard Business School, 1999).

16. More recently Beer and Eisenstat have developed and applied a methodology similar to Workout called Building Organizational Fitness. It attempts to integrate Theories E and O through a process of inquiry into O barriers to E objectives. See Michael Beer, Russell Eisenstat, and Ralph Biggadike, "Developing an Organization Capable of Implementing and Reformulating Strategy: A Preliminary Experiment," in *Organizational Learning and Competitive Advantage*, ed. Bertrand Moingion and Amy Edmondson (London: Sage Publications, 1996).

17. See Jay W. Lorsch, Cyrus F. Gibson, and John A. Seeger, "First National City Bank Operating Group (A)," Case 9-474-165, and "First National City Bank Operating Group (B)," Case 9-474-166 (Boston: Harvard Business School, 1995).

18. See Michael Beer and James Weber, "Asda (A)," "Asda (A-1)," "Asda (B)," and "Asda (C)." In mid-1999 ASDA was acquired by Wal-Mart. Although we don't believe that this event in any way changes the essential conclusions we draw from this case, it does prevent us from observing the performance of the company over a longer period of time.

19. The speech in the Asda (A-1) case is a paraphrase of what Norman said in an interview several years after this event took place. Extensive research in the company over several years showed that he largely enacted what he espoused at the beginning.

20. These views are recorded in a videotape of an interview with Norman and Leighton, Michael Beer, and James Weber, "Asda: An Interview with Archie Norman and Allan Leighton, April 1998, Video," HBS Product No. 499-506 (Boston: Harvard Business School Press, 1999).

21. See James Daly, "Editor's Note: Logging On, Cashing Out," *Business 2.0*, May 1999.

SECTION I

PURPOSE OF CHANGE

*Economic Value or
Organizational Capability?*

W HAT IS the overarching purpose that should guide change initiatives? Some have long argued that the proper, indeed the
only aim of any change effort should be to increase shareholder value,
what we call Theory E of change in the introductory chapter. This
perspective rests on the view that the continued survival of firms in a
competitive economy depends on their continued ability to satisfy
their shareholders. If a firm fails to do so, its shareholders will shift
their resources elsewhere, or will use the market for corporate control
to replace the existing management with a single-valued focus that
provides a clear basis for managers to make the trade-offs that they
must inevitably confront. Proponents of the shareholder-value view
would argue that this perspective is neither hostile to other stakeholders (such as employees) nor short-term in orientation. Their reasoning: Self-interested shareholders are no less interested in satisfied
and motivated employees, if such employees truly improve firm performance, than anyone else. Nor would shareholders favor short-term
changes that would compromise their long-run interests. Based on this
powerful economic logic, proponents of this view, as reflected by Michael Jensen's paper in this section, contend that shareholder value
provides the proper North Star to guide managers through the
difficult challenges of leading and managing change.

A countervailing view, reflected in Peter Senge's paper in this section, is that firms are better understood as organic, interdependent systems. Proponents of this perspective argue that the dynamics of such complex human systems cannot be reduced to a system of linear equations that derive from a single objective such as maximizing shareholder value. According to this view, even if one is interested in increasing shareholder value, one can best achieve this by building the organization's capability for dynamic adaptation—in short, by focusing on organizational learning, what we call Theory O of change in the Introduction. Enhancing an organization's adaptive capacity is, in this view, a better objective; because the knowledge necessary to achieve any objective (such as shareholder value) is neither static nor concentrated in the mind of one person. Organizations are open systems that are perpetually evolving, partly in response to their environments, partly because of the ingenuity and imagination of their members. The proper purpose of change must therefore be to enhance the organization's capacity to learn to respond better to its changing environment and to shape that environment. According to this view, what is required is a holistic view of the firm and its health that cannot be reduced to a single objective.

Each of these views rests on a different concept of the firm and on a different concept of the role of management. Joe Bower, in his commentary in this section, discusses these differences at some length. He concludes that both perspectives are in a sense too theoretical and don't adequately take into account the pragmatics of the general manager's job. He offers an alternative point of view that he argues is grounded more fully in the nature of general management.

I

VALUE MAXIMIZATION AND THE CORPORATE OBJECTIVE FUNCTION

Michael C. Jensen

Proposition: This house believes that change efforts should be guided by the sole purpose of increasing shareholder value.

L YING BEHIND this simple statement, which I have been asked to address, is a complex set of controversies on which economists, management scholars, managers, policy makers, and special interest groups exhibit wide disagreement. Political, economic, social, evolutionary, and emotional forces play important roles in this disagreement, as do ignorance, complexity, and conflicting self-interests. I shall discuss these below.

At the organizational level, the issue is as follows: Every organization attempting to accomplish something has to ask and answer the following question: What are we trying to accomplish? Or, put even more simply: When all is said and done, how do we measure better versus worse? Even more simply: How do we keep score?

At the economywide or social level the question is the following: If we could dictate the criterion or objective function to be maximized by firms (that is, the criterion by which executives choose among alternative policy options), what would it be? Or, even more simply: How do we want the firms in our economy to measure better versus worse?

In this light I prefer to restate the proposition I have been asked to address as follows:

> ***This house believes that in implementing organizational change managers must have a criterion for deciding what is better, and that better should be measured by the increase in long-term market value of the firm.***

I call this the value maximization proposition, and it has its roots in 200 years of research in economics and finance. "Stakeholder theory," the asserted (and currently popular)[1] main contender competing with value maximization for this objective function, has its roots in sociology, organizational behavior, the politics of special interests, and managerial self-interest. I say "asserted" contender because stakeholder theory is incomplete as a specification for the corporate purpose or objective function, and therefore cannot logically fulfill that role. I argue below that its incompleteness is not accidental. Stakeholder theory serves the private interests of those who promote it, including many managers and directors of corporations.

Briefly put, value maximization says that managers should make all decisions so as to increase the total long-run market value of the firm. Total value is the sum of the values of all financial claims on the firm— including equity, debt, preferred stock, and warrants.

Stakeholder theory, on the other hand, says that managers should make decisions so as to take account of the interests of all the stakeholders in a firm. And stakeholders include all individuals or groups who can substantially affect the welfare of the firm: not only the financial claimants but also employees, customers, communities, and governmental officials—and, under some interpretations, the environment, terrorists, blackmailers, and thieves.[2]

The answers to the questions of how managers should define better versus worse, and how managers in fact do define it, have important implications for the welfare of a society's inhabitants. Indeed, the answers provide the business equivalent of the medical profession's Hippocratic oath. It is an indication of the infancy of the science of management that so many in the world's business schools, as well as in professional business organizations, understand so little of the fundamental issues in contention.

With this introduction of the issues let me now move on to a detailed examination of value maximization and stakeholder theory.

The Logical Structure of the Problem

In discussing whether firms should maximize value or not, we must separate two distinct issues:

1. Should the firm have a single-valued objective? And

2. Should that objective be value maximization or something else (for example, maintaining employment or improving the environment)?

The debate over whether corporations should maximize value or whether they should act in the interests of their stakeholders is generally couched in terms of issue number 2 and is often falsely framed as stockholders versus stakeholders. The real conflict is actually an unjoined debate over issue number 1: whether the firm should have a single-valued objective function or scorecard. This confusion has led to widespread misunderstanding.

What is commonly known as stakeholder theory, while not totally without content, is fundamentally flawed because it violates the proposition that any organization must have a single-valued objective as a precursor to purposeful or rational behavior. In particular, I argue that a firm that adopts stakeholder theory will be handicapped in the competition for survival because, as a basis for action, stakeholder theory politicizes the corporation. It leaves its managers empowered to exercise their own preferences in spending the firm's resources.

We begin with a discussion of issue number 1, the necessity for a single-valued objective.

Issue 1: Purposeful Behavior Requires the Existence of a Single-valued Objective Function

A SIMPLE EXAMPLE
Consider a firm that wishes to increase current-year profits, p, as well as market share m. Assume, as in figure 1-1, that over some range of values of m, profits increase. But at some point increases in market share come only at reduced current-year profits—say because of increased expenditures on research and development, more advertising, or price reductions to increase market share reduce this year's profit. Therefore, it is not logically possible to speak of maximizing both

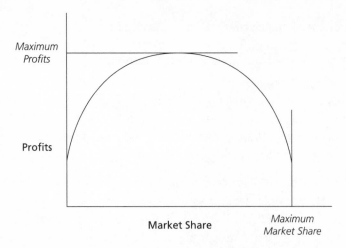

Figure 1-1   Trade-Off between Profits and Market Share. A manager directed to maximize both profit and market share has no way to
decide where to be in the range between maximum profits and
maximize market share.

market share and profits. In this situation it is impossible for a manager
to decide on the level of R&D, advertising, or price reduction, because
he or she is faced with the necessity to make trade-offs between the
two "goods" p and m with no way to do so. The manager knows that
the firm should be at least at the point of maximum profits or maximum market share, but there is no purposeful way to decide where to
be in the area where the firm can obtain more of the one only by giving
up some of the other.

Multiple Objectives Is No Objective

It is logically impossible to maximize in more than one dimension at
the same time unless the dimensions are monotone transformations of
one another. Thus, telling a manager to maximize current profits,
market share, future growth in profits, and anything else one pleases
will leave that manager with no way to make a reasoned decision. In
effect, it leaves the manager with no objective. The result will be
confusion and lack of purpose that will fundamentally handicap the
firm in its competition for survival.[3] A firm can resolve this ambiguity
by specifying the trade-offs among the various dimensions, and doing

so amounts to specifying an overall objective function such as $V = f(x, y, \ldots)$ that explicitly incorporates the effects of decisions on all the goods or bads (denoted by $x, y, \ldots$) affecting the firm. At this point, the logic alone does not specify what V is. It could be anything the board of directors chooses, such as employment, sales, or growth in output. But I argue below that social welfare and survival will severely constrain the board's choices!

Nothing in the analysis so far has said that the function f must be well-behaved and easy to maximize. If the function f is nonmonotone, or even chaotic, it makes it more difficult for managers to find the overall maximum; but even in these situations the meaning of "better" or "worse" is defined, and managers and their monitors have a principled basis for choosing and auditing decisions. Without a definition of the meaning of better there is no principled foundation for choice.

Issue 2: Total Firm Value Maximization Makes Society Better Off

Given that a firm must have a single objective that tells us what is better and what is worse, we then must face issue number 2—the question of what that definition of better is. (As I pointed out above, having a single objective does not mean that individuals or firms care only about one thing. This single objective will always be a complicated function of many different goods or bads.)

The short answer to the question of the definition of better is that 200 years' worth of work in economics and finance indicate that social welfare is maximized when all firms in an economy maximize total firm value. The intuition behind this criterion is simply that (social) value is created when a firm produces an output or set of outputs that are valued by its customers at more than the value of the inputs it consumes (as valued by their suppliers) in such production. Firm value is simply the long-term market value of this stream of benefits.

When monopolies or externalities exist, the value-maximizing criterion does not maximize social welfare. But the solution to these problems lies not in telling firms to maximize something else, but in defining and assigning the alienable decision rights necessary to eliminate the externalities. Under the Coase Theorem we know externalities can exist only if some alienable decision rights are not defined or assigned to someone in the private economy (see Coase 1960; Jensen and Meckling 1992).[4]

Maximizing the total market value of the firm—that is, the sum of the market values of the equity, debt, and any other contingent claims outstanding on the firm—is one objective function that will resolve the trade-off problem among multiple constituencies. It tells the firm to spend an additional dollar of resources to satisfy the desires of each constituency as long as that constituency values the result at more than a dollar. Although there are many single-valued objective functions that could guide a firm's managers in their decisions, value maximization is an important one because it leads under some reasonable conditions to the maximization of social welfare. Let's look more closely at this.

Value Maximizing and Social Welfare

Much of the discussion in policy circles over the proper corporate objective casts the issue in terms of the conflicts among various constituencies or "stakeholders" in the corporation. The question then becomes whether shareholders should be held in higher regard than other constituencies, such as employees, customers, creditors, and so on. It is both unproductive and incorrect to frame the issue in this manner. The real issue to be considered here is what firm behavior will result in the least social waste—or, equivalently, what behavior will get the most out of society's limited resources—not whether one group is or should be more privileged than another.

Profit Maximization

To see how value maximization leads to a socially efficient solution, let's first consider a simpler objective function: profit maximization in a world in which all production runs are infinite and cash flow streams are level and perpetual. This scenario allows us to ignore the complexity introduced by the trade-offs between current and future-year profits (more accurately, cash flows). Consider now the social welfare effects of a firm's decision to take resources out of the economy in the form of labor hours, capital, or materials purchased voluntarily from their owners in single-price markets. The firm uses these inputs to produce outputs of goods or services that are then sold to consumers through voluntary transactions in single-price markets.

In this simple situation a firm taking inputs out of the economy and putting its output of goods and services back into the economy increases aggregate welfare if the prices at which it sells the goods more than cover the costs it incurs in purchasing the inputs. Clearly the firm should expand its output as long as an additional dollar of resources taken out of the economy is valued by the consumers of the incremental product at more than a dollar. Note that the difference between these revenues and costs is profits. This is the reason (under the assumption that there are no externalities)[5] that profit maximization leads to an efficient social outcome.[6]

Because the transactions are voluntary, we know that the owners of inputs value them at a level less than or equal to the price the firm pays, or they wouldn't sell them. Therefore, as long as there are no externalities in the input factor markets, the opportunity cost to society of those inputs is no higher than the total cost to the firm of acquiring them. I say "no higher" because some suppliers of inputs to the firm are able to earn "rents" by obtaining prices higher than the value of the goods to them. But such rents do not represent social costs. Likewise, as long as there are no externalities in the output markets, the value to society of the goods and services produced by the firm is at least as great as the price the firm receives for the sale of those goods and services. If this were not true, the individuals purchasing them would not do so. Again, as with producer surpluses on inputs, the benefit to society is higher to the extent that consumer surplus exists (that is, to the extent that some consumers are able to purchase the output at prices lower than the value to them).

Therefore, when the firm acquires an additional unit of any input (or inputs) to produce an additional unit of any output, it increases social welfare at least by the amount of its profit—the difference between the value of the output and the cost of the input(s) required in producing it.[7] The signals to the firm are clear: Continue to expand purchases of inputs and sell the resulting outputs as long as an additional dollar of inputs generates sales of at least a dollar.

Value and Trade-Offs through Time

In a world in which cash flow, profit, and cost flows are not uniform over time, we must deal with the trade-offs among these items through time; for example, when capital investment comes in lumps that have to be funded up front although production will occur only in the future. Knowing whether society will be benefited or harmed requires knowing whether the future output will be valuable enough to offset the cost of having people give up their labor and capital and material inputs in the present. Interest rates give us the answer to this. Interest rates tell us the cost of giving up a unit of a good today for receipt at some time in the future. So long as people take advantage of the opportunity to borrow or lend at a given interest rate, that rate determines the value of moving a marginal dollar of resources (inputs or consumption goods) forward or backward in time.

The value one year from now of a dollar today saved for use one year from now is thus $\$1 \times (1 + r)$, where r is the interest rate. Alternatively, the value today of a dollar of resources to be received one year from now is its present value of $\$1 \div (1 + r)$. In this world an individual is as well off as possible if his or her wealth, measured by the discounted present value of all future claims, is maximized. When we add uncertainty, nothing of major importance is changed in this proposition as long as there are capital markets in which the individual can buy and sell risk at a given price. In this case it is the risk-adjusted interest rate that is used in calculating the market value of risky claims. The corporate objective function that maximizes social welfare thus becomes "maximize total firm market value." It tells firms to expand output and investment to the point where the market value of the firm is at a maximum.[8]

Stakeholder Theory

To the extent that stakeholder theory argues that firms should pay attention to all their constituencies, the theory is unassailable. Taken this far stakeholder theory is completely consistent with value maximization, which implies that managers must pay attention to all constituencies that can affect the firm.

But there is more to the stakeholder story than this. Any theory of action must tell the actors, in this case managers and boards of directors, how to choose among multiple competing and inconsistent constituent interests. Customers want low prices, high quality, expensive service, and so on. Employees want high wages; high-quality working conditions; and fringe benefits including vacations, medical benefits, pensions, and the rest. Suppliers of capital want low risk and high returns. Communities want high charitable contributions, social expenditures by firms to benefit the community at large, stable employment, increased investment, and so on. And so it goes with every conceivable constituency. Obviously any decision criterion—and the objective function is at the core of any decision criterion—must specify how to make the trade-offs among these often conflicting demands.

As I have said before, value maximization provides the following answer to the trade-off question: Spend an additional dollar on any constituency to the extent that the long-term value added to the firm from such expenditure is a dollar or more. Stakeholder theory as stated by (Freeman 1984) and others contains no conceptual specification of how to make the trade-offs among stakeholders that must be made. This makes the theory damaging to firms and to social welfare, and it also reveals a reason for its popularity.

Implications for Managers and Directors

Because stakeholder theory provides no criteria for what is better or what is worse, it leaves boards of directors and executives in firms with no principled decision criteria for problem solving. Firms that try to behave in accordance with stakeholder theory will eventually fail if they are competing with firms that are behaving so as to maximize value. If this is true, why do so many managers and directors of corporations embrace stakeholder theory?

One answer lies in these individuals' own personal short-run interests. Because stakeholder theory provides no definition of better, it leaves managers and directors unaccountable for their stewardship of the firm's resources. With no criteria for performance, managers cannot be evaluated in any principled way. So stakeholder theory plays into the hands of self-interested managers to pursue their own interests at the expense of society and the firm's financial claimants. By expanding the power of managers in this powerful and unproductive way, stakeholder theory therefore increases agency costs in the economic system. It is not surprising that so many managers like it.

By gutting the foundations on which the firm's internal control systems could constrain managerial behavior, stakeholder theory gives unfettered power to managers to do almost whatever they want, subject only to constraints by the financial markets, the market for control, and the product markets. Thus, it is not surprising that we find stakeholder theory used to argue for governmental restrictions on financial markets and the market for corporate control. These markets are driven by value maximization and will limit the damage that can be done by managers following stakeholder theory.[9] Current pressures for restrictions on global trade, as well as environmental campaigns, illustrate use of the arguments to restrict product market competition, as well.

Implications for the Power of Special Interests

In addition, stakeholder theory plays into the hands of special interests who wish to use the resources of firms for their own ends. With the widespread failure of centrally planned socialist and communist economies, those who wish to use nonmarket forces to reallocate wealth find great solace in the playing field that stakeholder theory opens to them. Stakeholder theory gives them the appearance of legitimate political access to the sources of decision-making power in organizations; and it deprives those organizations of a principled basis for rejecting their claims. The result is to undermine the foundations that have enabled markets and capitalism to generate wealth and high standards of living worldwide.

If widely adopted, stakeholder theory will reduce social welfare even as its advocates claim to increase it—just as in the failed communist and socialist experiments of the last century. And, as I pointed out above, stakeholder theorists will often have the active support of managers who wish to throw off the constraints on their power provided by the value criterion and its enforcement by capital markets, the market for corporate control, and product markets. Indeed, we have seen and will continue to see more political action limiting the power of these markets to constrain managers.[9] And such actors will continue using the arguments of stakeholder theory to legitimize their positions. Exposing the logical fallacy of these arguments will reduce their effectiveness. But because there is something deeper in the evolution of the human psyche that drives the attraction to stakeholder theory, it is worth delving further into the issue.

Conflicts between Family and Markets and Their Role in Stakeholder Theory

Stakeholder theory taps into the deep emotional commitment of most individuals to the family and tribe. For tens of thousands of years, those of our ancestors who had little respect for or loyalty to the family, band, or tribe probably did not survive. In the last few hundred years of humanity's existence, however, we have experienced the emergence of a market system of prices and private property rights on which they are based. This system for voluntary and decentralized coordination of human action has brought huge increases in the welfare of humans and in their freedom of action. As Frederick Hayek (1988) points out, however, we are generally unaware of the functioning of these systems, because no single mind invested or designed them—and because they work in very complicated and subtle ways.

> We are led—for example by the pricing system in market exchange—to do things by circumstances of which we are largely unaware and which produce results that we do not intend. In our economic activities we do not know the needs which we satisfy nor the sources of the things which we get. Almost all of us serve people whom we do not know, and even of whose existence we are ignorant; and we in turn constantly live on the services of other people of whom we know nothing. All this is possible because we stand in a great framework of institutions and traditions—economic, legal, moral—into which we fit ourselves by obeying certain rules of conduct that we never made, and which we have never understood in the sense in which we understand how the things that we manufacture function. (p. 14)

Moreover, these systems operate in ways that limit the options of the small group or family, and these constraints are not well understood or welcomed. Many people are drawn to stakeholder theory through their evolutionary attachment to the small group and the family. As Hayek (1988) puts it,

> Constraints on the practices of the small group, it must be emphasized and repeated, are *hated*. For, as we shall see, the individual following them, even though he depends on them for life, does not and usually cannot understand how they function or how they benefit him. He knows so many objects that seem desirable but for which he is not permitted to grasp, and he cannot see how other beneficial features of his environment depend on the discipline to which he is forced to submit—a discipline forbidding him to reach out for these same appealing objects. Disliking these constraints so much, we hardly can be said to have selected them; rather, these constraints selected us: they enabled us to survive. (pp. 13, 14)

Thus we have a system in which human beings must simultaneously exist in two orders, that of the microcosmos and that of the macrocosmos.

> Moreover, the structures of the extended order are made up not only of individuals but also of many, often overlapping, suborders within which old instinctual responses, such as solidarity and altruism, continue to retain some importance by assisting voluntary collaboration, even though they are incapable, by themselves, of creating a basis for the more extended order. Part of our present difficulty is that we must constantly adjust our lives, our thoughts, and our emotions, in order to live simultaneously within different kinds of orders according to different rules. If we were to apply the unmodified, uncurbed rules of the micro-cosmos (i.e., of the small band or troop, or of, say, our families) to the macro-cosmos (our wider civilization), as our instincts and sentimental yearnings often make us wish to do, we would destroy it. Yet if we were always to apply the rules of the extended order to our more intimate groupings, *we would crush them*. So we must learn to live in two sorts of worlds at once. To apply the name 'society' to both, or even to either, is hardly of any use, and can be most misleading. (Hayek 1988, p. 18)

Stakeholder theory taps into this confusion and antagonism and relaxes constraints on the small group in ways that are damaging to society as a whole. Such deeply rooted and generally unrecognized conflict between allegiances to family and tribe, and what is good for society as a whole has major impact on our evolution. The conflict in this case does not operate for the good.

Enlightened Value Maximization and Enlightened Stakeholder Theory

There is a way out of the conflict between value maximizing the stakeholder theory for those who are interested in improving management, organizational governance, and performance. It lies in what I call enlightened value maximization and enlightened stakeholder theory.

Enlightened Value Maximization

Enlightened value maximization recognizes that communication with and motivation of an organization's managers, employees, and partners is extremely difficult. What this means in practice is that if we tell all participants in an organization that its sole purpose is to maximize value, we will not get maximum value for the organization. We must give people enough structure to understand what maximizing value means, in such a way that they can be guided by it and therefore have a chance to actually achieve it. They must be turned on by it, in the sense that it taps into some desire deep in the passions of human beings—for example, a desire to build the world's best automobile or to create a movie or play that will affect humans for centuries. All these can be consistent with value maximization.

I believe there is a serious semantic issue here. Value maximizing tells the participants in an organization how they will assess their success in achieving a vision or implementing a strategy. But value maximizing says nothing about how to create a superior vision or strategy. Value maximizing says nothing to employees or managers about how to find or establish initiatives or ventures that create value. It only tells us how we will measure success in the activity.

Defining what it means to score a goal in football or soccer, for example, tells the players nothing about how to win the game. It just tells them how the score will be kept. That is the role of value maximization in organizational life. It doesn't tell us how to have a great defense or offense, or what kind of plays to create or practice, or how much to train and practice, or whom to hire, and so on. All of these critical functions are part of the competitive and organizational strategy of any team or organization. Adopting value creation as the scorekeeping measure does nothing to relieve us of the responsibility to do all these things and more in order to survive and dominate our sector of the competitive landscape.

This means, for example, that we must give employees and managers a structure that will help them resist the temptation to maximize the short-term financial performance (usually profits or, sometimes even more silly, earnings per share) of the organization. Such short-term profit maximization is a sure way to destroy value. This is where enlightened stakeholder theory can play an important role. We can learn from the stakeholder theorists how to lead managers and participants in an organization to think more generally about how the organization's policies treat all important constituencies of the firm. This includes not just financial markets but employees, customers, suppliers, the community in which the organization exists, and so on.

Indeed, it is obvious that we cannot maximize the long-term market value of an organization if we ignore or mistreat any important constituency. We cannot create value without good relations with customers, employees, financial backers, suppliers, regulators, communities, and the rest. But having said that, we can now use the value criterion for choosing among those competing interests. I say competing interests because no constituency can be given full satisfaction if the firm is to flourish and survive. Moreover, we can be sure, externalities and monopoly power aside, that using this value criterion will result in making society as well off as it can be.

Resolving externality and monopoly problems is the legitimate domain of the government in its rule-setting function. Those who care about resolving these issues will not succeed if they look to firms to resolve these issues voluntarily. Firms that try to do so either will be eliminated by competitors who choose not to be so civic minded, or will survive only by consuming their economic rents in this manner.

Enlightened Stakeholder Theory

Enlightened stakeholder theory is easy to explain. It can take advantage of most that stakeholder theorists offer in the way of processes and audits to measure and evaluate the firm's management of its relations with all important constituencies. Enlightened stakeholder theory adds, however, the simple specification that the objective function of the firm is to maximize total long-term firm market value.

I say long-term market value to recognize that it is possible for markets not to know the full implications of a firm's policies until they begin to show up in cash flows over time. In such a case the firm must lead the market to understand the full value implications of its policies, then wait for the market to catch up and recognize the real value of its decisions as they become evidenced in market share, employee loyalty, and finally cash flows and risk. Value creation does not mean succumbing to the vagaries of the movements in a firm's value from day to day. The market is inevitably ignorant of many of our actions and opportunities, at least in the short run. It is our job as directors, managers, and employees to resist the temptation to conform to the pressures of equity and debt markets when those markets do not have the private competitive information that we possess.

In this way enlightened stakeholder theorists would see that although stockholders are not some special constituency that ranks above all others, long-term stock value is an important determinant (along with the value of debt and other instruments) of total long-term firm value. They would see that value creation gives management a way to assess the trade-offs that must be made among competing constituencies, and that it allows for principled decision making independent of the personal preferences of managers and directors. Importantly, managers and directors also become accountable for the assets under their control, because the value scorecard provides an objective yardstick against which their performance can be evaluated.

Measurability and Imperfect Knowledge

It is worth noting that none of the above arguments depend on value being easily observable. Nor do they depend on perfect knowledge of the effects on value of decisions regarding any of a firm's constituencies. The world may be complex and difficult to understand. It may leave us in deep uncertainty about the effects of any decisions we may make. It may be governed by complex dynamic systems that are difficult to optimize in the usual sense. But that does not obviate the necessity of making choices (decisions) on a day-to-day basis. And to do this in a purposeful way we must have a scorecard.

The absence of a scorecard makes it easier for people to engage in intense value claiming activities at the expense of value creation. We can take random actions, and we can devise decision rules that depend on superstitions. All of these are unlikely to serve us well in the competition for survival.

We must not confuse optimization with value creation. To create value we need not know exactly where and what maximum value is, but only how to institute changes and strategies that cause value to rise. To navigate in such a world in anything close to a purposeful way, we have to have a notion of "better," and value maximization is such a notion. I know of no other scorecard that will score the game as well as this one. It is not perfect, but that is the nature of the world. We can tell (even if not perfectly) when we are getting better and when we are getting worse. If we are to pay any attention to the nihilists who call themselves stakeholder theorists, they must offer at least some way to tell when we are "better" other than their own personal values. In the meantime we should use their theory only in the form of enlightened stakeholder theory, as I describe above. In this way it is a useful complement to enlightened value maximizing (or value creating, for those who argue the world is too complex to maximize anything).

Discussion

In his comments in the following article, "The Puzzles and Paradoxes of How Living Companies Create Wealth: Why Single-Valued Objective Functions Are Not Quite Enough," Peter Senge makes many points. I agree with virtually all of them, including that in his title. Yes, a single-valued objective function is not quite enough to ensure the success of any organization.

Peter classifies his concerns as instrumental (the operationalizing of value maximization) and objective (the aim itself). He discusses at length what it means to "optimize," and I agree with nearly all of what he has to say except the notion that somehow these difficulties mitigate the importance of having a single-dimensional scorecard for evaluating whether we are doing better or worse. I say "scorecard" here because I think some of the difficulty is caused by the term "single-valued objective function" and by the implication that something is being optimized in a classical sense. It matters not whether a perfect model cannot predict in a complicated dynamic setting. We still have to have a definition of "better" in order to behave purposely.

Indeed, Peter emphasizes the importance of learning, and I agree with this emphasis. But learning cannot occur if we do not, as he says, "understand the longer-term consequences of alternative policies," and this is my point—one that Peter explicitly agrees with. Learning is important, and in fact I believe creating value requires such emphasis.

I also agree with the observation that people commonly want to take actions prompted by their intuition that will move them in the opposite direction of their real desires. But again, this is a problem of learning, not of the scorecard we use to determine whether people are moving in the right or wrong direction. Indeed, the absence of such a scorecard combines with people's defensive behaviors to inhibit learning about the counterproductive effects of their actions.

Peter raises concerns that I share about the tendency of human beings to resort to short-term value-destroying actions in the name of value creation. I would point out that the absence of a clear-cut value scorecard facilitates this behavior. This again is a learning problem—about causal theories affecting the relation between actions and results. Peter's example of the insurance company managers and their mistaken belief about the relation between litigation costs, profits, and value describes an all too common situation. Those managers were engaged in value-destroying activities and did not want to learn otherwise. The absence of clear-cut measures of value destruction are important to the continued survival of such fallacious theories.

I recall years ago a meeting of a board compensation committee on which I served. We were about to award the management of the company large bonuses for the tremendous job they had done in the previous year. I pointed out that the actions of the management had been associated with the destruction of half of the entire company value in the previous year. My fellow directors were stunned. They asked,

"How did you calculate that?" I explained; but the committee, with one abstention, awarded the bonuses anyway. I must say that the discussions about value continued and eventually did have an effect on policy matters at the board level. All this occurred in a company that espoused great allegiance to value creation, but never calculated value.

I share Peter's allegiance to Deming's exhortations to "eliminate numerical goals for the work force and numerical goals for management." In most cases these goals have value-destroying effects, yet they survive, and often people argue that they are there to create value. Theories can be wrong, and these are. But that does not invalidate the necessity to have a single-dimensional scorecard.

Peter raises what he calls objective problems with value maximization. He raises issues associated with the metaphor of a company as a living system rather than as a machine for making money. I like the analogy and would like to take it one step farther. Living organisms in the end have to generate enough calories to enable them to survive. They evolve in miraculous ways to do this. They emerge rather than being designed. But the grim reaper of death and extinction is always there to select out those organisms that fail the value-creation test of nature.

Organisms that expend more calories than they consume do not survive. Companies and economic and management systems are also like organisms, but the survival test often operates with a long time lag. It took seventy years for the misguided communist and socialist experiments of the twentieth century to fail. General Motors has been on the road to extinction since the early 1970s, and still it continues. We can do better, and here I disagree with Peter. Having the value-creation scorecard front and center in every organization will help, not hinder, progress. I have watched the alternative approach in countless companies, and the result is not pretty. ITT, Westinghouse, and many other fine companies are gone because they did not watch the value-creation/destruction scorecard closely enough.

Finally, Peter offers reference to *A Road Map to Natural Capitalism* (Lovins, Lovins, and Hawken 1999), which, he argues, suggests new ideas about capitalism and the redefinition and redesign of the function of corporations. When I read the article, what I see is the authors arguing that corporations are missing opportunities to increase value that are associated with husbanding natural resources. The tagline of the article says it quite well: "Business strategies built around the radically more productive use of natural resources can solve many environmental problems at a profit" (p. 145). The authors argue that "Some very simple changes to the way we run our businesses, built on advanced techniques for making resources more productive, can yield startling benefits both for today's shareholders and for future generations" (p. 146). They point to ignorance of opportunities by firms and to misguided tax, accounting, and regulatory policies as explanations for why value-creating opportunities are being missed by companies on a grand scale.

I find nothing in the Lovins et al. article or in what they advocate that is inconsistent with value creation. Whether the authors are right is another issue, but the problem does not seem to be that companies are being misled by the effort to enhance value. In fact, the authors are arguing that companies must take these opportunities for value creation. In their words: "The companies that first make the changes we have described will have a competitive edge. Those that don't make that effort won't be a problem because ultimately they won't be around" (p. 158).

Notes

1. Stakeholder theory, for example, has been endorsed by many professional organizations, special interest groups, and governmental organizations including the current British government. In her excellent article on the topic (1996) and her book (1994), Elaine Sternberg surveys the theory's acceptance by the Business Roundtable, its recognition by law in twenty-nine American states, and even its endorsement by the *Financial Times*.
2. See Freeman (1984, p. 53). "The . . . definition of 'stakeholder' [is] any group or individual who can affect or is affected by the achievement of an organization's purpose. . . . For instance, some corporations must count 'terrorist groups' as stakeholders."
3. See Jensen, Wruck, and Barry (1991) and Wruck, Jensen, and Barry (1991) for a case of a small nonprofit firm that almost destroyed itself while trying to maximize over a dozen dimensions at the same time.
4. In addition, we should recognize that when a complete set of claims for all goods for each possible time and state of the world do not exist, the social maximum will be constrained; but this is just another recognition of the fact that we must take into account the costs of creating additional claims and markets on time/state delineated claims. See Arrow (1964) and Debreu (1959).
5. By externalities I mean situations in which the full social cost of an action is not borne by the firm or individual that takes the action. Examples are cases of air

or water pollution in which a firm adds pollution to the environment without having to purchase the right to do so from the parties giving up the clean air or water. There can be no externalities as long as alienable property rights in all physical assets are defined and assigned to some private individual or firm. See Jensen and Meckling (1992).

In the case of a monopoly, profit maximization leads to a loss of social product, because the firm expands production only to the point where its incremental revenues are equal to a dollar, not to where consumers value the incremental product at a dollar. In this case, the firm produces less of a commodity than that which would result in maximum social welfare.

6. I am indebted to my colleague George Baker for this simple way of expressing the optimality of profit maximization.

7. Because suppliers generally earn surplus on inframarginal units and consumers earn surplus (value them more highly than price) on their inframarginal units, social welfare actually rises by more than the difference between the revenues and costs of the firm.

8. Although I shall not go into the details here, the same criterion applies to all organizations, whether they are public corporations or not. Obviously, even if the financial claims are not explicitly valued by the market, social welfare will be increased as long as managers of partnerships or nonprofits increase output, so long as the imputed market value of claims on the firm continue to increase.

9. Such stakeholder arguments, for example, played an important role in persuading U.S. courts and legislatures to limit hostile takeovers through legalization of poison pills and state control shareholder acts.

References

Arrow, K. J. 1964. The Role of Securities in the Optimal Allocation of Risk Bearing. *Review of Economic Studies* 31 (86): 91–96.

Coase, R. H. 1960. The Problem of Social Cost. *Journal of Law and Economics* 3 (October): 1–44.

Debreu, G. 1959. *Theory of Value*. New York: Wiley.

Freeman, R. E. 1984. *Strategic Management: A Stakeholder Approach*. Boston: Pittman.

Hayek, F. A. 1988. *The Fatal Conceit*, in *The Collected Works of F. A. Hayek*, ed. W. W. Bartley. Chicago: University of Chicago Press.

Jensen, M. C., and W. H. Meckling. 1992. Specific and General Knowledge and Organization Structure, in *Contract Economics*, ed. L. Werin and H. Wijkander. Oxford: Basil Blackwell. Reprinted in M. C. Jensen, *Foundations of Organizational Strategy* (Cambridge: Harvard University Press, 1998).

Jensen, M. C., K. H. Wruck, and B. Barry. 1991. Fighton, Inc. (A) and (B). Case 9-391-056. Boston: Harvard Business School.

Lovins, A. B., L. H. Lovins, and P. Hawken. 1999. A Road Map for Natural Capitalism. *Harvard Business Review* (May–June).

Sternberg, E. 1994. *Just Business: Business Ethics in Action.* Boston: Little, Brown.

———. 1996. Stakeholder Theory Exposed. *The Corporate Governance Quarterly* 2(1): 4–18.

Wruck, K. H., M. C. Jensen, and B. Barry. 1991. Fighton, Inc., (A) and (B) Teaching Note. Case 5-491-111. Boston: Harvard Business School.

2

THE PUZZLES AND PARADOXES OF HOW LIVING COMPANIES CREATE WEALTH

Why Single-Valued Objective Functions Are Not Quite Enough

Peter M. Senge

MIKE JENSEN (2000) argues that firm value maximization, whole value maximization, is optimal. Specifically, he argues that it's "logically impossible to maximize in more than one dimension at the same time." That doesn't mean that we don't have multiple "goods" or "bads" in our lives and in our organizations. But we must, in the end, specify the trade-offs among them. And that's what an overall "single-valued objective function" does. Without a clear, single measure for what is sought, it is not possible for people to make sound choices in which they rationally balance short-term and long-term gains, give up more of one valued objective in favor of another that is also valued, or draw the line where the costs of obtaining a desired outcome exceed the benefits. For example, suppose management tells a firm's members that it wants both more short-term profit and more growth in profit. This can leave people incapable of making sound choices if they are in a situation in which "in order to get more growth in profits, we have to sacrifice current profits." In essence, management is abdicating its responsibilities if it fails to clarify a single overarching objective that can inform sound trade-offs.

Given this stance, it is not surprising that Mike is highly critical of concepts such as "balanced scorecards" and stakeholder theories that present to people an array of often competing goals and performance measures. It is not that these ideas are completely wrongheaded. But they are dangerously incomplete, Mike argues, because they present people with many possible aims but with no way of making tough choices among these aims. So what on the surface looks like an advance toward a more systemic picture of the firm and of its interactions with a complex environment may actually lead to poorer decisions in terms of the long-term health of the firm and its contribution to society. Mike also points out that maximizing the total value of the firm, which he advocates, is not necessarily the same as maximizing shareholder return, because there can be sources of financial capital other than equity capital. Especially when there is risky debt, a firm may make decisions that create value for shareholders but transfer more value away from debt holders. Value maximization must always be in light of all of society's (financial) claims on the firm.

There are many aspects of this argument and of the concerns that lie behind it with which I agree. In particular, I find that most businesses are not nearly so concerned with profits as they purport to be. W. Edwards Deming used to say, "Does anyone care around here about profits?" To be sure, every businessperson talks a good talk on this subject. But my own observation is that profits, and particularly long-term wealth creation, are often well down the line among priorities that drive actual decisions—often well behind what is politically expedient; what helps a manager build power or avoid losing it; and the enormous anchor of habit, or "the way things have always been done." As a highly successful European CEO remarked to me over a few beers one evening, "I have never been around an organization where at least 50 percent of managers' energy wasn't devoted to keeping one another comfortable."

Not only do internal politics, ego-based executive decisions, and avoidance of conflict and self-examination dominate decision making; they debilitate commitment and squander the potential energy people might otherwise bring to their work. Most people care deeply about being part of a team and an organization that excels. They are frustrated when they see management that is incompetent or that is not focused on the health of the enterprise as a whole. Sadly, all too often, people accept this as "the way things are," and in doing so they become resigned and to some degree withdrawn. Work then becomes a mere job rather than an exciting adventure of contributing to a mission that matters and creating value as a consequence.

In response to the problem of firms dominated by self-serving managers rather than by goals of serving customers and creating wealth, a whole generation of purportedly "results-oriented" CEOs has emerged. These are people who excel at focusing people's attention on shareholder value—or at least project an image of themselves as excelling in that area. My own concern is that often these CEOs actually make matters worse. That is, they leave enterprises less able to focus their energies on shareholder value, shifting attention to their own "leadership" rather than to growing business capabilities throughout the enterprise. Jack Welch wannabes seem to abound in business today, both in the United States and in Europe, and I fear that most such "tough business leaders" actually undermine long-term generation of wealth rather than increasing it. They create environments of fear that stress short-term numerical goals. They often operate on one- to three-year time horizons, planning on moving on to their next assignment well before the longer-term negative consequences of their leadership come home to roost.

I think Mike Jensen shares many of these concerns. In talking with Mike, I found that we had a great deal in common in terms of our underlying concerns and the motivations driving our respective work. But we also have some differences. I see two sets of problems with the argument that what is needed is single-valued objective functions and a clear focus on maximizing value. One set is instrumental and concerns operationalizing value maximization. The other set is objective; that is, it concerns the aim itself.

Instrumental Problems with Value Maximization

The instrumental problem with value maximization is this: Accepting that increasing firm value is a legitimate overarching aim (although I will raise some questions about this below), it is unclear how management can best focus people's efforts and attention in order to reliably achieve progress in this direction.

Predictiveness Issues

My background and academic training is in nonlinear dynamic systems, and particularly in the "system dynamics" approach developed at

MIT by Jay Forrester. Studying nonlinear dynamics leads you to conclude that you don't maximize or, to use our term, optimize anything, because such systems are by nature nonpredictive.

It is important to understand that predictiveness in a nonlinear dynamic system is not the classic problem taught to us in school of not having enough information, or of having an imperfect model of the problem at hand. On the contrary, the problem with nonlinear dynamic systems is that even a "perfect model," a model that matches its referent system exactly, is not predictive, even given appropriate statistical criteria for predictiveness. The problem inheres in the characteristics of nonlinear multiple-feedback-loop dynamic systems: If you assume a nonlinear world, the system itself is not predictable in the sense of the "point predictions" of classical statistics.

Today many people recognize some of these ideas from chaos theory; there is widespread understanding that even deterministic nonlinear dynamic systems will produce unexpected behavior over time (for example, see Sterman 1989a). For me, I first came to understand the problems of prediction many years ago, from a computer simulation experiment included in Forrester's book *Industrial Dynamics* (1961). In this experiment Forrester simulated the same nonlinear dynamic model several times, with different sequences of random inputs. The statistical character of the stationary random noise was unchanged among the several simulations, and the deterministic part of the model was unchanged. Yet the different simulations diverged dramatically over time. The system model was oscillatory, and the oscillations generated in different simulations became completely out of phase after only one or two cycles. For example, in one simulation inventory levels would peak at month thirty-three, and in another they would be at a trough (Forrester 1961, p. 430).

The implications of this experiment were striking. Even a perfect model could not be expected to match the behavior of its referent system over time, in a point-by-point manner. Not only would it not match, it would not even be close. Because the problem stems not from imperfect knowledge but from the character of nonlinear dynamics, there is no reason to expect predictability ever to improve.

This realization had quite an impact on my thinking as a young student. Among other things, I never thought any more about optimization, even though my background was in engineering control theory.

If a perfect model cannot predict the future state of a system, how can the imperfect models we must always employ in a real setting do any better? If you cannot predict the future state of a system, how can you predict the consequences of one set of actions versus another on that state? Practically speaking, what does it mean to identify the actions that optimize or maximize some performance index, if there are such fundamental limitations to our ability to predict the consequences of any action?

Why Learning Is More Important Than Optimizing

One implication of these limits on predictability is that living in a non-linear world means giving up analytic abstractions like optimizing or maximizing and concentrating on learning *how* things can get better over time.

Ironically, these early computer simulations pointed to the need for a more *qualitative* as opposed to quantitative approach to understanding and improving complex human systems. They did not imply that there was nothing that could be learned, or that no guidance for effective policy and strategy was possible. On the contrary, the patterns of behavior generated by the different simulations in Forrester's experiment were quite similar—it was just the quantitative behavior that varied wildly. Moreover, differences between the simulated effects of alternative policies could be quite robust in the face of the quantitative unpredictability of the nonlinear model. In other words, policy set A could be quite superior to policy set B, even though you could not predict exactly the outcomes of either. This finding suggested a way to understand the longer-term consequences of alternative policies and strategies in a nonlinear system: Results cannot be predicted precisely, but the patterns shaping them can be understood.

This is why, for me, learning takes precedence over optimizing. The fundamental challenges of management are not about "finding the right answer" so much as about seeking better understanding of the consequences of our actions, and especially understanding of how we may be unwittingly heading in directions opposite to what we intend. Such understanding can in turn lead to significant improvement.

Now, Mike's response to these problems is that although optimization may no longer make sense in a nonlinear world, a single-valued objective function whereby you gauge improvement still does. After all, people do still need to make trade-offs, and having a clear shared idea of how we define "better" still matters. I agree that people need shared understanding of what "better" means, but I contend that agreeing on the objective function is a small problem relative to much bigger ones.

In particular, I worry that a singular focus on the goal of increasing or maximizing firm value will actually reduce the possibility of that goal's being attained. The root of these concerns lies in the unexamined and highly questionable causal theories that guide human actors in complex situations—theories that are likely to remain unexamined so long as management sees its job as focusing on value maximization rather than on learning.

The System Dynamics View of People's Theories in Use

One of the most recurrent findings of system dynamics studies of corporate policy and strategy is that conscious policies in complex systems are very often a primary source of the very problems those policies purport to solve. Forrester called this phenomenon "the counterintuitive nature of complex systems," arguing that human intuition consistently leads people to want to do virtually the opposite of what would really accomplish their aims (Forrester 1971). As Jay used to say, when confronted with a complex system, most people focus their efforts on the very parts of the system where there exists the lowest leverage for significant change; should they stumble onto a high-leverage policy lever, "They will usually push it in the opposite direction of what is needed." The implications of Forrester's view are that almost all corporations massively underperform, and that simply being more clear about the goals will do little if anything to help.

John Sterman of MIT has explored these basic problems with human decision making in numerous laboratory experiments. He has shown that people consistently misjudge even simple dynamic decision-making tasks (Sterman 1989b). Sterman's work falls within a large behavioral decision-making literature on cognitive biases and limits on rationality (e.g., Hogarth 1987; Kahneman et al. 1982; Simon 1979, 1982). Sterman has added to this literature the important point that, beyond biases and self-limiting heuristics, there appear to be "basic cognitive limits" to our abilities to understand the dynamics of nonlinear multiple-feedback-loop systems. We are used to seeing a world of simple linear cause and effect, and this mental frame consistently and often significantly misleads us when we are confronted with dynamic complexity. Sterman found that experimental subjects in a relatively simple production–distribution system with four interacting decision-making roles generated, on average, costs that were ten times higher than the feasible minimum. The problem was not lack of information; the benchmark cost against which the subjects' results were compared utilized the same information. The problem was not lack of clarity regarding the objective function; the subjects all faced an explicit single-valued performance measure. The problem was the subjects' inability to understand the feedback dynamics of their setting. Subsequent experiments have shown that different subjects, including experienced managers, have similar problems, and that markets with multiple firms do little better (Baaken 1993, Diehl and Sterman 1995, Kampmann and Sterman 1996, Paich and Sterman 1993).

Forrester and Sterman argue that the key problem is the inadequacy of the causal theories that typically guide our actions. We can have all the clarity in the world about the goal of improving firm value and yet have little ability to make decisions that will move us in that direction. If this is the case, our primary tasks in complex human systems are to become more reflective on the reasoning that guides our actions and to gradually improve our theories in use. This core learning challenge, in my judgment, dwarfs the problem of convincing people that they should try to improve firm value.

There is another important implication of the system dynamics view of our theories in use: namely, that firm value maximization will almost always become, by default, short-term profit maximization. The reason is that the complex feedback dynamics that bedevil our simplistic causal theories take time to play out. Given a short enough time horizon, many of these feedbacks can be ignored. This is why manipulating profits over the short term is much easier than building wealth over the long term. A simple causal theory may suffice for the former, while the latter requires a much more complex causal theory. For example, a manager does not require a complex theory to determine that cutting head count can boost short-term profits; only in the longer run do the negative effects on morale, risk-taking, and innovativeness, and the unintended loss of key people, affect new products and new revenue generation. Thus, whether intended or not, preaching value maximization will almost always lead to short-term profit maximization. It cannot do otherwise—unless it is linked to efforts to build better causal theories; that is, to learn.

The Immensity of the Learning Challenge in Realistic Settings

But preaching learning is also problematic, as many executives who advocate "learning organizations" have discovered. There are significant barriers to deep learning—to rethinking assumptions and practices that are taken for granted. In realistic decision-making settings, unarticulated and simplistic individual mental models interact with complex group dynamics and with social norms and assumptions. The following example illustrates the problems this can pose for collective learning.

Some years ago I worked with several colleagues in a large property and casualty insurance firm, attempting to understand the dynamics of claims management. Our aim was to develop and test simulation-based learning tools. Gradually, however, what emerged was a theory of the business that had disturbing implications. At one level the theory was relatively simple and intuitive. The cost structure of a typical claims operation reveals that somewhere between two thirds and three quarters of total costs are paid out as settlements and litigation costs; sometimes the figure is as high as 80 percent. The remainder are expenses, primarily salary and overhead for claims staff. In the eyes of most senior claims managers, settlement and litigation costs are outside their ability to control, whereas expenses are controllable. Consequently, emphasis is put on expense control. For example, each claims office in the firm reported monthly results on a common "scorecard," which featured "expense ratios" (expense dollars normalized by premium volume), along with "production ratios" (claims settled normalized by incoming claims) and related productivity statistics. As you might imagine, this scorecard created vigorous competition among the offices to show low expense ratios and high productivity figures.

But we came to conclude that these managerial practices were deeply flawed. Veteran claims adjusters disputed the idea that settlement and litigation costs were not controllable. Indeed, these adjusters argued that the traditional view of claims adjusting was based on the belief that the quality of investigation and record keeping could significantly affect settlement costs. The problem, in their view, was that quality standards had eroded steadily over many years. Such quality standards, applied to both technical analysis of claims and the interpersonal process of negotiation with claimants, were inherently nonquantifiable and could be met only by experienced adjusters and managers who engaged in continual reflection and vigilant oversight of adjusting practices. But experience levels had been declining for years. Few adjusters stayed on the job for more than a few years, and managers seeking advancement often moved out of claims and into higher-paying marketing and finance career tracks. The profession of adjusting, in the veteran adjusters' view, was becoming a nonprofession and was being replaced by the euphemistically labeled "claims processing"—the mechanical handling of large volumes of claims as quickly as possible, with little or no investigation and consequently with minimal knowledge of the facts and records, even in complex cases. This, the adjusters argued, also accounted for much of the growth in litigation costs, as insurance companies were ill prepared to defend themselves in court or upon "subrogation" from other insurers.

Gradually, we developed a dynamic theory of the long-term evolution, or more precisely devolution, of an industry over many years (Senge and Oliva 1993). As claims standards eroded and settlement and litigation costs increased, financial pressures increased, leading to increasing managerial emphasis on cost control. This emphasis became translated as expense control, reduced investment in people and skill levels, further deterioration of quality and profitability, and continued financial stress. This theory of long-term dynamics was backed up by industry statistics showing that settlement and litigation costs as a proportion of total costs had risen steadily over fifty years, while expense ratios had improved. Contemporary managers took pride in the improved expense ratios, citing modern information technology and other managerial innovations that had led to more and more rapid claims handling. Rising settlement and litigation costs were attributed to external factors, such as increasing technological complexity, rising societal litigiousness, and proliferating governmental regulations. Because these factors were seen as unconnected to insurance company practices, the primary response of insurers was to beef up their legal departments and lobbying efforts. Since this original study, subsequent studies have shown that similar vicious spirals may afflict many service businesses (Oliva 1996, Sterman and Oliva 1999). In settings where quality is inherently highly subjective and not easily reduced to quantitative measures, a vicious spiral can easily develop: underinvestment in professional capacity, erosion of quality standards, and increasing financial pressures due to rising costs of poor quality, all of which lead to greater expense control and continued underinvestment.

Now, this theory of the insurance business had potentially important implications for total costs and profits, especially over the long run. Although the theory contradicted much current thinking and practice, gradually the claims vice president and several senior staff became convinced—after more than a year of developing and testing dynamic models of the claims system—that it had merit. They saw it as potentially representing a significant shift in strategy and decided to bring the case for this shift to the company's top management.

What then ensued was a classic example of the perils of challenging established mental models. In a meeting with most of the top management, the claims VP laid out the basic logic of the theory, supported by views from veteran adjusters about eroding quality and the high costs of poor quality. He shared anecdotes of 100 percent overpayments on claims due to inadequate investigation, such as on claims based on inflated auto body shop estimates. Unnecessary losses in litigated claims (most of which are settled out of court in favor of claimants because insurers know so little about the facts) were still higher, he suggested. He argued that a strategy of rebuilding professional capacity in skilled adjusters and setting higher quality standards could hold the key to reversing the spiral of escalating settlement and litigation costs that afflicted the industry. As a hypothetical illustration of the leverage for increased profitability, he showed how the costs of doubling adjuster capacity would be offset by a modest 25 percent improvement in settlement and litigation costs. He argued that with such a strategy the firm could become a leader in the industry, further building its already strong financial position (the firm had risen to the top quartile of the industry over the preceding decade). His peers listened carefully. They seemed to grasp the logic of the argument. But they were decidedly reserved in showing any enthusiasm for its implications: the need to invest in more adjuster capacity in order to reap eventual reductions in total costs. After all, each manager was already being asked to cut back expenses in his or her own department. Expense control was not just a company norm but an industry norm. And they were all being judged by their commitment to that norm. Finally, one of the other VPs asked tersely, "Aren't our claims expense ratios already higher than those of any of our main competitors?"

With that question, the meeting came to an end. Of course, as all the VPs knew, the company's claims expense ratio was already high, relative to competitors'. And the claims VP was proposing that it should become higher still, perhaps significantly so. This proposal so contradicted the expectations and conscious intentions of all the VPs that it suddenly seemed almost ludicrous. Realizing this, the claims VP quickly grew much less impassioned in his advocacy—perhaps also realizing that he was on very thin ice in terms of his credibility with his peers. Although the senior claims management team remained convinced of the logic of their position, they also felt that to pursue it further could become a "career-limiting" strategy. They felt defeated and resigned. The weight of established thinking was clearly too great to overcome.

I do not think the problems in this case stemmed from lack of clarity about the aim of building the economic value of the firm, or from lack of commitment to this aim. I think the members of that management team felt they were adopting positions that reflected that very commitment. Indeed, the strength of their opposition to the claims team's radical strategy showed just how committed they were, at least in their own minds. Rather, I think this is a classic case of what the behavioral decision-making literature refers to as "anchoring and adjustment." It was impossible for the senior managers in this firm to consider anything but a minor adjustment to the core strategy of expense control. They were firmly anchored on this strategy, like most of their counterparts throughout the industry. The idea that a key to significant increases in profitability lay in what seemed like reversal of the core strategy was virtually undiscussable—especially among people with a great deal of personal investment in succeeding in that strategy. In essence, the emotional and cognitive demands made by radical proposals for increasing profitability exceeded the group's capacity for inquiry; and the limited capacity for inquiry determined what decisions were possible.

Now, it is very possible that our dynamic theory of underinvestment in professional capacity was wrong in some important ways that none of us could find. The point of my story is not to defend the theory but to reflect on it as a meaningful example of why it is so difficult to explicate and improve the causal theories underlying corporate policies. Although there undoubtedly were flaws in the theory our team had developed, it was at the least an explicit theory, one that was capable (through endogenous mechanisms) of recreating important aspects of history, and one that several highly experienced people had come to believe captured critical aspects of their professional experience. Yet in a direct confrontation with the implicit mental models of the management team, the theory had little chance.

This is the type of deep learning challenge that companies face all the time, especially in market settings where radical shifts in strategy and policy may be called for. I do not see where clarity on the objective function will help; in fact, it may even hinder. As with the insurance firm's managers—and I want to emphasize that this was a very successful firm—fear of loss of profitability may be so great that focusing on profit, or maximizing firm value, may even be actively counterproductive.

I believe Mike Jensen understands this argument. But I do not see how he has taken the implications of this cognitive problem into account in advocating for value maximization. It seems to me that the worst strategy is to ignore the problem: to simply advocate value maximization and hope that people then figure out what to do. If we are serious about building firm value, we cannot ignore the immense learning challenge this mandate presents.

What Can Management Do to Help People Focus Their Efforts Productively?

Focusing directly on value maximization appears to be a low-leverage strategy. What, alternatively, can management do to help people focus their efforts more productively?

I surely do not expect there ever to be a simple answer to this question; nor do I expect there to be any sort of exact science that offers guidance. But there may be some principles that will be helpful, or at least some suggestions as to why what is common practice today may be exactly the wrong thing to do.

First, just as focusing everyone's efforts on value maximization may not lead toward that aim, so too we should question management's abilities to parse this overarching aim into the optimal set of local goals. It is commonly seen as management's task to set local goals for local operations. So, for example, it is common to have management set cost-reduction targets for operations. After all, who else will figure out how to set local goals that are in line with overall profit and return objectives? But there are good reasons to question the wisdom of automatically ceding this task to management.

Deming (1982) used to exhort managers to "eliminate numerical quotas for the work force and numerical goals for management." But I know few organizations where this has happened. Most contemporary managers see Deming's directive as almost unthinkable—so wedded are we to the notion that one of management's most basic jobs is to set targets and to "motivate" people toward the attainment of these goals.

But perhaps blind faith in this hoary truism may be one of the primary reasons that firms fail to realize potential value growth. Most industry analysts would consider Toyota the world's superior automobile manufacturer. Its product quality and customer loyalty are unequaled. Virtually every major manufacturer has tried to imitate the famous "Toyota production system." From 1988 to 1998, Toyota's market capitalization roughly equaled the sum of the Detroit "big three." Clearly, Toyota has demonstrated a superior ability to create financial value relative to its major competitors.

In this light it is especially interesting that Toyota has a cost management system radically different from those of its U.S. counterparts. Based on in-depth study of Toyota's primary U.S. assembly facility in Georgetown, Kentucky, accounting theorist Tom Johnson points out that Toyota does not use a standard cost system to control operating costs. That is, although Toyota employs many measures related to costs and productivity, there is no use of cost information by management to "drive improvement." Instead, Johnson says, the Toyota philosophy of measurement is aimed at supporting people rather than controlling them. Echoing Deming, Johnson argues that when "business . . . drives the actions of its members with external targets and information designed to enforce goals defined by someone outside the members' community . . . it inevitably generates adverse feedback in a human social system that eventually causes the system to chronically underperform, at best, or totally collapse, at worst" (Johnson 1998, p. 4).

This finding suggests a second principle: People are truly motivated to learn without external pressures. Interestingly, Toyota is arguably the large firm most influenced by Deming (his portrait hangs in the lobby of Toyota's corporate headquarters). Not only has Toyota taken to heart Deming's admonition to eliminate numerical quotas, the company seems to have internalized Deming's belief in local workers' intrinsic motivation to improve: "The prevailing system of management has destroyed our people. People are born with intrinsic motivation, self-esteem, dignity, curiosity to learn, joy in learning" (Deming 1994). Deming believed that industrial-age institutions, starting with schools, destroy intrinsic motivation and curiosity through "management by objectives."

Third, learning should be made inseparable from working. In a forthcoming book, Johnson (2000) suggests that Toyota has discovered and embodied certain principles of living systems, and that this accounts for the company's unprecedented productivity and cost performance. Rather than operating by command and control, living systems develop awareness and feedback processes that allow local actions to support systemwide objectives. Johnson argues that the relentless use of fragmented quantitative information to drive performance undermines people's natural efforts to make sense of the relationships in their environment and hinders the natural evolution of feedback processes that increase intelligence. Relationships cannot be measured quantitatively. Yet understanding of those relationships is crucial for effective action. In effect, management by quantitative objectives creates a deep and pervasive distraction from the natural learning processes in which people would otherwise engage in order to increase their effectiveness. The real task of management is to find ways to improve and accelerate those learning processes.

Over many years Toyota has developed its own methods, many of which Johnson attempts to explicate. The essence of the approach is to immerse people in continually deepening their understanding of the complexities of the entire manufacturing process, to build awareness of how the process is functioning in real time, and simultaneously to deepen workers' sense of responsibility for the healthy functioning of the system as a whole. This is a highly labor-intensive process. As Johnson points out, when Toyota opened its Georgetown facility, 300 Japanese managers came to live with their U.S. counterparts for up to a year. The famous "Toyota production system" is in fact a learning system, inseparable from the knowledge embodied in the people who make up the system.

Lastly, none of this says that there should not be local goals, or that quantitative targets have no use. On the contrary, people intrinsically motivated to learn will often set challenging targets for themselves. For example, Toyota has a sophisticated system of target costing through which local units focus their improvement activities. If set locally by people immersed in continual learning, goals are less likely to cause the destructive fragmentation that arises when they are set by those disconnected from the processes whereby the goals will be realized. The key to local goal setting that serves the health of the whole is helping people at the local level see how they fit into the larger system. Only then can they shape a field of local goals consonant with systemwide health.

In our own work, we have concluded that management's job must include creating work environments where three types of learning capabilities can develop: individual and collective aspiration, reflectiveness and generative conversation, and systems thinking (Senge 1990, Senge et al. 1994). First, aspiration is vital to learning, because we all learn best when we are engaged in things that matter to us. Questions of purpose are always central for people. Although work settings rarely provide the opportunity for people to think about what matters to them, such thinking is vital to engagement, commitment, and perseverance. Many companies fail to tap immense reservoirs of human energy and ingenuity because they ignore simple, basic questions: Are people proud of the work they do? Do they know why the organization exists and how it seeks to serve in unique ways? What do they tell their children about what they do? Second, it is equally important that people become more able to reflect on and talk about their current reality. Oftentimes, telling the truth about reality is more difficult and more threatening than talking about our aspirations. We are used to expressing our views, but we are much less used to examining our actions and how they may be inconsistent with those views. Organizations are invariably full of "undiscussable" subjects, as Chris Argyris (1990, 1997) says—sometimes because of the personal threats these topics pose and sometimes because they simply conflict with unquestioned and unquestionable assumptions, like those of the insurance managers who could not imagine intentionally increasing expense ratios that already exceeded competitors'. Lastly, system thinking is needed in order to understand the complex interdependence of business realities. The fragmentation into arbitrary functions, the focus on pleasing the boss rather than understanding larger processes, and the perpetual attacking of problem symptoms while deeper systemic causes go unattended all frustrate people and limit learning in organizations everywhere.

Put slightly differently, two fundamental gaps characterize the difficulty of encouraging learning to increase firm value. First, managers' theories in use may not match their espoused theories. Second, people's theories in use may be very poor guidance for effective decision taking in a complex system. An example of the first gap occurs when managers espouse a commitment to building firm value but actually consistently take actions that are contrary because they are more interested in achieving other objectives, such as maintaining political power or reducing threat to themselves or others. The second gap arises because, as I explained earlier, our theories that connect actions and consequences are inadequate, given the dynamic, nonlinear world in which we must act. It is my experience that these two gaps are almost always both present, and their interaction creates the extraordinary learning challenges of real-world organizational settings. Dealing with these gaps requires individual and collective learning capabilities not found in traditional organizations.

In summary, once people recognize that focusing everyone's attention on firm value may not be the best way to generate firm value, they then tend to conclude that it is management's task to set up correct local goals to align local actions with systemwide performance. I am dubious of this conclusion. It presupposes an almost godlike level of understanding of the system as a whole that does not match my experience of managers, even highly competent ones. It also results in the imposition of goals from outside a work community on the members of that community, with the consequent reactions that Deming and Tom Johnson so eloquently characterize. In short, I see no substitute for the messy, ongoing process of everyone working together to make sense of the dynamic, nonlinear, highly interdependent realities in which work gets done. I believe there are tools and methods that can support this effort. I believe that companies like Toyota and many other cases that I have witnessed firsthand offer evidence of immense possibilities for improving firm value lying in this direction (for examples, see Kleiner and Roth 2000, Roth and Kleiner 1999, Senge et al. 1994).

Interestingly, I think Mike Jensen and I may agree that the fundamental responsibility of management is to continually improve the processes whereby this ongoing learning can take place. Mike has even explored, from the vantage point of his own theorizing, some of the implications of this concept for reallocating decision rights and decentralizing goal setting. Within a context of continually improving the learning processes that shape the field of goals and aspirations in an enterprise, by and large I have no problem with seeing building firm value as a guiding aspiration. My main concern stems from what I feel is misplaced and emphasis on value maximization when it is fragmented away from this larger learning process.

Objective Problems with Value Maximization

I also want to raise some questions about value maximization from a more philosophical viewpoint: questions about the aim itself. These are the objective problems I mentioned earlier. In particular, I would like to suggest that there is often a sort of machine worldview that underlies value maximization as a company aim. If we think of firms as living systems rather than as machines, it leads to a different metaphorical understanding of the roles of profits and value creation in the vitality of an enterprise. While in some sense this different understanding does not lessen the importance of value creation, it places it in a different context.

The Living Company

In a remarkable little book, *The Living Company* (1997), retired Shell executive Arie de Geus raises a host of provocative issues flowing from a simple question: What are the implications of seeing a company as a living being versus as a machine for making money?

For those of us growing up in industrial societies, the depth to which the machine metaphor penetrates our ways of thinking and talking is hard to appreciate. We speak casually of "management control systems" and "leaders who drive change" without ever stopping to ponder the images we are conveying. Companies that are underperforming are seen as "broken" and turnaround experts are brought in to "fix them." We know that if we applied these same ways of thinking in our families, we would be in big trouble. Yet we rarely stop to question them in organizations.

From a biological viewpoint, one of the differences between a machine and a living system stems from the fact that a living system creates itself, whereas a machine is created by someone or something else—the distinction made by biologists between *autopoiesis* and *allopoiesis*. In this sense, the status of a company is ambiguous. A company has founders, who in a sense created the firm as a legal entity. Specific managers create the company's formal policies and structures. But the present organization is also a human community. As a community it was no more created by its founders than the children in a school were created by the people who started the school. Although the company has formal structures and policies, the "operating structures" that shape what really happens are continually being enacted through the day-to-day actions of its members. There is no formal set of rules or guidelines that explicate the norms, goals, tacit sanctions, expectations, habits, and pressures that drive actual decisions; these live only in the human community that is the enterprise, and are continually reinforced by the actions of that community.

De Geus argues that those companies that have survived and thrived for a long time tend to see themselves more as human communities and less as machines. The backdrop for his commentary was a Shell study of companies that had survived for more than 200 years. De Geus suggests that these firms have a sense of identity, of what they stand for—a purpose and core values that transcend what they do. Curiously, this appreciation for continuity makes such companies tolerant of continual experimentation and novel ways of doing things: They continually grow the new in the midst of the old. They are sensitive to their environment, and they are conservative in their financing so as to allow for flexibility as that environment changes.

Interestingly, a conscious grasp of their organizations as living human communities rather than as machines also characterizes some of today's most successful leaders. I have already cited Toyota as an example of biological thinking in a manufacturing environment. Another example is the governance system created for Visa International, one of the largest enterprises in the world in terms of market value. Dee Hock, Visa's founding CEO, describes Visa's corporate organization as actually the current manifestation of a continual process of self-organizing, "like the body, the brain, and the biosphere" (Waldrop 1996). Owned by its members, governed by a constitution that sharply limits the power of its elected officers, and grounded in a statement of purpose and principles that are the core of that constitution, Visa also has sales that exceed $1 trillion; is growing at 20 percent a year; and has a market value, according to Hock, that would exceed $400 billion if it were a publicly traded company. "All organizations are merely embodiments of a very old, very basic idea—the idea of community," says Hock. "An organization's success has enormously more to do with clarity of a shared purpose, common principles and strength of belief in them than to assets, expertise, operating ability, or management competence, important as they may be" (Waldrop 1996).

Purpose and Function: Rethinking Value Maximization in a Living Company

What does the idea of the living company have to say about value maximization?

There is one more distinction from biology that can help here: that between design and emergence. Living systems have design characteristics that can often be thought of usefully in mechanistic terms. In this sense you might say that these biological mechanisms have certain basic functions, like maintaining glucose or temperature balances. It is very useful to understand the functioning of these systems. But in a living system these mechanisms are themselves emergent phenomena, created by the organism itself, not by some outside designer or builder.

The capabilities of a living system in any place and time arise from the interplay of design and emergence. For example, the human being can be remarkably creative in generating new behaviors in response to new challenges, but those behaviors do not include flying, because bodily flight is beyond the limits of our design. On the other hand, the genius of our design lies precisely in the possibilities for emergence it affords. Evolution has invested a few billion years in this design, precisely so that it becomes less and less predictable, more and more capable of emergence.

The distinction between design and emergence makes it possible to distinguish function and purpose. Function can be specified. It is embedded in design. Function has two meanings, one relating to the design of the organism and one relating to how the organism fits into larger living systems. A viable biological organism maintains conditions required for its healthy functioning. So, for example, the respiratory system *functions* so as to maintain oxygen levels in the human body. But the organism also has a function in service to the larger living community of which it is a member. The corporation as currently designed has clear requirements essential to viability. One of these is profits. Profits are to a corporation what oxygen is to a human—a necessary condition for viable functioning. But the corporation as currently designed also has functions determined by the needs of the larger social system. For example, the corporation has the function of creating a return on the financial investment society has made in it, which is why firm value is ultimately a societal concern.

But both of these functions are different from purpose. Purpose is emergent. It can never be specified by design. In the corporation as a human community, a sense of purpose continually evolves, a living embodiment of the organization's members' quest for meaning and purposefulness. You and I need oxygen to survive. But life is about more than breathing. So, too, can a corporation as a living community generate purposefulness. This is different from its function.

At present, from our prevailing economic perspective, maximizing value expresses the function of the corporation within society. It is important to understand this. This function can change only if there are distinct changes in design. But in a living system capable of self-awareness and self-organizing, design is subject to emergence. So the present corporate design can change if our sense of purpose changes.

To illustrate, one such possible design change may come from new ideas about capitalism (Hawken, Lovins, and Lovins 1999; Lovins, Lovins, and Hawken 1999). Industrial-age capitalism pays close attention to financial capital but ignores natural capital, the stock of service-generating capacity that nature has accumulated over four billion years on this planet. This is the capital that gives us water to drink, air to breathe, and soil in which to grow our food. Stewarding this capital, endeavoring to maximize return on this capital, would require significant design changes in the present-day corporation. This has been a blind spot of industrial-age capitalism. But as we continue to deplete the stock of natural capital, deteriorating ecosystems will lead to rising societal costs and concerns. Should a new sense of purpose for corporations emerge from these concerns, we might well redefine the design and function of corporations. If this happened, would it be sufficient to regard value maximization as a firm's single design function? What would a corporation whose function was both stewarding natural capital and financial capital look like? How would such a corporation's learning processes and control processes evolve? Today these questions are unanswered. But they are not addressed. Indeed, a growing number of firms are taking them very seriously.

Design and emergence coexist and continually interact in a living system. This is why building firm value and actualizing purpose can coexist healthily. But emergence alters design. As purpose evolves, so too will function. There is only one thing that can be said safely: As a living system, the corporation will evolve.

References

Argyris, C. 1990. *Overcoming Organizational Defenses.* Boston: Allyn and Bacon.

Argyris, C., and D. Schoen. 1997. *Organizational Learning: A Theory of Action Perspective.* Reading, MA: Addison Wesley.

Bakken, B. 1993. Learning and Transfer of Understanding in Dynamic Decision Environments. Unpublished Ph.D. dissertation, MIT Sloan School of Management.

de Geus, A. 1997. *The Living Company.* Boston: Harvard Business School Press.

Deming, W. E. 1982. *Out of the Crisis.* Cambridge, MA: MIT Center for Advanced Engineering Studies.

———. 1994. *The New Economics of Industry, Government, Education.* Cambridge, MA: MIT Center for Advanced Engineering Studies.

Diehl, E., and J. Sterman. 1995. Effects of Feedback Complexity on Dynamic Decision Making. *Organizational Behavior and Human Decision Processes* 62: 198–215.

Forrester, J. W. 1961. *Industrial Dynamics.* Cambridge, MA: MIT Press.

———. 1971. Counterintuitive Nature of Social Systems. *Technology Review.*

———. 1975. *Collected Papers of Jay W. Forrester.* Cambridge, MA: MIT Press.

Hawken, P., A. Lovins, and H. Lovins. 1999. *Natural Capitalism.* New York: Little, Brown.

Hogarth, R. 1987. *Judgment and Choice.* New York: Wiley.

Jensen, M. 2000. Value Maximization and the Corporate Executive Function. In *Breaking the Code of Change,* ed. M. Beer and N. Nohria. Boston: Harvard Business School Press.

Johnson, H. T. 1998. Using Performance Measurement to Improve Results: A Life Systems Perspective. *International Journal of Strategic Cost Management* 1(1): 1–6.

———. 2000. *Profit beyond Measure.* New York: Free Press.

Kahneman, D., P. Slovic, and A. Tversky, eds. 1982. *Judgment under Uncertainty: Heuristics and Biases.* Cambridge, U.K.: Cambridge University Press.

Kampmann, C., and J. Sterman. 1996. Feedback Complexity, Bounded Rationality, and Market Dynamics. *Sloan School of Management working paper.* Cambridge, MA: MIT.

Kleiner, A., and G. Roth. 2000. *Oil Change: Perspectives on Corporate Transformation.* New York: Oxford University Press. (Full document can be ordered from SoL Web page: sol-ne.org.)

Lovins, A., H. Lovins, and P. Hawken. 1999. A Road Map for Natural Capitalism. *Harvard Business Review* (May–June).

Oliva, R. 1996. A Dynamic Theory of Service Delivery: Implications for Managing Service Quality. Ph.D. thesis, MIT Sloan School of Management.

Oliva, R., and J. Sterman. 1999. Cutting Corners and Working Overtime: Quality Erosion in the Service Industry. Working paper. Harvard Business School, Boston.

Paich, M., and J. Sterman. 1993. Boom, Bust, and Failures to Learn in Experimental Markets. *Management Science* 39: 1439–1458.

Roth, G., and A. Kleiner. 1999. *Car Launch.* New York: Oxford University Press.

Senge, P. M. 1990. *The Fifth Discipline.* New York: Doubleday.

Senge, P. M., and R. Oliva. 1993. Developing a Theory of Service Quality/Service Capacity Interaction. In *Proceedings of the 1993 International Conference of System Dynamics,* ed. E. Zepeda and J. Machuca. Cancun, Mexico, 476–485.

Senge, P. M., A. Kleiner, C. Roberts, R. Ross, and B. Smith. 1994. *The Fifth Discipline Fieldbook.* New York: Doubleday.

Simon, H. 1979. Rational Decision Making in Business Organizations. *American Economic Review* 69: 493–513.

———. 1982. *Models of Bounded Rationality.* Cambridge, MA: MIT Press.

Sterman, J. D. 1989a. Deterministic Chaos in an Experimental Economic System. *Journal of Economic Behavior and Organization* 12: 1–28.

———. 1989b. Modeling Managerial Behavior: Misperceptions of Feedback in a Dynamic Decision Making Experiment. *Management Science* 35: 321–339.

Waldrop, M. M. 1996. The Trillion Dollar Vision of Dee Hock. *Fast Company* (Oct.–Nov.) 75–86.

3

THE PURPOSE OF CHANGE
A Commentary on Jensen and Senge

Joseph L. Bower

THE TITLE PROVIDED by the editors for this chapter captures in a special way the dilemma a general manager experiences when confronting the field called "organizational change." "What is that about?" he or she will mumble. "Aren't organizations changing all the time? The trick is to get them to change in the direction that you have in mind." For general managers, work life is all about *purposive change*—what it should be and how it should be accomplished. The academic study of this topic is the work of the field once called business policy and now usually called strategic management. That field has been my intellectual home for thirty-five years, so it is from the purposive change perspective that I approach the topic.

Purposive Change

Once we make the transformation of title it becomes remarkably easy to appreciate the presentations of Michael Jensen and Peter Senge. They each thought it necessary to explain the central role of purpose in their thinking about organizational behavior. It is also easy to understand why they had trouble posing their remarks in a debate format. They have completely different concepts of purpose. In fact, their arguments exist in separate dimensions of reality. In this commentary, after summarizing briefly the positions expounded by Jensen and Senge, I will address questions posed to the authors, provide additional context from my own research, and conclude by suggesting an appropriate way to address purposive change.

Michael Jensen tried in his presentation to explain that the problem in most change efforts is a lack of clear purpose. Viewing managerial effort from the perspective of an economist, Jensen points out that although a manager must deal with multiple constituencies, he or she cannot maximize multiple objectives. One can seek to maximize an objective function with several dimensions, but these must be capable of being traded into a single common measure that in turn can be maximized. Managers who speak as if they can maximize in several directions simultaneously are desperately confused. They will inevitably make a muddle of things. For example, the manager seeking growth in both current and future profits must realize that at some point growth in one will limit the other.

Jensen suggests that the answer can be found in value maximization. He argues that the problem with stakeholder theory is that it is incomplete. It simply tells company leaders that they must pay attention to all stakeholders, without clarifying what the trade-offs are among the stakeholders. Managers should invest in a stakeholder until the marginal benefit to the firm of doing so equates to other investments.

As summarized here, the argument may seem abstract. But Jensen's work has been motivated by a very concrete problem: value destruction. In his research he has documented the billions of dollars of wealth destroyed by firms in industries such as oil, chemicals, tires, and defense that have not paid attention to value creation as they managed investments and operations. In the context of this book, we could say that by not changing organizational practices in the face of changing markets, such firms have failed miserably in their actual intention to help stakeholders. Jensen's solution, the application of a rigorous organizational economics driven by value maximization, relies on performance-based incentives to align the interests of all parts of the organization with those of the owners.

In short, Jensen's prescription is for a firm to express its purpose in a fashion linked directly to the firm's long-term value. If the members of the organization are motivated by successful value creation, then they will drive appropriate change.

Peter Senge's analysis differs from Jensen's, not because he thinks value maximization unimportant, but because he sees purpose as a reason for being, not a formula for measuring economic value. For Senge, organizational change is about learning: learning to do new things or to do the same things for different reasons. People learn best when they *want* to learn—which is why organizational purpose is so important. When members comprehend an organization's purpose as distinct from what it does, they can understand why it may be important to change what the organization does in order to serve its purpose. More importantly, they may have a good idea of how their specific part of the organization should change the way it operates. Learning in an organization is difficult, in part because it is hard to communicate about sense making (how/why the world works), and in part because of complexity. In the realm of nonlinear dynamic systems, Senge maintains, you really don't think about maximizing value. But not thinking about purpose because it's complex will not do either.

For Senge, purpose is not so much targeting as answering the question: Why are we here? For example, the ultimate raison d'être for an insurance company he was studying was "because life is unfair." Everything else flowed from that motivating proposition. In turn, Senge's research is concerned with reflective conversation—"How do we talk to one another so that we can learn?" Learning, in turn, requires understanding complex systems. For example, health is hard to define or maximize, but we know how to improve health.

For Senge, the problem posed by learning, communication, and complexity is that it is very hard to link purposive managerial behavior with outcomes. A manager preaching value maximization may not only be irrelevant to what is happening in his organization; he may be counterproductive. Even if a manager accepts the maximization of value of the firm over time as a legitimate goal or objective function, Senge contends, focusing people's time and energies effectively is a very serious practical problem.

A General Management View of Change

What Jensen's and Senge's arguments represent are partial analyses of a problem more complex than either acknowledges. As many authors have described, purposive behavior in complex organizations has cognitive, economic, organizational, and emotional components that interact in important ways.[1] Strategic outcomes develop over time, influenced by activity occurring simultaneously at multiple levels of an organization, sometimes intentionally, sometimes unintentionally, and often in response to external shifts in markets and the broader environment. When we look at this complex activity through one lens, for example that of an economic model, we see much that is true. When we look at it through the lens of organizational learning, the overview seems correct, but the normative propositions that follow seem partial and very abstract. In either case, we miss a good deal of what is going on. For an academic, missing things is not a problem as long as one's analysis reveals more of the picture over time. But for the manager responsible for the whole picture, missing things can be a disaster.

The model summarized in figure 3-1 captures a good deal of the problem facing a manager contemplating purposive change. It views the company as a system for deploying resources.

To begin, the model suggests the extent to which judgments about purposive action are made from several *organizational perspectives*. Substantive analysis of a particular business activity involves at least its *technological and economic* aspects. These are examined from both corporate (top) and operating unit (bottom) perspectives, which can be quite different. For example, in 1970 General Electric was one of the three or four strongest challengers to IBM in the burgeoning computer market. The division managing GE's computer business had introduced time-sharing and had demonstrated significant technological and marketing capability. Within the computer division, various department managers were arguing the merits of specific technological and product developments. For example, the details of the transition from transistors to solid-state technology was debated in the late 1960s. The division's strategic plans called for considerable growth and profit. But when the corporation examined the same business, they saw that the financial resources to fund the business properly would take up a significant portion (perhaps 70 percent) of the company's

The Corporate Environment: The Capital Markets, The Talent Markets

Type of Activity	Technical – Economic Content	Commitment of Resources	Systemic Context (Structural, Cultural, and Cognitive)
Corporate	Developing plans and programs to shift the strategic domain and economic quality of the business portfolio in response to corporate goals, competition, and market response.	Decisions to allocate capital and people to one or another set of plans.	Building the organization and information, planning, and budgeting systems for measuring and rewarding business and management performance; the work environment; and the value premise.
Integrating	Translating and applying corporate plans to the concrete possibilities provided by the business units. Stimulating the modification of corporate plans to exploit unit opportunities.	The brokering of proposals. Selection of programs to support.	Adapting the corporate context to the needs of particular businesses and the abilities of particular managers. Changing the context.
Operating	Building plans and programs involving new processes, products, markets, and capabilities.	Proposals to obtain resources to support plans and programs. Sometimes called "championing."	"Making the system work" for this business at this time. Proposing changes in context.

The Business Unit Environment: The Markets for Products and Services

Figure 3-1 The Resource Allocation Process

cash flow for the foreseeable future, thereby denying many of GE's other business units adequate funding. The same plans for growth that spelled opportunity for the unit, therefore, provided a basis for the corporation's decision to exit the business.

The division and the corporate management had different views of value maximization. Both were correct ex ante. It is by no means obvious that GE would not have been a more interesting company had it funded the computer business and exited some of the activities that were only cut by corporate at the end of the next decade. Jensen describes this as a problem in aligning incentives. But it is also a problem in managing risk, in formulating strategy, and in thinking imaginatively about finance.

In its middle column the model describes the sponsoring, brokering, and commitment making associated with the actual *allocation of human and financial resources*. For example, the top managers of the GE computer division spent a good part of their time championing their business plans in various meetings with peers, financial staff, and corporate line managers. In effect, these managers were investing their credibility—their track record for delivering on promises for uncertain business futures—in the effort to persuade corporate managers who may have been skeptical of the promise of computers in the face of IBM. In turn the corporate managers were facing overwhelming demands for new resources from more than 100 GE businesses, all promising good returns. They knew that how they allocated resources would affect the future of these businesses and, therefore, the future records of the unit managers. Those records would determine the paths of those individuals' careers just as much as the outcome of the investment decisions would affect the course of GE.

The resource allocation skill of a very few managers can make an enormous difference to how a company performs over time. For example, at IBM in the 1960s, T. Vincent Learson and two or three lieutenants saw that the proliferation of IBM's product lines left it vulnerable to attack by competitors such as GE, which threatened to target specific elements of the line. Operating from a position that would be at the integrating level of the model, Learson engaged the company's leaders in study of the issue. With their approval he mobilized the leading technological talent of the company to focus on the problem, steered the crafting of a strategic solution based on breakthrough technology, and oversaw the development and introduction of a compatible line of computers that covered the market from one end to the other—a development of such staggering significance that the industry was transformed for a decade. In the face of great skepticism from the barons of the operation, Learson's track record of successful innovation enabled him to secure the continuous commitment of IBM's CEO, Thomas Watson Jr., and he wielded that commitment to focus the company's total resources on the challenge. "Engaged," "mobilized," "steered," "oversaw," "wielded": These verbs describe the artistic skills of a great leader of change. Such leaders energize and focus the efforts of the organization's key figures—corporate and technical—in a coherent way.

How would understanding the purpose of IBM help the managers involved with mobilizing, brokering, and judging the appropriateness of particular commitments? The problem was that a group of extremely intelligent and successful managers disagreed as to the wisdom of leapfrogging existing product lines that enjoyed near monopolistic market shares and were providing IBM with extraordinary profits. They all agreed to IBM's purpose. They disagreed as to the feasibility and desirability of achieving it through a single compatible line of computers. The idea that Learson began to champion in 1959 was not manifest in implementable conceptual designs until 1964. How does the idea of purpose help us to understand the managerial work involved during the interval between "discrepancy perceived and puzzle solved?"[2]

On the right, figure 3-1 lists many of the *systemic contexts* for managerial influence available to a corporation. The way jobs are defined and measured; the kind of information available; the way managerial performance is evaluated and rewarded; the style with which these administrative processes are conducted; the values that define the corporate purpose—all these elements combine to provide the context within which substance is analyzed and articulated and resources are committed. These forms of managerial influence are the meta–management tool kit. Bob Simons calls them the "levers of control."[3] They influence how specifics are managed. How this complex system of administrative influence is configured and how it is used constitutes another core element of the process of change.

During the 1960s, GE chief executive Fred Borch became convinced that he had no reliable basis for guiding the 100-plus divisions of GE or for allocating resources among their competing claims. The structural and strategic context of GE did not provide a sound basis for decision. All businesses were getting some support; but because the demands of a few, such as computers and nuclear power, were enormous, almost none were getting what they really needed to make GE a dominant force in any market.

Drawing on the best that America's strategy consultants had to offer, GE built a new system of Strategic Business Units (SBUs) for purposes of separating out strategic planning and resource allocation from the regular work of operating and budgeting. The company made heavy investments in management training and staff support so that the leadership of the SBUs could develop sensible long-term strategic plans. A matrix of business and industry attractiveness was devised so that it was finally possible to manage GE's portfolio of businesses. This changed structural context provided the necessary information, measures, and changed strategic perspective to enable management to make true choices among the demands from business units. It was this system that legitimized the exit from computers, for it revealed just how voracious were computers' demands for cash. GE finally had a way to manage complexity.

For all the elegance of the SBU structural device, GE's corporate performance tracked the stagnant performance of the U.S. economy during the 1970s. It was not until the protean, Learson-like executive Jack Welch took over GE and imposed a simpler conception of the businesses that the company began to respond. Welch acted in all three dimensions discussed above, and he has continued to act for over two decades—constantly prodding executives with carefully thought-through challenges, drastically revising the structure and work environment so as to expose management thinking and behavior and to empower the lowest levels of the organization, and acting decisively to prune businesses and commit new resources.

Perhaps most illustrative of the complexity of purposive change, Welch announced early in his tenure that GE would be number one or number two worldwide in every line of business in which they competed. "Fix it or sell it" was the mandate. There is a tremendous tendency in the business press to focus on the harsh objectivity of this charge to the troops. What is much more impressive is the way words were used to change the cognitive map of thousands of managers. Under the previous award-winning planning and organizational systems, heroic attempts to implant strategic thinking saw GE managers still focusing on doing "10 percent better than last year." What the concept of number one or number two worldwide did was shift the focus of managers away from internal concerns (with last year and other GE divisions) to external problems with markets and competitors. That shift in turn, was reflected in changed standards for resource allocation and in dramatic changes in the structural context.

These two long descriptive examples serve to illustrate the extent to which the purpose of a corporation is both constructed over time (Henry Mintzburg uses the more passive "emerges") and discovered over time as technology and the environment change. Did the purpose of GE change? The question is worthy of a fine teleological debate. What is clear is that GE executives at all levels came to understand more clearly that economic competitiveness required a global perspective and a dominant position in the market. It was also clear to executives that they would achieve this position or lose their role at GE. Indeed, their business unit might be sold.

From Jensen's perspective, the interests of GE's business unit managers and the corporate leadership became more clearly aligned, and the resultant improvement in firm value was tremendous. And some of the changes Welch made could be described in terms of Jensen's economics of organizations. But mechanisms involved in the profound shift in thinking brought about by the phrase "number one or number two in everything we do" are outside the value-maximization model. Similarly, while that shift in thinking undoubtedly represents learning, it probably represents better understanding as to *how* GE's purpose should be achieved rather than as to *what* that purpose is. Moreover, the powerful pedagogical effect of major shifts in the strategic portfolio and extensive delayering and destaffing are simply not accounted for in any systematic way.

It is one thing to recognize that a corporation is a complex nonlinear system interacting with a very rich and changing environment. It is another to provide a map of that system that permits managers to act in an intentionally rational fashion. The model I have presented captures several elements of the challenge of leading significant purposive change. Most important, managers at multiple levels are simultaneously working on technical and economic, organizational, and interpersonal aspects of the same issues. The pattern of resource commitments they make over time reveals what the purpose will be. At the same time, managers learn through doing and through reflecting on what specific ways of pursuing objectives are more successful than others.[4]

The 1980s and 1990s made the managerial challenge of purposive change particularly demanding, because radical shifts in market conditions took place. The globalization of product and service markets and the liberalization of financial markets have led to a dramatic increase in the number and capabilities of competitors. Free movement of technology, capital, and the knowledge and tools of professional management mean that the Schumpeterian gale of competition now comes from all points on the compass. It is no longer even clear that individual firms have the capacity to devise successful strategic responses to the conditions we face.

One of the most telling examples from my research comes from a trip to Europe taken by the twelve CEOs of Japan's major petrochemical companies in 1982. Led by MITI (Ministry of International Trade and Industry) officials, they visited the headquarters of the leading European producers. The purpose of the trip was very much like Welch's "number one or number two." The oil shocks of 1973 and 1978 had brought about a fundamental transformation of petrochemical economics and markets, but the executives of the Japanese firms would not lead the changes necessary—including mergers—to deal with the secular crisis. Two decades of steady growth had led these managers of Japan Inc.'s chemical sector to understand that markets always recovered. Temporary price-fixing (legal under Japan's laws) coupled with exports would carry a company across the pain of recessionary periods. But this was different. MITI's aim was figuratively to rub the noses of these company leaders in the reality of a worldwide secular crisis.

Unfortunately, comprehension on the part of the leaders would not be enough. MITI sought from these executives the kinds of actions that lay outside the repertoire of most Japanese managers. Understanding the necessity for major change—the now popular "burning platform"—is not enough. Nonetheless, it supports a huge business of economic and strategy consultants. Especially in countries where political barriers often hamper significant corporate change, disinterested technical expertise may be necessary to legitimize painful corporate moves.

Interestingly, even when there is understanding of the necessity for major change, my research suggests that action often requires a new leader. For a variety of reasons, an executive who has led a company into a problematic situation often finds it extremely difficult to break the many commitments that brought the company to its impasse. It is not so much that such executives do not comprehend the change in the world; it is that they cannot imagine the profound changes needed in their own organizations.

A poignant illustration of this phenomenon is provided by the comments of John Nevin, then the recently elected president of the tire manufacturer Firestone, describing a March 1980 meeting with outgoing CEO Richard Riley after Riley had read Nevin's restructuring proposal to Firestone's board.

> When Riley came in that morning, I wasn't surprised that he summoned me to his office. He said "John, I didn't sleep all night. I read that damn thing and I couldn't sleep. I guess I now fully understand why the board was so insistent that we go outside. That memo is so logical and the case is so compelling for what you're recommending that it just startles me that in six weeks you could do that paper and we weren't even close to those conclusions." So this was a very decent man who was *shocked*. This was going to involve the layoff of 15,000 people, and this was the guy who six months earlier had planned to grow.

To put Riley's problems in context, during the 1970s the several manufacturers in the U.S. tire industry managed to destroy several billion dollars of value.

A dramatic feature of the contemporary U.S. business scene is the shortened tenure of chief executives. Boards have become far less tolerant of value destruction and more accepting of the idea that a change in leader may be needed to get change in behavior. The same phenomenon appears to be moving globally as the capital markets liberalize.

What do the new leaders do? Programs of purposive change appear to follow a pattern. My studies show a sequence of moves that seem ordinary but in sum transform the system modeled in this chapter.

- The first stage is an assessment of the organization's businesses by means of existing information systems. Often this triggers installation of new, more transparent systems.

- Next comes a period of "fixing the portfolio." Business units are "fixed," closed, or sold, and the balance sheet improves as debts are reduced and new capital raised.

- As the economic situation is stabilized, attention turns to the values, goals, and standards that shape the work environment of the corporation.

- The processes by which operations and innovation are managed then get attention.

- Finally, it is normal today to see corporations seeking to build new businesses across existing divisional lines in order to serve customer needs more fully.

Much of the work of making this change happen is ad hoc, in the sense that it is guided by the wisdom of experienced practitioners and consultants rather than being grounded in research. In particular, after the pruning and reordering is done the critical work of growing the enterprise turns on factors such as communication, values, incentives, and recruitment and development of talent. Strangely enough, when one turns to the research literature for help in these arenas one finds relatively little that is directly helpful. Best practice is a better source of insight.

The reason for this dearth of useful work brings us back to the opening of this paper. Like the work of Jensen and Senge, most research is set in the context of a discipline. In such research the complexity of the modern business is acknowledged, as for example in Senge's "nonlinear dynamic system," but the detail is unspecified and unstudied or debilitatingly partial. If we understand that purposive change in a complex system means that most things are connected, then what we need is research that deals directly with those problems.

Elsewhere I have argued that

[good] process research should:

- Seek out natural experiments that control variety so that the relationships among a few of [the many variables in the system] can be studied;

- Conduct longitudinal studies of process using a shared model of strategic activity so that the work of different researchers can cumulate;

- Where possible, conduct comparative longitudinal studies.[5]

These precepts would be familiar to medical clinicians, who have moved their field forward remarkably. Treating the human body as a complex system, they have been able to improve the repertoire of interventions, despite models of the system that are progressively revealed as incomplete. Although specialists focus on specific organs or systems, they acknowledge the centrality of the system as an entity. The neurosurgeon may end an operation, not because the work is complete, but because the body is too vulnerable to permanent injury after fourteen hours of deep anesthesia. The dentist recognizes that emotional stress may cause temporary inflammation of the gums.

Business clinicians—academics or executives—also know their medium is a complex system. When they consider purposive change, they move knowing that action conceived in one dimension has consequences in many—*including the corporate purpose!* In the face of such complexity, it is easy to understand why a rigorous but partial theory is appealing. But it is fundamental to understand that the actors have no such good fortune. Their responsibility is to move their enterprise forward, generally through attempts at purposive change.

Notes

1. A short listing would include Graham Allison, *The Essence of Decision.* (Boston: Little, Brown, 1971); Joseph L. Bower, *Managing the Resource Allocation Process* (Boston: Harvard Business School Press, 1970); Mark S. Granovetter, Economic Action and the Social Structure: The Return of Embeddedness. *American Journal of Sociology* 91 (November 1985): 481–510.
2. These are Jerome Bruner's categories. Creative problem solving begins when we perceive a discrepancy between the existing state of the world and the possibility of a more desirable state. We "solve" problems by imposing on the discrepancy the form of a puzzle that is subject to solution. This is often done through metaphor. See, for example, Jerome Bruner, *The Process of Education* (Cambridge, MA: Harvard University Press, 1979).
3. Robert Simons, *Levers of Control* (Boston: Harvard Business School Press, 1995).
4. Don A. Schon, *The Reflective Practitioner* (New York: Basic Books, 1983).
5. Joseph L. Bower, "Process Research on Strategic Questions," in *Strategic Decisions*, ed. Vassilis Papadakis and Patrick Barwise (Kluwer, 1998), 30.

LEADERSHIP OF CHANGE

Directed from the Top or High-Involvement and Participative?

HOW SHOULD change initiatives be led? According to one view leadership is the force for change. In this view, the burden rests on an individual or handful of leaders at the top of the organization who have the vision and capability to drive change. Jay Conger's paper in this section reflects this top-down view. Conger argues that increasingly the nature of organizational change requires a perspective that cuts across organizational boundaries. Restructuring or reengineering cannot be entrusted to people lower down in the organization, who may have neither the organizationwide perspective, nor the resources, nor the political power to introduce such systemwide changes. Such changes have to be led from the top. Like generals on historic battlefields, only leaders who sit on the top of the hills have a broader view of the situation. Only they can enjoy the allegiance of the troops, who need to believe that someone is leading them. Only they can be entrusted with allocating resources that are beyond the scope of any individual unit.

Warren Bennis, in the next paper in this section, opposes this myth of the heroic leader as the force for change. He takes a very different view of the challenges that are confronting modern organizations. Bennis argues that organizations are becoming more complex, technologically sophisticated, and knowledge intensive. In these increasingly networklike organizations, it is an act of hubris of imagine that an individual or a small group of leaders at the top can possess the knowledge and wisdom to tackle the problems for which the organization must find solutions. Top executives must instead learn to walk in the crowd of leaders that exists in any organization. They must eschew decrees, orders, and grand plans and instead listen to and amplify the diversity of voices in their organization. It is only such distributed and participative leadership that will lead to successful change in the years ahead.

In the final paper in this section, Dexter Dunphy addresses and resolves the differences between these two perspectives on the leadership of change. He argues that both perspectives have merit. Rather than rejecting one or the other, the challenge is to find a way of holding the tension of the two together—of embracing a paradox. In some situations embracing this paradox requires recognizing that at different times, even in the same organization, one view may be more useful than the other. The key is to determine who has the relevant knowledge. Sometimes it can indeed be the leader at the top. On other occasions it will be lower-level members of the organization. While choosing the appropriate leadership style for the appropriate situation is one way of resolving the paradox, a more robust solution is to enhance the personal, professional, and organizational capabilities of everyone in the organization. It is only by investing in enhancing the stock and quality of leadership in our organizations that we can ultimately build the capability for ongoing change.

4

EFFECTIVE CHANGE BEGINS
AT THE TOP

Jay A. Conger

T HE QUESTION OF whether change is most effective when driven
from the bottom of an organization or from its uppermost levels
appears at first glance to be a well-worn and largely unproductive
point of discussion. As with most extreme positions, we think of these
polar viewpoints as more useful for sparking debate than for understanding reality. But in this particular case, an extreme position is a
valid one. Specifically, I will argue that top-led organizational change
has a far greater chance of achieving success than change driven by
lower levels.

The very nature of organizational change today favors a top-led
approach. For example, more and more change initiatives take place in
response to major shifts in corporate strategy or to a fundamental
reengineering of basic company processes. The implication is that
fewer and fewer change efforts are about incremental improvements
limited to isolated functions. Instead, change often has systemwide
ramifications and involves costly new systems and technologies. Given
the magnitude of this type of change and the often heavy accompanying investments, senior executives are far better positioned to lead organizational reinvention.

In this chapter I will explore in greater depth this character of organizational change today and its implications for the debate between

top-down and bottom-up approaches to change. Then I will turn to three critical levers that give senior management crucial tactical advantages over junior levels in most change efforts.

First, however, it is important to clarify the assumptions underlying my use of the term *top-led*. First and foremost, it is assumed that a top-led approach is not simply a CEO-driven approach. Rather, when describing top-led initiatives, I am referring to the *team* of senior executives. Second, I assume that the members of the executive team are talented and that they are highly sensitive to the changes unfolding in the world around them. This latter point is a tough requirement in itself. The chairman of one of the nation's most successful semiconductor manufacturers likes to say that "as a senior manager, I am subject to self-deception." What he is essentially pointing out is that there is a high probability that the senior team will themselves be blindsided by their own histories. Research appears to suggest that it is for this reason that major organizational and strategic changes are more often initiated by new leaders of the firm (e.g., Grinyer, Mayes, and McKiernan 1990; Virany, Tushman, and Romanelli 1992). It is clear that the CEO and his or her executive team must promote debate and candor within the organization. They must be willing to hear and to be challenged about their own paradigms of the company and their industry. They must reward people for the very things they themselves may have been punished for. In other words, they must demand unconventionality and countercultural perspectives. Cassandras are essential. As well, top leaders must be continually involved in data collecting on the state of customers and on the company's operations.

Essential to effective top-led change efforts is also the engagement of lower levels of the organization in the determination of appropriate local visions, operational goals, and tactics. In essence, junior levels are in the best position to successfully translate corporate strategies into effective operating initiatives. A purely top-down effort, in which there is little or no participation within the organization, is just as likely to end in failure as a purely bottom-up approach. Widespread participation and buy-in are essential to most successful change efforts.

Organizational Change Today: More Fundamental, Less Incremental

Stanford professor Jeffrey Pfeffer likes to describe today's management literature as falling into the "breathless" category: Every aspect of the business world is depicted as more rapid, more complex, more demanding, more competitive than ever before. So it is with a measure of trepidation that I propose that our world today is indeed different from that of previous decades.

Although we all share a degree of Pfeffer's cynicism, most academics and practitioners would agree that the magnitude of certain environmental forces has increased over the last few decades and in turn has heightened both the intensity and the complexity of change. Dramatic growth in the number of multinational competitors, more open markets around the world, and remarkable advances in technology are the leading contenders to explain today's hypercompetitive landscape. For example, the United Nations estimates that there are now more than 40,000 multinational corporations. Reflecting the greater openness of most markets, international trade grew between 1989 and 1997 at an annual rate of 5.3 percent and foreign direct investment increased at a rate of 11.5 percent (Yergin and Stanislaw 1998). On the technology front, the 1980s and 1990s saw remarkable advances in computer-assisted design engineering, mass production techniques, and electronic distribution, which have all accelerated the pace at which new products come to market. For example, in the 1970s new car model development cycles ran as high as ninety-some months from design to production models. By the mid-1980s Japanese producers had lowered the average cycle to forty-two months. Today we approach the possibility of twenty-two-month cycles. Given this element of speed plus a growing overcapacity in many industries and firms' ability to rapidly imitate competitors' innovations, many goods become commodities almost overnight.

The competitive landscape we are describing requires continual reinvention in company strategies and in the organizational architectures and cultures that support them. As a result, few industries today have the luxury of leisurely and incremental change. The pressure is instead for significant and frequent shifts in a company's strategy and for corresponding organizationwide changes. The vast majority of these strategic changes demand multifunctional changes. Change efforts therefore increasingly ripple across the firm rather than remain within the boundaries of a particular function. The implication is that a defining characteristic of successful change is its systemic nature; in other words, successful change produces major alterations in the reward, performance measurement, and operating systems that span the organization. This also implies that change is costly. One cannot fundamentally alter basic operating systems without incurring high capital investments.

In light of these defining characteristics of many of today's change efforts (need for speed; cross-functional nature; significant alterations in structures, systems, and corporate cultures; and high capital requirements), it is difficult to imagine how successful change outcomes can be produced by initiatives driven by the lower levels of an organization. For example, bottom-up approaches too often reflect the functional or departmental biases of the groups driving the change. As a result, such groups are often blind to the cross-functional implications of what they are proposing. From an implementation perspective, the limited power base of junior levels means that they rarely possess the political clout to produce broad buy-in from other functions. Nor do they have the authority to institute radical revisions in corporate performance measures and reward systems.

Beyond these dilemmas, there are additional problems. For instance, junior-level managers may lack the courage needed to set and achieve radical goals. It is not easy for individuals to establish demanding stretch targets for themselves when their own careers are on the line. There is an inherent bias toward setting targets that will be more easily attained and that can more reliably garner rewards. Finally, the lower levels of the organization have extremely limited access to capital. Yet, as noted earlier, many organizational change efforts involve expensive alterations in the information systems and technology-driven processes that span the entire organization.

Given the nature of organizational change today, organizations themselves have recognized that *top-down* change efforts are essential to their ability to adapt to a rapidly moving world. This recognition is evident in a recent national survey of Fortune 1000 companies conducted by the Center for Effective Organizations at the University of Southern California, which polls senior executives annually on human resources issues (Lawler 1998). The 1998 survey results show that the majority of respondents described their corporations as changing their strategies, structures, and information systems in major ways. Sixty-two percent of the respondents said that company change efforts were integrated companywide to a moderate or great extent. As a result, 89 percent of survey respondents said they were relying from a moderate to a very great extent upon top management–led change strategies. Only 15 percent of respondents described their change efforts as based to a great or very great extent upon a bottom-up implementation strategy. One particularly fascinating finding of the survey is that even employee involvement programs are seen as most successful when they are led by the top management team: [C]hange efforts that are tied to a business strategy, based on clear beliefs, have mission and values statements, are integrated, are long term, and are led by top management tend to have the most successful EI [employee involvement] programs . . . the evidence seems to show clearly that programs are most successful when they are led by the top, not when they are a bottom-up operation" (Lawler 1998, p. 137).

The Unique Advantages That Senior Leaders Bring to Change Efforts

Although senior managers possess numerous advantages over junior levels when it comes to implementing organizational changes, three particular ones stand out: (1) the senior team's breadth of perspective and strategy-formulation role; (2) attributions about leadership itself; and (3) the power of the top leadership's position. Each of these critical levers ensures that executive-led approaches have a higher probability of success in major change efforts.

The Generals Sit atop the Hills

Breadth of perspective is the first key advantage. Before the advent of modern communications and long-range weapons, battles were conducted with the commanding officers positioned high upon hilltops. From there they could more easily discern the movements of the enemy and those of their own troops. On the actual battlefield, in contrast, junior officers and their men commonly became confused about their positions and the movements of the opposing side, being surrounded by men, weapons, smoke, and terrain that afforded only an extremely limited perspective. For the actual combatants, then, it was impossible to have a broad strategic sense of how the battle was unfolding. Senior officers, removed from the mayhem and possessing a clearer line of sight, could make more apt judgments about appropriate tactics.

The analogy with corporations is clear. Given their focus on *overall* operations, senior corporate leaders by the nature of their positions possess a vantage point that oversees a fuller "battlefield." Their responsibilities often require them to take a multifunctional and multibusiness approach to decisions. As a result, senior leaders are less likely to have narrowly defined perspectives. They are also more likely to appreciate how the organization is an interlocking set of functions and systems—where changes in one will have implications for the others.

Given that today's change efforts usually have significant cross-functional implications, the senior team's breadth of perspective is a necessity if change initiatives are to have any chance of success. This point is nicely illustrated by a well-known classroom case study entitled Hovey and Beard. Dating back some time, Hovey and Beard has often been used to teach business students and managers basic lessons about organizational change. While it is a relatively simple case study of a toy company, its dynamics powerfully mirror the lessons of change in companies of any size. The case describes a small group within the company that had used worker participation to create change solely within their particular unit. The change ends up producing a dramatic improvement in the production of toys. As a result, bonuses go up within the department, the workers feel more involved, and soon everyone in the unit is quite happy with the initiative. The story ends, however, with the initiative being dismantled. The reason is that the change had implications for other departments—implications so significant that powerful forces beyond the unit were successful in erasing all traces of the new initiative. In a nutshell, employees in other departments came to resent the fact that the unit's production workers were now earning more than others in the factory. Besieged by demands that this inequity be addressed, management revoked the bonus, and the unit's production was restored to its former pace. The case is illustrative of many bottom-up approaches. Because they emanate from the interests of a single unit or function, they often fail to appreciate broader organizational ramifications. In addition, junior managers lack the political clout necessary to garner commitment from other departments and to institute systemwide changes that can sustain the change.

The "perspective" advantages of the senior team are also tied to their responsibility for setting corporate strategy. This activity not only affords them a view of their marketplaces but also the potential for an objective view of the corporation as a competitive entity. In other words, top leaders can conceivably reconfigure the entire corporation if a changing world so demands it. Jack Welch at General Electric is a powerful example of this point. When Welch took the helm at GE, half of the company's profits depended upon machine-age products: motors, wiring, appliances, many dating back to Thomas Edison. Several of these mature businesses were struggling, and of the 150-odd businesses only a handful were either number one or number two in their markets—the ultimate goal Welch set for all business units (Tichy and Sherman 1993). The company's stock mirrored this situation over the 1970s by losing some 25 percent of its value net of inflation. Through an aggressive acquisition and divestiture strategy and high performance targets, Welch successfully revamped the company's product and service lines. Now imagine for a moment frontline GE managers attempting to bring about so massive a change in the corporation. It would be extremely difficult. First, their interests would lie with their operating unit, not with the overall corporation. In other words, they would in most cases have little interest in setting themselves up for divestiture. Second, they would not have access to the capital or the political muscle needed to reconfigure the organization. Finally, they would lack the backlog of career experiences necessary to inform sound strategic decisions needed to successfully reposition the company.

The Romance of Leadership

Some time ago, a film came out entitled *Being There* and starring Peter Sellers. Sellers played the character of Chauncy, the not-so-intelligent gardener of a wealthy man. Unfortunately, his patron passes away one day, and Chauncy is left stranded for the first time in his working life. He leaves the confines of the urban estate and wanders about in the town. At one point he is struck accidentally by the bumper of a limousine. A lady passenger rushes to his assistance—in part, fearful that Chauncy may sue her for the accident. She takes him to her home, where he is made a house guest during his recuperation. In the process, the woman and her husband, a powerful industrialist, become enamored with Chauncy the gardener, whose name they have misunderstood as Chauncy Gardener. Through a series of wonderful misinterpretations, they come to believe that Chauncy is actually a remarkably wise man with great understanding of world issues. As the couple are friends of the American president, a meeting is arranged in which Chauncy advises the seniormost leader of the nation on economic policy.

This delightful spoof illustrates the power of the process we call attribution. In the film a simple gardener is propelled into the national spotlight simply because of a series of random events and mistaken attributions about who he is. In everyday life, too, human beings make powerful attributions about individuals that may or may not represent an accurate understanding of reality.

Attribution processes are particularly powerful when it comes to the formal leaders at the top of any firm. As members of an organization, we have a need to imagine that a single individual can play a heroic role in shaping the destiny of our company. Nowhere is this phenomenon more apparent than in the business press. Looking through the pages of most business journals, one could easily imagine that most successful companies are run largely by one individual. That person is usually the company CEO, who is given most of the credit (or blame) for the organization's good and bad times. Rarely will other executives or managers be mentioned in these articles. Yet in reality a single executive can never single-handedly run a corporation. For example, over the last few years, there have been innumerable articles on Gordon Bethune, the current CEO of Continental Airlines. From these pieces you would have to believe that Bethune was largely responsible for the successful turnaround of that airline. In reality, he did create the necessary climate for change. Often not mentioned, however, are the other executives he enlisted in his effort. Foremost would be his coarchitect in the turnaround, Gregory Brenneman, a former Bain &

Company consultant, whom Bethune appointed president of the airline and with whom he brainstormed many of the company's initial turnaround tactics (Bryant 1996).

In essence, this process of attribution reflects our need to explain events through the deliberate actions of individuals rather than seeing them as the efforts of a collection of individuals or as random events or the effects of natural forces. To maintain the illusion of control over our world, we need to create causal attributions for events. And because senior leaders are highly visible and have formal positions of authority, employees (and the press) have a strong tendency to attribute causality to them (Pfeffer 1977). Another example would be Lee Iacocca, former CEO of Chrysler and executive at Ford, who has been credited with the Ford Mustang and the turnaround of Chrysler. In reality, entire teams worked to create both the car design and the company turnaround. And this is the case in every story of corporate success or failure. Nonetheless, individuals in senior leadership positions come to symbolize the controlling or guiding force behind most events.

Senior leaders therefore have a unique advantage over more junior ones. They can harness the power of this attribution process. They have at their disposal a means of using events and their own behaviors to send messages throughout the entire organization about what is valued or where attention should be directed. This ability to harness attributions becomes particularly important in organizational change efforts. Specifically, individuals in corporations pay attention to what the senior leaders pay attention to. Executives' reactions to critical events; their comments; their modeling of behavior; what they measure and reward; and their criteria for promotion, recruitment, and termination—all garner enormous attention partly because of this "romance of leadership" phenomenon (Schein 1985). Senior leaders who are alert to this phenomenon and are systematic in paying attention to what they wish for outcomes can harness a powerful means of communication. They can also garner commitment to themselves and to their change agendas.

For example, one leader I studied needed to gain the commitment of his workforce to a large-scale change effort. He had been brought into the company from the outside and needed quickly to build a strong relationship with employees. Moreover, he knew that the workforce itself had historically been antagonistic toward management. To gain commitment to both himself and his change agenda, he performed two symbolic acts within his first week on the job. First, one evening he instructed all of the executives' secretaries to park in their bosses' reserved parking spaces the next morning and to remove the reserved parking signs in front of the spaces. From now on, he explained, these spaces would be for anyone who had a perfect attendance record, no matter what level in the company. The next morning word rapidly spread throughout the organization about what had happened. Next, one day later, the executive arrived at the production area early in the morning, check-in time for the workforce. Crowbar in hand, he began ripping the company time clocks off the wall. As stunned employees stood nearby, he explained to them that the company needed to trust them, and time clocks were a symbol of a lack of trust. Again, word of these actions spread rapidly throughout the company. It was becoming very clear to the workforce that their new executive was not going to build walls of status between himself and company employees but rather break them down. Through these actions and several others, the executive quickly won the commitment of the workforce and therefore was able to introduce many critical changes. In this case, the individual's actions took on tremendous meaning—far beyond any meaning of the simple actions themselves. He became heroic in the workforce's eyes. He also, of course, had sufficient power to avoid punishment for such actions. If a department supervisor had tried a similar set of actions, he would most likely have been terminated for insubordination.

Junior managers are therefore at a disadvantage when it comes to the "romance of leadership." Given their lower status and limited access to the limelight, it is difficult for them to develop similar attributions among other members of their organization—especially among peers and other units. They do not possess enough formal authority to be a natural point of projection for attributions or to avoid punishment for highly countercultural actions. Nor do their behaviors and actions simply receive the level of visibility needed to engender romantic or heroic notions. As a result, it is extremely difficult for low-level leaders to capitalize on attribution processes that might otherwise enhance their efforts to induce organizational change.

The Power of Position

Top-led change efforts have a third, and certainly the most obvious, advantage in their favor when it comes to driving change: power. Although power at the executive level is rarely as "powerful" as one might assume, because of political forces and organizational inertia, senior executives nonetheless possess more of it than junior levels. Specifically, the executive level can control rewards, performance measures, recruitment, information, and access to resources and people. These are the building blocks of organizations. For example, senior leaders can fill key positions with supportive change agents. Likewise, executives can remove opponents of the change who could block or slow down the initiative. Junior levels usually lack this degree of authority and power.

Positional power can have its greatest impact through alterations in the measurement and reward systems that span the corporation. This is one area where senior executives have a tremendous advantage over junior levels. For example, in the case of Continental Airlines, Gordon Bethune and Gregory Brenneman installed a companywide reward system designed to address the airline's poor on-time reliability. The incentive system rewarded Continental employees with bonuses whenever the airline finished among the top three carriers in on-time performance in the United States. Similarly, Jack Welch's team at GE established a new incentive system to address cultural barriers that stood in the way of his new corporate strategy—namely, the company's historical aversion to layoff. A restructuring fund run from the corporate center paid out the severance costs for the operating groups, which included lump-sum payments, training, and outplacement services. This restructuring fund was financed with the proceeds from the sales of operating units that had failed to obtain market leadership or which no longer fit the new strategic vision. This setup permitted the economic benefits from payroll reductions to appear on an operating unit's bottom line and produce the improved performance that Welch was demanding (Tichy and Sherman 1993). In both the case of GE and Continental, these major alterations in reward systems were essential to the success of the larger change strategy.

Executives can also use their positional power to obtain adherence to very demanding stretch targets. Early in his reign as CEO at Coca-Cola, Roberto Goizueta instituted a process nicknamed the Spanish Inquisition (Greising 1997). The objective was to instill greater rigor into Coke's planning process and to push company executives to far higher levels of performance. Goizueta transformed what historically had been a process with little rigor or accountability into a mandate for reform. He canceled the tradition of five-year plans, saying that no one could successfully predict the future that far out. Instead, he announced, there would be three-year plans, and managers would be held personally accountable for achieving their three-year targets. He also required his executives to file their plans in advance so that he could examine them in detail for weaknesses. In the end, most executives were required to redo their plans. It was out of numerous steps such as these that he forced performance: "Those who don't adapt will be left behind or out—no matter what level they are" (Greising 1997, p. 82).

In contrast, junior managers are in a difficult position when it comes to setting demanding stretch targets for themselves. For one, they run the risk of failure and in turn the possibility of losing their jobs or at least being penalized. Second, they may not believe in their own capacity to accomplish what appear to be dramatic performance improvements.

Along with the power to focus attention and mobilize individuals, senior executives also possess political clout. Their career paths have allowed them to garner political capital and in many cases have taught them how to use it effectively. They can deploy this power to gain access to critical resources and to shift attention to certain businesses, functions, and individuals. Junior managers, on the other hand, have had few opportunities to build up their political capital and often lack a sufficient base of experience to be politically savvy. Their political maneuvers are likely to have little or very limited influence on the levels above them or in the departments that flank them.

Finally, one of the most important advantages of positional power is access to resources. Given that many organizational changes today involve large capital investments, junior managers start at a serious disadvantage. They have limited access to capital and must compete against many others over the pool of funds. The doors to the board's finance committee are largely closed to them. Senior leaders, in contrast, have access not only to capital but generally to large sums of it. The more politically skillful executives also possess the power necessary to obtain capital from the finance committees of their companies' boards of directors.

Conclusion

This chapter has argued strongly that senior leaders are in the best position to orchestrate organizational change successfully. Nevertheless, I wish to close by reminding readers of an earlier point: Top-led changes do not exclude participation by the levels below. Ultimately, successful change efforts depend upon the ability of all levels to implement. Senior managers are generally too far removed from day-to-day operations to determine the most effective ways to implement strategic and organizational changes in every unit, function, or situation. It would be difficult and even inappropriate for top management to take responsibility for determining local structures, crafting local strategies and tactics, or making many operational decisions. These activities are usually best suited to those actually conducting the business. The process of involving junior levels in the translation of proposed goals and changes into local objectives and solutions also ensures that these levels feel ownership and a compulsion to make things happen. In the end, it is the effective integration of the unique advantages of both the upper and lower strata of an organization that determines the success of any change effort. Each level must see the value of the other and work to harness those advantages fully.

References

Bryant, A. 1996. The Candid Mr. Fix-It of the Skies. *New York Times* (Nov. 12): C1, C18.

Greising, D. 1997. *I'd Like the World to Buy a Coke: The Life and Leadership of Roberto Goizueta.* New York: Wiley.

Grinyer, P. H., D. Mayes, and P. McKiernan. 1990. The Sharpbenders: Achieving a Sustained Improvement in Performance. *Long-Range Planning* 23: 116–125.

Lawler, E. E. 1998. *Strategies for High-Performance Organizations.* San Francisco: Jossey-Bass.

Pfeffer, J. 1977. The Ambiguity of Leadership. *Academy of Management Review* 2: 104–112.

Schein, E. 1985. *Organizational Culture and Leadership.* San Francisco: Jossey-Bass.

Tichy, N. M., and S. Sherman. 1993. *Control Your Destiny or Someone Else Will.* New York: Doubleday.

Virany, B., M. L. Tushman, and E. Romanelli. 1992. Executive Succession and Organizational Outcomes in Turbulent Environments. *Organization Science* 3: 72–91.

Yergin, D., and J. Stanislaw. 1998. *The Commanding Heights.* New York: Simon and Schuster.

5

LEADERSHIP OF CHANGE

Warren Bennis

GETTING IMPALED on the horns of a false dichotomy is rather more fun than I had anticipated. The very idea of a debate, in which issues are egregiously oversimplified, can't help but lose the subtly nuanced distinctions we academics relish and thrive on. I am reminded of an old *New Yorker* cartoon showing Charles Dickens in his publisher's office, being told rather sternly by his editor: "Well, Mr. Dickens, it's either the best of times or the worst of times. It can't be both." Well, of course, Dickens knew it is always both. As F. Scott Fitzgerald famously noted, "The mark of an educated person is the capacity to hold two contradictory ideas simultaneously without rejecting either."

I was cast against type, so to speak, for this debate, and would have felt far more comfortable arguing the side opposite to the one I was assigned, a side more compatible with my own recent writing. But in the process of preparing for the debate I arrived at an unexpected conclusion: that the "resolution before the house, that all successful change must originate at the top"—call it top-down leadership—was not only wrong, unrealistic, and maladaptive but also, given the report of history, dangerous.

The Encompassing Tendency

The idea of top-down leadership is based on the myth of the trium-phant individual. This myth has become an encompassing tendency—an idea deeply ingrained in the American psyche and unfortunately fostered and celebrated in the daily press, business magazines, and much of academic and popular writing. My own work, at times, has also suffered from this deification of the icons of American business: the Welches, the Barneviks, the Gateses—fill in your own hero. Whether it is midnight rider Paul Revere or basketball's Michael Jordan or baseball's Mark McGwire, we are a nation enamored of heroes: rugged self-starters who meet challenges and overcome adversity. Our contemporary views of leadership are entwined with our notions of heroism, so much so that the distinction between "leader" and "hero" (or "celebrity," for that matter) often becomes blurred. In our society leadership is too often seen as an inherently individual phenomenon. It's Oprah and Michael (Jordan or Eisner) and Bill (Clinton or Gates) and Larry and Hillary. We are all victims of or witnesses to what Leo Braudy calls the "frenzy of renown."

Think of it: Can you imagine a best-selling magazine as popular as *People* called *System?* And yet we do understand the significance of systems. After all, it is systems that encourage cooperation and collaboration and systems that make change not only effective but possible. A shrinking world in which technological and political complexity increase at an accelerating rate offers fewer and fewer arenas in which individual action, top-down leadership, suffices.

And here is the troubling disconnect. Despite the rhetoric of collaboration, we continue to live in a byline culture in which recognition and status are conferred on individuals, not on the teams of people who make change possible. But even as the lone hero continues to gallop through our imaginations, shattering obstacles with silver bullets, leaping tall buildings in a single bound, we know that that's a false lulling fantasy and not the way real change, enduring change, takes place. We know there is an alternative reality. What's surprising is that this should surprise us. In a society as complex and technologically sophisticated as ours, the most urgent projects require the coordinated contributions of many talented people working together. Whether the task is building a global business or discovering the mysteries of the human brain, it doesn't happen at the top; top-down leadership can't hope to accomplish it, however gifted the person at the top is. There are simply too many problems to be identified and solved, too many connections to be made.

So we cling to the myth of the Lone Ranger—that great things are accomplished by larger-than-life individuals shouting commands, giving direction, inspiring the troops, sounding the tocsin, decreeing the compelling vision, leading the way, and changing paradigms with brio and shimmer. But this encompassing tendency is dysfunctional in today's world of burring, spastic, hyperturbulent change. And it will get us into unspeakable troubles unless we understand that the search engine, the main stem-winder for effective change, is the workforce and its creative alliance with top leadership.

A personal case in point. My colleague David Heenan and I wrote a book about the role of number two individuals in organizations: how they work and don't work. We thought it an original idea, one that was significant and astonishingly neglected in the literature. We entitled the book *Second Banana* and had chapters on some of the most famous and successful partnerships between ones and twos in corporate life; for example, the fabled relationship between Warren Buffet and his number two, Charles Munger, known for containing Buffet's enthusiasm about investments and referred to by Buffet as the Abominable No Man. And there was a chapter called "Banana Splits" on infamously unsuccessful partnerships, such as the widely publicized split between Michael Eisner and Michael Ovitz. All twelve of the publishers who reviewed the book declined. One put it rather nicely. He said, "Warren, no one in America wants to be number two." He also quoted Leonard Bernstein, who once proclaimed that "The hardest instrument to play in a symphony orchestra is second fiddle."

The Reality

Having presented the encompassing tendency—the myth—I will now present the reality. I will make my argument in an unorthodox way but one that I hope will be interesting and plausible. I will draw on sources a little out of the ordinary for management scholars: examples and analogies from poetry, history, and theater, as well as the more traditional experimental studies and business anecdotes. I'll start with an excerpt from a poem by Bertolt Brecht, the Marxist playwright.[1]

QUESTIONS FROM A WORKER

Who built the town of Thebes of Seven Gates?
The names of kings are written in the books.
Was it the kings who dragged the slab of rock?
And Babylon, so many times destroyed,
Who built her up again so many times?
Young Alexander conquered India.
All by himself?
Caesar beat the Gauls.
Not even a cook to help him with his meals?
Philip of Spain wept aloud when his Armada
Went down. Did no one else weep?
Frederick the Great won the Seven Years War. Who
Else was the winner?

On every page a triumph.
Who baked the victory cake?
In every decade a great man.
Who picked up the check?

So many reports.
So many questions.

"So many questions." That encompassing tendency again. And it shows up throughout history. In Plutarch's great biography of Cato the Elder, he wrote: "Rome showed itself to be truly great, and hence worthy of great leaders." What we tend to forget is that greatness lies within nations and organizations themselves as much as, if not more than, within their leaders. Could Gandhi have achieved his greatness without staying close to the people and representing their greatness of spirit? So many questions. . . .

Now for a contemporary business example. I wrote an article in which I quoted one of my favorite management philosophers, The Great One, Wayne Gretzky, saying, "It's not where the puck is, it's where the puck will be." Soon after I received a rather sour letter from the chairman and CEO of one of our largest Fortune 500 companies, who wrote: "I was particularly interested in what you characterize as the Gretzky factor. I think I know where the puck is going to be—the problem is, we've got thousands and thousands of folks who don't want the puck to go there, would rather that it wasn't going there, and in the event that it is going there, aren't going to let us position ourselves to meet it until after we've skated past. *In plain English, we've got a bunch of people that want the world to be the way it used to be—and are very disinclined to accept any alternative forecast of the future.*" (Emphasis mine.)

Now what's interesting about this "leader" is that (*a*) he was regarded as one of the most innovative and creative CEOs in his industrial sector, but (*b*) his unquestionable "genius" was ineffectual, because he lacked a critical mass of willing followers. And he had no followers because he was unable to generate and sustain a minimum degree of trust with his workforce, widely known to be resistant to and—no exaggeration—dyspeptic with his pre-Copernican ego and macho style.

If there is one generalization we can make about leadership and change it is this: No change can occur without willing and committed followers.

Let us turn now to social movements and how they are led and mobilized. Mohandas Gandhi's singular American apostle was Dr. Martin Luther King Jr., who was introduced to Gandhi's teachings as a graduate student at Boston University's Divinity School in the early 1950s. I had gone to college with Coretta Scott and got acquainted with her future husband while she attended the New England Conservatory of Music and I was in graduate school at MIT. Recently, upon reading John Lewis's book *Walking with the Wind,* I recalled how back then, light years ago, Coretta seemed the charismatic one and Martin, shy and bashful. Lewis, one of King's acolytes in the Civil Rights movement of the 1960s, now a Congressman from Atlanta and one of the most respected African-American leaders, tells us in his book how much of the movement was a team effort, a "band of brothers and sisters," and how Dr. King "often joined demonstrations late or ducked out early."[2] (I should add that Lewis was and is a devoted admirer of King.) Garry Wills's take on King is similar: "He tried to lift others up and found himself lifted up in the process. *He literally talked himself into useful kinds of trouble* [emphasis added]. King's oratory urged others on to heroic tasks and where they went he had to follow. Reluctant to go to jail, he was shamed into going—after so many young people responded to his speeches and found themselves in danger."[3] Don't be misled here. I'm not just reiterating one of those well-worn bromides about how leaders carefully watch where their followers are going and then follow them. I'm saying something quite different. I'm saying that exemplary leadership and organizational change are impossible without the full inclusion, initiative, and cooperation of followers.

I mentioned earlier that the top-down leadership tendency is also maladaptive, and I will return to that now. It's become something of a cliché to discuss the extraordinary complexity and ambiguity and uncertainties of our current business environment. As one of my CEO friends put it, "If you're not confused, you don't know what's going on." We need look no farther than to one of the contributors to this volume for convincing amplification of this point. At the risk of oversimplifying his important work on leadership, Ron Heifetz asserts that with relatively simple, "technical problems," leadership is relatively "easy"; that is, that top-down leadership can solve clear-cut problems.[4] But with "adaptive" problems—complex and messy problems such as dealing with a seriously ill cancer patient or cleaning up an ecological hazard—many stakeholders must be involved and mobilized. The truth is that adaptive problems require complex and diverse alliances. Decrees, ukases, orders *do not work.*

An elegant experiment dreamed up by one of the most imaginative (and least acknowledged) social psychologists of his day, Alex Bavelas, dramatizes if it does not prove this point. Imagine a simple, round wooden dining-room table, about ten feet in diameter, with plywood partitions walling off five people from visible sight of each other. The table is constructed so that participants can communicate only by passing messages written on three-by-five cards through narrow slots in the partitions. The cards are all color coded so that you can count how many messages are sent to whom and by whom. Also, the table is constructed so that different organizational forms can be simulated. For example, you can create a rough example of a typical bureaucratic, command-and-control organization by restricting the flow of messages to only one central person.

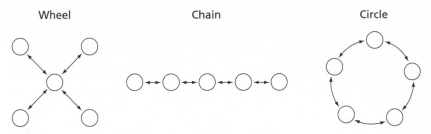

Figure 5-1 Three Organizational Models.

We experimented with this arrangement using three kinds of organizational models (figure 5-1): the Wheel, which more or less resembles the typical organizational pyramid; the Chain, a slight modification of the Wheel; and the Circle, where everyone could communicate to the two participants adjacent to them. Not quite a completely connected network, but one of equality. The problem to be solved was relatively simple. Each person was given a pill box containing six different colored marbles. They were what we used to called "puries"—pure white, pure blue, pure green, red, and so on, and easily identifiable. For each experimental trial, there was only one color that all participants had in common. On one trial, for example, it was the red; on another it was the green; and so on, randomly varied. There were fifteen trials. As soon as each participant thought he or she had the common color, the idea was to drop the marble down a rubber tube in the table so that the experimenter could measure not only the group's accuracy but also how long it took for all five people to deposit their marbles.

Our predictions were not surprising and they were confirmed. The Wheel, the form most like the top-down leadership model, was the most accurate and the most efficient; Wheel groups were very, very quick. We did notice that in our postexperiment questionnaire, the central person reported having the highest morale and was wildly enthusiastic about his or her role, whereas the other group members were, to be polite, pissed. Expectable and not particularly exciting results. So we decided to change the task to a more "adaptive" problem and substituted for the "puries" ambiguously colored marbles: cat's eyes, ginger ale-ish, bluish-green or greenish blue, all sorts of dappled colored marbles. . . . Again, our predictions were confirmed. That is, under these ambiguous conditions, the Circle was the most efficient

and accurate, and all members claimed relatively high morale. We repeated this form of the experiment about fifty times, and on only one
occasion did the Wheel perform better. In this one case, the central
person was an exceptionally gifted artist and writer. She was also taking
a minor in art history. Genius does happen. Once in a blue moon.

The connection between that primitive experiment and the messy,
changing business environment barely needs stating. But the experiment dramatically illustrates my point that none of us is as smart as all
of us; that the top-down model, in the present business context, is dysfunctional and maladaptive and, as I'll get to now, dangerous.

The dangers of top-down leadership, vivid examples of colossal
folly and disaster, are so numerous that one doesn't know where to begin. Stalin's communal farms? Niemeyer's Brasilia? Hitler's Holo-
caust? Chainsaw Al's follies? Napoleon's Russian campaign? Lyndon
Baines Johnson's Vietnam? Mao's Cultural Revolution? Maggie
Thatcher's poll tax? Perhaps the best source to turn to is Barbara
Tuchman's *The March of Folly*, an all too often ignored treasure for students of organizational behavior.

Tuchman argues that folly occurs when a governmental leader
pursues policies contrary to the self-interest of the nation. But to be
true folly, first, the policy must have been perceived as counterproductive *in its own time*, not merely in hindsight. Second, there must have
been feasible alternative means that were available. Tuchman takes her
concept of folly and refracts it through the prism of four major epochal
events: the Trojan horse escorted innocently (and stupidly) through
the gates of Troy by Priam's own warriors (who had heard from Cas-
sandra among others that it was probably a Greek ploy); the actions of
the Renaissance popes that brought about the Protestant Reformation;
the loss of the American colonies by George III; and LBJ's pursuit of
the Vietnam War. Tuchman writes: "Wooden-headedness, the source
of self-deception, is a factor that plays a remarkable role in individuals.
It consists in assessing a situation in terms of preconceived fixed notions while ignoring or rejecting any contrary signs. It is acting according to wish while not allowing oneself to be deflected by the facts. It is
epitomized in a historian's statement about Philip II of Spain, the sur-
passing wooden-head of all sovereigns: 'No experience of the failure of
the policy could shake his belief in its essential excellence.'"[5]

Where does all of this lead us in terms of organizational leadership? What should be clear by now is that postbureaucratic organizations require a new kind of alliance between leaders and the led. Today's organizations are evolving into federations, networks, clusters, cross-functional teams, temporary systems, ad hoc task forces, lattices, modules, matrices—almost anything but pyramids with their obsolete top-down leadership. Successful organizations—organizations that want to be in the phone book in the year 2005—will be led by leaders who encourage healthy dissent and values those followers courageous enough to say no. Success will go to the leader who exults in cultural differences and knows that diversity is the best hope for long-term survival and success. These new leaders will have, not the loudest voice, but the most attentive ear. Instead of pyramids, these postbureaucratic organizations will be structures built of energy and ideas, led by people who find their joy in the task at hand, not in leaving monuments behind.

Notes

1. From George Tabori, ed., *The World of Brecht* (Hollywood: Samuel French, 1962). © 1962 Stephen Brecht. Reprinted with permission from the estate of Bertolt Brecht.
2. John Lewis, *Walking with the Wind: A Memoir of the Movement* (New York: Simon and Schuster, 1998), 206.
3. Garry Wills, *Certain Trumpets* (New York: Simon and Schuster, 1994), 218.
4. Ronald A. Heifetz, *Leadership without Easy Answers* (Cambridge, MA: Belknap Press, 1994).
5. Barbara Tuchman, *The March of Folly* (New York: Knopf, 1984), 7.

6

EMBRACING PARADOX

Top-Down versus Participative
Management of Organizational Change

A Commentary on Conger and Bennis

Dexter Dunphy

ONE OF THE MOST hotly debated issues in the field of organizational change has been whether change is best developed participatively with the active involvement of all organizational members or
led from above by the CEO and top executive team. In particular, supporters of two very influential approaches to organizational change,
the organizational development (OD) and the sociotechnical systems
(STS) approaches, have argued strongly for widespread involvement
and participation by all organizational members in the planning and
implementation of change. In the 1960s and 1970s, OD was extremely
influential in the United States and STS in Europe. While these two
models of change differed in significant ways, they shared a common
ideology of bringing about corporate change participatively. Their
adherents viewed employee participation both as an ethical imperative and as the source of energy for change. Proponents of participative models were strongly committed to making change a collaborative
venture on the part of all who would be affected by the process;
the role of managers and other change agents was primarily to act as
catalysts.

In the 1980s, however, the dominance of these models was successfully challenged by the proponents of strategic management. Strategic management theory redefined organizational change as a process

of implementing corporate strategy. This approach placed the impetus for change, its planning, and the control of its execution firmly in the hands of the CEO and the top executive team. The top team was seen to have the perspective, the knowledge, and the power to reposition the organization strategically to take advantage of its dynamic environment. Employee participation was often viewed as useful in generating commitment to change and in ensuring that a strategic reorganization was actualized. However, as corporate repositioning frequently involved divestment of organizational units, downsizing, and significantly changes in the employee skill mix, employee participation also represented a potential threat to the effective implementation of strategy: Few would expect that such changes would be greeted enthusiastically by those most affected. Consequently the strategic management school stressed managerial control of the corporate change process— or, in some cases, indulged in the rhetoric of empowerment while largely ignoring it in practice.[1]

The Bennis and Conger Viewpoints

How do the Warren Bennis and Jay Conger articles line up with the historical viewpoints outlined above? Each is in fact an expression of one of these viewpoints.

Bennis's paper speaks for the OD viewpoint, as befits one of the outstanding leaders and contributors to this school of thought. Bennis attacks the top-down approach to corporate change, which he sees as based on "the myth of the triumphant individual." He correctly notes that heroic leaders can be wrong; after all, history is littered with the disasters such leaders created. Leaders are often "woodenheaded" and more motivated by greed, ego, the lust for power, and the yearning for fame than by the notion of contributing to human welfare or productivity. I am reminded of John Kenneth Galbraith's remark: "If all else fails, immortality can be assured by a spectacular error." Given that heroic leaders seem to have achieved immortality as much by spectacular errors as by spectacular successes, Bennis's unveiling of this myth seems appropriate.

Again, Bennis articulates a major OD value when he writes of the need for collaboration in a complex world where the cues around which we must make judgments are ambiguous rather than clear and simple. In such a world diversity and difference become resources; the more minds devoted to problems facing the organization as it changes, the better.

There is, however, a significant assumption hidden in Bennis's argument and, indeed, in the traditional OD viewpoint. It is true that leaders can be ignorant, wrong, and myopic in their viewpoints—but then so can other organizational members. It is true that more minds are often better than one—but only if they have relevant knowledge and are organized to share that knowledge and equipped to evaluate it. Bennis assumes that organizational members have the knowledge and capabilities to contribute effectively to organizational decision making around change, but members may be simply pooling their ignorance and pleading their special interests. Rather than assuming that participation is automatically undergirded by capability, we would do better to inquire about the circumstances in which organizational members do have the capability to contribute and those where they do not. I will return to this issue below.

Conger belongs to a later generation than Bennis and, as one might expect, is an articulate proponent for the strategic management model. He vigorously questions the capability of organizational members other than the senior executive team to initiate significant organizational change. A bottom-up approach to change, he argues, is futile—and he views those below the executive team with suspicion. Initiatives from below lack a systemwide perspective and will reflect "functional and departmental biases"; junior managers "may lack the courage needed to set and achieve radical goals"—and anyway don't have access to the resources critical to successful change. The essential role of junior managers is to "translate corporate strategies into effective operating initiatives"; in other words, to do what they're told. And they will be happy to do this, Conger implies, because of their propensity to attribute heroic qualities to those in power. (Often wrongly, it seems.) One wonders whether Conger would favor reintroducing, for junior managers and general employees, the prayer once recited each Sabbath by farmhands and household servants in Anglican churches— "God bless the squire and his relations and keep us in our proper stations"—but with the CEO and executive team replacing the squire!

Hiding in Conger's arguments for powerful leadership by the top executive team is another assumption: that there is one single-minded team at the top of the organization whose members are in substantial agreement with each other about the strategic reorientation of the organization. I shall return to this "unitary leadership" assumption below. Bennis also seems to assume this, although he is far less convinced than Conger that the unitary view necessarily embodies the highest strategic insight.

In all other respects, Conger's assumptions are the mirror image of Bennis's. For Bennis knowledge and wisdom about change reside primarily in the organizational members below the senior level, and leaders are a potential source of disaster. To tap organizational resources and overcome their own limitations, leaders need to ensure that organization members participate actively in all aspects of the change process. For Conger knowledge and wisdom about change reside in the CEO and the top team, while other employees are a potential source of error, inadequacy, and special interest pleading. To ensure that strategic change, generated in the top team, is not subverted, it is vital that other organizational members faithfully carry out the initiatives generated from the top of the organization.

Here we have two highly intelligent, competent academics with extensive practical experience in consulting to and researching major organizational change programs. Yet their views are contradictory. Who is right?

Embracing Paradox

What we are faced with here is a paradox. There are two imperatives in the modern organization. On the one hand, the rate of change demands that those who operate closest to the action, including employees who relate daily to customers' rapidly shifting demands, be empowered to make decisions to allow quick and effective organizational responses. It is also vital that frontline workers' accumulating and current knowledge of a volatile marketplace be taken into account when new strategic directions are debated and strategic change initiated. On the other hand, the rate of change also demands swift and decisive leadership action from the top of the organization. This action may involve closing down unprofitable plants, investing in new ventures, entering into alliances, and many other such strategic redirections. Some of these major shifts effectively disempower people by eliminating their jobs, closing down the operations to which they are committed, and significantly altering their responsibilities without their consent.[2]

It is tempting to try to resolve a paradox by rejecting one of the contrasting positions. But it is the nature of paradox that we can manage it only by embracing the contradiction and living, somewhat uncomfortably, in the tension between the alternatives. Long ago the Taoist sage Lao-Tzu pointed out that all opposites coexist, and the presence of each demands the other. For example, convex cannot exist without concave or, as in the Chinese symbol, yin without yang. We may wish to simplify reality by flying to one end of the dilemma and declaring it to be the whole truth. But, as H. L. Mencken once wrote, "For every problem there is a solution which is simple, direct . . . and wrong."

How then can we embrace, understand, and manage this uncomfortable paradox that underlies an effective approach to organizational change?

An Examination of the "Unitary Leadership" Assumption

We have noted that Conger and Bennis both assume unitary leadership of the modern corporation. For Bennis such leadership is a potential danger, while for Conger it is the prime asset in the conduct of corporate change. But how valid is this assumption?

There is no doubt that in some circumstances unitary leadership does exist and that in some of these cases the top team actively initiates and leads corporationwide change that successfully repositions the organization, resulting in improved performance.[3] Decisive top-down leadership is particularly important in corporate turnarounds where significant interest groups oppose change.[4]

However, it is also clear that in some cases unitary leadership does not exist and that structural trends in organizations are multiplying these instances. In the future we will need to check whether the assumption holds before assuming that Conger's model will work. What are these structural trends, and how are they modifying the control structures of organizations?

Increasingly organizations are emerging that are in reality coalitions, strategic alliances, consortia, networks, and virtual organiza-

tions. The vertically integrated bureaucratic organization is a threatened species, being replaced by what Handy refers to as "federal"
organizations and Quinn as "spiderweb" organizations.[5] These organizations often do not have a centralized, unitary command structure; at
the most, there may be a loose alliance around some common interest
and the challenge of developing a command structure for the conduct
of transitions.

For example, I have consulted to four competing organizations in
the mining industry that jointly own a common ore-processing facility.
The facility is controlled by a board consisting of representatives of all
four companies. In this situation a shared set of interests revolve
around having an efficient plant to serve the needs of all four companies. However, there are also strong conflicting interests relative to the
pricing of raw materials, shipping costs, sharing of leading-edge technology owned by a particular partner company, and so on. In these circumstances the unitary leadership assumption crumbles, rendering the
standard strategic model inadequate. Determining the goals of a major
program of organizational renewal for the processing plant involved
political maneuvering by the representatives of the partner organizations, negotiation of trade-offs between partners' conflicting interests,
and sensitivity to the cultural differences of multinationals head-
quartered in different nations with very different cultures. To have
assumed that unitary leadership existed at any point in this change
program would have led to the collapse of the change program.
The greatest challenge was to develop, through negotiation, sufficient agreement among the partners for a coherent change program
to be initiated and carried through in the shared facility. Such circumstances will be increasingly common as the process of globalization
continues.

Conger is correct in arguing that effective change programs proceed from a clear strategic intent. However, as the command structures of organizations become more tenuous and complex, developing
a consensual strategic intent is increasingly problematical.[6] Even in
traditional organizations, it was always dangerous to assume that the
executive team agreed on the direction of a proposed change program.
It is not only "junior managers" whose views represent functional or
departmental biases; experienced CEOs know that they have to work
hard to develop a corporate perspective on the part of their direct
reports.

In this regard I report the experience of one of my colleagues when he was first invited to attend the meetings of the top executive team of a certain organization. As he entered the boardroom on the first meeting, he noticed that there were two tables in the room. One table was rectangular; the other was round. Without hesitation, the executive team sat down at the rectangular table and the CEO sat at the head. There were eleven items on the agenda. After completing discussion of the first eight items, the CEO stood up and moved to the round table. The rest of the team followed. They then discussed the remaining three items and the CEO closed the meeting.

As they were leaving the room at the end of the meeting, my colleague asked the CEO: "Why the two tables, and why did you switch tables during the meeting?" The CEO replied: "Oh, I should have told you about that before the meeting. The first items on the agenda are primarily internal issues. We sit at the rectangular table, and I expect my managers to represent the interests of their divisions. However, the last items are important issues relating to the overall direction of the organization. We move to the round table, and at that point I expect my managers to put aside their sectional interests and to think like directors of the company, pursuing only what is best for the company as a whole."

The moral: Experienced CEOs don't assume a breadth of perspective on the part of their top team; they work to create it. The development of alliances and consortia only reveals more clearly the political process that is always involved in constructing a consensual strategic intent among a top executive team, and it demonstrates the need for CEOs and change agents to develop strategies to facilitate the consensus-making process. Strategic leadership by the top executive team is a vital component of organizational renewal—but it often has to be generated rather than taken for granted.

Whatever Happened to "Positive Attribution" and Loyalty?

Conger becomes almost lyrical in describing how organization members of the project positive attributes onto their formal leaders, invoking the figure of Chauncy Gardener in the film *Being There*. Certainly I have worked with organizations where one or more charismatic leaders attracted the respect and projective identification of the majority of organization members. But currently I see many more organizations where formal leaders are viewed with cynicism, indifference, or antipathy and where loyalty to the organization and its leaders is a scarce commodity. Little wonder, given the record of top-down restructuring and downsizing over the last decade and the feeding frenzy of acquisitions, mergers, and divestments undertaken for short-term financial gain and with disregard for the interests of employees.

In Australia, for example, on average one in two employees were "retrenched" each year over a recent eleven-year period. Ex-employees are unlikely to attribute heroic characteristics to those who sacked them. But it is not simply those who have gone who carry grief, resentment, and anger with them to the next workplace (if there is one). As Cascio has shown, a "survivor syndrome" characterizes those who remain in the organization. Their morale drops; they become self-absorbed, risk averse, and less productive; and they too distrust management.[7] Survivors are likely to see the next managerial-driven "organizational renewal" program as a signal for yet another round of restructuring, downsizing, and cost cutting—a round in which they too will lose their jobs or end up working even more hours for the same pay.

In this regard I take Marc Jones's point about modern capitalism's creating a dualistic structure, which he sees as made up of, on the one hand, a "complex and technologically sophisticated intensive sector" and on the other hand "the grunge economy," a "heterogeneous collection of contingent and informal activities" in which a class of "grunge" workers are materially disadvantaged and disenfranchised.[8] Grunge workers are unlikely to respond to management change initiatives with positive attribution. At best they may conform to directives, but their attitudes and skills will make participation a waste of time and effort. In this case, management get the return commensurate with its investment in the capabilities of the workforce.

What Does Employee Participation Offer?

The term *strategy* was derived from military usage, and Conger develops the military analogy in discussing the positional power of formal organizational leaders, particularly of the CEO. He refers to generals sitting atop the hills, thus having a broader perspective than those fighting hand-to-hand on the battlefield. However, that broader perspective often did not necessarily lead to more insightful military decisions, as Dixon shows in his book *On the Psychology of Military Incompetence*.[9] The long view is a necessary but not sufficient factor in strategic success. Outstanding military leaders do two other things that Conger does not mention: They systematically build the capabilities of their forces in advance of the need to use them, and they work relentlessly to build the commitment of their forces, checking constantly to measure how loyalty is holding up. A reading of the lives of outstanding military figures such as Nelson, Wellington, and Lafayette shows this. They understood that they could not win just by sitting on hills when the battles were fought. When the time arrived to supervise the battle, they needed troops with the capability to fight effectively and the commitment to do so; they also needed runners to bring back timely news on what was happening at points where they couldn't see clearly. (Battles aren't always fought in broad daylight in bright sunshine and within view of the commander.)

The issue of the capability of organizational members, in particular, brings us to a critical examination of Bennis's assumption that the workforce necessarily has the capability to participate effectively in the strategic change process.

Bennis has a strong belief in the potential of employees to contribute to the formulation and implementation of organizational change. In my own work in organizational change, I have been impressed many times by the untapped talent that emerges at all levels of organizations. However, I also bring to mind general employees whose lives centered around simple repetitive tasks such as packing cookies in cartons or peeling and slicing ginger root for bottling in syrup. In many of these cases these people often had little interest in, understanding of, or contribution to make to the formulation and implementation of strategic change—or even of simple changes in their own immediate work environment. I am reminded of the film *Zorba the Greek* when Zorba, played by Anthony Quinn, is asked, "What work do you do?" He replies: "I have head, hands, feet—they do the work for me. Who the hell am I to choose!" This is not an unusual attitude on the shop floor, particularly in Tayloristic workplaces.

As we move into knowledge-based organizations, however, there are fewer people who respond like Zorba. In service organizations with a high-technology base, financial services for example, we typically find a workforce composed of intelligent, highly informed and educated people who often understand their segment of the market better than management does, both in operational and strategic terms, and who want to influence the direction and process of organizational change. The top executive team that fails to involve these people (or their representatives) is running a high-risk strategy. The top team may have a broad overview of the business; but in a complex organization with a dynamic technology base and diverse, turbulent, fast-moving markets, management needs some good "runners" to update them on what often isn't obvious from the lofty heights of the hill. Also, as Bennis points out, when it comes to making strategic change happen, the top team is quite impotent without the mindful, motivated commitment of an informed workforce. If we extend the military analogy farther, a great deal of a commander's success depends on the intelligent interpretation of strategic intent in a concrete situation by the leaders of frontline units. "Doing what you're told" is no substitute for mindful, adaptive action.

So the capabilities of the workforce are critical for participation in change to have successful outcomes. Ironically, however, the top teams in some organizations are pursuing a strategy of dumbing down the workforce by creating new versions of Taylorism, creating a world of grunge work where employees are deprived of initiative and subject to the moment-to-moment control of computer programs. Many "call centers" are examples of this pattern. These are the new mechanistic organizations, and we should not be surprised if in them participation produces no positive input into strategic change programs. This is an inevitable consequence of managers' decision not to invest in personal, professional, and corporate capabilities.

A 1998 study by Turner and Crawford shows how vital investment in corporate capabilities is to successful organizational reshaping.[10] The study was a quantitative and qualitative analysis of 243 cases of organizational change. The analysis included performance indicators. The authors identify five essential capabilities for long-term performance and divide these capabilities into two fundamental groupings. One group, Operational Capabilities, enables an organization to operate effectively on a day-to-day basis. The second group, Reshaping Capabilities, enables an organization to change effectively in order to improve future performance. The study showed that investment in these corporate capabilities makes a major difference to an organization's long-term success. In particular, the Reshaping Capabilities (Engagement, Development, and Performance Management) ensure that a critical mass of the organization's members collectively understand the intended changes, become committed to them, grow confident in their ability to succeed, and are empowered to take action. This action takes place throughout the organization, not just at the top.

Other studies support the notion that organizations that invest in the capabilities of their employees and in their technical and human systems perform better in the medium to long term. Conversely, those that liquidate their human capital experience a performance decline.[11] This finding illustrates that we can no more assume that employee participation in change necessarily enhances the change process any more than does direction by the top team. Participation by knowledgeable, skilled, and motivated members of the organization does enhance a change project; participation by uninformed, unskilled, and unmotivated members of the workforce does not. To make participative change work we have to invest in it, putting our money, time, and attention where our mouth is. Rhetoric about participation and empowerment only breeds cynicism and external conformity. Real change depends on inner commitment brought about by trust in the top team's strategic judgment and in its determination to build the knowledge and skills of organizational members.

Working the Paradox

We are now in a position to embrace and work the paradoxical relationship of executive leadership and employee participation in change. As Bennis concludes in his article, "postbureaucratic organizations require a new kind of alliance between leaders and the led." This is very close to Conger's conclusion that "it is the effective integration of the unique advantages of the upper and lower strata of an organization that determines the success of any change effort."

We do need a unified executive team who develop a strategic intent, and we need opportunities for other organization members to participate fully in the strategic process. However, the purposeful consensus required by a challenging vision and strategy for change must be built rather than assumed. In knowledge-based organizations it must be informed by the in-depth insights of the skilled professionals who make up the organization as well as by the strategic overview of the top team. We also need the active participation of other organization members. However, to participate effectively they must be knowledgeable and capable and have the skills they need to make a genuine contribution. This occurs only where the top team systematically invests over time in a range of key personal, professional, and corporate capabilities that support meaningful participation.

Samuel Goldwyn once remarked: "I don't want any yes-men around me—I want everyone to tell me the truth even if it costs them their jobs." Goldwyn was rather more frank about his attitude toward those who differed from him than are many managers who share the same authoritarian instincts. The kind of highly interactive system that underlies effective organizational renewal thrives on difference and diversity, as Bennis points out. It demands a climate of trust and mutual respect that is easily destroyed by unilateral control and management by fear. However, this kind of system is not therefore less tough-minded where business strategies are concerned; in fact, recent research has demonstrated that short-term, cost-cutting approaches that degrade human and environmental resources have poor business outcomes.[12] As this evidence sinks into the minds of business leaders, financial analysts, and investors, we may see the emergence of the integrative alliance between senior executives and other organizational members that Bennis and Conger hope for. But this will not happen spontaneously through the magic of market forces. It will come about through the committed action of those who have the insight to see the need, the will to invest the necessary time and resources, and the organizational power to make the alliance happen. A new century may be the time to attempt to forge this interactive partnership and use it to support continuous, sustainable corporate renewal.

Notes

1. Bernard Burnes, *Managing Change: A Strategic Approach to Organizational Dynamics* (London: Pitman, 1996); Dexter Dunphy and Andrew Griffiths, *The Sustainable Corporation: Organizational Renewal in Australia* (Sydney: Allen and Unwin, 1998).

2. Doug Stace and Dexter Dunphy, *Beyond the Boundaries: Leading and Recreating the Successful Enterprise* (Sydney: McGraw Hill, 1994), 12–13.

3. Dexter Dunphy and Doug Stace, *Under New Management: Australian Organizations in Transition* (Sydney: McGraw Hill, 1990); Doug Stace and Dexter Dunphy, *Beyond the Boundaries;* John P. Kotter, *Leading Change* (Boston: Harvard Business School Press, 1996).

4. Stace and Dunphy, *Beyond the Boundaries.*

5. Charles Handy, *The Age of Unreason* (Boston: Harvard Business School Press, 1990); James B. Quinn, *Intelligent Enterprise* (New York: Free Press, 1992).

6. Steven W. Floyd and Bill Wooldridge, "Managing Strategic Change: The Foundation of Effective Implementation," *Academy of Management Executive* 16, no. 4 (1992): 27–39; Michael Beer, Russell A. Eisenstat, and Bert Spector, "Why Change Programs Don't Produce Change," *Harvard Business Review* 68, no. 6 (Nov.–Dec. 1990): 158–166.

7. Wayne Cascio, "Downsizing: What do we know?" *Academy of Management Executive* 7, no. 1 (1993): 95–104.

8. Marc Jones, "Blade Runner Capitalism: 'A New Narrative of Globalization,'" in *Rethinking Globalization(s)*, ed. Preet S. Aulakh and Michael G. Schecter (London: Macmillan, 1998).

9. Norman Dixon, *On the Psychology of Military Incompetence* (London: Jonathan Cape, 1976).

10. Dennis Turner and Michael Crawford, *Change Power: Capabilities That Drive Corporate Renewal* (Sydney: Business and Professional Publishing, 1998).

11. J Collins and Jerry Porras, *Built To Last: Successful Habits of Visionary Companies* (London: Century, 1994); Arie de Geus, *The Living Company: Habits for Survival in a Turbulent Business Environment* (Boston: Harvard Business School Press, 1997); Charles Egan, *Creating Organizational Advantage* (Oxford: Butterworth Heinemann, 1995); Dunphy and Griffiths, *The Sustainable Corporation.*

12. Dunphy and Griffiths, *The Sustainable Corporation*, Chapter 6, 140–170.

FOCUS OF CHANGE
Formal Structure and Systems or Culture?

ORGANIZATIONAL CHANGE efforts vary in the extent to which they focus on formal organizational arrangements such as structure and systems and the extent to which they acknowledge and deal with culture. By *culture* we mean the deeply held beliefs of employees, and in particular the moral meaning and legitimacy that people ascribe to the old order. Theory E leaders who want to spur rapid changes in their firms' economic fortunes typically rely on changes in formal organizational arrangements. Theory O leaders, who see as their purpose the development of organizational capabilities, focus on processes for development of coordination, competence, and commitment.

In this section Jay Galbraith argues cogently that in many circumstances, particularly when top management faces a change in strategic direction, management must make changes in formal organizational arrangements so as to reallocate power, influence, and decision rights quickly. Galbraith illustrates the importance of structure by describing the systematic organizational transformation of professional services (PS) firms from a focus on geography (offices) and function to a focus on global customers. These firms appointed global account coordinators and worldwide customer teams. While acknowledging the value of softer organization development interventions as the appropriate focus in some less radical circumstances, and as supporting interventions even in radical structural transformations, Galbraith contends that dramatic shifts necessitate starting with structure.

Larry Hirschhorn, in his chapter, makes the case that there is good reason to be skeptical about the effectiveness and sustainability of structural change. Many companies go through cycles of reorganization, each cycle spurred by the failure of the previous structure, suggesting that these structures never really took hold. Hirschhorn argues that using formal structure and systems to change behavior cannot yield sustained improvements in performance. Instead, managers must attend to the culture of the organization—the set of beliefs and values that gave the old order legitimacy. Hirschhorn says that leaders who want to legitimize new formal organizational arrangements—to imbue them with moral meaning—must develop what he calls a "counterstructure." This is a coalition-building mechanism designed to undermine the legitimacy of the inherited organizational structure. In this way the transformation of the old order *also* develops a new basis for cohesion and commitment. In addition, focusing on how the task and work must change, the counterstructure provides a safe way for aggression to be mobilized—a necessary ingredient in fostering change.

Allan Cohen offers a synthesis. He maintains that almost all major organizational changes, whether led by structural or by cultural change, fail to achieve what was intended within the anticipated time and budget. Cohen believes there is no universal formula. There are circumstances under which structure and systems should be the focus, and circumstances under which behavior and beliefs should be the focus. In all cases, he argues, the choice of structure or behavior for initial emphasis will depend on the extent to which behavior has to change. And if behavior has to change, structure and process interventions have to be integrated. For this, Cohen points out, the top team's own effectiveness will be critical.

7

THE ROLE OF FORMAL
STRUCTURES AND PROCESSES

Jay R. Galbraith

THIS CHAPTER will argue that under many circumstances, changing formal organizational structures and systems is central to the success of the overall change process. The first section will set the context by identifying which circumstances require structural changes. It will also define what is meant by "being central to the change effort" and by "formal structure and systems." The next section will use the example of global professional service firms, which are changing to serve the global customer, shifting from country-based profit centers to customer-focused profit centers. The last section presents the ideal of an organization: a reconfigurable organization, designed from the beginning to be quickly and easily changeable.

The Centrality of Change Levers

Meaningful organizational change requires the combined use of many change levers. For some circumstances, however, the organization's formal structure and systems can be the central lever.

The organizational development (OD) movement in the 1960s was one of the first groups to propose that soft means such as team building and improved interpersonal relationships were superior to hard means such as formal restructuring for driving organizational change. Hal Leavitt (1965) tried to address the debate with his chapter in March's *The Handbook of Organization.* Leavitt quite cleverly conducted an argument with himself. He created a manager with a problem who solicited proposals from consulting firms representing the OD viewpoint, the operations research (OR) or mathematical school, and the traditional general management consulting viewpoint. For the same problem the manager received three very different proposals, each reflecting one firm's specialty. Leavitt argued that although each proposal was not completely wrong, each was only partially correct. In order to solve the problem and create meaningful change, the manager should adopt all of the proposals. That is, the manager had to change the personal relationships as suggested by the OD firm, the information systems as suggested by the OR firm, and the structure as suggested by the traditional firm.

Leavitt's point was that one does not produce real change by relying on a single means such as reward systems or structure. Organization designs are integrated systems consisting of structure, formal systems, informal processes, reward and measurement systems, and human resources practices. Effective change requires changing a combination of policies, or all of them, to create a new and integrated design. And all of the policies must also be aligned or mutually reinforcing. Leavitt's ideas have since been translated into organization design models such as the author's star model (Galbraith 1978, 1995) and the McKinsey 7S model.

While acknowledging the need to use combinations of hard and soft levers of change, one can still make an argument that under some circumstances a hard or a soft approach may be more central to the success of a change. There are two arguments that can be made for this centrality. One argument is about leverage. That is, under some circumstances, a manager can produce more change by changing the formal structure than by changing culture. Under these conditions, if change could be measured along an index, a greater proportion of the variance of the index could be attributed to structure change. In other words, the manager gains more leverage by using changes to the formal structure. Or there will be little change if the structure is not changed. Other supporting changes still need to be made to things like culture and rewards, but it is the structure change that is the star of the show.

The second argument is about sequence. A change lever is more central when it is the first lever to be used. In this manner the first lever shapes and drives the subsequent change efforts. A combination of change levers is eventually used, but the first one takes the central position by starting the change.

A case for formal restructuring can be made that satisfies both of these arguments. But first, what are the conditions under which formal structure can be central?

Changes to formal structure and systems play a central role when substantial shifts in strategic direction are involved. At the extreme these shifts may require alterations in the legal structure of assets of the company through mergers and acquisitions. For example, Monsanto transformed itself from a traditional chemical company to a life sciences company based on biotechnology. To execute this change, Monsanto spun off its traditional chemical businesses, acquired seed and biotechnology companies, and formed a joint venture with Cargill. The company could not have accomplished this type of transformation by focusing solely on cultural change and team building.

The best discussion of internal structural changes required by changes in strategic direction is Chandler's (1962) classic study. In his historical analysis of strategy and structure, Chandler showed that companies did not succeed in diversifying until they adopted a multidivisional structure. Using a similar premise, Stopford and Wells (1972) and Egelhoff (1988) showed that structure changes are needed when a firm transitions from a national company to a multinational company. In all of these cases the execution of the strategic change requires a change to the formal structure of power in the company. Formal structures and systems concern the power dimension in the organization. In this context, power is the capability to allocate and coordinate the limiting resources. Usually the limiting resource is money or a type of money, such as capital. Formal structures create positions of power that control the allocation of funds to research and development, advertising, and other uses. The capital budgeting process is a formal system for managing this limiting resource on a companywide basis. Changes in strategic direction require a redistribution of this power.

On the other hand, it is possible to make large changes that do not involve shifts in strategic direction. A company may stay in its existing business but desire to be more family friendly or more innovative. In these cases, structural changes are more likely to be supporting rather than central to the overall change. Similarly the case of Asda, discussed by Michael Beer and Nitin Nohria in the introductory chapter of this book, involved a major change but not a new strategic direction. Asda was a sick company that was revitalized or turned around, but in the end it remained (or returned to being) a mass merchandiser to the low end of the grocery market in the United Kingdom. There were some structural changes at Asda, but they were not central to the transformation.

The next section will elaborate on this strategy/structure argument by presenting a current example: a profound change in strategic direction being taken today by professional service firms.

Changing Structure at Professional Service Firms

Professional service firms such as advertising agencies, accounting firms, investment banks, consulting firms, and executive recruiters are all being transformed. The force that is shaping them is the global customer. In order to serve this global customer, professional service firms are restructuring themselves. And changes to formal structure and systems are central to such restructuring. Let us look first at the leverage argument for this centrality, then at the sequence argument.

The Leverage Argument

The force that is driving change at professional service (PS) companies is the fact that for PS firms, today's customer is a globally present customer. Since 1985 the process of globalization has been driven by foreign direct investment (FDI). The result of FDI is that more companies and therefore more customers have presence in more countries than ever before. In addition, these customers want only one or at most a few providers of professional services everywhere they are present. For example, the customer wants one audit firm, one systems integrator, two ad agencies, and a couple of banks to serve it worldwide. But PS firms who want to serve this global customer are faced with a challenge, because for decades they have been organized by country. Their basic profit centers are country-based and are run by country managers. Global customers do not care how PS firms are organized as long as they receive seamless service. But delivering seamless service across country profit centers is the challenge.

As a result, many PS companies have changed or are changing from country profit centers to customer and customer segment profit centers. And increasingly, PS firms that want to serve the global customer will be at a competitive disadvantage if they are organized by country when competitors are organized by customer. One systems integrator changed its structure after directly experiencing this disadvantage. This firm's managing director for Europe encountered a situation in which a Spanish bank announced that it was outsourcing its information technology around the world and asked systems integrators to bid on global IT management. The managing director for Europe received the bank's request and found it to be an attractive bidding opportunity. The very next day, he received a call from his Spanish managing partner. The Spanish partner advised the managing director that fifty professionals from EDS had arrived in Madrid overnight and were working on a proposal for the bank. The managing director was shocked: He was just beginning what he called the "begging process" of asking country managers to free up people and send them to Madrid to work on a proposal. The first arrivals would take a week, and the full team would not be in place for a good two weeks. Even then it was not certain that the best talent would be working on the proposal. The bank, also impressed with the speed of the EDS response, awarded the contract to them. The systems integrator convened a study team and eventually restructured its profit centers around customers. It is now focusing on "integrated speed to serve the customer."

This example reveals the need for PS firms to change their power structure. When a firm is organized by country profit centers, the power to allocate and coordinate the limiting resource (talent) resides with the country manager. And when the most profitable clients are local clients, country profit centers constitute the most effective structure. But when the most profitable client is the global customer, country managers optimizing their local profits will not arrive at the best or the fastest allocation of talent for the firm. In order to service Nestlé, a team of sixty people from sixty countries is needed. Persuading sixty country managers to make available the kind of talent that Nestlé wants is an arduous task. And of course Nestlé is one of hundreds of global clients, all of whom want the same top talent. As a result, systems integrators, investment banks, and IT outsourcing firms such as EDS, IBM, and Andersen Consulting have all organized around customer groups: consumer goods, banking, and so on. In addition, they collect specialized talent in regional resource pools to respond to pan-European opportunities. The power to allocate and coordinate talent now rests with the heads of global customer–focused groups.

If PricewaterhouseCoopers (PwC) wants to serve this global customer and yet maintains its country partnerships, it will be at a competitive disadvantage when responding to opportunities generated by the global customer. With talent resources locked up in country silos, it cannot respond fast enough with a team that is competent enough and complete enough. But it cannot go to Nestlé and say, "We can serve you in forty-six of your sixty subsidiaries, because fourteen of our country managers opted out." IBM will serve Nestlé in all sixty countries. PwC can build networks across countries, change country manager mindsets, create a global culture, and train people in cross-cultural skills, all of which are good things to do; but it will lose to the others if it maintains its country profit centers. The high-leverage change approach is to change the formal structure and profit accounting systems to customer-based units. Then the power structure and the strategy are aligned. Then changes to global cultures, networks, and mindsets will support the central change and make it even more successful.

The argument can also be made that preemptive structure changes can lead to competitive advantages. Conversations with investment bankers suggest that investment banks that have organized by customer and industry profit centers are winning business from banks that are organized by country. Merrill Lynch apparently was a first mover. They wanted to enter the top rank of investment banks. They acquired a group and let them focus on the oil and gas industry. After some success they converted other industry groups into profit centers. The other investment banks soon followed Merrill Lynch. Customers then discovered that these specialists knew more about their industry and about them. The U.S. investment banks took this advantage into Europe. European banks still viewed Europe as a portfolio of countries. The U.S. banks saw a portfolio of cross-border customers and industries. When Ciba-Geigy and Sandoz merged to form Novartis they hired U.S. banks and not the Swiss banks that were their shareholders. Why? Because the U.S. banks had done the mergers of Bristol-Myers Squibb, SmithKline Beecham, Pharmacia & Upjohn, and Glaxo Wellcome. They had the in-depth knowledge and understood the value of merged pharmaceutical companies. The U.S. investment banks' preemptive moves to customer-focused formal structures had given them major advantages. European banks are now merging to get the size needed to afford to specialize by industry.

The Sequence Argument

The sequence argument can also be made to support changing formal structures as the central change lever. Let us take the same example of professional service firms and the globalization of their customers. Most PS firms were traditionally organized by country and by service or product lines, as described earlier. Figure 7-1 shows an investment bank with countries as primary profit centers. Within each country, re-lationship managers served customers and called on specialists in the service or product lines when the customers needed their services. The product lines, such as foreign exchange (Fx) and mergers and acquisitions (M&A), were the secondary profit centers. By the late 1980s, however, global customers wanted cash management and Fx to be pro-vided in every country where they were present. These customers be-gan to select PS firms for their ability to provide integrated service. Many of the large multinational PS firms saw that they needed to change their organizations and build a capability to coordinate across countries. To do this, the PS firms employed formal structures: inte-grating mechanisms such as teams and coordinators. They mobilized these mechanisms in a sequence of steps. As an example, consider the six-step sequence described below.

1. A FEW CUSTOMER TEAMS
An initial step taken by many PS firms is to create approximately five customer teams to serve customers around the world. The firms care-fully choose the five customers most desirous of this global service. The account manager serving the customer's headquarters is the team leader. A team member is also selected in each country where the cus-

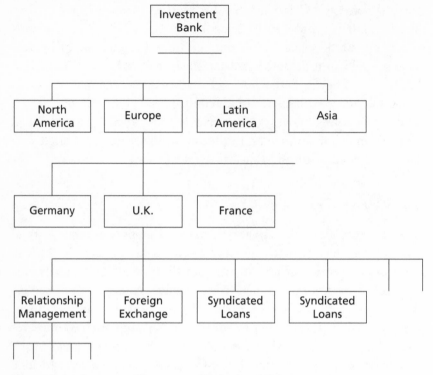

Figure 7-1   Structure of Investment Bank, circa 1990

tomer wants service. This team then puts together and executes an integrated customer strategy and plan. Two things usually result from this effort. One is the intended outcome: better coordination across countries to deliver integrated service to the global customer. The other is the opening up of new opportunities: first, the opportunity to drive organizational change, and second, the opportunity to build organizational capability.

The first opportunity is provided by satisfied customers. They can become a genuine force for change. If they have been carefully selected, these customers should respond positively to improved service across countries; but they will also indicate that more effort is needed to meet their needs. This outside force, an increasingly satisfied customer that still wants more, can be used to change country-focused mindsets.

Then there is the opportunity to expand and build upon the capability already created. With each customer team consisting of 50 to 60 people, between 250 and 300 people have now become aware of and part of the change effort. There are now 300 people who are trained in cross-border customer strategies, who understand the needs of the global customer, and who have cross-border networks and personal contacts. The 300 people too can become a positive force for change. They will have had different experiences. Most experiences should be positive, if people were chosen and recruited on the basis of skills and interests. Some of these people will enjoy the experience and want more. Some will find that serving local clients is more to their liking and can opt out. For the observant management, the customer teams serve as an audition to find cross-border talent. Some people will be good at this new effort and others not. Managements that see their task as identifying new leadership can use the teams as an opportunity to do so. And finally, the effort provides a learning experience. By collecting team members' and customers' experiences and ideas, management can improve the customer team structure next time.

These two outcomes are produced at each step in the change sequence. To summarize, the first outcome is the improved execution of some task. This outcome remains the intended purpose of the change. But the second outcome is the opportunity for management to engage outsiders such as customers, change mindsets of the doubters, train agents of change, build personal networks, select and develop new leaders, and improve the process. Managements that capture these opportunities can use changes to the formal structure and systems to drive and shape organizational change.

2. MORE CUSTOMER TEAMS

A next step would be to expand from a handful to a dozen or so customer teams. Again the firm selects those customers that want integrated service. The firm can solicit volunteers or carefully select team members who are interested in cross-border work. The previous team members can also solicit their colleagues to join. Usually the firm can make these team assignments attractive. In professional service firms, people are interested in personal growth and opportunity. Working on a team serving a global customer can be a route to learning and development not available with local clients. The multinational customer is usually the most advanced customer. Management can also see that work on global customer teams is recognized and rewarded in the countries.

Outcomes from this effort should resemble those from the first step. The difference is the larger number of people involved. Instead of a few hundred, this time a thousand or more people are trained in serving global customers and building their networks. A couple of dozen satisfied customers are asking for more. A critical mass of change agents is being built.

3. GLOBAL ACCOUNTS COORDINATOR

The next step is to create a position on the management team to coordinate the efforts to serve the global customer. At a minimum this change gives the global customer a voice or a champion on the management team. Someone of higher status can now appeal to recalcitrant country managers. The global accounts coordinator will expand the number of teams again. But perhaps most important, the coordinator can fund and build a customer-focused infrastructure.

One task is to create a common process for building global customer plans and strategies. Initially some experimenting by customer teams is useful. But the countries soon get overwhelmed with fifteen different planning formats. The coordinator can collect best practices from the various teams and set up a task force staffed with veterans of global teams to create common guidelines, forms, and processes. The common process makes it easier for customer teams and country management to work together.

The next task is the design and building of customer-based information and accounting systems. The question always arises, "Are we making any money serving these global customers?" With country-based accounting systems and profit centers, it is usually impossible to tell. Depending on whether the countries have compatible systems or not, this change can be a major effort requiring central funding and leadership from the global accounts coordinator. But in the end the customer teams will have information with which to measure their progress, compare their performance with other teams, and demonstrate global profitability.

A way to combine these two tasks is to generate revenue and profit targets for customers in the planning process. The teams can have revenue and profit goals for their global customers in each country. Perhaps more importantly, the goals can be added up in each country. Then each country manager can have revenue and profit goals for local clients and global accounts and can get credit for and be held accountable for these targets. The accounting system must connect the costs and revenues associated with each global customer. For example, an account team in the London office of one of the Big Five audit firms like PricewaterhouseCoopers worked for a year to win the global audit of a big U.K. firm. The team succeeded in winning the contract, but most of the work for the next few years would be in the North American subsidiary and in a recent acquisition in Australia. That meant that the work plus the costs to win the business were incurred in the U.K., but the revenues were booked in North America and Australia. With customer profit accounting, the U.K. can identify the revenues and costs and receive credit. The targets can be adjusted for these disconnects. Thus, in addition to being a champion for the customer, the global accounts coordinator can create the processes and information systems to manage the global customer as well as continuing to develop and identify talent and leadership on the teams.

4. GLOBAL ACCOUNTS GROUP

As the number of global accounts and teams exceeds several hundred, the role of the global accounts coordinator can be expanded and taken on by a department or a group. Customers and teams are grouped into broadly defined industry categories such as consumer products, financial services, oil and gas, pharmaceuticals and life sciences, multimedia, and so on. Although these groupings facilitate supervision of accounts, their main purpose is customer satisfaction. Customers want auditors and consultants who understand their business. Bankers do not want to teach their auditors about derivatives. Pharmaceutical companies assume their consultants know what the Human Genome Project is all about. So the global accounts activity can be expanded and specialized by customer segment.

The global accounts group usually leads an effort to establish a common segmentation scheme across the company. In large countries like Germany, the U.K., and Japan, customer segments are probably already in use. What is important is to have compatible schemes across the countries. Then a one-to-one interface can be established to facilitate communication between countries and within industries. The global accounts group usually includes global industry coordination: A global industry coordinator is selected for each industry that is common across the countries.

Many companies experience the need for global coordinating but have few people who are qualified to fill the roles. But if a company has followed the steps presented in this chapter and used the opportunity created by the initial customer team implementations, the company should have grown its own talent by now. An audit firm can serve as an example. A young Swiss auditor was identified as a talented performer on audits of banks in Zurich. When a global team was created for Citibank, the auditor, who had experience in audits of Citibank's subsidiary, became the Swiss representative on the Citibank team. Based on good performance, the auditor agreed to an assignment in the U.K. The move gave the auditor the opportunity to work in the London financial center. While in London the auditor served as the U.K. representative on the Credit Suisse global team. His next assignment was to lead an in-depth audit of the Credit Suisse First Boston investment bank in the United States. The auditor was then made partner of the audit firm and returned to Zurich. From there he was selected to be the global accounts team leader for Credit Suisse. After several years in the team leader role, the auditor became the global coordinator for the financial services customer segment. The firm assessed the auditor in each assignment for audit performance and knowledge of the financial services industry as usual. But it also assessed his teamwork skills, relationships with customers, ability to influence without authority, cross-cultural skills with customers, and cross-cultural skills and leadership of the cross-border team. Based on his experiences and training courses, the auditor was qualified to move into the global coordinator role.

5. GLOBAL ACCOUNTS UNITS IN COUNTRIES

A next step, designed to shift more power to the teams serving global customers, is to carve out global accounts units within countries and dedicate them to the global customers. The other country units will serve local customers. The global units report to the global accounts coordinator and to the local country manager. These country units place dedicated talent in the service of the global customer.

In some small countries, the country management may be reluctant to create a dedicated unit and share in its direction. They may have a surplus of profitable local business and prefer to avoid the multinationals. In these cases several PS firms have created joint ventures between the headquarters and the local country management. Usually the dedicated unit is funded from headquarters and staffed initially with expatriates. After a couple of years, the local management usually notices that the unit is quite profitable. In addition, they notice that the unit is a positive factor in recruiting; many new hires are attracted by the opportunity to work with global firms. In this way the creation of a global customer joint venture changes local mindsets. Local management eventually takes over the staffing and shares in the administration of the global unit.

6. Customer Profit Centers

A final step is the establishment of customers and customer segments as the line organization and profit centers. All of the global units report to the global industry units. The countries manage the local business and serve as geographic coordinators.

Citibank followed a similar stepwise process with its commercial banking business. Starting in 1985, the bank reestablished its World Corporations Group (WCG), which managed global corporations across its country profit center structure. The group created a team for each global account. Team members were subsidiary account managers (SAMs), and the team leader was a global account manager (GAM). The number of Citibank customers qualifying to become global accounts increased to around 450. The WCG created a customer-focused planning system and an accounting system to track customer revenue, cost, and profit across countries.

In 1995 Citibank conducted a strategy study. The realization was that they were a bank (took deposits and made loans) in more than 100 countries. The nearest competitor was Hongkong & Shanghai Bank, with presence in around 43 countries. Citibank's global presence was a competitive advantage that could not be matched by competitors. Citibank chose to become a cross-border bank. They would focus on global products, foreign exchange and cash management, for global customers. Each of 1,300 global customers became a profit center. The bank collected these customers into global industry groupings for administration. The customer-focused planning process is now called

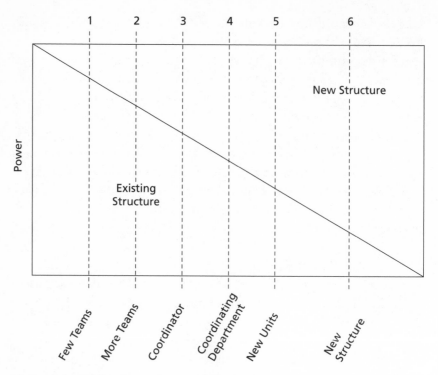

Figure 7-2   Shifting Power Incrementally to a New Structure

COMPASS and is placed on an intranet. Thus, in about twelve years, Citibank shifted from country profit centers to customer profit centers. They evolved their strategy, structure, and systems. They drove the change with formal integrating mechanisms such as customer teams and global account coordinators before completing it with the establishment of a new formal structure.

In general, management can drive a change process to transform any existing organization into any new organization using the sequential approach. Each step in the sequence makes an incremental shift in the power structure, as shown in figure 7-2.

Each increment corresponds to the change in one of the six steps outlined above. Starting with a few teams and moving to stronger coordinating units, the steps effect the transfer of power from countries (existing structure) to customers (new structure). At each step new work is accomplished. In the PS firms the new work was cross-country coordination to provide integrated service to the global customer. At each step there is also the opportunity to drive and shape the change process. With teams (steps 1 and 2), a few hundred and then a thousand people learn about the global customer. They learn how to create strategies that competitors cannot match. A percentage of the participants will become advocates for change and will lobby the nonbelievers. Through the teams a thousand people will build networks of personal contacts.

Management's role is to seize the opportunity and drive the change. They may sponsor a formal development program, such as training sessions for team members. These sessions can facilitate more learning and networking; also, management and customers can attend and get feedback from the participants. But most important is the opportunity for management to select and develop the talent and leadership for the new strategy and structure. By observing and reviewing the teams, management can identify people with the skills for and interest in cross-border work. Who are the best potential team members? Who can be a team leader? Who can develop into a global industry coordinator?

The coordinator roles (steps 3, 4, and 5) shift more power to the new structure and deliver more service to the customer. But the other opportunity is to develop processes and information systems to support the new organization. In addition, the coordinator teaches management about the new strategy. The company must shift from managing a portfolio of countries to managing a portfolio of customers. How will they make trade-offs and set priorities? At each step management has the opportunity to change the soft factors to support the change. They can develop the talent, build the networks, change the mindsets, and ultimately create a cross-border customer-focused culture.

In summary, formal structures and systems are central to changes in strategic direction. They are the high-leverage factor for these strategic changes. Through the use of integrating mechanisms, changes to the power structure and systems can drive the change process. Under these conditions formal structure can be central to change from both leverage and sequence viewpoints.

But there is probably a more powerful way that formal structures and systems can be central to change; that is, through the design of organizations to be more easily changeable. The change at Citibank took twelve years. Today many companies do not have that amount of time. Can we make organizations quickly reconfigurable into new forms?

The Reconfigurable Organization

The theory of organizations has always identified some types of organizations as being more easily changeable than others. Perhaps the earliest concept was Burns and Stalker's (1961) distinction between mechanistic and organic types of organization. Today there is renewed interest in organizations that are organic, flexible, agile, or reconfigurable. These are organizations that are designed from the beginning to be quickly and easily changeable. Even a little success in this endeavor would go a long way toward reducing the enormous amounts of time, effort, and pain associated with current change efforts.

The basic premise is to apply organization design thinking to create an organization that can move easily from one design to another. These moves result in combinations and then recombinations of skills, competencies, and resources. These skills and resources may be internal and owned by the firm, or they may be external and come from different companies. In a single-business company, these skills and resources are functional skills and resources that are combined in different ways for different products and for different customers. A single-business consumer food company will serve as an example to illustrate this approach to design and the alignment of the design policies.

Strategy

The food company in our example adopted a strategy for which a reconfigurable organization was appropriate. In the consumer food industry, competitive advantages do not last long. Sustainable advantage comes from a sequence of short-term advantages. The company competes by moving from one temporary advantage to another. The company then needs to move from one organization design to another. That is, in order to exploit a sequence of temporary advantages, the firm needs to configure and reconfigure different combinations of skills and resources. Any firm considering this type of organization should confirm that it has a strategy that requires a reconfigurable organization for execution. For example, the professional services firms discussed earlier need a flexible capability to assemble and disassemble teams in order to provide solutions to the global customer.

Structure

The structure of the reconfigurable organization consists of a stable part and a variable part. The stable part consists of "homes" for specialists in functions, which also host generalists on rotating assignments. These homes would typically be functions in the single-business company. Each home would be responsible for the long-term development of the talent and resources in its care.

The variable part of the structure consists of integrating mechanisms and networks across the functions. Initially, the food company had two teams for different product lines. They were like the standard cross-functional teams used by most firms today. But then this company discovered an ingredient that allowed it to maintain the taste of its products but lower their fat content. Management targeted the health segment of the market for this new ingredient. A team was put together to reformulate and rebrand the current products for the health segment. This new team was both cross-functional and cross-product.

When the new products were successful, the company used them to lead it into new channels of distribution. Some of these channels, such as vending machines, required different packaging. A new channel team was formed to manage this effort. This team was cross-product and cross-functional but did not have an R&D representative. New product development was not undertaken for the new channels. The team had an operations representative but used an outside co-packer with packaging flexibility to supply some of the channels.

The new ingredient had potential in other food categories in which the company had little experience. They therefore set up a joint venture with another food company that served these other categories but did not have the new ingredient. Both firms provided complementary competencies. This joint venture also was managed by a cross-functional team with heavy R&D representation from our company.

Then a couple of customers (food stores) recognized the company's new competency and asked them to manage their aisles in the company's category. The food company created a cross-functional, cross-product team to implement the category management plan for each customer. Again no R&D members were needed.

At the end of the period, the food company was organized by function, by product, by segment, by category, by channel, and by customer. They were considering some commodity teams to encourage more usage of common materials in various products.

Thus, the company was able to configure different teams across functions to implement different sources of advantage. The teams and partnerships make up the variable and reconfigurable part of the structure; the functions are homes and constitute the stable part.

Formal Processes and Systems

The formal processes and systems used by the food company also included stable and variable practices. These formal processes and systems consisted of the horizontal processes, the processes for coordinating and allocating the limiting resource, and the information systems to support them.

The horizontal processes were stable: the order fulfillment or order-to-cash process of supplying customers, and the new-product development process. Both processes were cross-functional and were designed by cross-functional project teams. All teams used these stable processes. The new product development process received particular emphasis. About 500 people were trained in its use. The sessions not only communicated the process but built the cross-functional networks to support the teams.

The formal systems for allocating and coordinating limiting resources were both stable and variable. The limiting resource is very often money, and the stable formal process for allocating funds is the budgeting process. The food company's budgeting process was a standard one. But in the short run the limiting resource changes and is usually not money. For the food company the limiting resource was often R&D talent who knew the new ingredient. Frequently priorities needed to be decided for the use of these specialists. Which products would they work on? Which factories got their support? And how much time was available for the joint venture? But when the new products took off, demand exceeded supply and new limits were encountered. Which customers would get supplied through which channels? Capacity bottlenecks occurred and disappeared. They occurred in the factories and they occurred in distribution. The food company dealt with these bottleneck decisions in their Monday morning meeting. The size, membership, and length of the meeting would flex with the agenda. The meeting consisted of as few as seven people and as many as twenty-one. The concept was to get everyone around the table who had information about and a stake in the bottleneck agenda item. The guideline was to get a total company view with as few people as possible and decide the issue as quickly as possible. Top management would attend but not run the meeting; they acted mainly as tie breakers on tough issues. The meeting was thus a flexible, hierarchical decision process for prioritizing the ever changing limiting resource.

This flexible decision process was supported by an equally flexible accounting system. Profitability could be determined by product, segment, category, channel, and customer. This data could be called out to aid in the setting of priorities. The system also gave teams an ability to set targets, build in accountability across functions, and monitor their progress. So there were both stable processes to provide continuity and variable processes to provide flexibility.

Flexible Human Resources Systems

Human resources practices to support a reconfigurable organization represent another important policy area. The most important of these practices are the measurement and reward system and the recruiting, hiring, and development process.

Compensation systems have historically been complicated and rigid. Today there is interest in designing "nimble reward systems" (Lawler 1994; Ledford 1995). These compensation systems involve more judgment in assessing performance and in assigning raises and bonuses. Performance is based on teamwork plus functional work. Salaries are based more on individuals' skills and competencies and less on job descriptions. There is greater use of one-time awards and less use of annuity awards. The whole system is designed to encourage more skill learning and more and faster change.

The practices of recruiting and hiring receive a great deal of effort. The idea is to find people who will fit into the reconfigurable organization. Some people are specialists and will reside in the functional homes. Others will be generalists and will rotate. These latter people are usually interviewed by people from many functions. They will subsequently spend time in several functions and then work on cross-functional teams. Over time, the hiring, development, promotion, and reward processes create a cross-functional culture that supports reconfigurability.

Thus, by creating an aligned set of policies for strategy, structure, formal processes, and human resources practices, companies can make their organizations more easily and quickly changeable. The formal design of the reconfigurable organization is central to its effectiveness.

Summary

This chapter has argued that changes to the formal structure and systems of an organization are central to strategic change processes. These changes to structure are central both from the standpoint of leverage and in terms of the sequence of steps that drive the change effort.

A company can use a sequence of implementations of integrating mechanisms to move from an existing structure to a new one. Each implementation both coordinates new work and creates the opportunity for building the organizational capability that will be required by the new structure. Each implementation shifts the power, step by step, from the existing to the new structure.

The ultimate achievement is the design of the easily and quickly reconfigurable organization. These designs use stable and variable structures, stable and variable systems, and human resources practices that support this flexible structural form.

References

Burns, T., and G. M. Stalker. 1961. *The Management of Innovation*. London: Tavistock.

Chandler, A. D. 1962. *Strategic and Structure*. Cambridge, MA: MIT Press.

Egelhoff, W. G. 1988. *Organizing the Multinational Enterprise*. Cambridge, MA: Ballinger Publishing Co.

Galbraith, J. 1978. *Organization Design*. Reading, MA: Addison-Wesley.

———. 1995. *Designing Organizations*. San Francisco: Jossey-Bass.

Lawler, E. E. 1994. From Job-Based to Competency-Based Organizations. *Journal of Organization Behavior* 15: 3–15.

Leavitt, H. 1965. Applied Organizational Change in Industry. In *The Handbook of Organizations*, ed. J. March. New York: Rand-McNally.

Ledford, J. 1995. Designing Nimble Reward Systems. *Compensation and Benefits Review* (July–August).

Stopford, J. M., and L. T. Wells. 1972. *Managing the Multinational Enterprise*. New York: Basic Books.

8

CHANGING STRUCTURE IS NOT ENOUGH

The Moral Meaning of Organizational Design

Larry Hirschhorn

THE ORGANIZERS of the "Breaking the Code of Change" conference asked me to address the question of how and whether executives can change an organization's structure in the hope of changing its performance. There is reason to be skeptical. Many companies go through cycles of centralizing and decentralizing, of organizing around product versus organizing around function, of creating or eliminating matrix organizations. Each restructuring is frequently propelled by dissatisfaction with the previous one, suggesting that no structure really takes hold. Often a new leader, hoping to put his or her stamp on an organization, restructures it simply to upend old coalitions and decrease their power. Yet these coalitions persist nonetheless, because they get the job done.

In this paper I will argue that leaders cannot attain sustained increases in performance by using formal structure and systems as the principal instruments of change. Instead, they have to attend to the culture of the organization—the set of belief systems and values that over time give the old order legitimacy. To accomplish this leaders must develop what I call a counterstructure: a series of interlocking mechanisms that undermine the inherited organizational structure while at the same time providing a new basis for cohesion. The counterstructure is often a temporary scaffolding that works by revivifying the work itself, providing a safe way in which aggression can be mobilized, and building a new psychological contract between leaders and employees. The counterstructure is thus a two-pronged intervention into the life of the organization: It creates new relationships, and it does so by mobilizing and directing feelings in new ways.

My argument is based on the following propositions:

- Organizational structure is a social construction.

- People imbue structure with moral meaning.

- Moral meaning is expressed as a set of promises we make and obligations we experience. It is the basis for the psychological contract between employees and the organization.

- People sensibly resist changes to this moral order.

- Crisis creates the preconditions for change.

- To take advantage of crisis, leaders must create a counterstructure.

- The counterstructure facilitates aggression, whereas the structure inhibits it.

- The work itself and the linking of affection to aggression limit the psychologically violent possibilities of the counterstructure.

- In the absence of real crisis, a virtual crisis based on people's passion for a new idea or product may establish the basis for the creation of a counterstructure.

The essay is divided into four sections. The first argues that an organizational structure is a moral order and thus socially constructed. The second discusses the dynamics of the counterstructure by examining the Asda grocery store chain case that was presented on the first day of the conference. The section presents the four elements of change that I hypothesize are required to overturn a moral order: a crisis, a counterstructure, a return to the work itself, and the combination of aggression and affection. I explore the last element by studying how Allan Leighton, the second in command at Asda at the time of the turnaround, took up his role at the conference itself. The third section briefly discusses the role of a "virtual crisis" in stimulating change, and the fourth summarizes the argument.

Structure as Moral Order

An organizational structure is an abstraction; it does not exist in the sense that a dollar bill, a client, or a television set exists. You cannot enter a headquarters office and hope to locate its structure on one of its floors. Structure is shorthand for a set of interlocking relationships that people believe they have with one another. That is, it is socially constructed.

The Social Construction of Structure

Consider, for example, the concept of the lame-duck leader. This leader has the trappings of authority, and subordinates officially report to him or her, but in their hearts they no longer feel loyal to this individual or accountable to his or her demands. People no longer attach the meaning of leadership to his or her person. In this sense a structure is a social construction: an agreement to impute certain meanings to people, roles, and practices. This is why there can be such enormous discrepancies between how people appear to behave and what they actually experience. For example, in many companies supervisors go through the motions of appraising their employees, using standardized forms that appear to be scientifically constructed. But in fact the appraisals and rewards supervisors give depend largely on custom, standards of fairness, and the comfort or discomfort they feel with particular employees.

Although structure is a social construction, however, it is not simply a matter of whimsy. On the contrary, the most important meaning that people impute to a structure is a moral one. The structure as they experience it entails a set of obligations, promises, rights, and duties that bind people together in a series of shared practices. Through structure people experience a psychological sense of community. The marketplace itself is amoral. It rewards capital without regard to people's sense of dignity, fairness, rights, or obligations. However, an enterprise, if it is to have a modicum of stability and a capacity to execute long-term plans, creates a moral order as a buffer against the marketplace. This is why, for example, managers in most settings are not free to fire an employee unless they follow certain procedures; for example, giving fair warning and carefully documenting an employee's misconduct or failure to perform. This is also why mergers and acquisitions so frequently fail: They destroy the moral basis for cooperation.

Unions emerged in part to secure a moral order—"a fair day's pay for a fair day's work"—through political means. Similarly, the rise of the divisionalized corporation can be interpreted as a political construction in the service of moral ends. Alfred Sloan, who, as head of General Motors, introduced this form of corporate organization, was all too aware of how founder Will Durant had almost bankrupted GM through his buccaneering and his unpredictable conduct. The divisionalized form would protect the company and its members against the arbitrary exercise of leadership from headquarters.

Finally, insofar as firms are finding it increasingly difficult to guarantee employment, they are looking for new ways to create a set of moral obligations. For example, one reason that firms increasingly spend money to educate employees is not simply to make them more productive but to find ways of expressing and discharging an obligation to them. Without these new obligations, corporate executives worry (sensibly) that employees will feel absolutely no loyalty to the firm.

Crisis and the Collapse of a Moral Order

The notion that people are reluctant to embrace new organizational arrangements because they "resist change" is too glib. People impute to an existing structure a moral meaning—the sense that the structure embodies principles of justice and fairness. It is for this reason that they do not relinquish it easily. For example, when executives change from a functional to a product-led organization, they are disrupting an entire network of promises and obligations that tied people to one another. This network of promises and obligations made it possible, for example, for a subordinate to sacrifice vacation time to help a superior look good by completing a project ahead of time. The subordinate does this in the expectation that he will be treated in a similarly generous manner when in the future he needs help. The reorganization violates these implicit agreements.

Let me suggest the following hypothesis. People relinquish a moral order only when it has seriously lost legitimacy, when it is no longer experienced as an arrangement that secures its members' future. Yet even then they do so warily. (This is a familiar process in the annals of war. In the wake of North Vietnam's victory in the Vietnam War, for example, many U.S. political institutions lost their ability to command loyalty—but only after significant cultural conflicts, many of which are still with us.) In business, this hypothesis suggests that an organizational structure no longer represents a moral order when the business itself is in crisis. A crisis renders all obligations and promises suspect, because the organization as a whole has an uncertain future. Indeed, one of the cases prepared for the conference and discussed on the first day, the case of Asda, was just such a story.

The Case of Asda

Asda, a large British grocery store chain with outsized stores, experienced a significant fall in operating profits from a high of 242 million pounds in 1989 to 163 million pounds in 1991. The company was in danger of defaulting on several loans; it was 700 million pounds in debt; interest expense rose about 120 million pounds in this period; and the share price fell from 120 in September 1989 to about 30 in early October 1991. The board brought in Archie Norman as the CEO to turn the company around. Three months after his arrival, Norman hired Allan Leighton, with whom he had never worked before, to be his second in command. Norman and Leighton collaborated in transforming the stores. The case of Asda points to four elements that I propose are essential to the successful transformation of an organization: a felt crisis, the development and deployment of counterstructural mechanisms, a set of practices that revivify the work itself, and a leader who can combine aggression with playfulness. Let me examine these elements in some detail.

The First Element: Crisis

When leaders take over an organization in crisis, they are often puzzled by the inertia they encounter. Why aren't the employees motivated by a sense of crisis to take action? Inertia has three roots. First, people are tied to the network of promises and obligations they have worked in. They are wary of abandoning a moral order that has sustained them, so they tend to wait for signs that the crisis will pass. Second, people feel demoralized and unable to act. Third, they begin to make their own personal plans to abandon ship while they can still garner resources from the firm, such as outplacement assistance. (Indeed, in many cases the leaders themselves abandon ship by liquidating the corporation. This was Al Dunlap's expertise.)

The three roots of inertia suggest that to mobilize employees, leaders must create a new moral order, or at least the promise of one, that also offers people potentially productive work. In other words, leaders cannot ask employees to surrender one moral order without offering another in its place.

The Second Element: The Counterstructure

How do leaders accomplish this? They do so by creating what I call a *counterstructure*. The case points to five processes Norman and Leighton put in place to build this counterstructure. Four processes attacked the chain of command; the fifth attacked the split between store managers and traders.

First, Norman and Leighton recognized that they could not possibly transform the stores, which were insufficiently profitable, if they worked through the chain of command. Instead, they created a store renewal program through which the top leadership could take charge of particular stores so as to redesign their format, their pricing, and their management process. Second, Norman began showing up in stores unannounced, notebook in hand, and talking with employees on the floor. He no longer honored the store managers' rights to advance notice, throwing them off balance and increasing the felt power of the store managers' subordinates, who could now talk directly to the boss. Third, he introduced a "Tell Archie" program, under which employees wrote in with suggestions that were forwarded to the relevant managers for response. He then personally reviewed each of these responses, turning back those he felt were inadequate. In each of these programs Norman bypassed the chain of command.

These processes obviously gave Norman greater direct control over the stores; but, equally important, they created a psychological contract between Norman and store employees that bypassed middle management. Norman, Leighton, and the top team became the center of a new moral community in which the top leaders promised to reward employees who supported them. The moral dimension of this relationship is seen in their fourth undertaking: In 1992 Norman and Leighton formed a soccer team composed of themselves and other managers, and played other departments and fifty store teams in a "Monday Night Football" program. As Norman describes it, "The stores come to Leeds and it is a very big deal. After the game we go out for pizza and beer and we chat. It has been very successful and we have learned a great deal."[1] In other words, Norman created a psychological sense of community outside the boundaries of the work, in which employees met on an equal footing and the talented, whatever their rank, excelled and were noticed.

THE SHITM

Most striking of all was the fifth process Leighton introduced: the SHITM. It is worth quoting him at length here.

> In December 1993, we invented this thing called a SHITM (Stores Head office Interactive Trading Meeting), which was a meeting that I chaired every month at Asda House. It included all the regional managers, traders and distribution people. And everyone hated it, but it was fantastic because we put all of the issues on the table. The meeting was very tense and confrontational: regional managers would accuse traders of wasting their time and dumping things on the stores, and the traders would get defensive and try to explain themselves. Then the traders would get their chance and go right back after the regional managers, telling them how they were messing up. And I would let them build to a fever pitch before calming them down. To make it entertaining we had this thing called the plank on this big table and it was like walking the plank. I asked the traders whom they wanted on the plank and they would pick a regional manager. The regional manager would get on the plank and the traders would attack him and every time he didn't have an answer he would go further out on the plank. It became one of the totems and you would even hear managers outside the meeting saying we need to get someone on the plank. (pp. 12–13)

There are four features of this description that I want to focus on. First, Leighton has created a counterstructural mechanism to overcome the organization's split between store managers and traders. Second, the acronym SHITM, derived from a rather strained wording that purportedly describes the meeting ("Stores Head office Interactive Trading Meeting"), evokes the stuff that hits the fan when conflicts explode. (Interestingly, the case writers chose not to comment on this self-evident link.) Third, Leighton describes with confidence his ability to manage the event's affectivity: to "let them build to a fever pitch before calming them down." Fourth (and this is one way in which he managed the affectivity), Leighton devised a ritual, walking the plank, that turned the meeting into a game and let people laugh.

I suggest that these features of the event highlight Leighton's ability to mobilize aggression, not for destructive purposes, but in order to solve organizational problems. Aggression, by which I mean the exercise of psychological force to take something apart, is required if an organization is to upend practices and norms that are counterproductive. For example, Leighton used the plank to overcome the inhibitions people feel in criticizing one another. This highlights an important complementarity between a structure and a counterstructure. People experience an organizational structure as moral insofar as it inhibits psychological violence—the arbitrary exercise of psychological force without recourse to community standards and ideas of fairness. Structure inhibits this kind of aggression by circumscribing it with rules and procedures. Thus, for example, the rules and practices that govern disciplining an employee proscribe a manager's arbitrary conduct or vindictive behavior. *Structure inhibits aggression, but counterstructure facilitates it.* Structure protects a moral community; counterstructure hopes to create a new community by destroying the old one.

In this sense my concept of the counterstructure differs somewhat from Bushe and Shani's concept of parallel structures,[2] as well as from Gilmore and Krantz's use of the term.[3] The latter, for example, argue that leaders should develop parallel structures to initiate a change, but that to implement the change they should return to the regular hierarchy. In the situation I am describing here, the counterstructure permanently undermines the regular structure.

The Problem of Violence

But what prevents behavior sanctioned by the counterstructure from turning into the exercise of arbitrary psychological violence? It is easy to imagine that some participants in the SHITMs felt unfairly shamed and violated, even if they appeared to share in the general mirth. What stops the process from spinning out of control? I suggest that two elements are essential here: the "work itself" as a moral anchor, and the ability of the leader to combine aggression with playfulness.

The Third Element: Back to Basics and the Work Itself

As the Asda case writers show, Archie Norman's strategy for turning the organization around was to go "back to basics." This meant refocusing the employees' attention on the customer's experience of food, even on its sensuous qualities. In redesigned stores fresh food displays were significantly enhanced; fruit and vegetables were piled high to give the impression of abundance and selection; the bakery and meats walls were removed and the work areas revealed so that customers could watch bread being baked and meats being cut fresh, packaged, and put on the shelves. Store layout was also changed. Store managers had once placed clothing at the front of the stores, because this was the higher-margin merchandise. Consequently, many customers thought of Asda as a nonfood store with some food, rather than as a food store with some clothing. Fresh produce was now placed at the front so that this was the first item customers saw upon entering a store.

A focus on the work itself helps delimit aggression in two ways. First, it delimits arbitrary action, because in the end all actions must enhance the work itself; in this case presenting good and tastefully displayed food to the customers so that they will buy it. Power must be exercised in the service of the task rather than in the service of a particular leader's fantasy or grandiose ambitions. In this sense the work itself introduces reason or rational argument as a counterweight to arbitrary conduct. Second, the work itself, when it represents value to customers, becomes the way in which the enterprise takes up a position in the moral order of society; that is, as an institution that has a right to social resources because it provides a valued service. Within the enterprise, the commitments people make to one another and the obligations they engender are increased in moral value because the work itself has evident value to customers. This is what we mean when we say an organization and its leaders have integrity.

Yet the work itself may be insufficient to counterbalance arbitrary conduct or psychological violence, particularly when it is still being articulated. In the Asda case Leighton's particular ability to integrate aggression and playfulness also helped suppress the potential for psychological violence latent in a counterstructural mechanism. How did he do this?

The Fourth Element: Combining Aggression and Playfulness

What do we mean by integrating aggression with playfulness? Leighton was of course deadly serious in the pursuit of his objectives. But in creating a game within the very serious SHITM, he formed a relationship to his subordinates based on laughter. Laughter is constructive; it binds us together by helping us open up to one another without at the same time feeling unduly vulnerable. We often use the phrase "hearty laughter," and in laughing we open up our hearts. Indeed, hearty laughter can open the way to the "affair of the heart"; there is a relationship between laughter and affection. And as we shall see shortly, Leighton used the word "heart" in describing his conception of an organization.

To get better insight into this laughter–aggression combination, let us consider the interaction between Allan Leighton and the participants in the "Breaking the Code of Change" conference. Leighton attended the conference and was asked to address its participants after the Asda case was discussed. Not surprisingly for a man clearly comfortable with aggression, he began confrontationally. This is how the transcript reads.

> There is a big difference between us. I think there might be four or five of us in this room who actually do this and there are a number of you in this room who talk about it quite elegantly. And there is a big difference between the two things, and never forget it (applause and laughter). (p. 1)[1]

This is a familiar critique of pointy-headed academics; but instead of the group's reacting sullenly or defensively, there is applause and laughter. Why? I propose two hypotheses. First, the participants accepted Leighton's critique because, after all, he had made himself a subject for discussion. He *was* the case and we owed him one. Leighton knew that he had a right to our consideration because he had taken the risk of exposing himself. In this sense he re-created in a small moment a process he had used at Asda. By taking personal risks, leaders create a sense of obligation among community members. This in turn gives them the right to aggress in the service of a task—in this case, the task of clarifying the case.

Second, I also believe that we laughed because we experienced his ability to play with aggression. He was not so much spoiling for a fight as he was enjoying it. His capacity to enjoy the fight was itself infectious and made his confrontational performance part of a game we could all play. This was in microcosm the process he had used in managing the SHITM.

THE AUDIENCE RESPONDS
This last hypothesis is confirmed by another interaction. One member of the conference critiqued him, saying,

> There is not a model of an organization in what I've heard here today. The only thing it seems that we have to know is it is all about psychology and individuals. In other words, you are not talking about what is important. (p. 8)

Leighton replied:

> Let me come back to you on that George, because I agree with part of what you are saying, but I don't agree with all of it. And the reason I don't agree with it is because you missed the point again (laughter). It's very hard for you and lots of others to actually see into this and to be able to put any real analysis around it all, and that makes it even more powerful to me. And that's why I think it is a real piece of competitive advantage. (p. 9)

The laughter here reflected the pleasure participants took in Leighton's thrust and parry, particularly the way in which his first comment, "I agree with part of what you are saying" was a feint for his later comment, "you missed the point again." But later in the interchange another participant came back at him, suggesting that he could not really be capable of engaging people, of leading them, because he in fact had attacked George. "And you begin by saying George I agree with you, however you misunderstand the point. And I began to believe that if that's what you do back home, when someone challenges you, I can't see how you reached 80,000 people and do the kind of thing you're saying you do."

In response Leighton, in thrust-and-parry fashion, dodged the bullet and said, "I agree with you"; laughter and applause again followed. He then added, "my point is I am particularly trying to rile George." In other words, he was having fun. The participant, persisting, then said, "you just said that my strategy was to rile George, so a part of your strategy is to keep the strategy you use secret." To which Leighton replied, "I am completely lost now," once again to laughter (p. 9).

Heart versus Love

How can we characterize what Leighton does? Consider here an earlier interaction between Leighton and another participant at the conference. After some opening remarks, the participant commented that "what you are saying is that it is all about love." Leighton replied, "No, I wouldn't say it's all about love, I think it is all about success. No, I don't like that." The participant replied, "Well you talk about heart," and Leighton replies, "Yes, it is in the heart, I think organizations have hearts" (p. 3).

The distinction between *heart* and *love* is relevant here. For in addition to conveying the idea of affection, *heart* also connotes a position of passion, of being engaged fully, that always entails some aggression as well as affection. Leighton legitimately objected to the participant's first comment, because it described only half of what he did.

Indeed, several times Leighton argued that no one has really been able to describe how one manages people to create change. For example,

> It's the bit that nobody understands, it's very difficult to teach, it's all in the people, it's absolutely all in the people. And nobody yet I have ever come across has ever really been able to get to the bottom of this. And certainly you have not been able to get to the bottom of it, to teach people how to get people to do things for them willingly and well who are just ordinary people. And that is the code to crack. (p. 2)

I suggest that what Leighton was saying was that he has intuitively learned how to combine aggression with playfulness, so that in launching potentially violent counterstructural processes, he could keep them productive and pleasureful. Nonetheless, as his masterful performance at the conference suggests, integrating aggression and playfulness requires much skill and presence. Perhaps one reason major organizational change efforts fail is that many leaders, however smart, ambitious, and aggressive they are, lack heart.

The Four Elements Again

To summarize, the case of Asda and Leighton's presentation point to four elements that are pivotal in any process of organizational transformation: a felt crisis, the development and deployment of counterstructural mechanisms, a set of practices that revivify the work itself, and a leader who can combine aggression with playfulness. The crisis indicates that the organization's historic mission, made concrete in the work itself, no longer has value in the marketplace. This loss of value sets in a motion a process through which the organization's leaders and the organizational structure appear increasingly illegitimate. This process sets the stage for the work of opposing the structure with a counterstructure, in this way establishing the conditions for developing new work practices. These practices in turn establish the basis for a new moral community within the organization and for a new moral as well as economic relationship to the marketplace.

Virtual Crisis?

The most problematic of the four elements I have described is the "felt crisis." Does this mean that in the absence of a crisis there can be no organizational transformation that takes hold? If, as the conference organizers hoped we could do, we want to "break the code" of organizational change, can we discern a pattern only when crisis sets the stage?

One way to address this question is to ask another. Can there be a "virtual" crisis? That is, can people experience the urgency of a crisis even as the organization continues to appear successful? Let me propose the following hypothesis.

A virtual crisis is possible only when members of a coalition linked to a leader translate their sense of personal urgency into an organizational one. This sense of personal urgency is typically experienced as a passion, an emotional conviction that a particular idea, product, or strategy must be pursued. The conviction gives birth to the feeling that the current situation is profoundly unsatisfying. This is the sense in which one person can experience as a crisis a situation that others experience as satisfactory.

A psychodynamic conception of passion provides another insight into how a sense of crisis can be stimulated and expressed even when conditions are objectively satisfactory. Personal passion and its accompanying sense of urgency are built upon a feeling that the individual lacks something profound, that he or she is incomplete. *The passion is thus the expression at the same time of a personal crisis.* This is the basis for romantic passions, and it can also trigger the creativity that may follow on from a midlife crisis. It is this psychological sense of incompleteness that stimulates the sense of urgency and, when communicated to others, creates an experience of both crisis and opportunity. Thus, we may modify the four-element formula for breaking the code of change by substituting a virtual crisis for a real one—the virtual crisis based on the passions shared by the members of a potentially dominant coalition.

Nonetheless, we do well to be wary of these passions; because in the absence of a real crisis, we cannot easily distinguish a passion that has resonance from mere personal ambition or opportunism. This is why, for example, organizations create so many hurdles to the acceptance of a new idea, method, product, or strategy. In this context we should again appreciate the positive aspects of the resistance to change.

In Sum

I have suggested that the case of Asda and Allan Leighton's presentation of self at the conference provide one answer to the question, What are the underlying elements, the genetic code of successful organizational transformation? My answer has been based on the nine propositions I recapitulate here:

- Organizational structure is a social construction.

- People imbue structure with moral meaning.

- Moral meaning is expressed as a set of promises we make and obligations we experience.

- People sensibly resist changes to this moral order.

- Crisis creates the preconditions for change.

- To take advantage of crisis, leaders must create a counterstructure.

- The counterstructure facilitates aggression, whereas the structure inhibits it.

- The work itself and the linking of playfulness to aggression limit the psychologically violent possibilities of the counterstructure.

- In the absence of real crisis, a virtual crisis based on people's passion for a new idea or product may establish the basis for the creation of a counterstructure.

Implications for Organizational Change

This analysis of Allan Leighton's role in the transformation of Asda and his role at the conference underscores the conclusion that leaders cannot hope to change an organization's performance simply by changing its structure. Instead, sensitive to the moral meanings of the inherited structure, leaders must find a way to attack this structure while simultaneously providing a new basis for the organization's moral legitimacy. This means returning to the work itself while linking the necessary aggression to playfulness and affection. I suggest that the story of Asda is becoming increasingly relevant. Employees today are increasingly self-managing. To be effective, knowledge workers rely increasingly on the relationships that they themselves develop and cultivate. Employees, rather than the organization, increasingly "own" the structure; they develop "property rights" in it. Leaders who hope to change these relationships in the interests of improving the organization's performance and viability are thus at risk of depriving workers of their rightful property. But leaders who are experienced as thieves cannot long sustain their own moral legitimacy. The counterstructure becomes an extremely important mechanism for sustaining legitimacy while effecting change.

Notes

1. Asda. Case 9-498-007, p. 5, (Boston: Harvard Business School, 1998).
2. Gervase R. Bushe and A. B. Shani, *Parallel Learning Structures: Increasing Innovation in Bureaucracies* (Reading, MA: Addison-Wesley, 1991).
3. Thomas N. Gilmore and James Krantz, "Innovation in the Public Sector: Dilemmas in the Use of Ad-Hoc Processes," *Journal of Policy Analysis and Management* 10, no. 3 (1991): 455–468.

9

INITIATING CHANGE

The Anatomy of Structure as a Starting Point

A Commentary on Galbraith and Hirschhorn

Allan R. Cohen

JAY GALBRAITH and Larry Hirshhorn address the power and the limitations of utilizing new structures to make organizational change. At one level, they are addressing different parts of the structural elephant, choosing as examples differing change situations and coming, therefore, to opposite conclusions about starting with structure. Different premises, different (but both correct) conclusions. Both Galbraith and Hirschhorn agree that structure alone is not enough, a conclusion that is hard to escape for anyone who has more than a few experiences with major organizational change. And both make vivid use of change examples to support their arguments.

Galbraith, however, asks when structure is central to change, whereas Hirschhorn argues that only through the promise of meaningful, productive work will people respond to a new structure. Galbraith addresses changes designed to create better fit between environment and reporting structure, but Hirschhorn addresses changes designed to overcome collective paralysis. And though Galbraith focuses on structural changes, he describes important gradual shifts in attitudes and skills that accompany and undergird successive new structures; Hirschhorn, in contrast, describes the change process and its sequence. A central difference, as I see it, is that Galbraith treats power neutrally, as the ability to allocate resources, whereas Hirschhorn treats power as an inherently dangerous ability to be arbitrary.

Hirschhorn sees the moral meaning attached to structure as perceptual, "socially constructed," a view that underplays several other possible factors, including actual differences in sanctioned power. For example, Hirschhorn attributes collective inertia in the face of crisis only to the ties of obligations and promises, demoralization, and escape planning. But inertia could also be due to other factors, such as failure to recognize crisis ("it's just cyclical and things will return to normal"), lack of newly requisite skills, not knowing what to do, an action-inhibiting culture, and so on. Yet Hirschhorn's action model rings true even if the diagnosis is restricted.

The Complexities of Viewing Structure

Listening to Galbraith and Hirschhorn, and then reading their papers, brings a ridiculously simple and incredibly difficult question to mind: Just what is organizational structure? Galbraith acknowledges that there is more to structure than reporting relationships and lines on organization charts, but he focuses on that part of structure to make his arguments. Hirschhorn says that "structure is a social construction," giving short shrift to the actual differentials in power over resources that some organizational structure confers. But structure is about the formal elements of organization, the rules and procedures that are designed to guide or restrict the behavior of people. As one conference participant stated, structure is what is left when people are removed from the organization. That makes it more than a social construction, though organization members certainly do invest any set of rules and procedures with their own meanings.

Even this model of structure can be misleading. Although structure is the formal system of rules and regulations, over time practices emerge from the way people behave that take on the elements of requirements even though they are not written down. Thus, structure can include the organization's prescribed roles, job assignments, rules for proceeding, decision-making powers, reporting relationships, communication channels, hiring and retention practices, career paths, and other practices that attempt to channel people towards organizational ends. Yet the minute we begin to talk about structure, there is a tendency to slide into using the term as if it means only the boxes and lines in the organization chart, the picture that is supposed to tell people whom they may talk with, whom they have to take orders from, and who has the right to make certain decisions. The very word *structure* makes us picture only a certain part of the skeleton of an organization—as if it were only the bones of an animal that constituted its structure, and not also the nervous, circulatory, digestive, muscle, and other systems that make it a unique totality. To be accurate, and to be genuinely helpful in determining appropriate change strategy, we need to keep on the radar screen all the elements of structure, not just one of them.

Furthermore, as Hirschhorn reminds us, structure is not just about the intended rules of the organization, but also about its "moral order"—the meaning invested in rules and relationships by organization members. It is shortsighted to treat structure as just what can be written down about how things are supposed to work.

Perhaps most important, it is imperative to recognize that there is no structure that guarantees specified behavior will result; people are extraordinarily clever at circumventing any structure to accomplish what they prefer. Similarly, even cumbersome, wrongheaded structures that inadvertently work against desired tasks are sometimes overcome by determined people who want to get the needed work done. We are all more than the elegant designs of the would-be masters of creating the perfect organization.

The design of purposive organizations such as businesses, of course, is a device for attempting to instruct members in what they are supposed to do to accomplish organizational goals. As soon as two or more people come together, a structure will emerge, deliberately or through practice, with some purposes in view. The larger the organization, the more that structure needs to be conscious, to serve as a mechanism for coordinated effort. And trying to change behavior of members by changing structure is not a new invention:

> We trained hard—but it seemed that every time we were beginning
> to form up into teams, we would be reorganized. I was to learn that
> later in life we tend to meet any new situation by reorganizing, and

> a wonderful method it can be for creating the illusion of progress
> while producing confusion, inefficiency, and demoralization.
>
> —*Petronius Arbiter*, 66 A.D.

Experienced change agents, however, recognize that the best-laid plans can, and probably almost always do, go astray. The conference on "Breaking the Code of Change" is living proof that very smart and well-established professionals still do not have a universal formula for planned change. There are remarkably few good examples of major organizational changes that achieved what was intended in anywhere near the time or budget anticipated. I believe that statement is true whether the change agents started with structure or with processes or with attitudes. In the balance of this paper, I will try to explain some of why that is true and, based on the examples in the Galbraith and Hirschhorn papers and others I have observed, to offer a few useful propositions about when to use structure as a starting point and when to make it a supportive element for change.

Nature of Change and Success Requirements

As both Galbraith and Hirschhorn acknowledge, structure and process are both necessary; so the question becomes one of sequence and emphasis. When is it more appropriate to start with structural change, and when with organizational and interpersonal processes? For purposes of analysis, this paper will assume a conscious and deliberate change effort, even though in practice it is often difficult to pinpoint actual beginnings.[1]

Galbraith concludes that structure is the key, preferred initial lever for change when there is a need for a shift in strategic direction. His main example is of a professional service firm that has to become more global to serve customers that have become more global and want service that responds rapidly to their problems wherever they occur. Leaving aside the question of whether this is a strategic shift or merely a matter of execution, it may be instructive to survey some of the major reasons why companies initiate major organizational changes. Table 9-1 lists common motives for change and requirements for its successful implementation.

Table 9-1
Reasons for Change and What Is Needed to Accomplish It

Reasons to Initiate Change	Requirements, Solutions
Better serve global customers (Galbraith example)	Reorganize to get people to the customer for bids, service
Strengthen product, business portfolio	Buy and sell units, companies
Counter product or business cycles	Diversify, add businesses
Speed product development, make more responsive	Reorganize or create new roles for closer co-ordination among sales, research, design, and manufacture; colocation
Reduce costs dramatically (Scott Paper)	Reengineer, using processes and information technology; eliminate duplication; use TQM to eliminate errors; eliminate non-value-added activities, products; reduce service
Reduce time required for decisions	Eliminate layers, streamline processes, create autonomous units, delegate decision-making power
Reduce cycle times	Eliminate steps, decentralize decisions
Increase entrepreneurial initiative at all levels	Foster attitudes, skills, and support structures that encourage innovation, proposals
Unify customer interface	Establish one face to the customer, account management, call center
Create better combination of expertise and customer need, geography, product specs	Install matrix organization
Provide more attractive service to customers (Asda)	Reward attention; alter roles, knowledge; get closer to customers by location, technology, processes
Increase cross-selling	Increase individual product knowledge, incentives, team formation

Although the list in table 9-1 is not completely comprehensive, almost all major change efforts are initiated to address problems of the magnitude shown. Like both Galbraith and Hirschhorn, I assume that eventually both structure and behavior will have to change: both the system and the individuals. But not all change efforts require equal amounts of both. Some can achieve rapid progress just by regrouping resources, before critical behavior changes kick in, as was the case in Galbraith's professional service firm. Rapid deployment of professionals to focus on customers in transnational territories quickly altered competitive ability, even though many attitudinal and skill changes eventually had to accompany the changes in reporting relationships.

As we examine the list, it is clear that certain of the requirements for implementation are centrally about how individuals behave. Others are more about placing decision-making power in different hands. For example, when a company decides to diversify by acquisition, the decision about which companies to buy can be made by a relatively small group of executives and can be implemented rapidly, before all the details of how newcomers and existing employees will relate to each other are dealt with. This conclusion is not meant to minimize the human complexities of absorbing acquisitions or merging cultures, but the sequence almost by definition has to start with the structural change of adding one or more units. If, on the other hand, acquisitions are an attempt to gain scale or market coverage, there will be far more need for accompanying behavioral changes.

From these examples we can derive the first proposition:

> *The less dependent a change is on new behavior rather than on reallocation of human and financial resources, the better it is to start with structural interventions.*

Similarly, organizations that over time proliferate product offerings, with separate sales forces for varied lines, often get to a point where too many different people are calling on a single customer, causing duplication and confusion. IBM and many computer companies bumped into this problem at particular points in their development and decided that customers would respond better if there were a single point of contact that could connect to all of the seller's resources. Whether the attempted solution was account management or a sales force consolidation/reorganization, altering the structure could have a relatively rapid impact, because there was literally a change in who made contact.

It isn't that such a reorganization automatically serves customers better—considerable training, adjustment of reward systems, and customer "training" will be necessary—but that the first structural change is almost a necessary starting point. That some salespeople and their managers are resistant or angry because their relationships (invested with meaning) are broken is to some extent beside the point; these employees may leave or rail against top management, but unless they possess special and irreplaceable knowledge or have unusually close ties to the purchasing decision makers, the change can proceed quickly. As with the global reconfiguration Galbraith describes, the individual and related changes can follow. Thus,

> *The more a change requires a new set of players in place, the more desirable it is to start with structural interventions.*

> *When structure not only alters formal power but reduces the necessity for contact with others, it is easier to lead with structural changes.*

At the other extreme, think about the challenge of changing a formerly bureaucratic organization to a more entrepreneurial structure. I was involved with a recent attempt to do this at Siemens Nixdorf, the German computer company, and can testify to the difficulty of changing behavior and cultivating new attitudes—willingness to spot opportunities, to take the risk of making a business plan, to embrace ambiguity, to use influence rather than authority—as well as of teaching the skills necessary for such initiative. It took many related supporting activities, including some structural ones such as open meetings, idea fairs, a matrix design, an internal venture capital fund, and so on; but the new structures could not be particularly effective without accompanying behavioral and attitudinal changes.

In similar fashion, many organizations have tried to speed decision making and take out costs by eliminating layers of management. This structural change is highly limited by the skills of those who remain and by their willingness and ability to make decisions, delegate responsibility, develop the talent below, encourage initiative, and so on. Even more daunting is the challenge of predetermining which members of the layer being eliminated have special knowledge that doesn't show up in the organizational chart, could be effective in other roles, or are needed for the connections they make among different units in the company. Formulaic slashing based on numbers of people supervised doesn't always lead to the best decisions, and can set off unanticipated problems and delays.

Even in a situation such as a new division created to facilitate decision making close to the customer instead of buried in deep functional stovepipes, where a new set of people (or established people in new roles) can perform the work required without great cooperation from existing personnel, the new decision makers will not be very effective if they do not have the requisite skills or knowledge. The ability to act as a general manager, balancing competing interests and making sensible trade-offs, requires experience in such a role; and smart functional managers often do not learn that ability without new general management experience.

In schemes to create one face to the customer, another form of new role creation, the interface person or unit must have the skill to understand customer needs, relate them to available products or services, and make the connection. If the company's "one face" does not have the right experience to make reasonable judgments, creating this new role will not satisfy the customers' desires for simplicity of transactions. Thus the next proposition about the timing of structural changes:

> ***Starting with structure is likely to be a weak launch tactic if people in new roles do not have the necessary skills to make appropriate decisions.***

Structure change may be necessary early to bring potentially appropriate people together, as in an effort to speed decisions by taking out layers or colocating units; but if the change is to be effective when skills are low, there will need to be considerable support—clear leadership, training, coaching, process consultation, organization development. The new structure may increase need, and therefore readiness, for learning.

Further, those in new roles such as that of account manager will sooner or later need the relational skills to gain cooperation from the independent or formerly independent units that provide the services. In the case of a centralized customer interface, the need for relational skills is likely to come sooner. In the case of an attempt to speed up decisions by creating new units, the work may be doable in the beginning as members are released from layers of management, but it will eventually require the building of good working relationships and other forms of cooperation among the new unit members. New structural connections do not automatically translate into good service.

Starting with structure is likely to be a weak launch tactic if people in new roles do not have the relational skills or prior connections necessary for those roles.

A variation of the relationship problem occurs in situations in which newly assigned managers are dependent on the goodwill of existing personnel in order to be effective. Attempts to obtain better decisions by creating a matrix organization and shifting power to lower levels of the organization often founder on the unwillingness of higher-level managers to stop functioning hierarchically, or on the reluctance of those in other arms of the matrix to strive for balanced decisions rather than defending their area at all costs.

Power is, of course, not just a matter of formal authority; it can reflect relative amounts of knowledge, access to other decision makers, or prior relationships. Even when new people are given increased formal power, as is the case in several of the types of solutions listed in table 9-1, they may still be dependent on nominally less powerful employees for information or connections.

Starting with structure will not work effectively if the decision makers in the new structure are dependent on other organization members who do not understand the new structure or do not choose to cooperate for fear of losing power.

My own experiences leading change as chief academic officer at Babson College, during the seven years (1991–98) when we launched and successfully implemented radical curriculum reforms, provide another instructive experience. Academic institutions have their idiosyncrasies, but they are quite similar to other professional organizations in which the key service deliverers are mostly experts with far more knowledge than the nominal leaders or managers. For one thing, control of many of the most important processes rests with the professionals, not the managers; faculty, for example, control curriculum, the classroom, and personnel decisions. Change in academic organizations is reputed to be more difficult than moving graveyards![2] Yet at Babson dramatic change proved to be possible.

The changes at Babson did not start with structure. Consistent with Hirschhorn's thesis, felt crisis—helped along by a new president from Xerox, a strategic planning process involving feedback from customers, and constant reminders from the chief academic officer—was the starting point. Early in the process, however, many of the strategic planning subgroups came to the same conclusion: Unless the college changed its governance system, the rules and processes by which curriculum decisions were made, there was little point in recommending significant changes. This conclusion led to a reversal of the cumbersome (and tiresome) traditional practice of having all decisions made by the entire faculty. For each major program a new decision-making body (DMB) was formed, consisting of five faculty elected at large, two students, and the appropriate dean. Each DMB was empowered to make all decisions for its program—after scanning the environment, monitoring program relevance, consulting, and informing widely. The power was formally decentralized, although a fail-safe mechanism provided for appeal to the whole faculty. The new rules, however, placed the burden of appeal on those who dissented from change, instead of on those who proposed it.

The new governance system turned out to work: not because controversial decisions were forced through by a tiny minority, but because the belief that change was now possible freed the imagination and initiative of faculty innovators who had previously assumed that the low probability of success made attempting change not worth the effort. The radical changes (full integration of first-year M.B.A. courses; parallel consulting experiences throughout the first year; an overseas requirement; a competence-based undergraduate curriculum, including integration among core business courses and across business and liberal arts) led to many supporting structural and process changes, without which the whole effort would have collapsed. Collaborative teaching, for example, required new skills for faculty members, more time allocated for group planning of courses, new hiring and tenuring practices, much more supportive leadership coupled with more honest evaluation, and so forth. As with any complex change, a full array of organizational devices (and considerable new resources) were necessary to sustain the change.

We can conclude that

Where complex new behavior is needed and there is high dependency on the goodwill of organization members, change will require both structural and process interventions, each stimulating and supporting the other. Structural interventions are unlikely to be a viable starting point for change.

Problems in Change Agents' Internal Processes

My discussion of major changes thus far has assumed that the proposed changes are appropriate to the needs of the organization for better, faster, more effective action. But in some cases flawed decision-making processes in and among change agents make this assumption invalid. As Hirschhorn says, "Power must be exercised in the service of the [organization's] task rather than in the service of a particular leader's fantasy or grandiose ambitions." There are no guarantees that even appropriate changes will be implemented willingly, but more fundamental is the problem of getting key decision makers to work together effectively to diagnose problems and decide what changes to pursue. In large organizations it is seldom one leader who determines changes; a top team will almost always be involved, though certainly it may be driven by the top person.

In *Power Up*[3] David Bradford and I describe an organization we call Pharmco, in which the top management group was quite dysfunctional. The COO blamed the CEO for periodic interference and the next level down for not being able to get past parochial interests. The CEO believed that the COO was too soft and took too long to act on business problems; in turn the team members blamed the COO for not standing up to the CEO and the CEO for being unavailable and making arbitrary decisions. Collectively they were paralyzed.

Until they did some work on their own processes, intermingled among their discussions about the need to streamline offerings, speed up product development, and cut costs, the Pharmco management group could not make sensible decisions about how to proceed. Once they did make a start at learning to confront one another and talk about the complex relationships among the top team, they were able to make good decisions about which product division to sell off, what organizational changes to make, and where to make them. The process they followed had most of the four elements that Hirschhorn deems necessary: They had a felt crisis, came to see their structure as "illegitimate," and developed a counterstructure to address the business concerns. (There were other elements at work, which I will not describe here but which were within the general traditions of organizational development and consistent with Hirschhorn's approach.)

The propositions that can be derived:

> *If the problem-finding and decision-making processes of the team launching change are ineffective—driven by politics, conflict avoidance, territoriality, or defensiveness—then no change design is likely to be appropriate or successful.*

> *Structural change should not be the lead intervention if relationships among decision makers are too strained to allow accurate diagnosis and appropriate decision making. In such a case, work on the team's process should come first.*

> *The discussion of problems and possible changes—structural and process—may serve, however, as a vehicle to surface dysfunctional relationships, which can then be worked on as a first step to proper decision making.*

Any major change effort will be enhanced by the willingness of the drivers of change to be honest and open—about the reasons for the change, the goals, the processes to be used, the likely and then the actual glitches, the modifications that are being made to the change plan, and the lessons the change agents are learning from the experience. Only in a very few change situations, such as addition of an autonomous new unit, can structure alone produce desired results. To alter structure alone would be like performing heart surgery looking only at the organ itself, without monitoring the other vital systems of the body. Living organisms are both structures and processes; and whenever change starts, to sustain life both structures and processes will soon be involved.

In this context it is important to credit Hirschhorn's insights about the use of humor to manage the tensions arising from changes that affect established relationships. His clever analysis of Allan Leighton's actions both at Asda and at the conference is a potent reminder that change is a personal process, both in effects on recipients and in its leadership. People's abilities to engage in new thinking, absorb inevitable anger and frustration, and keep going are helped immeasurably by humor. The use of humor is a humanizing device that allows for dissent without total disruption, and its mastery is one of those seldom acknowledged "competencies" that make an enormous difference in leader effectiveness.

Summary and Conclusions

The discussion has addressed the contingencies of leading with structure or process. Whether and how to proceed depends upon the effectiveness of the change team and the degree of behavioral change necessary for implementation. Table 9-2 suggests the implications of the combinations.

The old reliable escape phrase of action-oriented social scientists—it all depends—once again rears its head. Although all major changes will eventually require both structural and process fixes, systems and individual modifications, each major change effort is likely to be more effective if it starts with the right kind of intervention. Beginning with structure has the advantage of being comprehensive and less

Table 9-2
Implications of Required Behavior Change and Leadership Team Effectiveness

	Quality of Leadership Team	
	Good	*Poor*
BEHAVIOR CHANGE REQUIRED	Implement process and structure together	Do not launch
BEHAVIOR CHANGE NOT REQUIRED	Move rapidly	Lead with structure

people dependent; but in some situations it will lead to wasted effort or even inappropriate structures, if there is not prior or accompanying work on the relationships and processes among decision makers and those affected. Structural launches work best when there will be low need for interaction or low dependency on established organization members or customers so that effective changes can start at once. Effective implementation, however, will always sooner or later depend on establishment or reestablishment of relationships, including the kind of careful interpersonal work that Hirschhorn recommends. And where no effective action can take place until a new "moral meaning" is generated, change efforts should begin with a close look at the meanings participants attach to existing relationships, the creation of a clear felt need for change, and the development of new ways of working that allow for more fruitful discussion of changes.

The latter kind of work is much more difficult than restructuring. It calls for exquisite interpersonal skills on the part of the change agent; perhaps for that reason, among others, it is seldom the preferred choice of top management. Far too often, top executives gravitate quickly to structural changes as the first and, if they can get away with it, the only change intervention. I have often seen examples of executives moving to structural change to solve what is essentially an individual problem; instead of dealing directly with a problematic but established powerful individual, they invent a new structure to work around the person. Then they can say, "It's not you, it's just that we needed to get closer to the customer/cut costs/become more global" and so on. Restructuring becomes a substitute for interpersonal courage, and the opportunity to build greater honesty and directness in the organization is lost.

This is not to ignore the many good reasons for avoiding direct confrontation of long-term managers who have contributed a great deal and still have a following.[4] It would be foolhardy to alienate numerous people in the organization unnecessarily in order to remove or render harmless a former contributor. Too often, however, executives assume that a direct but supportive approach would backfire. Hirschhorn calls structure a defense against aggression and arbitrariness in organizations. (I believe this is why bureaucracy was invented: to overcome paternalistic/personalistic behavior.) But structure can also be a defense against straight talk.

In the long run, straight—but supportive—talk is part of what makes organizations healthy and amenable to the openness to learning needed to sustain ongoing and appropriate adaptation to environmental changes.[5] Without straight talk, many organizations become out of touch and paralyzed. Others become "Dunloped"; that is, temporarily whipped into shape but unable to grow. Both extremes force new, painful changes rather than building resiliency and adaptiveness.

Notes

1. See Rosabeth Moss Kanter, *The Change Masters* (New York: Simon and Schuster, 1983).
2. Joseph Zolner, "Moving the Academic Graveyard: The Dynamics of Curriculum Reform at Babson College" (Ed.D. Dissertation, Harvard Graduate School of Education, 1996).
3. David L. Bradford and Allan R. Cohen, *Power Up: Transforming Organizations through Shared Leadership* (New York: Wiley, 1998).
4. For a vivid example of just such a delicate political situation, see Chapter 9, "Lessons from a Determined Influencer: The Rise, Fall—and Eventual Resurrection—of Monica Ashley and 'Project Hippocrates,'" in Allan R. Cohen and David L. Bradford, *Influence without Authority* (New York: Wiley, 1990).
5. See "Power Talk: A Hands-On Guide to Supportive Confrontation," in Bradford and Cohen, *Power Up.*

PLANNING OF CHANGE
Planned or Emergent?

A NY SIGNIFICANT change effort involves a process of getting from here to there—from an old state to a new state. But there are competing views on how we can best get from here to there. In the first paper in this section, Sumantra Ghoshal and Christopher Bartlett contend that what is required is a systematic plan of action that carefully sets out and sequences the various stages of change. Indeed, Ghoshal and Bartlett suggest a particular sequence of change initiatives. They contend that the first stage of any change process should focus on improving the performance of each of the individual units of the organization. A strong organization, they argue, cannot be built upon a foundation of weak parts. In the second stage, the emphasis can then be shifted to capitalizing on the potential synergy among the parts and building integrative mechanisms that make the whole greater than the sum of the parts. Like other proponents of planned and systematic change, Ghoshal and Bartlett claim that the process of change cannot be left to evolve on its own accord. It is also a mistake, they say, to believe that there are many paths to the same destination.

Karl Weick, in the next paper in this section, takes a very different view. He contends that organizations are in fact constantly evolving. There are always efforts, experiments, and other types of change initiatives ongoing at both the periphery and the center of the organization. People closest to the marketplace and to the inner workings of the organization are always tinkering to make it better. The trick is to recognize this perpetual flux and amplify it. Change must be more emergent than planned. It must build upon the naturally occurring changes in small pockets of the organization and find a way of diffusing and spreading that change throughout the organization. Grand plans for programmatic change to get from here to there may get you no-where, because they can readily be rejected by the organization's body politic. In Weick's view it is far better to amplify what exists than to impose from without.

Andrew Pettigrew, in chapter 12, attempts to synthesize these two views. Drawing upon his own detailed longitudinal studies of change in organizations, Pettigrew argues that the change process can take on a different character at different times. On some occasions it is more emergent, and properly so. On others it is more planned and program-matic, and again properly so. The danger is to employ a process unsuited to external conditions. When the demands placed by the external environment are urgent and require systemwide change, a systematic battle plan is called for. An emergent process is just not fast enough. In contrast, when the challenge is to enhance performance by building capability, and when time is not a critical constraint, a more emergent process may be suitable.

10

Rebuilding Behavioral Context

A Blueprint for Corporate Renewal

Sumantra Ghoshal and Christopher A. Bartlett

M OST COMPANIES around the world have tried to reinvent them-selves—some more than once—over the past decade. Yet for every successful corporate transformation, there is at least one equally prominent failure. General Electric's dramatic performance improvement stands in stark contrast to the string of disappointments and crises that have plagued Westinghouse; the ascendance of Asea Brown Boveri (ABB) to global leadership in power equipment only empha-sizes Hitachi's inability to reverse its declining fortunes in that busi-ness; and Philips's successful revitalization since 1990 only highlights its own agonizingly slow turnaround in the preceding ten years.

What accounts for the success of some corporations' renewal ef-forts and the failure of so many others? How were some organizations able to turn around transformation processes that had clearly stalled out? In the course of five years of research into the nature and implica-tions of the radically different organization and management models that emerged in the 1990s, we studied more than a dozen companies as they implemented a succession of programs designed to rationalize their inefficient operations, revitalize their ineffective strategies, and renew their tired organizations.[1] In the process, we believe we gained some insight into the reasons why some firms were able to make rec-ognizable progress in their process of transformational change while others only replaced the dead weight of their bureaucracies with change program overload.

In observing how the successful corporate transformation processes differed from those that struggled or failed outright, we were struck by two distinctions. First, successful transformation processes almost always followed a carefully phased approach that focused on developing particular organizational capabilities in appropriate sequence. Second, the successful companies' management recognized that transformation is as much a function of the behaviors of individuals within the organization as it is of the strategies, structures, and systems that top management introduces. As a result, rather than becoming preoccupied with downsizing and reengineering programs, these leaders focused much of their attention on the changes required to fundamentally reshape what we will describe as their companies' behavioral context.

A Phased Sequence of Change

The problem with most companies that have failed in their transformation attempts is not that they tried to change too little, but that they tried to change too much. Faced with the extraordinary demands of their highly competitive and rapidly changing operating environments, engineers have eagerly embraced the flood of prescriptive advice that consultants and academics have offered as solutions—typically in the random sequence of a supply-driven market for management fads. According to one survey, between 1990 and 1994 the average company had committed itself to using 11.8 of 25 such currently popular management tools and techniques—from corporate visioning and Total Quality Management programs to empowerment and reengineering processes.[2] Despite this widespread frenzy of activity, the study found no correlation between the number of tools a company used and its satisfaction with its financial performance. The authors did conclude, however, that most tools "could be helpful" if the right ones were chosen at the right time and implemented in the right way.[3]

Although such a conclusion borders on the self-evident, we would endorse the importance that it gives to the sequencing and implementation of activities in a change process. In many companies we have seen frontline managers bewildered in the face of the multiple and inconsistent priorities imposed on them. In contrast, we observed that the companies that were most successful in transforming themselves into more flexible and responsive organizations pursued a much simpler and more focused sequence of actions.

One of the most widely recognized of these phased transformation processes has been Jack Welch's revitalization of General Electric. Following his emphasis on downsizing, delayering, and portfolio pruning in the early and mid-1980s, Welch shifted his focus to more developmental and integrative activities in the late 1980s. By the early 1990s he had began to create what he described as a "boundaryless and self-renewing organization." Although he has faulted himself for not moving faster, Welch has remained firmly convinced of the logic that ordered the sequence of his actions and of the need to make substantial progress at each stage before moving to the next.[4]

Our study results suggest that as a model for corporate transformation, the GE example has broad applicability. It rests on the simple recognition that the performance of any company depends on two core capabilities: the strength of each of its component units and the effectiveness of their integration. This is as true of the integration of individually strong functional groups along an organization's value chain as it is of the synergistic linking of a company's portfolio of business units or the global networking of its different national subsidiaries. This assumption defines the two axes of the corporate renewal model shown in figure 10-1.

As they face the renewal challenge, most companies find themselves with a portfolio of operations that can be represented by the circles in figure 10-1: a few high-performing but independent units and activities (represented by the tightly defined but separate circles in Quadrant 2), another cluster of better-integrated operations that despite their better integration are not performing well individually (depicted by the looser, overlapping circles in Quadrant 3), and a group of business units, country subsidiaries, or functional entities that don't perform well individually and are also ineffective in linking and leveraging one another's resources and capabilities (illustrated by the ill-defined unconnected circles in Quadrant 1).

The overall objective of the transformation process is to move all the entities in the portfolio—high performance and high integration—and into Quadrant 4 and find ways to prevent them from returning to their old modes of operation. But although the goal of developing an

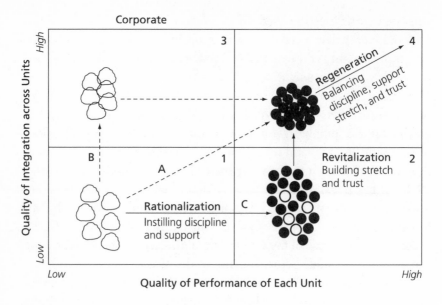

Figure 10-1   Corporate Transformation Model

organization built on well-integrated efficient operating entities is clear, the path to this organizational nirvana is not well defined. Yet it matters immensely.

Some companies—General Motors in the 1980s, for instance—tried to take the direct route as represented by the dotted diagonal Path A in figure 10-1. While intellectually and emotionally appealing, this bold approach of trying to improve performance on both dimensions simultaneously has typically ended in failure because of the fact that the complex and often contradictory demands it involves overload the organization. GM discovered this during the 1980s when it pressured its five auto divisions to boost their individual market share and profitability while simultaneously improving cross-unit synergies. It turned out that the demands of coordinating body styling and chassis design often conflicted with each division's ability to respond to the needs and opportunities of its own particular market segment. As with GM, IBM's late 1980s attempt to improve both unit performance and corporate integration also caused that company's transformation program to stumble.

Other companies—Philips in the late 1980s, for example—followed a more focused path, pushing first for integration on the assumption that better synergies among units would help each improve its individual performance. However, this change model, represented by Path B in the figure, has also proved unsuccessful. In a bold reorganization, company president Cor van der Klugt declared Philips's consumer electronics, professional electronics, components, and lighting businesses the company's "core interdependent" operations and tried to create structures and processes that would help them manage their perceived interdependencies. As the company soon discovered, however, it was extremely difficult to integrate operations that were themselves struggling with enormous internal difficulties. And even where linkages succeeded, connecting uncompetitive individual businesses served mostly to emphasize and reinforce the liabilities of each. As corporate performance continued to decline and a new CEO was appointed to try another approach, Philips managers concluded, with typical gallows humor, that "four drunks do not make an effective team." It was a lesson that was unfortunately lost on Daimler-Benz, which continued its efforts to integrate its diverse and overstaffed operations until a new top management team signaled a change in direction for the struggling transformation program in 1995.

It is the third option, Path C in figure 10-1, that we believe defines the most effective sequence of transformational change processes. This is the path Jack Welch followed as he steered GE through the ongoing series of change processes that he initiated in the early 1980s. As we reviewed this much admired transformation of one of the world's largest corporations, three distinct phases of active were evident— phases we define as rationalization, revitalization, and regeneration. In the *rationalization* phase Welch focused on strengthening the performance of each of the company's businesses, attempting to make each "number one or number two" in its industry. Over a period of five years he sold or closed operations valued at almost $10 billion and acquired new businesses worth $18 billion. He stripped away the heavy superstructure of sectors and groups that had long burdened frontline units, and he made drastic cuts in the size and responsibilities of corporate staffs. This streamlining cost the company some ability to integrate and coordinate activities across units, but Welch's primary concern was to give the engineers of the core businesses the freedom to develop new strategies and to control their operations. By creating a sense of organizational clarity and managerial simplicity, he felt more able to hold units accountable for the results.

By the mid-1980s, with most of the acquisitions and divestitures completed, Welch moved into a second phase, which we call *revitalization*. With thirteen businesses running strongly at the company's core, he began to look for ways he could link them to exploit potential scale economies, to leverage their individual resources, and to capture opportunities for cross-unit learning. Beginning with his top-level Corporate Executive Committee meetings, he worked to develop an environment for interunit collaboration that would demonstrate the concrete benefits of cooperation. He pushed his senior executives to agree to some high-visibility symbolic agreements—getting sixteen pounds of GE plastics into every GE refrigerator, for example, or having the engineers from the locomotive division help resolve a serious design problem in the appliance business. Over the next several years, Welch pushed collaboration deeper into the organization through his "boundaryless" and "best practices" programs designed to open minds, clear communication channels, and eliminate parochial attitudes that had insulated functions, isolated businesses, and separated operating units from one another.

Almost two decades after he began, Welch had rationalized the organization and then revitalized its business, and began to see the emergence of the kind of organization that he hoped to leave to his successor—one that continuously replenished and renewed itself. In the closing years of the 1990s, he initiated actions that moved GE into the third phase of transformation, one that would imbue the organization with a capability that we call *regeneration*. As he challenges GE employees to move their traditional industrial businesses into the fast-growing e-commerce—an initiative he calls destroyyourbusiness.com—Welch is trying to develop an organization with the ability to balance the tensions and management paradoxes implicit in each unit's drive to achieve superior individual performance while simultaneously collaborating with other units to leverage the organizationwide benefits of integration. Like the first two phases, this one is demanding profound behavioral change among the people of General Electric.

A New Behavioral Context

The major constraint in any corporate transformational process—and the reason for the need for carefully sequenced stages—lies in the capacity of people to accommodate change. Indeed, the companies that were most successful were those that recognized that behavioral change was not just an outcome of the transformation but its driving engine. These were the companies that focused their attention beyond the conventional concern about restructuring the hierarchy and reengineering its processes, and devoted most of their attention to the more subtle and demanding task of changing individual attitudes, assumptions, and behaviors.

This realization struck Jack Welch in the mid-1980s, a few years after he had initiated the bold and effective delayering and downsizing program that had eliminated several layers of GE's hierarchy and reduced its payroll by 70,000 employees. Although he had been extraordinarily successful at meeting his initial objectives, Welch understood he could not achieve his long-term goals unless he won the minds and changed the behaviors of many frontline employees. Workers were suspicious and even cynical about the motivations of the man they had begun to call "Neutron Jack." In 1985 Welch acknowledged, speaking to a group of employees, "A company can boost productivity by restructuring, removing bureaucracy, and downsizing, but it cannot sustain high productivity without cultural change."

Successful corporate transformation, as Welch recognized, could not simply be imposed from the top through macro change programs. It also had to be built up from the bottom through activities designed to ensure that everyone understood and supported the change. An effective change process needs to focus simultaneously on the company's "hardware"—its business configuration and organization structure—and its "software"—the motivations, values, and commitments of the company's employees. In other words, together with the changes in structure and systems, managers need to also change what we call the behavioral context of the company.

As we observed GE and other companies evolve through the long and painful process of transforming bureaucratic hierarchies into self-renewing organizations, we became aware of the importance not only of the sequencing of macro processes—rationalization, revitalization, and regeneration—but also of the changes to individual behavior that supported those broader initiatives. The kind of performance-driven actions implicit in Welch's call for speed, simplicity, and self-confidence, for example, were different from the more collaborative behaviors he was trying to elicit in his subsequent emphasis on "a boundaryless organization." Our observations suggest that the four vital elements of the transformational behavioral context were discipline, support, stretch, and trust—and that these elements were most effectively developed sequentially, in a way that supported the three stages of renewal. Instilling individual discipline and support, for example, is crucial to managing the company through the rationalization phase. Instilling stretch and trust is essential to managing revitalization. And integrating and balancing the four elements is the key to continuous regeneration.

Rationalization: Building Frontline Initiative

Of all the companies we studied, the one that faced the most daunting transformation challenge was AT&T. Forced to divest itself of 70 percent of its assets in an antitrust settlement, compelled to battle formidable global competitors in a suddenly deregulated business, and confronted with an industry being fundamentally restructured by the converging technologies of computers and telecommunications, AT&T was a dinosaur on the brink of extinction for the first few years after the company's 1984 breakup: Within four years its near monopoly of long-distance telephones had been reduced to a 68 percent share, its once highly profitable equipment business was staggering under the attack of aggressive competition, and its computer business was floundering in a struggling partnership with Olivetti. It was at this time that Bob Allen was appointed CEO. Allen launched a series of initiatives that illustrate the kinds of actions that have been most effective in the first stage of transforming a classic bureaucracy into a self-renewing organization.

In a radical departure from the focus on cross-unit integration that had until then been the centerpiece of AT&T's "single enterprise" strategy, Allen broke up the company's large and unwieldy organization into twenty-one business units, each responsible for developing its own business model and for delivering its own results. To reinforce this restructuring, he implemented a rigorous Economic Value Added (EVA) system that recorded and reported the return on capital for the newly created business units, each of which was required to manage not only its profit and loss account but also its own balance sheet. The business unit managers, in turn, created more than 100 focused product groups, each with its own P&L, thereby fragmenting AT&T into more than 100 distinct management units. According to Allen, the dramatic improvement in AT&T's performance over the next five years, reflected in a 200 percent increase in the company's market value, would not have been possible without this restructuring.

But powerful though his macro structural and systems changes were in framing the rationalization process, Allen did not believe that by themselves they would create the changes in individual values and activities that he believed were required. Extremely sensitive to the fact that competitive defeats, personnel cuts, and operating losses had led to a widespread decline in motivation and confidence among AT&T's once proud and successful people, he wanted to help them "learn how to win again." He did this by creating an environment that simultaneously reestablished norms of self-discipline and offset those hard-edged demands with a context of support and encouragement.

Building Discipline

Of the many actions that Allen initiated to shift the internal context from one focused on compliance to one of self-discipline, the three that seemed to have the most pronounced influence were a set of un-ambiguous performance standards; a commitment to frequent, de-tailed, and desegregated feedback; and a process of clear and consis-tently applied rewards and sanctions.[5]

With the introduction of EVA, Allen sent a powerful message to the organization that financial success could no longer be negotiated in Washington in discussions among lobbyists, lawyers, and regulators, but instead would have to be won in the marketplace through the ac-tions of frontline managers. Through management's relentless insis-tence that each business prove its economic viability and strategic po-tential, business heads were motivated to translate their broad EVA objectives into internal performance benchmarks and clearly defined individual targets right down to the front lines of their operations. In this way, EVA became more than just a mechanical control system; it became the basis of a behavioral context that fostered a norm of fulfilling commitments and meeting tough standards—a discipline that was not widely observed in the predivestiture AT&T.

Once the organization is focused on unambiguous performance

standards, the next vital element for any leader trying to build a discipline-based organization is to create an effective feedback process to ensure that individuals see exactly how they are measuring up. AT&T accomplished this through a new accounting system that gave each unit frequent, detailed, and desegregated feedback designed to "ruthlessly expose the truth about performance." Again, it was not so much the system as the way it was used by senior management that was key to shaping the desired behavioral context. Through their practice of conducting open reviews within each unit and between business units and corporate staff, Allen and his top team were able to define clear standards, clarify expectations, and provide honest and timely evaluations of performance. Both the intensity and the quality of this review process greatly contributed to the institutionalization of discipline as an established behavioral norm.

The third common contextual element in organizations that developed a strong sense of individual discipline was a consistently applied set of rewards and sanctions clearly linked to the performance standards. At AT&T, the EVA system was designed with a strong, direct linkage to the compensation system, a characteristic that gave it early credibility and teeth. Equally important, the linkage was reinforced by the way senior management implemented the system: not only by their awarding performance-based bonuses of up to 50 percent of base salary, but also by their willingness to replace managers and even sell or merge units unable to meet their EVA targets. The replacement of several key nonperforming managers with outsiders from high-discipline organizations provided a strong reinforcement to the emerging norm stating that AT&T managers deliver on their commitments.

Embedding Support

Over time, however, such unalloyed emphasis on results can become corrosive. In the course of our study, we found that the rationalization process was more likely to be protected from individual burnout or organizationwide rejection if the hard-edged tools of discipline were counterbalanced and complemented by management's willingness to nurture and support the initiatives of those spurred into action by the rigorous demands of the discipline-based context.[6] As AT&T discovered, a commitment to legitimate empowerment, access to resources, and a management style based on coaching and guidance proved most effective in creating such an environment of support.

One of Bob Allen's first objectives was to break the sense of control and dependence that often characterized the relationships between superiors and subordinates at AT&T. At the same time that he was holding business units accountable for their performance, for example, he was also radically decentralizing responsibility by giving unit leaders the authority to make fundamental changes in their businesses' strategy and operations. The new accounting system proved to be of great importance in this effort. Instead of being designed primarily around senior management's control needs, reports were explicitly developed to provide desegregated information to support the activities and decisions of operating-level managers. Additionally, however, the system provided AT&T's senior management with an effective early warning tool that gave them confidence to loosen their control, knowing they had timely and reliable information that would allow them to intervene before major problems developed.

This systems change was reinforced by Allen's huge commitment to training new managers to use the data and accept the responsibilities they were being given. Furthermore, Allen took personal responsibility for appointments to all key positions, and he ensured that his selections were individuals who had reputations as delegaters and developers. But his most powerful empowerment message was provided by his own personal management style. He described his philosophy in these terms:

> I have never thought that I could be so knowledgeable about our businesses and markets that I could make the decisions. I have always been an advocate of shared decision making. In fact, I believe this is one of the reasons I am CEO.

As most companies soon realized, empowerment was legitimized only when those given responsibility were given access to the resources they needed to implement their newly delegated decisions. Again, Bob Allen initiated radical change by decentralizing many of the assets and resources that had traditionally been controlled at the corporate level. In a major restructuring of Bell Laboratories, for example, he gave the business units control over the budgets for more than 80 percent of the labs' employees, thereby giving them direct access to and influence over AT&T's enormous technological resources. In the view of middle-level managers, it was this increased access to financial and technological resources that was key to the company's rapid transition from a highly centralized bureaucracy to a more flexible organization where those deep in the operations could initiate and drive action rather than just write proposals and await approvals.

To provide substance to the norm of empowerment and to validate the redeployment of assets and resources, senior managers must be willing to step back from their historic role as the organization's chief planners and controllers, and must redefine their core responsibilities in more supportive terms. In the new environment of radically decentralized responsibility and authority, they must provide the coaching and guidance that separates legitimate empowerment from the knee-jerk version that often ends up as abdication. It is this third element of a supportive behavioral context that presented Allen with his most critical challenge. Starting with his own actions and those of his colleagues on the Executive Committee, he tried to model the desired coaching role and supporting relationship. When managers tried to escalate issues for his decision, Allen persistently responded that his opinion was not really relevant and encouraged the questioner to work through the problem.

To help spread this management model, he broadened the evaluation criteria for all senior managers to include a new development measure: "people value added" (PVA), which was given the same weighting as the well-established EVA measure. This was supported by a 360-degree assessment process and a carefully designed complementary feedback process, which Allen applied first to himself and his top management team before rolling out into the company.

It was through a broad array of such tools, programs, and individual actions that AT&T's management team was able to create a supportive environment that smoothed the hard edges of the highly discipline-oriented context simultaneously being developed. It was through these actions in the rationalization process that Allen and his team were able to bring about the changes in AT&T that saw a $1.2 billion loss in 1988 change to a $4.6 billion profit in 1994.

Revitalization: Integrating Cross-Unit Relationships

For most companies, the initial tightening of ongoing operating performance is only the first stage of a long transformation process. For although this rationalization phase can improve the productivity of a company's resources, some very different efforts and abilities are required to restart its growth engine. At AT&T, for example, the fragmentation of the organization into disciplined business units allowed the company to reduce waste and cut expense, but it also led to the creation of twenty-one highly autonomous business units (BU) run by what one manager described as "a bunch of independent BU cowboys." Yet in order to grow—whether by expansion into the dynamic new infocom business growing at the intersection of the computer, communications, consumer electronics, and entertainment industries, or by exploiting the fabulous potential of the emerging Chinese market—the twenty-one entities would have to operate as one AT&T.

Between 1993 and 1995 AT&T struggled to turn around the momentum of its highly successful rationalization process by creating the integrating mechanisms necessary for the revitalization phase. They initiated several structural measures, from a new regional management structure designed to integrate the disparate initiatives of the twenty-one business units in Europe, Latin America, and the Asia Pacific region, to cross–business unit project teams to address the emerging multimedia, data communication, and other business opportunities that lay at the intersection of two or more business units. At the same time, to create the supporting integrative behaviors, the company invested a huge amount of effort in embedding a shared vision that focused on how the different parts of AT&T could collectively allow people to communicate with one another "anytime, anywhere," and in articulating a set of shared values as a "common bond" that could tie the whole organization together. After two years of effort, however, the company was finally forced to abandon this effort and to organize itself into three separate entities—an outcome that demonstrated the enormous difficulties of managing the transition from the rationalization to the revitalization phase.

Whereas AT&T failed in revitalizing its businesses by leveraging their interdependencies, ABB, the Swedish–Swiss electrotechnical giant, is farther down the path and will serve to illustrate some of the key requirements for managing this second phase of the renewal process. At his first meeting with his top 200 executives, and just months after his appointment as CEO of the $17 billion company formed through the merger of Asea and Brown Boveri, Percy Barnevik announced his vision for the new organization: to be "global and local, big and small, radically decentralized with central reporting and control." For the first couple of years, however, Barnevik focused his attention on only one part of each of the three dualities: He wanted to build the new company on a solid foundation of small, local, radically decentralized units. To break the back of the old bureaucracies and to strip out excess resources, Barnevik radically restructured ABB into 1,300 legally separate companies, giving them control over most of the organization's assets and resources. At the same time, he slashed the old hierarchies from eight or nine levels to a structure that had just three management levels between himself and the front line. Although somewhat more radical, these early actions were very similar to those taken by Bob Allen at AT&T.

By the early 1990s, however, Barnevik and his team began to pay more attention to the challenge of ensuring ABB's long-term growth. This was a task that would require the revitalization of activities in a mature set of business operations through the integration of independent units and numerous acquisitions into a single company. It was at this stage that ABB's management, working to capture the benefits of the company's size and reach, began to focus on the other half of the three dualities. By becoming more effective at linking and leveraging the resources of the 1,300 local companies, ABB used its global scale and scope to build new capabilities in existing power-related businesses; to develop new business opportunities in areas such as environmental engineering; and to enter new markets such as eastern Europe, India, and China.

Just as the behavioral change required for rationalization is facilitated through certain changes in structure and process—through fragmenting the organization into smaller units and developing a rigorous financial control system, for example—the behavioral context that supports revitalization also requires some changes in the organizational hardware. At ABB the organizational structure designed to create the tension that drives revitalization is provided by a carefully managed global matrix with a complementary overlay of boards, committees, and task forces at all levels of the organization.

But beyond changes in organizational hardware, just as the rationalization phase needs the behavioral software of discipline and support for effective implementation, the revitalization phase needs a behavioral context of stretch and trust to motivate the vital cross-unit integration. The experiences of ABB provide a good example of how these two attributes of behavioral context can be shaped to drive an organization through this second phase of corporate transformation.

Creating Stretch

Stretch is an attribute of an organization's context that enhances people's expectations of themselves and of the company. It is the antithesis of timidity and incrementalism. Stretch is the boldness to strive for ambitious goals rather than settling for the safety of achievable targets. In observing the revitalization efforts at companies such as GE, Intel, and ABB, we identified three elements that were at the core of the most successful efforts to create this environment of raised personal aspiration and extraordinary individual effort. A company needs, first, to develop a sense of shared ambition that energized the organization; next, to establish a set of unifying values able to reinforce individuals' commitment to the organization; and third, to provide employees with a sense of personal fulfillment by linking their individual contributions directly to the larger revitalization agenda.[7]

To decouple individuals from the parochial interests that drove performance in the rationalization stage, companies need to provide a powerful motivation for collaboration. In most organizations this implies creating a shared ambition that exceeds the organization's ability to achieve without cooperation: stretching the collective reach beyond the individual grasp. At the broadest level, Barnevik did this by building a corporationwide commitment to making ABB "a global leader— the most competitive, competent, technologically advanced, and qual-

ity minded electrical engineering company in our fields of activity."
But rather than leaving it as a broadly framed vision statement unconnected to the organization's day-to-day operations, Barnevik and his
top team embedded this commitment as shared ambition by going on
the road to communicate and translate it so that each operating unit
bought in on its implications for their own particular objectives.

While ambition can be highly energizing, it is only when the organization's objectives connect with individuals' basic belief systems that
the required personal commitment is likely to be enduring. This is the
role that a set of unifying values can play for a company. To create
such an individual-level commitment to its corporate ambition, ABB
has framed its ambition within a broadly defined set of organizational
values. For example, the company has a stated objective "to contribute
to environmentally sound sustainable growth and make improved living standards a reality for all nations around the world." Depending on
management's actions, such a statement has the potential to become
either a source of unifying personal commitment or a source of cynicism. At ABB Barnevik ensured that the stated values were not just put
on display in the annual report but documented in the company's *Mission, Values and Policies* book, referred to by insiders as "the policy bible." More importantly, these values became the basis for face-to-face
discussion between top management and employees at every level of
the organization; and they were demonstrated in the actions of corporate leadership as they acquired environmental management capability
and made massive commitments to investments in the developing
world.

Finally, management must deal with the fact that modern societies
in general and large corporations in particular provide individuals with
very few opportunities to feel as if they are making a difference. To
create a sense of stretch, companies need to counteract the pervasive
meaninglessness that individuals feel about their contributions and replace it with a sense of personal fulfillment in work. To do this they
must be able to link the macro revitalization agenda to the tasks and
contributions of each individual.

Although radical decentralization at ABB and other similar companies makes it easier to relate overall corporate challenges to the performance of individual units and thus the actions of particular people,
it is often the integrating channels and forums that provide the most

powerful means for creating personal fulfillment. These overlaid devices give top management the opportunity to invite the heads of national companies to serve on the internal boards of other units or even on worldwide business boards. Similarly, local functional heads may have the opportunity to serve on one of the functional councils that the company uses to identify and transfer best practice worldwide. Through such service these individuals are able to see firsthand how their role fits into the larger objective and, more importantly, how their efforts are contributing to the broader agenda.

Developing Trust

A readiness to link resources and leverage capabilities is central to the revitalization process, and this kind of intensively collaborative behavior cannot be induced solely by stretching people's goals and expectations. Like discipline, stretch lends a hard edge to the behavioral context that gives rise to individual energy and enterprise; but in its raw form stretch can also lead to organizational exhaustion. In this second stage of the renewal process, the appropriate quality offsetting stretch is trust, a contextual characteristic vital to the nurturing of the collaborative behavior that drives effective revitalization.[8]

Unfortunately, the level of trust in a company just emerging from a major rationalization process is often quite low, with autonomous units finding themselves in intense competition for scarce resources, and once loyal employees feeling that their implicit contracts with the company have been violated by serial layoffs and cutbacks. Most of the companies we studied seemed to accept this erosion in individual and group relationships as an inevitable by-product of a necessary process. Although they tried to minimize the impact of loss of trust during the rationalization phase, they tended to leave the task of rebuilding individual and intergroup trust to the revitalization stage, when frequent and spontaneous cooperation among individuals and across organizational units became essential.

In our observations we found that the key characteristics of an organizational environment that supported such trusting behavior were a bias toward inclusion and involvement, a sense of fairness and equity, and a belief in the competence of one's colleagues. Involvement is one of the most critical prerequisites of trust, allowing companies to build both organizational legitimacy and individual credibility. At ABB the organization's extensive use of integrative forums provided the infrastructure for routinely bringing managers together to discuss and decide on key issues. As suggested earlier, key local company managers were appointed to their business area boards, where they participated in major decisions affecting their business's global strategy and operations; functional managers' membership on worldwide functional councils gave them a major role in deciding the policies and developing the practices that governed their area of expertise.

This bias toward inclusion and participation extended beyond formal boards and committees, however. ABB's senior managers made employee involvement an integral part of their daily operating style. For example, in the relays business we studied, the new global strategy was not formulated by the global business manager and his staff or even by the more inclusive business area board. It was developed by a group of managers who had been drawn from deep in the worldwide operations and asked to define the business's objectives, options, and priorities as they appeared to those closest to the customers, the technologies, and the competitive markets. The process of developing the relays strategy document and its subsequent approval by top management created a strong bond among those on the team and a sense of trust in their superiors. The new relationship was reflected in and confirmed by the informal contract that developed around the strategic blueprint the team and top management had developed together.

Such widespread involvement in the activities and decisions relating to issues beyond their direct control created an organizational openness that was vital for a sense of organizational fairness and equity, the second component of a trust-building context. The formal matrix organization was the core design element that management believed allowed ABB to cope with the dilemmas inherent in its objective to be "global and local, big and small, radically decentralized with central control." The matrix demanded that an organizational norm of fairness and equity be developed to resolve the tension implicit in the structural dualities and to manage the conflicting demands in the strategic paradoxes those dualities reflected. The function of the numerous boards, teams, and councils was not only to allow widespread involvement but also to create the channels and forums in which often conflicting views and objectives could be surfaced, debated, and resolved in an open and reasonable manner.

But fairness cannot simply be designed into the structure; it must be reinforced through management words and actions, particularly those of the most senior-level executives. Backed by the "policy bible's" commitment to build employee relations on the basis of "fairness, openness, and respect," the constant stream of decision making surrounding ongoing plant closings, employee layoffs, and management reassignments was conducted by ABB's senior management in an environment of transparency and rationality rather than through backroom political maneuvering. The resulting perception of fairness protected, indeed enhanced, the feeling of trust despite the inherent tensions and the painfulness of the decisions.

Finally, trust requires people to believe in the competence of their colleagues and particularly of their leaders, for it is in these people that individuals place their confidence as they let go of the traditional safety of incrementalism to achieve the new stretch targets. At ABB Barnevik set the tone in his selection of his senior management team. Recognizing that their drastically delayered and radically decentralized organization placed a huge premium on a high level of competence at all levels, he personally interviewed more than 400 executives from both Asea and Brown Boveri. His aim was to ensure that ability assessment rather than horse trading dominated the selection process for the top positions in the newly merged companies. Barnevik's actions not only provided a model that influenced the whole selection and promotion process, but also sent a signal that the identification and development of human resources was a vital management responsibility.

This revitalization process, supported by greater cross-unit integration, allowed ABB to leverage the one-time productivity gains from the massive rationalization program of the 1988–90 period and, by developing new product and market areas, to weather the recession that caused almost all of its competitors to retrench in the early 1990s.

Regeneration: Ensuring Continuous Learning

The hardest challenge facing companies that have undertaken effective rationalization of their operations and revitalization of their businesses is to maintain momentum in the ongoing transformation process. This is particularly difficult in companies that have been through the two processes in succession and are striving to maintain an internal context

that supports both the individual initiative needed in frontline operations and the collaborative team-based behaviors required for resource
linkages and best-practice transfers across individual entities.

In the final state of self-renewal, organizations are able to free
themselves from the embedded practices and conventional wisdoms of
their past and continually regenerate themselves from within. As in the
earlier stages of the transformation, the challenge in the regeneration
phase is not just to change structures or processes but, rather, to fundamentally alter the way managers think and act. As ABB executive vice
president Göram Lindahl saw it, this final stage in the transformation
process would be achieved only when he had succeeded in a long, intense development process he described as "human engineering,"
through which he hoped to change engineers into capable managers,
and capable managers into effective leaders. "When we have developed all our managers into leaders," he explained in an interview with
us, "we will have a self-driven, self-renewing organization."

Despite several promising signs of self-renewing behavior with
their respective organizations, top executives at GE and ABB would
readily acknowledge that they have not yet fully achieved this state of
self-generated continuous renewal. Indeed, of the many companies
that have undertaken organizational transformation programs since
the early 1990s, few have moved much beyond the rationalization
stage, and even fewer have successfully revitalized their businesses in
the manner our model describes. Nonetheless, in our study we were
able to observe a handful of companies that had reached the stage of
being able to constantly regenerate themselves by developing new capabilities and creating new businesses on an ongoing basis.

In most of these companies, such as 3M in the United States or
ISS, the Danish cleaning services company, in Europe, this elusive self-
regenerative capability was based on long established and deeply embedded corporate values and organizational norms, often linking
back to the influence of the founder or other early leaders. But we observed a few companies in which a more recent transformation process
had led to the creation of an impressive self-regenerative capability. A
good example was Kao, the Tokyo-based consumer package goods
company.

For the first fifty years of its life, Kao had been a family-run soap
manufacturer. It eventually expanded into detergents in the 1940s,

modernizing by unabashedly copying leading foreign companies; even Kao's corporate logo was amazingly similar to Procter & Gamble's famous moon and stars symbol. It was only after Dr. Yashio Maruta took over as president in 1971 that the company gradually developed a self-regenerative capability. As Maruta said to us in an informal interview, "Distinct Creativity became a policy objective, supporting our determination to explore and develop our own fields of activity." By 1990, after Kao had expanded into personal care products, hygiene products, cosmetics, and even floppy disks, the firm was voted one of Japan's top ten excellent companies—along with Honda, Sony, and NEC, and ahead of such icons as Toyota, Fuji Xerox, Nomura Securities, and Canon.

In our analysis of Kao and of other successful self-regenerating companies such as 3M, ISS, Intel, and Canon, we developed some notions about two key management tasks that inevitably played a central role in the development of such capabilities. The first was an ability to integrate the entrepreneurial performance-driving behavior shaped by discipline and support with the equally vital cross-unit integrative learning framed by stretch and trust. The second was the somewhat counterintuitive task of keeping these basic contextual elements in a state of dynamic disequilibrium—so as to ensure that the system never became locked into a static mode of reinforcing and defending its past.

Integrating the Contextual Frame

Dr. Maruta always introduced himself first as a Buddhist scholar and second as president of Kao, and he saw these two roles as inextricably interlinked. Over the years he embedded two strong Buddhist principles as the basis of Kao's self-regenerating capability. The first core principle was an absolute respect for and belief in the individual, a value that was supported by an explicit rejection of elitism and authoritarianism and an active encouragement of individual creativity and initiative. The other pervasive principle was a commitment to have the organization function as an educational institution in which everyone accepted dual roles as teacher and student. It was at this level of corporate philosophy and organizational values that the vital entrepreneurial and collaborative behaviors were legitimized and integrated at Kao.

Reflecting the strong belief that the ideas and initiatives of individual managers were what drove performance, Maruta created an organization in which all employees were encouraged to pursue their ideas and seek support for their proposals. Central to this corporate environment was one of the most sophisticated corporate information systems in the world. Instead of designing IS at Kao to support top management's need for control, as with most such systems, Maruta spent more than twenty years ensuring that the primary purpose was to stimulate operating-level creativity and innovation. For example, one internal network linked the company directly with thousands of retail stores, allowing marketing managers not only to monitor market activity and trends but also to provide retailers with analyses of store-level data as an added service. Kao also developed an artificial intelligence–based market research system that processed huge volumes of market, product, and segment data to generate clues about customer needs, media effectiveness, and other key marketing questions. And a third information-gathering process, based on Kao's consumer life research, combined a traditional monitoring of product usage in a panel of households with an ongoing analysis of calls to the customer service telephone bank. Managers used the integrated output to define new-product characteristics and fine-tune existing offerings.

In launching the company's new Sofina line of cosmetics, the new-product team used these and other data resources and intelligence systems to define a product–market strategy that defied the industry's conventional wisdom. They developed a uniquely formulated product line based on technical data and scientific research rather than on new combinations of traditional ingredients; they positioned the line as skin care rather than on the more traditional image platform; they sold it through mass retail channels rather than through specialty outlets; and they priced it as a product for daily use rather than as a luxury good.

Although respect for and encouragement of individual initiative was central to Kao's philosophy, so too was the commitment to organizationwide collaboration, particularly as a means of transferring knowledge and leveraging expertise. This educational commitment was aimed at maximizing what Maruta described as "the power of collective accumulation of individual wisdom" and relied on an organization that was "designed to run as a flowing system."

Throughout the organization there was much evidence of this philosophy, but one of the most visible manifestations of Kao's commitment to the sharing of knowledge and expertise was the widespread use of open conference areas known as "decision spaces." From the tenth-floor corporate executives' office down, the norm was that important issues were discussed openly in these decision spaces and that everyone interested, even passersby, could join in the debate. Likewise, research and development priorities were worked out in weekly open meetings; and projects were shaped at laboratories' monthly conferences, to which researchers could invite anyone from any part of the company. In all of these forums, information was freely transferred, nobody "owned" an idea, and decision making was kept transparent.

Through such processes individual knowledge in particular units was transferred to others, in the process becoming embedded in organizational policies, practices, and routines that institutionalized learning as "the company way." Similarly, isolated pockets of expertise were linked together and leveraged across other units—in the process developing into distinctive competencies and capabilities, on the strength of which new strategies were developed.

The vital management role at Kao was to create and maintain an internal environment that not only stimulated the development of individual knowledge and expertise to drive the performance of each operating unit, but also supported the interunit interaction and group collaboration to embed knowledge and develop competencies through organizational learning. This environment constituted a delicately balanced behavioral context in which the hard-edged norms of stretch and discipline were offset by the softer values of trust and support. The result was an integrated system that Maruta likened to the functioning of the human body. In what he termed "biological self-control," he expected that the organization he had created would react as the body did when one limb experienced pain or infection: Attention and support would immediately flow to any weak spot without being asked for or directed.

In this state, the organization became highly effective at developing, diffusing, and instutionalizing knowledge and expertise. But although a context shaped by discipline, support, stretch, and trust was a necessary condition for organizational regeneration, it was not sufficient. A second force was needed to ensure that the contextual frame itself remained dynamic.

Maintaining a Dynamic Imbalance

Less obvious than the task of creating a behavioral context that supports both individual unit performance and cross-unit collaboration is a complementary management challenge: to prevent such a system from developing a comfortable level of "fit" that leads it toward gradual deterioration. The great risk in a finely balanced system of biological self-control such as the one developed by Kao is that it can become too effective at embedding expertise and institutionalizing knowledge. This capability risks becoming a liability when unquestioned conventional wisdom and tightly focused capabilities constrain organizational flexibility and strategic responsiveness, leading the system to atrophy over time.

In recent years the popular business press has been full of stories of once great companies that fell victim to their own deeply embedded beliefs and finely honed resources—the so-called "failure of success" syndrome. Digital Equipment's early recognition of a market opportunity for minicomputers grew into a strong commitment to its VAX computers that blinded DEC management to the fact that the segment they were serving was disappearing. Similar stories have been played out in hundreds of other companies, from General Motors and Volkswagen to Philips and Matsushita. They are stories that underscore the key role top management must play in preventing the organizational context they create from settling into a comfortable static equilibrium.

Flying in the face of the widely advocated notion of organizational fit, the top-level managers in the self-regenerating companies we saw were concerned about the need to do what one of them described as "putting a burr under the saddle of corporate self-satisfaction." These leaders saw their task as almost the opposite of their historically assumed role of reinforcing embedded knowledge in policy statements of "the company way" and reaffirming well-established capabilities by designating them as core competencies. While creating a context in which frontline and middle management could generate, transfer, and embed knowledge and expertise, such leaders were in a sense working to counterbalance and constrain that powerful process. By challenging conventional wisdom, questioning the data behind accumulating knowledge, and recombining expertise to create new capabilities, top managers at companies like Kao, Intel, ISS, and 3M created a sense of dynamic imbalance that proved to be a critical element in the process of continuous regeneration.

Maruta and his colleagues at Kao maintained this state of slight organizational disequilibrium through two major devices: a micro process aimed at providing continuous challenge to individual thinking, and a macro process based on regular realignment of the broad organizational focus and priorities. With regard to the former, Maruta was explicit about his willingness to act as a counterbalance to the strong unifying force of Kao's highly sophisticated knowledge-building process. He repeatedly told the organization, "Past wisdom must not be a constraint, but something to be challenged." One approach that Maruta adopted to prevent his management team from too readily accepting deeply ingrained knowledge as conventional wisdom was his practice of discouraging managers from making references to historical achievements or established practices in their discussion of future plans. As one senior manager we talked to emphasized, "If we talk about the past, the top management immediately becomes unpleasant." Instead, Maruta constantly challenged his managers to tell him what new learning they had acquired that would be of future value. "Yesterday's success formula is often today's obsolete dogma," he said. "We must continually challenge the past so that we can renew ourselves each day."

At a more macro level, Maruta created a sense of dynamic challenge by continually alternating his emphasis on rationalization and revitalization. Soon after assuming Kao's presidency in 1971, he initiated the so-called CCR Movement, a major corporate initiative aimed at reducing workforce size through widespread computerization. In the mid-1970s Maruta followed this efficiency-driven initiative with a total quality management (TQM) program that focused more on organizationwide investments and cross-unit integration to improve long-term performance. By the early 1980s, an office automation thrust returned attention to the rationalization agenda—which, by the mid-1980s, was broadened into a total cost reduction (TCR) program. By the late 1980s, however, top management was reemphasizing the revitalization agenda, and the company's TCR slogan was reinterpreted as "total creative revolution," an effort requiring intensive cross-unit collaboration.

Through this constant shifting between rationalization and revitalization agendas, Maruta was able to create an organization that not only supported both capabilities, but embedded them in a dynamic imbalance, thus ensuring that no mode of operation singly became viewed as the dominant model. It was an organizational context that was vital for ongoing business regeneration.

Leading the Renewal Process

Managers in many large companies around the world recognize the need for the kind of radical change we have described. Yet most shy away from taking the plunge. The European head of one of the largest American companies provided us with what is perhaps the most plausible explanation for this gap between intellectual understanding and emotional commitment to action: "The tragedy of top management in large corporations is that it is so much more reassuring to stay as you are, even though you know the result will be certain failure, than to try to make a fundamental change when you cannot be certain that the effort will succeed."

Many books and articles on corporate transformation suggest that the process is inherently complex and messy. That is true. But many also ascribe to the process a mystical characteristic, with the claim that no generalizations about it are possible. This is not true. We have seen numerous companies make effective and sustainable change toward the self-regenerative capability we have described. In all such cases—Motorola, GE, AT&T, Philips, ABB, Lufthansa, and several others—we have observed the same sequential process, with distinct though overlapping phases of rationalization, revitalization, and regeneration. At the same time, companies that have tried alternative routes, such as IBM, Daimler-Benz, DEC, and Hitachi, have made little progress until a change of top management led them to something closer to the model we have described. Similarly, when such a phased approach failed, as it did under Douglas Danforth at Westinghouse, it was because changes in the organizational hardware were not matched with changes in the behavioral software. The model we have presented is general, we believe. And although we have inferred it from our observations of practice, recent theoretical advances suggest that the particular sequence we have proposed is necessary to break down the forces of organizational inertia.[9]

This does not mean that leading a company through such a renewal process will be easy or quick, or that it will be painless. The metaphor of a caterpillar transforming into a butterfly is a romantic one, but the process is not a pleasant experience for the caterpillar. It goes blind, its legs fall off, and its body is torn apart as the beautiful wings emerge. Similarly, transforming a hierarchical bureaucracy into a flexible, self-regenerating company can be painful, and it requires enormous courage from those who must lead the process of change. We hope the road map we have provided will help kindle this courage. We hope we have taken some of the air of mysticism and uncertainty away from what is unambiguously the most daunting challenge facing corporate leadership today.

Notes

1. The full conclusions of the research project are detailed in The Industrialized Corporation (New York: Harper Business, 1997).
2. Results are from the Bain & Company/Planning Forum Survey reported in Darrell K. Rigby, "Managing the Management Tools," *Planning Review*, Support–October 1994, 20–24.
3. Ibid.
4. Jack Welch had described this logic in a presentation at the Harvard Business School in 1989. The logic can also be inferred from the detailed descriptions of the changes in GE in Noel M. Tichy and Stratford Sherman, *Control Your Destiny or Someone Else Will* (New York: Doubleday, 1993). For a descriptive account of GE's transformational change under Welch, see Christopher A. Bartlett and Meg Wozny, "GE's Two Decade Transformation: Jack Welch's Leadership," Case 9-399-150 (Boston: Harvard Business School).
5. Past research on organizational climate has highlighted the importance of standards, feedback, and sanctions in building organizational discipline; see, for example, George H. Litwin and Richard A. Stringer, *Motivation and Organizational Climate* (Cambridge, MA: Harvard Business School, 1968); Richard T. Pascale, "The Paradox of Corporate Culture: Reconciling Ourselves to Socialization," *California Management Review* 13, no. 4 (1985): 546–588; and G. G. Gordon and N. DiTomaso, "Predicting Corporate Performance from Organizational Culture," *Journal of Management Studies* 29, no. 6 (1992): 783–798.
6. The importance of support in enhancing corporate performance has been em-

phasized in Richard Walton, "From Control to Commitment in the Work-place," *Harvard Business Review* (March–April 1985). For a more academically grounded analysis of the organizational requirements to create this attribute of behavioral context, see R. Calori and P. Sarnnin, "Corporate Culture and Economic Performance: A French Study," *Organizational Studies* 12, no. 1 (1991): 49–74.

7. G. Gordon and N. DiTomaso have shown the positive influence that ambitious goals can have on organizational climate; see their "Predicting Corporate Performance from Organizational Culture" note above. The importance of values and personal meaning are highlighted in J. Richard Hackman and G. R. Oldham, *Work Redesign* (Reading, MA: Addison-Wesley, 1980); and in K. W. Thomas and B. A. Velthouse, "Cognitive Elements of Empowerment: An Interpretative Model of Intrinsic Task Motivation," *Academy of Management Review* 15 (1990): 666–681.

8. The importance of trust features prominently in the academic literature on organizational climate; see, for example, J. P. Campbell, M. D. Dunette, Edward E. Lawler, and Karl E. Weick, *Managerial Behavior, Performance and Effectiveness* (New York: McGraw-Hill, 1970). For a more recent contribution on the effect of trust, see R. D. Denision, *Corporate Culture and Organizational Effectiveness* (New York: Wiley, 1990).

9. See, for example, R. P. Rumelt, "Inertia and Transformation," in *Resource-Based and Evolutionary Theories of the Firm*, ed. Cynthia M. Montgomery (Boston: Kluwer, 1995).

11

Emergent Change as a Universal in Organizations

Karl E. Weick

THE BREATHLESS RHETORIC of planned transformational change, complete with talk of revolution, discontinuity, and upheaval, presents a distorted view of how successful change works. The hyperbole of transformation has led people to overestimate the liabilities of inertia, the centrality of managerial planning, and the promise of fresh starts, and to underestimate the value of innovative sensemaking on the front line, the ability of small experiments to travel, and the extent to which change is continuous.

To create a richer picture of organizational change, this chapter makes the case that emergent, continuous change forms the infrastructure that determines whether planned, episodic change will succeed or fail. I will begin by describing emergent continuous change and contrasting it with planned, episodic change. I will then argue that preferences for either style of change are affected by assumptions about inertia, programmatic change, and unfreezing. Emergent change tends to be valued more highly when inertia is seen as a peripheral rather than as a central issue in organizational effectiveness; when the foundations of change are seen to consist of animation, direction, updating, and dialogue rather than of programmatic directives; and when sensitivity to ongoing processes of change leads people to favor intervention strategies of rebalancing rather than strategies of unfreezing.

The Nature of Emergent Change

To understand the nature of emergent change in organizations, consider a few real-world examples and a few theoretical conceptualizations.

Emergent Change in Practice

Here's what emergent change looks like in everyday life.

An executive at Macquarie Bank in Australia describes an emergent style of change when he says, "We never stay still, but we don't change in quantum leaps—our corporate culture would preclude that; running a business on partnership concepts means that policy decisions are not too dramatic, they evolve" (Stace and Dunphy 1994, p. 98).

A manager of the chemical division of a major oil company reviews his unit's ongoing initiatives that anticipate corporate-sponsored transformation: "When [the CEO] began to focus on how he wanted to run the corporation, mission–vision–values came along. I drew a picture for my troops. One box portrayed the company-wide mission–vision–values, and an overlapping box contained our mission and guiding principles. I said, 'Isn't seventy percent of it the same?' 'Yeah.' 'And isn't this different stuff better?' 'Yeah.' 'So what's the big deal?' 'Nothing.' Actually I think that most of us at Chemical are proud that the company sort of adopted the path that we were on" (Kleiner and Roth 1998, p. 6).

Kentucky Fried Chicken (KFC), in the early (1970s) stages of its internationalization, encouraged entrepreneurial frontline operations that created continuing change; this produced innovations such as chicken nugget experiments and new kitchen designs. However, all of these innovations were dropped when, in the 1980s, formal analytic management processes were installed at corporate headquarters to produce planned change. Much of the planned change amounted to reinvention of changes that had previously been accomplished and then abandoned. In the words of the KFC–

Japan president, "We kept thinking there were lots of ways they (corporate) could have learned from us. We felt our twelve-piece minibarrel could be a success elsewhere. And our small store layouts with their flexible kitchen design seemed ideal for U.S. shopping malls. We were even experimenting with chicken nuggets in 1981—well before McDonald's introduced them—but were told to stop" (Ghoshal and Bartlett 1997, p. 72).

Allan Leighton and Archie Norman, in their attempts to revitalize the Asda supermarket chain, set a direction in which they wanted the firm to move; but the changes themselves were a mixture of local deviations, open-ended experiments, and formalization of informal tactics that worked. In a description that has as much figurative value as it has literal accuracy, Leighton characterized the message this way: "We told people to pile produce up, see how much sells, and not worry about waste" (speech at the August 1998 Harvard Business School conference).

Examples much like these are found in Waterman's (1987) discussion of "informed opportunism" (pp. 24–70) and "tiny steps" (pp. 225–228); in Brown and Eisenhardt's (1998) discussion of "growing the strategy" (pp. 191–215); in Kouzes and Posner's (1987) discussion of "small wins" (pp. 217–238); in Collins and Porras's (1994) discussion of "opportunistic experimentation" (pp. 140–168); and in Peters's (1997) discussion titled "You Can't Live without an Eraser" (pp. 75–121). The recurring story is one of autonomous initiatives that bubble up internally; continuous emergent change; steady learning from both failure and success; strategy implementation that is replaced by strategy making; the appearance of innovations that are unplanned, unforeseen, and unexpected; and small actions that have surprisingly large consequences.

Emergent Change in Theory

What is interesting theoretically about the preceding examples is the emergent quality of change in each description plus the fact that change is ongoing, continuous, and cumulative. Orlikowski (1996) provides a rich summary of the qualities these examples share:

Each variation of a given form is not an abrupt or discrete event; neither is it, by itself discontinuous. Rather, through a series of ongoing and situated accommodations, adaptations, and alterations (that draw on previous variations and mediate future ones), sufficient modifications may be enacted over time that fundamental changes are achieved. There is no deliberate orchestration of change here, no technological inevitability, no dramatic discontinuity, just recurrent and reciprocal variations in practice over time. Each shift in practice creates the conditions for further breakdowns, unanticipated outcomes, and innovations, which in turn are met with more variations. Such variations are ongoing; there is no beginning or end point in this change process. (p. 66)

As people experiment with "the everyday contingencies, breakdowns, exceptions, opportunities, and unintended consequences" of work (p. 65), they improvise, produce ongoing variations, and enact micro-level changes.

Emergent, continuous change, when contrasted with planned change, can be defined as "the realization of a new pattern of organizing in the absence of explicit a priori intentions" (Orlikowski 1996, p. 65). The basic argument is that as accommodations and experiments "are repeated, shared, amplified, and sustained, they can, over time, produce perceptible and striking organizational changes" (p. 89). These "striking organizational changes" are often equated with emergent strategy, and the processes that led up to them with emergent strategizing. Examples of such analyses are found in Eden and Ackermann's (1998) work on strategy maps; Mintzberg, Ahlstrand, and Lampel's (1998) discussion of "strategy formation as emergent process" (pp. 175–232); Czarniawska and Joerges's (1996) discussion of "the travel of ideas" (pp. 13–48); and Sayles's (1993) discussion of "strategy from below" (pp. 130–153).

Comparison of Planned Change and Emergent Change

The power of emergent change to enhance adaptability in changing environments derives from the liabilities of planned change plus the advantages of emergent change.

Stated in synoptic form, the liabilities of planned change include a high probability of relapse; uneven diffusion among units; large short-term losses that are difficult to recover; less suitability for opportunity-driven than for threat-driven alterations; unanticipated consequences due to limited foresight; temptations toward hypocrisy (when people talk the talk of revolution but walk the talk of resistance); adoption of best practices that work best elsewhere because of a different context; ignorance among top management regarding key contingencies and capabilities at the front line; and lags in implementation that make the change outdated before it is even finished.

The advantages of emergent change include its capability to increase readiness for and receptiveness to planned change and to institutionalize whatever sticks from the planned change; sensitivity to local contingencies; suitability for on-line real-time experimentation, learning, and sensemaking; comprehensibility and manageability; likelihood of satisfying needs for autonomy, control, and expression; proneness to swift implementation; resistance to unraveling; ability to exploit existing tacit knowledge; and tightened and shortened feedback loops from results to action.

The preceding mirror-image lists suggest conditions under which emergent changes are less effective and planned changes more so. Thus, emergent changes can be slow to cumulate; too small to affect outputs or outcomes; less well suited for responding to threats than for exploiting opportunities; limited by preexisting culture and technology; deficient when competitors are wedded to transformation; better suited to implementation in operations, plants, and stores than to strategy, firm-level, or corporate change; diffuse rather than focused; insufficiently bold or visionary; wedded to a teleological view of change ("intent" drives change), which means that other "engines" such as dialectical, life-cycle, or evolutionary change may be overlooked (Van de Ven and Poole 1995); and unlikely to generate a shift from one frame of reference to a totally different one. By contrast, planned change may be better able to capture attention and focus it on a single direction. Planned change affords a pretext and cover for changes that may be peripheral to the transformational vision but are seen as desirable to make anyway; it is usually aligned with the distribution of power in the organization; it conveys to key stakeholders the impression of being a rational program; it allows a more informed choice among options for implementation; and, because it consists of an explicit, compact mandate, it may be easier to diffuse, although this very solidity may also make it easier to attack and/or avoid.

The content of these lists is not news, although they are seldom assembled this way for the sake of comparison. What is news is that each list constitutes a reasonably coherent argument for a distinct style of change. These arguments constitute a mindset toward change that practitioners often share with researchers. Furthermore, the language of these mindsets may be embodied in organizational cultures as a dominant logic of change. Each set of arguments is supported by a deeper set of assumptions. I turn now to discussion of three of them: inertia, programmatic change, and unfreezing.

The Assumption of Inertia

Pivotal in discussions of change are assumptions about inertia. I argue that an appreciation of the pervasive influence of emergent change fluctuates as a function of how one thinks about inertia. The greater the attachment to the idea that organizations build up inertial structures and are held in place by those structures, the greater will be the reliance on planned change rather than emergent change. According to this line of thinking, inertia is an "inability for organizations to change as rapidly as the environment" (Pfeffer 1997, p. 163). This inability to change rapidly has been attributed to a variety of factors, including dense interdependencies that are difficult to change (Gersick 1991), habitual routines (Gioia 1992), complacency induced by success (Miller 1993), top management who have been in place too long (Virany et al. 1992), and outdated technology (Tushman and Rosenkopf 1992). All of these attributions are basically variations on the idea that the seeds of inertia lie with "a system of interrelated organizational parts that is maintained by mutual dependencies among the parts and with competitive, regulatory, and technological systems outside the organization that reinforce the legitimacy of managerial choices that produced the parts" (Romanelli and Tushman 1994, p. 1144). These interdependencies tend to become tighter during a period of relative equilibrium. The problem is, this tightening often occurs at the expense of continued adaptation to environmental changes. As adaptation lags behind environmental change, effectiveness decreases, pressures for change increase, and the firm begins to enter a period of crisis. As pressures continue to increase, they may trigger an episode of planned change during which activity patterns, roles, responsibilities, and personnel are altered. These alterations then become the basis for a new equilibrium period.

Representative descriptions of planned change efforts that are consistent with this scenario can be found in Miles's (1997) insightful presentation of four major corporate transformations; Tushman and O'Reilly's (1996) discussion of discontinuous changes in strategy, structure, and culture at Apple as it moved from the leadership of Steve Jobs through that of John Sculley, Michael Spindler, Gil Amelio, and back to Jobs; and Bate's (1990) discussion of culture change at British Rail.

Images of Inertia Reflected in Images of Organization

The basic images of organizations that people have in mind, when they argue that firms are susceptible to inertia and therefore require transformational interventions, are actually quite complex. Organizations that develop inertia and require planned change to undo it are viewed as entities that (1) move from one state to another in a forward direction through time, (2) move from a less developed state to a better-developed state, (3) move toward a specific end state often articulated in a vision, (4) move only when there is disruption and disequilibrium, and (5) move only in response to forces planned and managed by people apart from the system (Marshak 1993). The basic image is that of a solid structure, held together by tight interdependencies, whose direction is inertial and is subject to redirection only by the application of a substantial set of forces.

It is possible, however, to portray organizations in a different manner, one that makes the role of inertia much less central in the determination of change. In this alternative portrait, more attention is paid to processes of organizing than to structures of organization. Coordination is viewed as a dynamic process that tends to unravel and therefore has to be reaccomplished continuously. The constant tension between unraveling and reaccomplishment is an ongoing prod to emergent, continuous change. When people reaccomplish the coordination that ties their activities together, they tend to alter it slightly so that it fits better with changing demands from internal and external sources. This continuous updating tends to produce units that change just as rapidly as their environments. Hence, inertia is no longer a problem. Which means it is no longer a determining factor in change.

When inertia is less central, a different and more meaningful story of organization, organizing, and change can be told. This narrative depicts organizations as follows (Marshak 1993): (1) Organizations go through periods of ebb and flow that repeat themselves; in these periods processes unravel and then need to be reaccomplished. (2) Organizations move in an orderly sequence through cycles whose disruption creates a crisis. Typically, units try various strategies, identify strategies that seem to work, and remember and repeat those that work, all of which produces an orderly evolutionary cycle of variation/selection/ retention. (3) Organizations are preoccupied with journeys and directions rather than with destinations and end states. That is, top management provides the direction and leaves the front line to provide the sensemaking and experiments that move the unit in that general direction, in ways that are responsive to local contingencies. (4) Organizations view effective change as interventions that restore balance and orderly sequences. In other words, effective change does not replace one state with another but rather restores adaptive sequences that had been disrupted; for example, a mandate imposed from the top might preempt experimentation, which would produce the less balanced sequence selection/retention, which would then need to be restored to the more adaptive sequence of variation/selection/retention. And (5) organizations accept the reality that nothing remains the same forever. For example, people do not expect that they will be able to fix the organization once and for all and put design problems behind them.

Nuance in the Image of Inertia

The picture of inertia that results when emergent change and organizing are conceptualized in terms of process, flow, and structuring (rather than structures) is quite different from that associated with planned change. For example, organizational routines are assumed to unfold in a repetitive manner by those who worry that this repetition blunts adaptation and can be reversed only by planned change. Routines are portrayed quite differently, however, by those who talk about emergent change. Investigators such as March and Olsen (1989, p. 38), Feldman (1989, p. 130), and Nelson and Winter (1982), have found that so-called routines actually consist of sequences that unfold in slightly different ways each time they are enacted. This variation tends to be responsive to subtle environmental changes, which means that adaptability is preserved rather than lost.

Likewise, mechanisms of inertia are seen by those who advocate planned change to reside in patterns of dense, tight interdependence that can be altered only when attacked forcefully from the outside. Again, these dense patterns are viewed differently by those who talk about emergent change. The latter tend to see organizational interdependencies as more transient, temporary, and loose. This is because the organizational forms that are more salient for them include events in which alliances form and reform continuously (e.g., Browning, Beyer, and Shetler 1995), or in which innovations generated internally that go unsupported become the occasion for people to leave the firm and form their own company around those innovations (e.g., Martin 1997). The elaborate system of stable, mutual dependencies that Romanelli and Tushman describe is less characteristic of network organizations with their chronically salient large set of alternative partners.

It is also true that views regarding the importance of inertia, and of the type of change that is necessary to deal with it, may covary with the standpoint of the observer. From a distance (the macro level of analysis composed of the big picture captured by upper management), when observers watch the flow of events that constitute organizing, they see what looks like repetitive action, routine, and inertia dotted with occasional episodes of revolutionary change. But a view from closer in (the micro level of analysis composed of particular details captured by the front line) suggests ongoing adaptation and continuous adjustment. Although these adjustments may be small, they also tend to be frequent across units, which means they add up swiftly and can alter structure and strategy. Some students of change (e.g., Orlikowski 1996) treat these ongoing adjustments as the essence of organizational change and argue that emergent change is the infrastructure of all change. Other students (e.g., Nadler et al. 1995) describe these ongoing adjustments as incremental variations on the same theme and lump them together as typical of epochs of convergence, during which interdependencies tighten. Convergence is interrupted sporadically by epochs of divergence—sometimes termed revolution, deep change, or transformation.

From a middle standpoint halfway between near and distant, emergent and planned change begin to become indistinguishable. Thus, people in middle management who see fragments of frontline detail and fragments of a bigger picture are in the odd position of being the most savvy about what actually goes on in change, yet the least able to do anything about it.

The Assumption of Programmatic Change

Planned change often takes the form of off-the-shelf standardized solutions that focus on one issue and are driven through the organization by directives from top management. As Beer and his colleagues (1990) demonstrate, these attempts at revitalization amount to false starts, because they fail to have simultaneous impact on three important drivers of effective change: coordination, commitment, and competence. My analysis here is in the spirit of Beer and colleagues' search for fundamentals. But I differ in my list of fundamentals because I start from a different place.

I assume that change engages efforts to make sense of events that don't fit together (Weick 1995). Sensemaking involves "the meaningful linkaging of symbols and activity, that enables people to come to terms with the ongoing struggle for existence" (Prus 1996, p. 232). The four bare-bones conditions required for successful sensemaking are that people (1) stay in motion, (2) have a direction, (3) look closely and update often, and (4) converse candidly. My working hypothesis is that these conditions are activated more often by emergent change than by planned change, which is why I feel that emergent change is crucial in revitalization. This hypothesis derives from the basic requirements for sensemaking.

If sensemaking is drastically simplified, this question captures it: How can we know what we think until we see what we say? People need to act in order to discover what they face, and they need to talk in order to discover what is on their mind. The "saying" involves action and animation; the "seeing" involves directed observation; the "thinking" involves the updating of previous thinking; and the "we" that makes all of this happen takes the form of candid dialogue that mixes together trust, trustworthiness, and self-respect. Sensemaking appears to be the root activity when people deal with an unknowable, unpredictable world. In these dealings, they produce continuous ongoing change. Thus, effective sensemaking and effective emergent change are tied together closely. The more fully sensemaking activities are activated, the more effective the change.

The basic story in successful change seems to go like this. Faced with an important surprise (e.g., unexpected loss of market share), crisis (e.g., inability to meet loan covenants), or interruption (e.g., shutdown due to unsafe practices), people try to make sense of what is happening and adopt some program to remedy the trouble. It makes no difference what program they choose to implement, because any old program will do—as long as that program (1) *animates people* and gets them moving and generating experiments that uncover opportunities; (2) *provide a direction;* (3) *encourages updating* through improved situational awareness and closer attention to what is actually happening; and (4) *facilitates respectful interaction* in which trust, trustworthiness, and self-respect (Campbell 1990) all develop equally and allow people to build a stable rendition of what they face. Whether the chosen program involves economic value added, or total quality, or the creation of a learning organization, or transformation, or teachable points of view, or action learning or culture change or whatever, effectiveness will improve or decline depending on whether the program engages or blocks the four components of sensemaking. These components by themselves are sufficient to produce change. But they require a pretext for activation; there needs to be some kind of surprise and some kind of content to set them in motion. Both of these requirements, a surprise and a program, are met in virtually all of the cases described in this book. Nevertheless, it is the thrust of my argument that there is nothing special about the content of any one program per se that explains its success or failure in producing change. What matters is the extent to which the program triggers sustained animation, direction, attention/updating, and respectful interaction. It is these four activities that make it easier or harder for people collectively to make sense of what they currently face and to deal with it.

The successful engagement of these four driving forces is not inevitable. Planned change often produces animation and some direction, but not necessarily closer attention and updating or interaction in which people listen, speak up, and maintain self-respect while dealing with differences in interpretations. Most change programs ignore one or more of these driving forces. Consider a run-of-the-mill change intervention. When a new program is imposed on people, they have to keep the business going—usually by continuing with the older way—while they get accustomed to running it the new way. When they attempt this juggling act, people typically implement rather than experiment, pay attention to compliance rather than to effects and outcomes, and listen rather than speak up. When interventions inhibit animation, direction, attention, and dialogue, ambiguity increases. As a result, the rate of change is slowed rather than accelerated, because people are distracted by their efforts to reduce ambiguity. The problem is, they don't have access to the tools they need to manage ambiguity. People face ambiguity without action that tests hunches, without a general direction that allows local adaptation, without close attention to details and consequences, and without candid dialogue to build a consensual picture of what is happening. If the ambiguity persists, this situation becomes increasingly stressful. And stress has the unfortunate effect of forcing people back onto overlearned earlier routines that are the very tendencies the change initiative was supposed to abolish.

In a change process that works, people tackle new tasks and discover new capabilities. They continue to move in the direction of greater alignment of personal and organizational values. They continue to notice, now in greater detail, just how much top management neglected and has left as their legacy for the units to clean up. And they become increasingly willing to speak up about what really needs to be remedied. All four of these activities—animation, direction, attention, respectful interaction—are crucial for adaptation, learning, and change in a turbulent world. But they are also the four activities most likely to be curbed severely in a hierarchical command-and-control system.

Furthermore, there is no guarantee that highly touted planned change programs will necessarily recognize, restore, or legitimize animation, direction, attention, or respectful interaction. Thus, an important message of this essay is that if a change program leaves these elements untouched, it will fail. A further message is that emergent change is more likely than planned change to engage all four simultaneously.

The Assumption of Unfreezing

If people want to change a system in which they feel inertia runs deep, then their best bet is to start with Kurt Lewin's prescription for change: unfreeze–change–refreeze. As Hendry (1996) notes, "Scratch any account of creating and managing change and the idea that change is a three-stage process which necessarily begins with a process of unfreezing will not be far below the surface. Indeed it has been said that the whole theory of change is reducible to this one idea of Kurt Lewin's" (p. 624). We sometimes forget that Lewin presumed that there was high resistance to change and that strong emotions are often needed to breach the resistance. "To break open the shell of complacency and self-righteousness it is sometimes necessary to bring about deliberately an emotional stir-up" (Lewin 1951, quoted in Marshak 1993, p. 400). But although strong emotions may provide "major sources of energy for revolutionary change" (Gersick 1991), they may also degrade cognition and performance in ways analogous to those of stress (Driskell and Salas 1996).

Another message of this essay is that if you take emergent change more seriously and inertia less seriously, then you'll discover a broader range of options for change than those associated with planned change. If a problem of declining organization performance is diagnosed as one of inertia, then it makes sense to design an intervention that unfreezes the inertia, makes a change, and finally refreezes and institutionalizes the change. But if change is continuous and emergent, then the system is already unfrozen. Further efforts at unfreezing could disrupt what is essentially a complex adaptive system that is already working. In a system where continuous emergent change is happening, ineffectiveness lies not in inertia but in processes whose steps have gotten out of sequence or are unevenly accomplished, or in which some steps have momentarily disappeared. Continuous change may have lost its continuity or run into blockages.

If ineffectiveness is attributed to disruptions in continuous change, then a more plausible change sequence would be freeze, rebalance, unfreeze. To freeze continuous change means to make a disrupted sequence visible and to show patterns in what is happening—to uncover the causal sequence embodied in a process in order to spot vicious circles (Senge 1990). Freezing may also consist of a marginal gloss of real-time interaction in which people discover that their intentions and assumptions are at odds with what they produce (e.g., Argyris 1990). To rebalance means to reinterpret, relabel, and resequence steps so they unfold with fewer blockages. And finally, to unfreeze after rebalancing is to resume emergent change, complete with its improvisation and learning, in ways that are now more attentive to local changes, more resilient to anomalies, and more flexible in their execution.

One reason it is tough to alter a pattern of emergent change is that this requires a demanding set of diagnostic and intervention skills. People find it difficult to "see" processes, sequences, and patterns in a flow of events (Pettigrew 1997). What they are looking for, basically, are small inputs that have large consequences. Conversations are a good example of small inputs that can enlarge. As Ford and Ford (1995) put it, "The macrocomplexity of organizations is generated, and changes emerge, through the diversity and interconnectedness of many microconversations, each of which follows relatively simple rules" (p. 560). It is harder for people to see the power of process than it is for them to see the power of things, frequencies, stabilities, structures. Furthermore, for people to intervene meaningfully in emergent change, they need considerable linguistic skills to capture and label a flow of events, resequence and relabel that flow, and then release the revised flow.

Skilled change agents recognize adaptive emergent changes, make them more salient, and reframe them (Bate 1990). As Rorty (1989) observed, "a talent for speaking differently rather than for arguing well, is the chief instrument of cultural change" (p. 7). For example, Wilkof and her colleagues (1995) report on their attempt to intervene in the relationship between two companies in a difficult partnership. Wilkof's initial attempts to improve cooperation focused on feeding back problems from a traditional data collection. This tactic failed and led to the discovery that although there were technical or structural solutions available, the actors could not agree on them, because of vastly different cultural lenses and diametrically opposed interpretations of meaning. The consultant, therefore, changed her strategy. She began meeting independently with the actors from each organization. In the meetings she would meet each condemnation not with data or argument but with an alternative interpretation from the cultural lens of the other company. She calls the process "cultural consciousness raising." Wilkof and colleagues underscore the importance of helping people learn to interpret the actions of others not as technical incompetence but as behaviors that are consistent with a particular cultural purpose, meaning, and history. The power of this intervention can be understood in the context of Schein's (1996) observation that "The most basic mechanism of acquiring new information that leads to cognitive restructuring is to discover in a conversational process that the interpretation that someone else puts on a concept is different from one's own" (p. 31). Barrett and colleagues (1995) and Dixon (1997) have made similar arguments to the effect that the most powerful change interventions occur at the level of everyday conversation.

The power of conversation, dialogue, and respectful interaction to reshape ongoing change has often been overlooked. We are in thrall to the story of dramatic interventions in which heroic figures turn around stubbornly inertial structures held in place by rigid people who are slow learners. This is a riveting story. It is also a deceptive story. It runs roughshod over capabilities already in place, over the basics of change, and over changes that are already under way.

Summary and Conclusions

Emergent change consists of ongoing accommodations, adaptations, and alterations that produce fundamental change without a priori intentions to do so. Emergent change occurs when people reaccomplish routines and when they deal with contingencies, breakdowns, and opportunities in everyday work. Much of this change goes unnoticed, because small alterations are lumped together as noise in otherwise uneventful inertia and because small changes are neither heroic nor plausible ways to make strategy.

If leaders take notice of emergent change and its effects, however, they can be more selective in their use of planned change. To take notice means to become more aware of personal assumptions about inertia, because these assumptions color not just one's views of change but one's views of what is an effective organization. It is hard to see the value of emergent change unless you also see the organization in terms of structuring rather than structure, flexible routines rather than rigid routines, and loosely coupled interdependencies rather than tightly coupled ones.

The wise leader sees emergent change where others see only inertia and pretexts for planned change. The wise leader also sees that emergent change is most effective when people have the resources they need to produce it. One way to think about such resources is in terms of the question, What is valued in this firm? Emergent change, and its close relative sensemaking, are likely to be more effective when the culture of the corporation makes it clear that people are valued when they experiment with job descriptions (animation), implement a directive strategy in a novel manner (direction), rewrite requirements that no longer fit the environment (attention and updating), and speak up when things aren't working (dialogue). In a traditional command-and-control system, it is hard for upper management to walk the talk of those four prerequisites. It is that very difficulty that leads top management to favor planned change. Planned change is more centralized and easier to control from the top, which means it is easier talk to walk. The problem is, when top management opts for planned change, it often discards some of its best innovators, some of its best innovations, and some of its most adaptive processes.

Thus, a new "code of change" could be the recognition that organizational change is not management induced. Instead, organizational change is emergent change laid down by choices made on the front line. The job of management is to author interpretations and labels that capture the patterns in those adaptive choices. Within the framework of sensemaking, management sees what the front line says and tells the world what it means. In a newer code, management doesn't create change. It certifies change.

The moral of emergent change would seem to be that if something is not invented within the organization, it should be regarded as suspect. When consulting gurus sweep in with their promises of magical transformation through programs invented elsewhere, the wise manager thinks twice before allowing that show to unfold. The informed hesitancy springs from a deeper appreciation that mundane transformation may already be under way in the guise of unnoticed emergent change. Those emergent changes need to be noticed, labeled, and legitimized rather than displaced by the vendor-driven flavor of the month.

References

Argyris, C. 1990. *Overcoming Organizational Defenses: Facilitating Organizational Learning.* Boston: Allyn and Bacon.
Barrett, F. J., G. F. Thomas, and S. P. Hocevar. 1995. The Central Role of Discourse in Large-Scale Change: A Social Construction Perspective. *Journal of Applied Behavioral Science* 31: 352–372.
Bate, P. 1990. Using the Culture Concept in an Organization Development Setting. *Journal of Applied Behavioral Science* 26: 83–106.
Beer, M., R. A. Eisenstat, and B. Spector. 1990. *The Critical Path to Corporate Renewal.* Boston: Harvard Business School Press.
Brown, S. L., and K. M. Eisenhardt. 1998. *Competing on the Edge.* Boston: Harvard Business School Press.
Browning, L. D., J. M. Beyer, and J. C. Shetler. 1995. Building Cooperation in a Competitive Industry: Sematech and the Semiconductor Industry. *Academy of Management Journal* 38: 113–151.
Campbell, D. T. 1990. Asch's Moral Epistemology for Socially Shared Knowledge. In *The Legacy of Solomon Asch*, ed. I. Rock, 39–52. Hillsdale, NJ: Erlbaum.
Collins, J. C., and J. I. Porras. 1994. *Built to Last.* New York: Harper.
Czarniawska, B., and B. Joerges. 1996. Travels of Ideas. In *Translating Organizational Change*, ed. B. Czarniawska and G. Sevon, 13–48. New York: Walter de Gruyter.
Dixon, N. M. 1997. The Hallways of Learning. *Organizational Dynamics* (spring): 23–34.
Driskell, J. E., and E. Salas, eds. 1996. *Stress and Human Performance.* Mahwah, NJ: Erlbaum.
Eden, C., and F. Ackermann. 1998. *Making Strategy.* London: Sage.
Feldman, M. S. 1989. *Order without Design.* Stanford: Stanford University Press.
Ford, J. D., and L. W. Ford. 1995. The Role of Conversations in Producing International Change in Organizations. *Academy of Management Review* 20, no. 3: 541–570.
Gersick, C. J. G. 1991. Revolutionary Change Theories: A Multilevel Exploration of the Punctuated Equilibrium Paradigm. *Academy of Management Review* 16: 10–36.
Ghoshal, S., and C. A. Bartlett. 1997. *The Individualized Corporation.* New York: Harper.
Gioia, D. A. 1992. Pinto Fires and Personal Ethics: A Script Analysis of Missed Opportunities. *Journal of Business Ethics* 11: 379–389.
Hendry, C. 1996. Understanding and Creating Whole Organizational Change through Learning Theory. *Human Relations* 49: 621–641.

Kleiner, A., and G. Roth. 1998. Perspectives on Corporate Transformation: The OilCo Learning History. Society for Organizational Learning Working Paper 18.009. Cambridge, MA: MIT.

Kouzes, J. M., and B. Z. Posner. 1987. *The Leadership Challenge.* San Francisco: Jossey-Bass.

Lewin, K. 1951. *Field Theory in Social Science.* New York: Harper and Row.

March, J. G., and J. P. Olsen. 1989. *Rediscovering Institutions.* New York: Free Press.

Marshak, R. J. 1993. Lewin Meets Confucius: A Review of the OD Model of Change. *Journal of Applied Behavioral Science* 29: 393–415.

Martin, R. 1997. Cascading Choices. Unpublished manuscript, University of Toronto.

Miles, R. H. 1997. *Leading Corporate Transformation.* San Francisco: Jossey-Bass.

Miller, D. 1993. The Architecture of Simplicity. *Academy of Management Review* 18: 116–138.

Mintzberg, H., B. Ahlstrand, and J. Lampel. 1998. *Strategy Safari.* New York: Free Press.

Nadler, D. A., R. B. Shaw, and A. E. Walton. 1995. *Discontinuous Change.* San Francisco: Jossey-Bass.

Nelson, R., and S. Winter. 1982. *An Evolutionary Theory of Economic Change.* Cambridge, MA: Belknap Press.

Orlikowski, W. J. 1996. Improvising Organizational Transformation Overtime: A Situated Change Perspective. *Information Systems Research* 7, no. 1: 63–92.

Peters, T. 1997. *The Circle of Innovation.* New York: Knopf.

Pettigrew, A. M. 1997. What Is Processual Analysis? *Scandinavian Journal of Management* 13, no. 4: 337–348.

Pfeffer, J. 1997. *New Directions for Organization Theory.* New York: Oxford University Press.

Prus, R. 1996. *Symbolic Interaction and Ethnographic Research.* Albany, NY: State University Press.

Romanelli, E., and M. L. Tushman. 1994. Organizational Transformation as Punctuated Equilibrium: An Empirical Test. *Academy of Management Journal* 37: 1141–1166.

Rorty, R. 1989. *Contingency, Irony, and Solidarity.* New York: Cambridge University Press.

Sayles, L. R. 1993. *The Working Leader.* New York: Free Press.

Schein, E. H. 1996. Kurt Lewin's Change Theory in the Field and in the Classroom: Notes toward a Model of Managed Learning. *Systems Practice* 9: 27–47.

Senge, P. 1990. *The Fifth Discipline.* New York: Doubleday.

Stace, D., and D. Dunphy. 1994. *Beyond the Boundaries.* Sydney: McGraw-Hill.

Tushman, M. L., and C. A. O'Reilly III. 1996. The Ambidextrous Organization: Managing Evolutionary and Revolutionary Change. *California Management Review* 38: 1–23.

Tushman, M. L., and L. Rosenkopf. 1992. Organizational Determinants of Technological Change: Toward a Sociology of Technological Evolution. *Research in Organizational Behavior* 14: 311–347.

Van de Ven, A. H., and M. S. Poole. 1995. Explaining Development and Change in Organizations. *Academy of Management Review* 20, no. 3: 510–540.

Virany, B., M. L. Tushman, and E. Romanelli. 1992. Executive Succession and Organization Outcomes in Turbulent Environments: An Organization Learning Approach. *Organization Science* 3: 72–91.

Waterman, R. H., Jr. 1987. *The Renewal Factor.* Toronto: Bantam.

Weick, K. E. 1995. *Sensemaking in Organizations.* Thousand Oaks, CA: Sage.

Wilkof, M. V., D. W. Brown, and J. W. Selsky. 1995. When the Stories Are Different: The Influence of Corporate Culture Mismatches on Interorganizational Relations. *Journal of Applied Behavioral Science* 31: 373–388.

12

LINKING CHANGE PROCESSES TO OUTCOMES

A Commentary on Ghoshal, Bartlett, and Weick

Andrew M. Pettigrew

RESEARCH AND WRITING on organizational change is undergoing a metamorphosis. In 1985 an extended critique of the literature on change argued that research on organizational change was largely acontextual, ahistorical, and aprocessual (Pettigrew 1985). Since then considerable advances have been made both in empirical and theoretical work on organizational change. Many more studies now seek to link the context, content, and process of change (Pettigrew 1987). More recent writing acknowledges that context and action are inseparable, that any adequate theory of change has also to explain continuity, and that any study must include a time series in order to expose such dualities (Greenwood and Hinings 1996; Van de Ven et al. 1989). Furthermore, this new interest in time and process has triggered a new curiosity about the pace and sequencing of action in change processes (Gersick 1994; Kessler and Chakrabarti 1996; Pettigrew et al. 1992).

Meanwhile, theoretical developments have been taking place. The punctuated equilibrium view of change is under greater critical scrutiny alongside the more determinist interpretations of institutional theory (Greenwood and Hinings 1996; Sastry 1997). Recent writing by Brown and Eisenhardt (1997, 1998) seeks to blend evolutionary theory and complexity theory in order to expose and explain how innovation may occur "at the edge of chaos." And in an ambitious theoretical and empirical program, Lewin and his associates (1999) are seeking to develop a coevolutionary theory of organizational adaptation that portrays firms and populations of firms changing as a consequence of managerial actions, institutional influences, and environmental pressures. Important work has also been done in industrial economics by Milgrom and Roberts (1995) and by Ichniowski and colleagues (1997). These authors develop a line of thought that leads through contingency theory and configurational theory and points to the significance of coherent rather than piecemeal change for positive performance effects (Pettigrew and Whipp 1991). The precision of statement of the Milgrom and Roberts' theoretical work is a considerable advance on existing work seeking to link change actions with change outcomes.

One ingredient in the aspiration to "break the code of change" is the hope of generating knowledge that will underpin effective practice in change management. In order to do this we will have to be considerably more ambitious in our research on change than we have thus far. Part of this new boldness may entail discarding established dichotomous concepts such as planned and emergent processes. We may also have to extend our empirical questioning beyond analysis of the factors and processes that affect the success of change interventions, to look at much bigger questions about the relationship between change and organizational performance. That is the core theme to be pursued in this commentary on the chapters by Sumantra Ghoshal and Christopher Bartlett and Karl Weick.

This chapter is in four parts. The first part offers characterizations and brief critiques of the Ghoshal and Bartlett and Weick chapters. Debates about planned versus emergent change have been analytically and practically significant, but perhaps now they need to be complemented by a wider vocabulary that seeks to link the context, content, and process of change to change outcomes.

The second part picks up the importance of context and argues for the significance of customization as a core part of the practice of change management. This section indicates the importance of customization (alongside a range of other factors) in explaining the differential success of change initiatives. However, the fate of individual change programs needs to be linked to the wider performance of organizations. This issue the third section tackles by drawing on the results of recent European research on new forms of organizing and company performance (Whittington et al. 1999). The fourth and final section argues that the new competitive landscape demands not only new and more flexible forms of organizing but also a new social production of knowledge by scholars interested in innovation and change. Here the challenge of meeting the double hurdle of scholarly quality and relevance is overlaid by a new urgency—the need to conduct mapping studies on a global scale to capture the what of change, with longitudinal processual studies to help explain the why and how of change. Breaking the code of change is a big challenge. If scholars are to be influential in that process, we will need to make very big contributions of knowledge generation and diffusion. That will entail a fundamental questioning of our scholarly routines, and especially of how we tackle the coproduction and codissemination of management knowledge.

Planned and Emergent Change

There is a long tradition in the social sciences and in management and organization theory of using bipolar modes of thinking: dichotomies, paradoxes, contradictions, and dualities. Dichotomies are remembered; they are powerful simplifiers and attention directors, as the influence of Burns and Stalker's (1961) mechanistic and organic systems and Lawrence and Lorsch's (1967) differentiation and integration of structures testify. Dichotomies also tease. They may promise much analytically but deliver little in empirical analysis or practical application. Dichotomies may thus conceal as much as they reveal.

As Janssens and Steyaert (1999) have persuasively argued, although these various bipolar theories all imply two distinct and indissoluble concepts, they have slightly different meanings. Thus, paradox can imply apparent contradiction—but no choice may be called for, because the contradictory elements are both accepted. A dilemma is often seen as an either/or situation in which one alternative must be preferred over other attractive alternatives (Hampden-Turner 1986). Dualities, on the other hand, "reflect opposing forces that must be balanced, properties that seem contradictory or paradoxical but which in fact are complementary" (Evans and Doz 1992, p. 85). But what does "balanced" mean in the resolution of tensions and dualities? In a recent discussion of his exploration/exploitation duality, March (1999) notes that "balance is a nice word, but a cruel concept" (p. 5). He rightly argues that defining an optimum mix of exploration and exploitation is difficult or impossible. It involves trade-offs across space and time, people and levels in a system. In other words, the experience of dualities and their management is likely to be highly context sensitive.

The duality of planned versus emergent change has served us well as an attention director but may well now be ready for retirement. Karl Weick's sharp and lucid prose extracts the maximum from exposing the liabilities of planned change and the virtues of emergent change processes. Weick contends that planned changes have a high probability of relapse and regression; may precipitate uneven diffusion through a system; invite unanticipated and negative consequences; and tempt the initiators of change into hypocrisy, detachment, and delusion. Emergent change processes, on the other hand, can deliver flexibility—the capability to build receptive settings for change and the sensitive customization of action to meet local conditions. Emergent processes may be breeding grounds for learning and experimentation and can be compatible with local needs for autonomy, control, and swifter implementation. Most crucially, the language of emergent process can facilitate an executive mindset for change that is avowedly dynamic; and in today's competitive landscape thinking dynamically is one of the ingredients that encourage acting dynamically. So banish nouns and use verbs. Change and organization are static nouns, Weick argues; we need the dynamic vocabulary of changing and organizing if we are to take charge of a changing world.

Having been urged to be polemical, Weick does it well. But the polemicism directs our attention away from the mutualities and complementarities of planned and emergent change. In their introduction to this volume Michael Beer and Nitin Nohria use the Asda case very effectively to show that Archie Norman and Allan Leighton were able to combine a planned approach to change (Beer and Nohria's Theory E) with a more emergent process of change (roughly equivalent to Beer and Nohria's Theory O). Beer and Nohria commit themselves prescriptively to the view that E and O in combination is the best change strategy for firms that want to develop sustained competitive advantage. Where this is not feasible, Beer and Nohria recommend to begin with E and follow with O.

At the moment such prescriptive theorizing about the use of complementary or sequential change strategies rests on a very thin knowledge base. Until very recently scholars of innovation and change have been curiously uncurious about the pace and sequencing of change. (For some recent examples see Gersick 1994; Kessler and Chakrabarti 1996; and Pettigrew et al. 1992.) However, a sequence model of change is precisely what is on offer in the Ghoshal and Bartlett chapter in this volume. Ghoshal and Bartlett argue that the kind of transformation process that is likely to lead to performance improvement must reshape the behavioral context of the organization and must do this in a carefully phased sequence. Drawing on anecdotal information from a select group of high-profile successful firms, Ghoshal and Bartlett present the three Rs of change sequencing: First rationalize, then revitalize, and finally regenerate. The Jack Welch era at General Electric is used to exemplify the three phases, each era building on the strengths and limitations of the previous one. Thus, the core activities of linking and leveraging businesses in the revitalization phase help to exploit the potential of the slimmed-down organization from the rationalization phase and build some of the trust essential for regeneration. Ghoshal and Bartlett admit that it is not easy to find examples of successful regeneration, but they quote 3M, ISS, and Kao as good exemplars of regeneration and their three-phase sequence model.

If dualities have their virtues as attention directors and simplifiers, so do tripartite modes of expression. Ghoshal and Bartlett are not the first and will not be the last thinkers to adopt the trinitarian form of communicating. Dividing the world into threes is a powerful literary device, combining as it does not only isolatable sequences but also progression through three phases toward some higher order of things. Hegelian logic, for example, took us through thesis and antithesis to the climax of synthesis. For Ghoshal and Bartlett the point of greatest interest is regeneration, but only if that can deliver enhanced corporate performance.

Ghoshal and Bartlett's writing is clear and compelling. But the combination of descriptive analysis and prescription means that it is difficult for the reader to disentangle what the authors have found empirically from what they would like to see. The authors do not feel it necessary to inform the reader about their research strategy, method, or data sources. Did they rely on published sources of information about the organizations they quote, or did they collect primary data themselves, and if so from whom, and when? There is little evidence to link the adoption of the three Rs phase sequence to the enhanced performance of the organizations they cite. Since the publication of Peters and Waterman (1982), it is now widely regarded as fallacious to study the determinants of organizational performance in a case study sample that includes just one end of the distribution, be it high or low performers. Presumably there are case examples of firms that have improved their performance without using the Ghoshal and Bartlett sequence of rationalization, revitalization, and regeneration. There may also be firms that have used such a sequence and not delivered performance improvement. In the absence of such related findings and analysis, the Ghoshal and Bartlett thinking on change sequencing remains conjectural.

Successful Change Programs

Ghoshal and Bartlett make a strong case for the importance of sequencing in the management of change: It seems intuitively sensible first to rationalize, then revitalize, and then regenerate. But their problem is that they have presented neither the database nor the process information to link such sequencing behavior to firm performance. What is known about the interrelated set of factors that contribute to the success of change initiatives? Indeed, what is success in the management of change?

Definitions of success can include ratings of the quantity, quality, and pace of change. There may well be trade-offs among those three, with quantity and pace achieved at the price of the quality of the process. A poor-quality process may deliver change in a particular episode, but at the expense of reducing the capability and willingness of that part of the organization to contemplate further change in the future. If the goal is sustainable change, the notional success may in reality be a failure. Success can be realistically addressed only against self-proclaimed targets. But what targets? Some of the wilder transformational targets of business process reengineering (BPR) might have been attainable had they been more modestly expressed as process improvement and simplification.

Judgments about success are also likely to be conditional on who is doing the assessment and when the judgment is made (Pettigrew 1985, 1990). Most change processes do not attract universal acclaim. There is likely to be a mixed bag of supporters, doubters, and opponents, and individuals may move between these groups over time.

A further difficulty in assessing what is known about the success of change initiatives arises from the now voluminous literature on this subject. A great deal of the most accessible literature is written by practitioners and consultants, who are hardly disinterested observers of the processes they describe and proclaim. And the academic literature also has its limitations. Few academic researchers studying change processes collect time series data, and many do not include an outcome variable such as success or failure, or impact on performance. These two limitations constrain what we can conclude from research studies about success factors in change efforts.

In a review of the published literature on BPR implementation, Ascari and colleagues (1995) draw out a range of factors linkable to successful BPR development. The list includes factors such as care in building preparedness for change before the launch of the initiative; clearly articulated change goals and a company mission that emphasizes customer focus; understanding and commitment on the part of top management; the availability of a clear and respected change leader; an appropriate pace of change managed by the use of high learning–high impact pilot projects; and business objectives that drive the change process and not vice versa. Yet statements of BPR success have, of course, to be placed alongside consultant estimates that around 70 percent of BPR interventions do not meet expectations (Bashien et al. 1994).

The theme of persistent and consistent top-level support permeates much of the literature on change. The withdrawal of a key product champion, or shallow commitment from a fragmented and therefore incoherent top management team, will rapidly destabilize change efforts (Pettigrew and Whipp 1991). Paradoxically, zones of relative continuity and comfort are necessary for effective management of change. For the top this means developing a coherent and sustainable direction for the business and holding key executives in place long enough to see major change initiatives through. It may also require the top to clarify and communicate what is not going to change (for the time being) while the current change initiative is in process.

All change processes are influence processes. All influence processes require awareness of, if not action in, the political processes of the organizations. Change and politics are inexorably linked (Pettigrew 1973, 1975). This means that at the top, middle, and lower reaches of the organization, campaigning, lobbying, coalition building, and the sharing of information, rewards, and recognition are all fateful for change through all the various unpredictable stages and loops of the innovation journey.

Leading change is not just about individual leadership. Neither is it just about building a coherent team at the top and pressuring the levels below. Pressure from the top is essential to break any bonds of inertia, and crises are often constructed as attention directors to build a climate for change. But leadership is also about followership. The top get weary pushing for change if there is no reciprocal and reinforcing pressure from below. Important linkage mechanisms between leaders and potential followers arise when leaders create opportunities for a marriage between top-down pressure and bottom-up concerns. Top-down pressure seems to deliver more when that pressure is selectively and astutely orchestrated at the local level and linked in a coherent and sensitive fashion to bottom-up concerns (Pettigrew et al. 1992).

The content of change initiatives requires customization at lower tiers to match local circumstances and thereby script in local psychic energy. Customization does have risks: It may initially slow the process down, because learning and adaptation have to occur in many localities. It may cost more and bring dangers of incoherence as standardized templates and methods are altered to reflect operational circumstances. Without a clear purpose and strategic framework for the change program, customization may also precipitate suboptimal grabs for autonomy at the periphery. This is particularly likely when there is a climate of low trust and poor communication between the center and the periphery. However, customization is a key factor in linking strategic and operational change. For many firms it has been a risk worth taking to build in local identification and commitment to central purposes.

The global, long-term, and intangible nature of many change initiatives means these are long journeys that require persistence and patience and an investment rather than a cost view of people at work (Pettigrew and Whipp 1991). In a survey of total quality management (TQM) in the West and Japan, *The Economist* (The Cracks in Quality

1992) noted that unlike their Japanese counterparts, many Western firms had abandoned TQM after two years. Major Japanese firms had been investing in quality programs for thirty years or more. In the absence of such quality consciousness and behavior, many Western firms have sought ways of compromising between short-termism and long-termism. One such approach is to create and publicize intermediate successes or "islands of progress" along the change journey. Such stepping stones require that the firm first give real thought to operationalizing the intangibles of, for example, quality and culture change, then use such operational indicators to assess progress over time. Change initiatives can seem to be all input and process and no output. Without successful intermediate outcomes, even the most committed travelers get weary on what begin to feel like interminable journeys.

Thus far this discussion of success has linked together the complementary effects of persistent and consistent top-level support; skill in leading change and in linking strategic and operational change; customization aimed at drawing in the commitment and psychic energy of operational levels; and the use of operational indicators to create and publicize intermediate successes. Evidence also indicates that a range of additional factors may help sustain change initiatives long enough for companies to harvest real benefits. Beer and his colleagues (1990) and many others have drawn attention to linkage between a change initiative and the critical path of the business as a necessary though not sufficient condition for success. Some research evidence (Pettigrew 1985) suggests that inclusive project team management is beneficial in allowing change teams to bridge with key people and problems. "To change the world one must live with it" is the motto of the inclusive change team, which seeks to keep one foot in the present as it coaches and challenges the organization into the future.

Reward and recognition systems can be a powerful lever to pull in corporate settings. All too often, however, this lever is pulled too little and too late. Organizations moving from a quantity to a quality culture are unlikely to be persuaded just by rhetorical statements at the top. Unless and until the old quantity-based reward and recognition system is itself changed and begins to reflect the quality culture, it is very unlikely that the bulk of the organization—particularly its most ambitious members—will walk easily into this new future.

Two final success factors can play their part in sustaining change initiatives: episodic versus continuous process views of changing, and coherence in the management of the overall process of change in the organization. Research on the cognitive aspects of organizations has drawn our attention to the way individual and collective thought processes can shape the way managers respond to problems (Hodgkinson and Johnson 1994; Huff 1990). One example of such cognitive structuring is the tendency for managers to think of and act on problems as projects or episodes. Thus, major change issues that clearly have a continuous rather than an episodic presence may be treated as substantially time-limited events. The effect of this is twofold. First, the project mode implies that the intervention has a clear beginning and a finite end. For example, "We dealt with the quality issue between 1988 and 1991 and transformed our processes between 1996 and 1998." Second, this way of breaking up change interventions has the effect of limiting any possibility of constructing a continuous process view of change in the organization. This in itself can limit the success potential of any change strategy that has deeper and longer-term ambitions. Breaking this episodic management approach can, however, be extremely difficult indeed—especially in engineering and retail-dominated firms, where there is often a deep culture of project and operational management.

The final success factor relates to coherence in the management of overall processes of change. Research in the U.S. and U.K. private sectors by Kanter (1983) and Pettigrew and Whipp (1991) has clearly linked segmentation and incoherence to organizational inertia, and integration and coherence to change capability. Coherence has many facets and presents many challenges. There is purposive coherence—the placing of any change program in the context of the longer directional path of the firm; business coherence—linkage of the change initiative to the short-term critical path of the business; and political and policy coherence—unity emanating from a well-chosen and interpersonally effective top management team and, crucially, from the trust and understanding fostered by sound mechanisms for linking strategic and operational change.

In today's business world the pressures for change are such that firms no longer have the luxury of handling changes sequentially. Most organizations are in the business of managing change concurrently—tackling a simultaneous change agenda on a moving stage. This kind of complexity raises real challenges: Firms struggle to maintain direction, coherence, and operational effectiveness under the strains of multifaceted change agendas (Pettigrew and Whipp 1991). A key aspect of coherence is the skill and will to focus a multifaceted change agenda onto a subset of issues that are profoundly important and not merely urgent or politically expedient. Within this limited subset may lie many change initiatives. And the boundaries between these initiatives require careful and constant monitoring and adjustment if the purposes, methods, and success criteria of one are not to get in the way of those of the others. These big issues of coherence can be overseen only by the highest level of management. The isolation and management of this metalevel task is a key factor in firms that properly treat the management of change as a means to building and sustaining competitive performance.

Linking Change to Organizational Performance

It is one thing to catalogue the interrelated factors that shape the fate of change initiatives. It is a much bigger and more intractable problem to argue that a particular pattern of change initiatives contributes to organizational performance. Small-sample studies that look at only high performers are unlikely on their own to offer convincing evidence of a change–performance link. This leaves the student of change with two options, which ideally should be combined. Option one is to carry out large-sample studies over time to elucidate any association between firms' patterns of change and their financial performance. Such a research strategy would allow us to link the what of change to firm performance, but it would tell us very little about the process and context of changing. For this second related change agenda we would need option two: an associated set of longitudinal comparative case studies with matched pairs of high- and low-performing organizations. Such case studies would allow us to answer questions about the process, context, and customization of change strategies relative to performance.

As yet there are still few longitudinal studies attempting to link change processes and practices to firm performance. A study conducted in the late 1980s by Pettigrew and Whipp (1991) examined the process of managing strategic and operational change in four mature industry and service sectors of the U.K. economy: automobiles, publishing, investment banking, and life insurance. We chose a pair of firms in each of the four sectors, making a total of eight. Each pair was made up of a higher and a lower performer in the same broad product market. This approach avoided the business literature's tendency to glorify successful organizations and allowed us to make direct comparisons between the similarities and differences in the change strategies adopted by high and low performers. We collected real-time data (documents and 150 interviews across various levels of management) in the chosen firms between 1985 and 1990. We then complemented these five years of real-time analysis with a cross-level of analysis (firm, sector, political, and economic context) of the eight organizations over the period 1960–1985. From the resulting thirty-year time series we were then able to isolate the set of interconnected factors that explained the different performance levels of the organizations. In summary, the high-performing organizations differed from the lower-performing ones in the way they (1) conducted environmental assessment, (2) led change, (3) linked strategic and operational change, (4) managed their human resources as assets and liabilities, and (5) managed coherence in the overall process of competition and change. Because we had a thirty-year time series, it was possible for us to employ these five interrelated factors in two analytic roles. We could use them both to explain the differential performance of firms in one era of business development and to account for firms' loss or gain of performance relative to their peers over time.

Such studies are still rare in management research. They require big commitments from funding bodies, teams of management researchers, and sustained cooperation from the organizations under investigation. Any particular study also has its limitations, and the major limitations of our (Pettigrew and Whipp 1991) study were the relatively small sample of firms under longitudinal investigation and the fact that the firms were located within a single economy. In more recent work we are attempting a global study of innovative forms of organizing and company performance that combines the mapping of organizational change in Europe, Japan, and the United States with detailed analysis of eighteen case studies in Europe (Pettigrew 1999; Pettigrew et al. 1999; Whittington et al. 1999).

The research is being led from Warwick Business School and is being carried out with colleagues from Oxford University, Erasmus University (the Netherlands), ESSEC (France), IESE (Spain), Jonkoping University (Sweden), St. Gallen University (Switzerland), Duke University (United States), and Hitotsubashi University (Japan).

Known as INNFORM, this program of research has three major aims:

1. to examine the extent to which new forms of organizing have been implemented among large and medium-sized firms across Europe, the United States, and Japan;

2. to test the performance effects of adopting new organizational forms; and

3. to examine the managerial processes involved in moving from more traditional forms of organizing.

These three aims encapsulate a set of progress, performance, and process questions that have required us to use a multimethod research strategy and to collect temporal data. During 1997 we mailed a standardized survey instrument to the chief executives of large and medium-sized (i.e., with more than 500 employees) independent domestically owned firms throughout western Europe. For the United Kingdom, these were the largest 1,500 independent businesses by employment; for the remainder of western Europe, these were about 2,000 large and medium-sized firms sampled in proportion to home-country GDP. The overall response rate was 13.1 percent, comparable to rates in other recent European surveys of organizational change (Coulson-Thomas and Coe 1991; Ezzamel et al. 1996). Tests for the U.K. sample indicated no response biases for size, industry, or profitability. Similar surveys in Japan also covered the time points 1992 and 1996. A U.S. survey conducted in 1998 covered the time points 1993 and 1997.

Discussion of new forms of organizing in contemporary business often rests on some well-known suppositions about the changing competitive context of business and likely firm adaptations to that context. Hitt and colleagues (1998) argue that the principal drivers of the new competitive landscape are technology on the one hand and globalization on the other. The results are hypercompetition, the blurring of industry boundaries, greater knowledge-intensity, and discontinuous change. It is suggested that this competitive landscape renders anachronistic traditional efficiency-oriented vertical structures and triggers the current search for new organizational practices in which flexibility, knowledge creation, and collaboration are essential characteristics (Brown and Eisenhardt 1998; Volberda 1996).

The process and performance aims of the INNFORM program have the dual purpose of mapping on an international scale the extent of development of new forms of organizing and testing for the performance consequences of such organizational changes. Existing empirical research on adaptations to new technology and globalization have tended to draw on oft-repeated case examples such as ABB (Bartlett and Ghoshal 1993) or GE (Tichy and Sherman 1995) and/or to portray responses in terms of ideal type forms of organizing such as the federal form (Handy 1992), the cellular form (Miles et al. 1997), or the individualized corporation (Ghoshal and Bartlett 1998). Such formulations are helpful simplifiers, but their apocalyptic tone tends (in the absence of broadly based evidence) to overstate the speed and magnitude of changes under way. The INNFORM study findings may have the potential to address such questions as: To what extent are new forms of organizing actually happening? Are any such developments supplanting or supplementing existing forms? And, in the time period of our analysis (the early to late 1990s), was the pace of change incremental or radical in character?

In the standardized survey instrument administered in Europe in 1997, we asked the chief executives of firms to indicate the character of their organization in 1992 and to compare the organization on the same indicators in 1996. We have decided to capture organizational changes under the three headings: changing structures, changing processes, and changing boundaries. Within each of these three broad areas we have in turn measured three indicators of perceived change. Figure 12-1 captures the nine indicators of change in our survey. Existing literature on new forms of organizing does much to support widespread organizational innovation in the areas of changing structures, processes, and boundaries. The literature also suggests that these moves are likely to be mutually reinforcing. Flatter structures demand more interactive processes; interaction is concentrated within more tightly drawn organizational boundaries; moreover, focus reduces the need for tall hierarchies of control. These multidimensional changes may work best together, not singly.

Structures

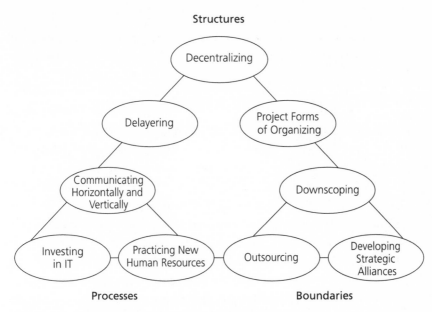

Figure 12-1   New Forms of Organizing: Multiple Indicators

Our western European results indicate widespread movement toward more fluid and decentralized organizational structures. The direction of change was not always one way, however, and movement was greater in some indicators than in others. Underlying these structural changes were considerable process changes: Firms were investing in greater horizontal and vertical interactions, facilitating these changes by big investments in information technology, and in turn supporting the hard infrastructure of IT with the soft infrastructure of personnel change. There was also evidence that new types of competition, and the new forms of organization designed to cope with them, are reshaping the scope of firms as well. Outsourcing and alliance formation increased markedly over 1992–96, with 65 percent of firms claiming increases in both indicators. Diversification trends, however, were complex, with only 11 percent of firms reducing their diversification (i.e., downscoping) over this period. Broadly, our findings indicate incremental rather than radical change in firm behavior. Firms are supplementing existing forms rather than supplanting them. Across Europe there is evidence of a common direction of change, but firms in different European countries reveal both different starting points for change and sometimes variation in the pace of change. A more detailed presentation and analysis of these trends in change are provided by Ruigrok and colleagues (1999) and Whittington and colleagues (1999).

Claims have been made for the performance benefits of all the dimensions of change with which we are concerned here. Rather than analyzing the impact of these various changes in a simple multivariate comparison (Nohria 1996), however, we are approaching performance payoffs in a more holistic fashion, using the notion of "complementarities" (Milgrom and Roberts 1990, 1995). We follow Ichniowski and colleagues (1997) by examining the performance of integrated systems of organizational variables rather than just examining pairwise relationships. In their analysis Ichniowski and colleagues (1997) proposed "four systems" of human resource practices organized in terms of a hierarchy of completeness. These researchers found the most complete system of practices to have the greatest performance effects and, when combined in the same equation, to exhaust the efforts of component variables taken individually—some of which on their own have negative impacts.

We take a similar approach. Thus, we transform individual companies' design variables into aggregate variables on the three main dimensions of organizational change—structure, processes, and boundaries. We then explore complementarities between dimensions by comparing the performance relationships of these singly and in various "system" combinations. We deemed individual companies to be either high or low on these three change dimensions according to a common set of rules (Whittington et al. 1999).

Thus, we classified the firms in our sample according to whether they were:

Changing structures	(A)
Changing processes	(B)
Changing boundaries	(C)

We found that 50 percent of the firms were making sets of boundary changes, 28 percent sets of process changes, and 20 percent sets of structural changes.

We then examined four systems of change:

System 1 (A+B+C)	4.5 percent
System 2 (A+B)	9.3 percent
System 3 (B+C)	14.3 percent
System 4 (A+C)	11.2 percent

Very few firms in our sample combine significant change on all three dimensions, as in System 1. It seems that holistic or systemic transformation is still very rare, involving less than one in twenty European firms.

Although only a few companies carried out the full multidimensional raft of innovative practices, our econometric analysis (Whittington et al. 1999) demonstrates that these System 1 firms enjoyed significant performance benefits, with a performance premium of more than 60 percent. On the other hand, firms that combined only parts of this full system of theoretically complementary practices tended to obtain no significant performance payoffs. Indeed, just combining structure and boundary changes without complementary process changes (System 4) was found to have negative effects on performance. IT investment is the only innovation taken singly that offered positive performance benefits over and above those available to the full system. And the biggest performance benefits are obtained by firms that align themselves with their strategic objectives through a systemwide set of complementary changes.

These are noteworthy findings, which in time we shall be able to confirm or disconfirm from our Japanese and U.S. surveys. However, at the moment the complementarities approach of Milgrom and Roberts (1995) is essentially static and aprocessual in character. We know little of the what, why, and how of the creation and re-creation of complementary changes in firms over time, or of how managerial choices and change processes may deliver the performance effects identified from the European survey results. In firms where complementary changes are intended or emerge, how did they evolve and why? What were the initial set of complements, why were they chosen, how were they justified, and through what processes were they embedded in the organizational consciousness? What combination of context and action, leadership, intent and "muddling through with a purpose" created the desire for this degree of change? How were any risks assessed and defrayed? Were the seeds of any complementary approach linkable back to the heavy hand of history in any particular firm or sector? What was the sequence of changes over time, and indeed was the change process overlapping or simultaneous as much as sequential? Was there any evidence of the cycling and recycling of change attempts to build the complements over the long term? How did firms reconcile the short-term need for performance improvement with the need to build long-term complements and underlying capabilities to ensure accumulating virtuous circles of performance improvement? How was any evident performance improvement explained and turned back to reinforce the continuing pursuit of holistic change?

To try and answer these major questions, the INNFORM program has carried out eighteen case studies in European firms (eight in the U.K., four in Switzerland and Germany, two in the Netherlands, and two each in Spain and Sweden). These case studies have been designed with two main objectives in mind:

1. To analyze the processes and practices of the emergence of new forms of organizing. The first eight of these case studies are published in Pettigrew and Fenton (2000).

2. To examine how and why the subset of our firms that attempted complementary change managed the process over the time period from the late 1980s to the late 1990s.

What is striking about the evidence from our case studies is that attempts to build complementary changes are also engendering dualities in the firms making such attempts. For example, our sample of cases have been investing in both hierarchies and networks, driving performance accountability upward and greater horizontal integration sideways, and centralizing and standardizing while also encouraging decentralizing and customizing. These dualities create rising levels of complexity, which in turn are being met by cries for simplification.

It is also clear that complements do not arise and develop instantaneously. There are always important tracers built into the past as well as seeds in the present and aspirations for the future. The cases also show evidence of sequential and overlapping change as well as simultaneous innovation. Building complements, sustaining them, and utilizing them to deliver performance are processes not amenable to any simple phase model of restructuring, revitalization, and renewal

(Gouillart and Kelly 1995) or of rationalization, revitalization, and re-generation (Ghoshal and Bartlett, chapter 10 of this volume). These processes defy the analytic prison of any simple language. Rather we see processes of continuity and change filled with striking intentions, bold strokes and long journeys, overlapping phases, reversals, and cycles of attentiveness and inattentiveness. But all in a relatively consistent system of thought and action, concept and delivery, characterizable as complementarities in action.

Breaking the Code of Change: Some Lessons for Research

Writing on the natural and social sciences, Webster (1994), Ziman (1994), and Gibbons and colleagues (1994) have indicated some fundamental changes in the way knowledge is produced. Changing aspects include who is involved in the production of knowledge; the process of knowledge production and types of available knowledge; and new settings and opportunities for knowledge production, dissemination, and use.

The title of John Ziman's 1994 book, *Prometheus Bound: Science in a Dynamic Steady State*, indicates his skepticism about the trends he so sharply describes. Ziman comments in his preface that many scientists and scholars look back with nostalgia to a more relaxed and spacious environment for academic research. In that bygone era scientists had social space for initiative and creativity, and time for ideas to grow and mature. There was an atmosphere receptive to debate, criticism, and innovation, and respect for specialized expertise. However, Ziman's pragmatism outweighs the "fruitless sentiment" of nostalgia: "The real question is not whether the structural transition [in knowledge production] is desirable or could have been avoided: it is how to reshape the research system to fit a new environment without losing the features that have made it so productive in the past" (pp. vii–viii).

But what are the broad elements of this structural transition in science? For Gibbons and his colleagues (1994), the move is from a Mode 1 to a Mode 2 form of knowledge production, with Mode 2 still emerging alongside Mode 1 and supplementing rather than supplanting it. Michael Gibbons and his coauthors characterize Mode 1 as discipline driven. Here the research problems are framed and solved within a disciplinary context, are set within a linear process of discovery and dissemination, involve teams that are homogeneous in terms of skills and experience, and feature discipline-directed quality control. In Mode 2 the research problem is framed in the context of application. Here research is transdiscipline driven, allows a process of diffusion to occur during knowledge production, is heterogeneous in terms of teams' skills and experience, and is more socially and politically accountable than the discipline-driven control process of Mode 1.

Eschewing an ideal type of analysis, Ziman observes a similar trend outlined by Gibbons and his associates. Thus, Ziman's picture of modern science is a tapestry of more management, more evaluation, greater interdisciplinarity, more emphasis on application, more networking and collaboration, more internationalism, and more specialization and concentration of resources. Although neither Ziman nor Gibbons and coauthors directly address the field of management research, it is clear that the trends they refer to bear on the conduct of research in management in the early 2000s. As knowledge producers we need to consider how we are to engage with the new production of knowledge, critically examine our practice of knowledge production, and take advantage of all the new opportunities this changing intellectual, social, and political context is presenting to us.

For management researchers the new competitive landscape and new forms of organizing are not just out there to be studied; they are also in here, demanding from us a new social production of knowledge. We need to address the power of "ands"—not only in recognizing and managing the dualities present as organizations seek simultaneously to build hierarchies and networks, but also as we tackle the double hurdles of scholarly quality and relevance (Pettigrew 1997). This means moving the agenda on from studies of change processes and beginning to master questions about the relationship between change processes and change outcomes. The management of performance is at the center of organizational life in the private and not-for-profit sectors. Policy and research in the performance area meet around the central but still largely unanswered question in the study of management and organizations—why do certain institutions regularly out-perform their peers? Both theory and empirical studies of complementary change are bound to be crucial in addressing this issue. Such studies now need to be conducted on a global scale to capture the what of change, and combined with longitudinal processual studies to clarify the why and how of changing. In sum, breaking the code of change also represents a big challenge for the community of scholars interested in the theory and practice of change.

References

Ascari, A., M. Rock, and S. Dutta. 1995. Re-engineering and Organizational Change: Lessons from a Comparative Analysis of Company Experiences. *European Management Journal* 13, no. 1: 1–30.

Bartlett, C., and S. Ghoshal. 1993. Beyond the M-Form: Towards a Managerial Theory of the Firm. *Strategic Management Journal* 14 (special issue): 23–46.

Bashein, B., M. L. Markus, and P. Riley. 1994. Business Process Re-engineering: Preconditions for Success and Failure. *Information Systems Management* 11 (spring): 7–13.

Beer, M., R. A. Eisenstadt, and B. Spector. 1990. *The Critical Path to Corporate Renewal*. Boston: Harvard Business School Press.

Brown, S. L., and K. Eisenhardt. 1997. The Art of Continuous Change: Linking Complexity Theory and Time-Paced Evolution in Relentlessly Shifting Organisations. *Administrative Science Quarterly* 42: 1–34.

———. 1998. *Competing on the Edge*. Boston: Harvard Business School Press.

Burns, T., and A. M. Stalker. 1961. *The Management of Innovation*. London: Tavistock.

Coulson-Thomas, C., and T. Coe. 1991. *The Flat Organization*. London: British Institute of Management.

The Cracks in Quality. 1992. *The Economist* (18 April): 67–68.

Evans, P., and Y. Doz. 1992. A Paradigm for Human Resource and Organization Development in Complex Multinationals. In *Globalizing Management*, ed. V. Pucik, N. M. Tichy, and C. V. Bartlett. New York: Wiley.

Ezzamel, M., S. Lilley, and H. Willmott. 1996. The View from the Top: Senior Executives' Perceptions of Changing Management Practices in UK Companies. *British Journal of Management* 7, no. 2: 155–168.

Gersick, C. J. G. 1994. Pacing Strategic Change: The Case of a New Venture. *Academy of Management Journal* 37: 9–45.

Ghoshal, S., and C. A. Bartlett. 1998. *The Individualised Corporation*. London: Heinemann.

Gibbons, M., C. Limoges, H. Notwotny, S. Schwartzman, P. Scott, and M. Trow. 1994. *The New Production of Knowledge*. London: Sage.

Gouillart, F. J., and J. N. Kelly. 1995. *Transforming the Organization*. New York: McGraw-Hill.

Greenwood, R., and C. R. Hinings. 1996. Understanding Radical Change: Bringing Together the Old and the New Institutionalism. *Academy of Management Review* 21, no. 4: 1022–1054.

Hampden-Turner, C. 1981. *Maps of the Mind: Charts and Concepts of the Mind and Its Labyrinths.* New York: Collier.

Handy, C. 1992. Balancing Corporate Power: A New Federalist Paper. *Harvard Business Review* (November–December): 59–72.

Hitt, M. A., B. Keats, and S. M. DeMarie. 1998. Navigating in the New Competitive Landscape: Building Strategic Flexibility and Competitive Advantage in the 21st Century. *Academy of Management Executive* 12, no. 4: 22–42.

Hodgkinson, G., and G. Johnson. 1994. Exploring the Mental Modes of Competitive Strategists. *Journal of Management Studies* 31, no. 4: 525–551.

Huff, A., ed. 1990. *Mapping Strategic Thought.* Chichester, UK: Wiley.

Ichniowski, C., K. Shaw, and G. Prenushi. 1997. The Effects of Human Resource Management Practices on Productivity: A Study of Steel Finishing Lines. *American Economic Review* (June): 291–314.

Janssens, A., and C. Steyaert. 1999. The World in Two and a Third Way Out? The Concept of Duality in Organization Theory and Practice. *Scandinavian Journal of Management* 15: 121–139.

Kanter, R. 1983. *The Change Masters: Corporate Entrepreneurs at Work.* New York: Counterpoint.

Kessler, E. H., and A. K. Chakrabarti. 1996. Innovation Speed: A Conceptual Model of Context, Antecedents and Outcomes. *Academy of Management Review* 21, no. 4: 1143–1191.

Lawrence, P. R., and J. W. Lorsch. 1967. *Organization and Environment.* Boston: Harvard University Press.

Lewin, A. Y., C. P. Long, and T. N. Carroll. 1999. The Co-Evolution of New Organization Forms. *Organization Science* (October): 4.

March, J. G. 1999. *Organizational Intelligence.* Oxford: Blackwell.

Miles, R. E., C. C. Snow, J. A. Matthews, and H. J. Coleman. 1997. Organizing in the Knowledge Age: Anticipating the Cellular Form. *Academy of Management Executive* 11: 4, 7–20.

Milgrom, P., and J. Roberts. 1990. The Economics of Modern Manufacturing. *American Economic Review* 80, no. 3: 511–528.

———. 1995. Complementarities and Fit: Strategy, Structure and Organizational Change in Manufacturing. *Journal of Accounting and Economics* 19, no. 2/3: 179–208.

Nohria, N. 1996. From the M-Form to the N-Form: Taking Stock of Changes in the Large Industrial Corporation. Working paper 96.054, Harvard Business School Division of Research, Boston.

Peters, T. J., and R. H. Waterman. 1982. *In Search of Excellence: Lessons from America's Best Run Companies.* New York: Harper and Row.

Pettigrew, A. M. 1973. *The Politics of Organizational Decision Making.* London: Tavistock.

———. 1975. Towards a Political Theory of Organizational Intervention. *Human Relations* 28: 191–208.

———. 1985. *The Awakening Giant: Continuity and Change in ICI.* Oxford: Blackwell.

———. 1987. Context and Action in the Transformation of the Firm. *Journal of Management Studies* 24, no. 6: 649–670.

———. 1990. Longitudinal Field Research on Change: Theory and Practice. *Organization Science* 3: 267–292.

———. 1997. The Double Hurdles for Management Research. In *Advancement in Organizational Behavior: Essays in Honour of Derek S. Pugh*, ed. T. Clarke. London: Dartmouth Press.

———. 1999. Organizing to Improve Company Performance. Warwick Business School Hot Topics Paper, 1, 5. February.

Pettigrew, A. M., E. F. Ferlie, and L. McKee. 1992. *Shaping Strategic Change.* London: Sage.

Pettigrew, A. M., S. Massini, and T. Numagami. 1999. Innovative Forms of Organizing in Europe and Japan. Working paper, CCSC. Coventry, UK: Warwick Business School.

Pettigrew, A. M., and R. Whipp. 1991. *Managing Change for Competitive Success.* Oxford: Blackwell.

Pettigrew, A. M., and E. Fenton, eds. 2000. *The Innovating Organization.* London: Sage.

Ruigrok, W., A. M. Pettigrew, S. Peck, and R. Whittington. 1999. Corporate Restructuring and New Forms of Organising: Evidence from Europe. *Management International Review* 39 (special issue): 41–64.

Sastry, M. A. 1997. Problems and Paradoxes in a Model of Punctuated Organizational Change. *Administrative Science Quarterly* 42: 237–275.

Tichy, N. M., and S. Sherman. 1995. *Control Your Destiny or Someone Else Will: How Jack Welch Is Making General Electric the World's Most Competitive Corporation.* New York: HarperCollins.

Van de Ven, A. H., H. L. Angle, and M. S. Poole. 1989. *Research on the Management of Innovation.* New York: Ballinger/Harper and Row.

Volberda, H. W. 1996. Toward the Flexible Form: How to Remain Vital in Hypercompetitive Markets. *Organization Science* 7, no. 4: 359–374.

Webster, A. 1994. International Evaluation of Academic–Industry Relations: Contexts and Analysis. *Science and Public Policy* 21: 72–78.

Whittington, R., A. M. Pettigrew, S. Peck, E. Fenton, and M. Conyon. 1999. Change and Complementarities in the New Competitive Landscape: A European Panel Study, 1992–1996. *Organization Science* (October): 4.

Ziman J. 1994. *Prometheus Bound: Science in a Dynamic Steady State.* Cambridge, UK: Cambridge University Press.

SECTION V

MOTIVATION FOR CHANGE
Do Financial Incentives Lead, or Do They Lag and Support?

T HERE ARE VIRTUALLY no fundamental changes in organizations that do not also involve some changes in the reward system. The reward system consists, of course, of multiple levers, from informal and intangible rewards such as recognition and political support to more formal arrangements such as the promotion and financial incentive system. In the 1990s financial incentives became an important and often the central motivating mechanism in change management. But this general consensus about the importance of financial incentives raises the question of whether incentives should be utilized to drive change early in the change cycle, or employed later in the change cycle to support earlier inventions.

Karen Wruck argues not only that financial incentives are important but that they must play a leading and central role in motivating change. She uses in-depth case studies to argue that misalignment of rewards in the old order creates dissatisfaction. And this dissatisfaction, she contends, is essential for behavior to change, particularly given the defensive routines in organizations that enable management to rationalize old assumptions and behavior. Financial incentive systems, Wruck posits, work to improve the economic value of the firm by (1) improving productivity, (2) promoting productive turnover in personnel, (3) mobilizing valuable specific knowledge by allowing ef-

fective decentralization, and (4) helping overcome organizational inertia and opposition to change. Wruck argues that all of these interdependent factors demonstrate how incentives help create economic
value, which she regards as the principal objective of the firm.

Gerald Ledford maintains that although financial incentives
should be employed to manage change, they should be used as a lag
intervention. Through a case study of change, he illustrates how financial incentives used too early may motivate behavior that is later
discovered to be inappropriate. Ledford holds that the definition of
strategy and consensus about it must come first. Because strategy, according to scholars such as Henry Mintzberg, emerges from the interaction of the firm with its environment as opposed to being created
through planning, early commitment to an incentive scheme may have
unintended and undesirable effects. In addition, a change in the financial incentive scheme does not occur without much controversy and
considerable investment of time and money as well as the potential
erosion of trust and commitment—another argument made for delaying changes in incentives until later in the change cycle. Of course,
embedded in this argument is the assumption that management will
employ other interventions early in the change process to motivate required behavior.

Ed Lawler provides a synthesis for Wruck and Ledford's opposing
views. He offers a contingency framework, arguing that the timing and
type of compensation system a firm employs depend on the firm's need
to (1) develop motivation for change, (2) facilitate implementation
through requisite skill enhancement and learning development, or (3)
motivate operational effectiveness once the firm has been realigned
with new economic goals and strategy.

13

COMPENSATION, INCENTIVES, AND ORGANIZATIONAL CHANGE

Ideas and Evidence from Theory and Practice

Karen Hopper Wruck

ACADEMICS AND practitioners from a wide range of backgrounds agree that bringing about sustainable, productive change in organizations is difficult. They disagree, however, on why this is the case. Consequently, they disagree on the most effective approaches to analyzing and solving organizational problems, and on the most effective approaches to implementing solutions. At the heart of the disagreement are differences over the factors that motivate individuals to change their behavior. Behavioral changes on the part of individuals are required for organizational change, and compensation systems affect behavior. Thus, it is critical to consider the role that compensation systems play in the process of organizational change.

To discuss the ways in which compensation systems facilitate effective organizational change, I must first define what I mean by productive or effective change. (I will use the two terms interchangeably.) *Productive change* is not a normative term subject to interpretation. In other words, it is not based on whether or not various individuals or groups think a particular change effort is good or bad, fair or unfair, painless or painful. Productive change is change that creates value for the organization and its owners, and in doing so creates value for society.

Because resources, including human resources, are scarce, social welfare depends on the ability of organizations and individuals to utilize resources efficiently or, equivalently, in ways that create value. A firm creates value when the value of the goods and services it produces is greater than the value of the resources it consumes. Assuming that prices accurately reflect the costs and benefits to society of the consumption of a particular resource, the value created by a firm is value created for society. This is the case in the absence of externalities and monopolies, and in the presence of well-functioning markets.[1]

This chapter will show why establishing a strong, positive relation between rewards and performance is critical to bringing about value-creating organizational change. Thus, if a firm's incumbent compensation systems do not tie rewards to strong performance *as it is defined in the new regime*, they must be redesigned. I will argue that this redesign can and should be implemented early in the change process. By early I mean *after* managers identify and adopt an overarching objective for the firm, but *before* they have completely specified how that objective translates into a new strategy and/or structure.

The ways in which effectively designed and implemented compensation systems help organizations create value can be grouped into four broad categories. Specifically, effective compensation systems

1. improve the motivation and productivity of employees,

2. promote productive turnover in personnel,

3. mobilize valuable specific knowledge by allowing effective decentralization, and

4. help overcome organizational inertia and opposition to change.

In the rest of this chapter, I will examine each of the four ways in which changes in compensation systems promote productive organizational change. Clearly, there is interdependence among the four items. For example, overcoming organizational rigidities helps bring about productive changes in individual and group behavior. Other interdependencies will become obvious in the discussion that follows. Nonetheless, each of the four ways in which compensation systems work to bring about change can be productively discussed as a separate mechanism.

Before I continue, it is important to point out that by *compensation system* I do not mean simply monetary payment. This definition is far too narrow to encompass all the things that human beings value or detest about organizational life, and so cannot capture all that affects their motivation and incentives. Rather, I define rewards and punishments broadly to encompass both the monetary and the nonmonetary. Thus, rewards and punishments include the satisfaction or dissatisfaction generated by participation in one's job, including the benefits of changes that make a job easier or safer, public recognition, the value of interactions and relationships with peers, raises, promotions, bonuses, profit-sharing plans, and equity ownership programs. All these items are valued by individuals and so provide motivation and incentives.

For managers considering the redesign of their firm's compensation systems, however, monetary rewards are a strong place to start—not because individuals value money over other types of rewards, but because money represents a claim over the goods and services that employees value. This means that employees can take the rewards from their work and spend them in a way that exactly meets their preferences. Thus, in general monetary rewards provide more flexibility and likely more utility for employees per dollar expended than less flexible rewards. Put differently, monetary rewards set in motion a decentralized process that allows each employee, at relatively low cost, to tailor rewards to his or her preferences. The only other alternative that provides such flexibility is for the managers to learn the tastes and preferences of individual employees and reward them accordingly—an approach too costly to be feasible.

I also want to make clear that my position is *not* that a redesign of compensation systems is the only necessary change a firm must make to turn its performance around. Neither is it my position that if the appropriate changes in compensation systems are implemented, all else will follow. Indeed, some of the organizations I have studied attempted to follow this approach. It ended in disaster.[2] To foster effective and lasting change, however, it is ultimately necessary to bring about changes in human behavior, ideally at all levels of the organization. Individuals, alone or in groups, are the ones who will identify and implement solutions to the problems facing an organization. And it is individuals who will prosper or decline as a result of the organization's success or failure. This makes individuals—their motivation, incentives, and the effectiveness of their learning and communication—the most important element in the change equation. Compensation systems, through their influence on individual behavior, play a pivotal role in the change process.

Finally, it is worth pointing out that the relation (or lack thereof) between pay and performance affects behavior in all organizations. All organizations have rewards and punishments. All individuals, groups, and business units have performance. It is natural to observe whether and how the two are related, and to draw inferences from these observations. It is clear, then, that managers do not get to choose whether or not their organization will have a reward and punishment system that affects the motivation, incentives, learning, and communication of their employees. But they do have a choice about whether and how to manage it.

Throughout this paper I use ideas and evidence from practice. I present these examples to illustrate not what is typical but what is possible—the bad and especially the good. It is my hope that these examples will stimulate both ideas and action among scholars and practicing managers.

I draw my examples from a broad range of sources including press reports, research articles, books, and my own studies of organizations in the process of change. In particular, I draw on the experiences of two companies I have studied in depth: Cooper Cameron and Cytec Industries. In my analysis of Cooper Cameron, I draw heavily on a study I conducted with Steve Kaplan and Mark Mitchell.[3] In my analysis of Cytec, I rely on a series of cases written with Sherry Roper.[4] All three of these coauthors deserve special thanks for their contributions to this paper.

Both Cooper Cameron and Cytec are publicly traded on the New York Stock Exchange. In 1998 they had sales of $1.9 billion and $1.4 billion, respectively. Each firm became public following a spin-off from a larger, better-known parent company: Cytec in December 1993 from American Cyanamid (acquired by American Home Products in 1996) and Cooper Cameron in July 1995 from Cooper Industries (publicly traded on the NYSE).

What makes Cooper Cameron and Cytec particularly interesting for students of organizational change is that they both have long histories as businesses, but short histories as independent public companies.

Cooper Cameron is in oil field service and petroleum equipment production. Its oldest business was founded in 1921. Cytec is a spin-off of American Cyanamid's specialty chemicals businesses. American Cyanamid was founded in 1907 as an agricultural chemicals company. By the 1920s, it had diversified into specialty chemicals.

Following their spin-offs, managers at both Cooper Cameron and Cytec faced a major challenge. Their companies could not be successful public companies if they continued to operate according to the status quo. For one thing, each of them had a history of operating losses and therefore of being "subsidized" by the parent firm's other operations. Major organizational change was necessary, and it had to occur quickly. There was no longer a parent organization to provide cover and support. The challenge was particularly tough because both firms operated in very competitive, highly cyclical industries.

Because each firm had a long history, there was baggage from the past to overcome along many dimensions, from culture to organization structure to relationships with customers. Because each company was independent, however, managers were unconstrained as to the approaches they could take to facilitate effective change. They did not have to concern themselves, as do managers of large divisions of larger public companies, with how their approaches would be received by headquarters. Neither did they have to consider whether or not their policies and practices were consistent with policies and practices set at some higher level of the organization. Thus, their change efforts provide a fascinating laboratory in which to observe what is possible at well-established companies in the absence of internally imposed constraints—and, of course, in the absence of internal support to the extent it would have existed.

As public companies, both spin-off firms produced dramatic turnarounds in operating performance. Between 1995 and 1998, the first four years following its spin-off, Cooper Cameron's operating profit before depreciation (OPBD) increased more than fourfold from $79 million to $323 million. Four years after its spin-off, Cytec had moved from an OPBD of –$95 million (1993) to $216 million (1996). By 1998 Cytec's OPBD had increased to $264 million.[5] Both firms had only modest increases in their asset base during this time, so the performance improvement is attributable largely to improvements in operating efficiency. This performance is outstanding, even relative to that of other spin-off firms.[6] Looking in detail at the ways in which managers brought about this improvement is, therefore, one way to learn about cutting-edge practice.

The discussion that follows is structured around the four ways in which compensation systems facilitate productive organizational change, as enumerated above.

Compensation Systems, Motivation, and Productivity

The most straightforward of the four ways in which compensation systems facilitate organizational change is through their effect on the motivation and productivity of individuals in the organization. Although the effect of compensation systems on motivation and behavior has historically been the subject of debate, researchers today generally agree that compensation systems encourage individuals to engage in more of the behaviors that are rewarded and fewer of behaviors that are punished. Edward Lawler of the University of Southern California and his colleagues have conducted perhaps the most comprehensive set of studies on the effects of compensation systems on behavior. Summarizing the findings of this work, Lawler states that "when pay is based on performance it can be a powerful motivator. . . . My research over the years has consistently shown that rewards can have a major impact on employee motivation and the skills that individuals develop (or do not). As a result, [rewards] can have a critical impact on an organization's effectiveness."[7]

This is not to say that compensation systems are always designed in a way that elicits productive behaviors and wise decision making. There are numerous examples of rewards systems that lead to counterproductive behaviors, ranging from the top levels of organizations to their shop floors. Perhaps the most famous examples are situations in which compensation systems have been alleged to have played roles in motivating individuals to commit fraud. In the world of finance, for example, rogue traders Nick Leeson of Baring Brothers (now liquidating) and Joseph Jett of Kidder, Peabody (later acquired by General Electric) engaged in trading that was disastrous in the longer run, but generated substantial cash bonuses for the traders in the short run.[8] An older but classic example in the case of Heinz, where managers engaged in accounting fraud to achieve profit targets.[9]

There are also many examples from manufacturing environments where individual piece-rate compensation (in environments where quality could not be easily monitored and/or where group cooperation was valuable) rewarded poor performance. Perhaps the best-documented study was conducted by Donald Roy, who found a reduction in productivity of 36 percent due to the perverse incentives provided by a poorly administered piece-rate system.[10] Disastrous occurrences along these lines led a number of quality gurus to dismiss all pay-for-performance systems as counterproductive.[11] A conclusion that, although understandable, is incorrect.[12]

A more sensible interpretation of the evidence on compensation systems, offered by George Baker, Michael Jensen, and Kevin Murphy (1988), among others, is not that compensation systems don't work but that they work too well.[13] Put in simplistic terms, in organizations you get what you pay for in terms of individual behavior. Thus, I suggest that a firm's incumbent compensation system is a terrific place to look to understand an organization's current state of affairs. Until an organization redesigns its compensation system, which in many organizations becomes a sacred cow, undesirable behaviors and poor decision making will either persist or, after a brief period of change, resurface.

Below, I examine compensation systems at Cooper Cameron and Cytec. Pre-spinoff, there was a substantial gap between desired and actual behavior at all levels of the organization. The gap can be explained by elements of the compensation system that were "hidden" from top management's view. These hidden elements were not explicit parts of the reward system, but they affected behavior and morale, nonetheless. Identifying compensation's hidden elements is an important part of the organizational change process. It leads to a better understanding of current behavior and provides a basis for the design of a more effective compensation system.

Uncovering the Hidden Elements of Compensation

Part of what makes compensation systems difficult to manage is that the minutiae matter. It is the details of the design, implementation, and administration of a compensation system that determine its success or failure. We know that there are many ways to misunderstand, misdesign, and mismanage compensation systems. What is less well understood, but equally important, is that managers often do not have a full understanding of how their compensation system is actually functioning. This is because in addition to the explicit and actively designed part of the system, there is an additional implicit or hidden part that takes on a life of its own. And this hidden part can overwhelm the system.

Both Cooper Cameron and Cytec managers reported that the compensation system of their former parent firm was ineffective. The ineffectiveness stemmed not from the explicit design of the compensation system but from the hidden part. In other words, the unintended consequences of the reward and punishment system were the dominant drivers of behavior. Following their spin-offs, top managers of both firms addressed this problem immediately by implementing new and very different compensation systems that provided incentives for productive organizational change. These incentives were not present in the parent firms.

The two critical elements of Cooper Industries' compensation system were its reliance on the Hay system and its program to assess management performance, called the Management Development and Planning (MD&P) program.[14] Under the Hay system each job is assigned a number of points based on measures of job size, including number of persons managed and size of the budget under a manager's control. The objective of the system is to allow cross-job comparisons to assure that the firm is paying similar compensation to managers with similar jobs. Cooper Industries' top managers viewed the Hay system as valuable, because its uniform pay scales allowed managers to move equitably between divisions.

Unfortunately, one hidden consequence of the Hay system is that it creates incentives for managers to increase personnel and other resources under their control. Under the Hay system, increasing the size of your job increases your compensation. Taken in combination with Cooper Industries' long-established strategy of growth through acquisition, the Hay system resulted in a situation in which the company rewarded managers for empire building, in effect growing the firm beyond its optimal size. While empirically establishing the optimal size of an organization is not possible, the findings of my study with Kaplan and Mitchell are consistent with the hypothesis that Cooper Industries did indeed destroy value by becoming too large.

Cooper Industries' MD&P program also had an undesired hidden effect on motivation. Under MD&P each manager developed detailed goals for the forthcoming year. Based on an assessment of his or her attainment of these goals, a manager could earn a bonus of up to 20 percent to 40 percent of base salary (depending on rank). Cooper Industries' top managers viewed the MD&P program as extremely valuable, because it "uncovered existing or potential management gaps and identified people worthy of succession."[15]

But in interviews conducted with Cooper Cameron managers, a different picture of the compensation system emerged. In general, Cooper Cameron's managers experienced Cooper Industries' bonus allocations as independent of performance—theirs or the company's. MD&P was, therefore, a source more of frustration than of motivation. Here is a sample of managers' comments:

> There is one word that best describes Cooper's compensation system: mystery. It was an absolute mystery. I never knew why my salary was what it was. Bonuses were even more mysterious.

> Cooper paid bonuses, but no one knew why they got what they got. It was kind of like getting a Christmas turkey.

> We commiserated about it all the time. We would cry on each other's shoulders; we didn't understand it. We put trust in the division president to get us a decent bonus.

Cytec managers also described hidden aspects of their former parent firm's compensation plan that provided poor incentives.[16] The most frequent mentioned feature was an inward-looking mentality focused on making one's superior "happy." Although taking actions to improve performance will sometimes be highly correlated with one's superior's happiness, this will not always be the case. And in cases of conflict between the two, it was clear to Cytec managers which one the typical American Cyanamid employee would choose. An important part of compensation at American Cyanamid was job security, and the company attracted individuals who valued this characteristic. Perhaps not surprisingly, Cytec managers described American Cyanamid's culture as bureaucratic and conservative. Many reported that a job-for-life mentality was common among employees at all levels of the organization, and that people were not held accountable for the outcome of their decisions. For example, one top manager commented:

> When I was working as a division manager in the late 1980s, one of the things I had to do was to bring in a guy and tell him that we were selling his business and that he was going with it. He was really upset. The reason was that he just couldn't contemplate the possibility of leaving Cyanamid.
>
> When someone is that worried about staying at a company, they start to care more about making their boss happy than about making the right decisions. They aren't willing to take risks, even when it's the right thing to do. That's how it was at Cyanamid.

Another Cytec top manager expressed the following view:

> Cyanamid was very inwardly focused. By necessity a lot of energy was devoted to feeding information upward. I didn't spend as much time on it as others did, and sometimes that was a problem. . . . People tried to figure out what management's vision was and then tried to please them.

It is difficult to imagine that substantive organizational change could have taken place in either organization without substantial revamping of both the explicit and the hidden compensation systems. Had change efforts taken place in the face of Cooper Industries' "mysterious" compensation system or of American Cyanamid's system based on pleasing one's superior, they would likely have come to naught or generated only temporary change.

A Brief Comment on Other Streams of Research

There are at least two well-known streams of research on compensation on which I have not relied because subsequent researchers have refuted their validity. The Hawthorne experiments, conducted in the 1920s and 1930s, established the first stream of research. The Hawthorne researchers concluded that the social aspects of work are more important to productivity than economic rewards or physical aspects of the work environment.[17] Their work was and is highly influential, launching the "human relations approach" to human resources management.

Subsequent researchers critiqued the experimental design and reanalyzed the data generated by the Hawthorne studies. Their work demonstrated that in many instances the experiments strengthened the relation between pay and performance. The original researchers did not intend for this to be the case. Nonetheless, this later finding raised the possibility that observed increases in productivity were attributable to economic rewards rather than to the social aspects of work. In addition, increased information feedback, rest pauses and shorter hours were also associated with increased rates of output.[18]

The second stream of work contends that extrinsic rewards—that is, rewards originating from external sources, including compensation—actually *reduce* productivity. Underlying this analysis is a "hydraulic" model of motivation. Under the hydraulic model, extrinsic motivators, in particular monetary rewards, drive out intrinsic motivation. Primary research supporting a hydraulic model of motivation was conducted by Edward L. Deci and popularized by others, most notably Alfie Kohn.[19]

Subsequent researchers, however, produced evidence inconsistent with Deci's work and Kohn's interpretation of it. Edward Lawler, for example, reports that his research "contradicts the thinking of those motivational theorists who argue that pay systems can only be a source of dissatisfaction and that they cannot motivate employees to perform at a high level."[20] Teresa Amabile, whose work on creativity Kohn (incorrectly) cited as evidence supporting his view of motivation, finds that appropriately administered extrinsic rewards enhance rather than diminish creativity in the workplace.[21] In summary, it is well established that both intrinsic and extrinsic motivation contribute positively to productivity.

Although both intrinsic and extrinsic motivation are important, as a practical matter it is sensible for managers to focus primarily on extrinsic rewards. Extrinsic rewards do pose a management challenge, but they are simpler to understand and work with than the intrinsic: It would be infeasible to gain insight into all the factors affecting the intrinsic motivation of each individual in the firm's employ.

Compensation Systems and Productive Turnover

Compensation systems serve as a selection device, or a way to attract and retain individuals with the desired skill and attribute set, to an organization.[22] It stands to reason, therefore, that changes in a compensation system will change the set of individuals that are attracted to and retained by the organization. When managers' goal is to transform an organization, part of that transformation involves turnover of personnel. Individuals who cannot work well or do not enjoy working in the new environment will leave. Individuals who were not attracted to the old environment may well be attracted are to the new. Such turnover is desirable and will positively influence the performance of the firm.

The redesign of compensation systems is a powerful mechanism that decentralizes the turnover process. It does so by capitalizing on the process through which individuals self-select in or out of an organization. If individuals know more about their own skills and abilities than do potential employers, relying on self-selection will help the firm attract and retain a better workforce.

A few examples, somewhat oversimplified, help illustrate how self-selection through compensation systems works. For example, for a firm where long-term employment is valuable, a compensation system offering a wage profile that is low relative to market in the early years of employment and high later on will attract individuals planning on a long career with the firm. It will not attract individuals who, for example, plan to work for a short time before returning to graduate school. A compensation system with a strong pay-for-performance component will attract individuals who believe they can perform in a way that will allow them to earn the payoff. But individuals who know that their skills will not allow them to achieve the payoff will view the expected compensation as low. To such individuals an organization offering less contingent pay would be more attractive.[23]

Managers undertaking change efforts can harness the power of compensation system design to attract and retain the "right" individuals, and to help individuals who do not work well in the new regime select out of the firm. The sooner a new, effective compensation system is implemented, the sooner this process can begin. Postponing the implementation of new compensation systems forces managers to live with the counterproductive effects of the incumbent system on productivity and self-selection.

The Power of Self-Selection in Practice

The experience of our spin-off firms confirms the importance of the design of compensation systems in attracting managers with the "right" characteristics and motivating them to create value. Each firm faced a different challenge. In the case of Cooper Cameron, the challenge was to attract talented top managers from outside the parent firm to join the soon-to-be-independent company. In the case of Cytec, the challenge was to attract the "right" group of incumbent managers to lead the spin-off.

Cooper Cameron's CEO and CFO were both hired from outside the firm six months before the spin-off. At that time these individuals were serving as CEO and CFO, respectively, for a public company in a related industry that was in the process of being sold. These hires brought Cooper Cameron depth of management and years of experience in running a publicly traded company. The CEO and CFO are individuals who, by their own admission, would not have considered working as division managers. Thus, making Cooper Cameron a freestanding public company granted it access to a new pool of managerial talent. Cooper Industries' top management felt that this infusion of experience and skill was necessary to turn around Cameron's performance.

The new top managers have strong views on the type of compensation package that is both attractive to them and best for the firm. It is based on an approach to executive compensation that is very different from Cooper Industries' "mysterious" bonuses. The new compensation system relies heavily on bonuses tied to objective performance goals and on equity-based compensation. In fact, the CEO and CFO insisted that they be compensated *solely in stock options*. The year following the spin-off, top managers and directors owned 4.87% of

Cooper Cameron's stock—almost 6.5 times more than the corresponding total for Cooper Industries.[24]

At Cytec, the power of self-selection became apparent when American Cyanamid began to put together a top management team for the soon-to-be-independent company. Some managers had a choice of whether to go with the spin-off or continue with American Cyanamid—and not all of them chose to go. Self-selection based on the firms' compensation system was an important determinant of who went to work at the spin-off firm. Among the concerns expressed by managers were job security, benefits, and the structure of pay packages. Taking a position at Cytec required giving up a generous Cyanamid retirement and benefits plan; taking on a pay package that was riskier, because it was strongly tied to stock price performance; and giving up what was expected to be a "job for life."[25] The decision to go to Cytec revealed a great deal about individuals' willingness to take on risk and about their confidence in their ability to manage effectively in a challenging situation.

Cytec's top management comprised nine former Cyanamid managers, each with a long career at the former parent. In fact, taken together Cytec's top management team had 193 years of work experience at Cyanamid. Nonetheless, Cytec's top executives identified themselves as individuals who were not of the Cyanamid mold—they described themselves as more entrepreneurial and more confident of their abilities. Their subsequent performance lends credibility to their self-assessment. As one executive put it:

> What's surprising about our spin-off is that although the management team is steeped in experience with Cyanamid, we wanted to make radical changes. . . . On paper, we didn't look any different than many Cyanamid managers, but we were. We were mavericks.

Cytec's top management believed that the design of their pay package would help create a performance-oriented culture and improve the firm's performance. The new management compensation package consisted of three components: salary, an annual bonus, and long-term compensation. The long-term compensation plan ran for three years and was based on targeted earnings and cash flow. Awards under the long-term plan consisted of grants of restricted stock (called performance shares) and cash payouts (called performance cash). Salaries and target bonuses were set below the industry median and were paid in cash. Long-term compensation was set between the median and the 75th percentile. This combination meant that a larger portion of management compensation was "at risk" than the industry norm. Nonemployee directors also received stock and stock options as part of their compensation. Cytec's CEO commented:

> I am very pleased to have the lowest salary of my peer group and one of the best upside packages. Our compensation plan reflects our management philosophy. If we create value for shareholders, we do well. If we don't, we do poorly.

As part of its change in compensation systems, the company encouraged equity ownership at all levels of the organization. Employees could purchase Cytec stock through a savings plan in which the company matched every $1 invested with an additional $0.75. By the end of 1994, the year after the spin-off, employees had purchased approximately 14 percent of the company's stock.

Not everyone, however, preferred the experience of working in the "new" organization to working for American Cyanamid. Following its spin-off, Cytec experienced substantial turnover in its management ranks. But not all managers, particularly lower-level managers, had had the right to choose whether or not to go with the spin-off; so perhaps this turnover is not surprising. We would expect individuals who did not like or could not adjust to the new work environment to leave the organization, some voluntarily and some involuntarily.

In the final analysis, managers viewed the turnover as beneficial to the organization's change efforts. Cytec's chief financial officer explained:

> Some people were so "Cyanamized" they just couldn't change. Every time you wanted to try something new there was a fight.

Another top manager explained why, in his view, the turnover was both necessary and productive:

> Ultimately, two thirds of the general managers and a somewhat smaller proportion of the top management team had to change. We

struggled a lot with trying to be compassionate and giving people enough time to change. It was a difficult call, in part because in the beginning, before we had established ourselves, we ran the risk of having too many new people too early. In the end, we might have been too compassionate, because the reality was that people had to leave in order for the organization to change.

The Details Matter: When Self-Selection Backfires

Again, it is worth emphasizing that managers must pay close attention to the details of the design, implementation, and administration of a compensation system. These details also determine the success or failure of a compensation system as a selection mechanism. Although the optimal amount of turnover is not zero, not all turnover is good. Compensation systems can be set up in a way that induces turnover among the wrong group of people. For example, in an effort to reduce the size of the workforce, many organizations adopt voluntary early retirement packages that pay generous severance; but managers often express dismay that the "wrong people" take the package. And a 1991 Conference Board study confirms that it is not uncommon for self-selection to backfire. In a survey of employees of downsized firms, 22 percent reported that the "wrong people" had left the company.[26] It is simple to explain why this happens. Talented individuals with strong alternative employment opportunities can take an early retirement package and move on to another rewarding job. To individuals with more limited alternatives, the retirement package is less attractive.

For example, in 1991 General Motors announced that it would cut 74,000 jobs, among them a substantial number of white-collar positions. The company relied on attrition and an early retirement package. By 1993 12,000 white-collar workers had left the firm. Analysts noted, however, that "the problem is that the wrong people are taking the buyouts." To counter this problem, GM eliminated that program and introduced a new program that required departures to be approved on a case-by-case basis. An analyst commented that "the approval process will keep the most valued employees from leaving. It may also prevent labor shortages caused when too many people leave a certain business unit within GM."[27]

Compensation Systems, Decentralization, and the Mobilization of Specific Knowledge

The power and productivity of decentralized decision making has been widely recognized. Studies of organizational change are replete with examples illustrating the benefits organizations reap through effective decentralization.[28] Indeed, numerous organizational change movements, including total quality management, employee empowerment efforts, and increased reliance on self-managed teams, rely on the effectiveness of decentralized decision making as a path to improved performance. What is often overlooked is the fact that the redesign of a firm's compensation system is a key determinant of whether efforts to decentralize are productive or counterproductive.

Well-designed compensation systems play a critical role in both mobilizing the benefits and controlling the costs of decentralization. A primary benefit of decentralization is better decision making due to improved utilization of specific knowledge. By specific knowledge I mean knowledge that is both valuable to decision making and cost to transfer among individuals.[29] Each individual in an organization has specific knowledge regarding his or her work and, in addition, the ability to create more knowledge. The fundamental characteristic of specific knowledge is its lack of transferability; it cannot be communicated to coworkers or managers without destroying or diminishing its value. It is impossible, therefore, for managers to specify with precision what each individual must do differently to bring about effective change. Thus, change efforts can harness valuable specific knowledge only by decentralizing decision making, at least to some extent.

Decentralization would pose few problems if all employees were so-called "perfect agents"; that is, individuals whose own interests automatically aligned themselves with the objective of the organization. This is, however, not the case. By definition, decentralizing decision making allows individuals more discretion; and because they are self-interested, this discretion increases the potential for individuals to make decisions that are at odds with the goals of the organization.[30] Successful change efforts require that individuals become informed, educated, and motivated to mobilize their valuable specific knowledge to move the organization toward its new objective. A well-designed compensation system is the most important tool managers have to align the objective of the individual employee with the objective of the organization. It follows that a new compensation system is a necessary complement to a new allocation of decision rights. Managers who leave their compensation systems untouched run the risk of exacerbating, rather than solving, their firm's performance problems.

Our spin-off firms illustrate the importance of compensation system design in determining firm performance. What is remarkable about the turnaround efforts led by the managers of these firms is that they were not undertaken after intensive internal studies or studies performed by outside consultants revealed problems of which managers were formerly unaware. The changes were made, in large part, based on knowledge that had been present in the organization for many years. A critical difference, credited by managers, was a new compensation system that mobilized the effective use of that knowledge. The experience of these firms illustrates what is possible in organizations when existing specific knowledge is mobilized effectively. Their pre-spin-off performance illustrates the converse: how value can be destroyed by a company's failure to utilize knowledge effectively.

In general, increased decentralization requires a tighter link between pay and performance, and relatedly a focus on measuring performance outcomes rather than monitoring inputs (such as effort or specific actions taken). For this kind of compensation system to be effective, employees must have or develop the skills necessary to make good decisions and solve problems as they arise. If the requisite skills are not there, managers will have to invest time and resources in communication and educational efforts. It is my observation not only that such efforts can pay off in terms of making a compensation system more effective, but that a feedback loop works in the other direction. A well-designed compensation system fuels employees' interest in building their skills and so heightens the effectiveness of efforts to improve communication, on-the-job learning, and problem-solving skills.

Communication, Learning, and Problem Solving

Effective communication, a learning-oriented work environment, and effective problem-solving efforts are valuable elements in organizational change efforts. They are three important ways to promote the creation of new specific knowledge and the mobilization of latent specific knowledge. By increasing motivation and incentives, a well-designed compensation system increases the effectiveness of all three elements. In doing so, it increases individuals' ability to make productive contributions to the firm. The implementation of a new compensation system sends a strong message that the mission or direction of the organization has changed substantially and, consistent with this, that the organization will function differently going forward. It encourages individuals to get on board with change and to learn, among other things, what the new goal or mission of the organization is and how their decisions and behavior will affect the organization's progress toward that goal.

My study of practice confirms this point. Many of the companies I have studied implement new compensation systems early in their change processes and concurrently launch intensive communication and educational efforts.[31] Managers of these firms could have undertaken these efforts separately. In conversation, however, they insist that the interplay between compensation and communication, learning, and problem-solving creates a powerful, persistent force for effective change that neither alone could generate.[32]

When I discuss this interplay with students, colleagues, and managers, many are skeptical. They argue that the firms I have observed must be "different," because, in general, employees would be incapable of understanding the "complex" performance measures that are typically a part of pay-for-performance plans. For readers who share this skepticism, I offer an interesting case study: the pay-for-performance plan of Cain Chemicals as documented by Michael Jensen and Brian Barry.[33]

Cain Chemicals was created through a leveraged buyout of seven chemical plants from various firms. Immediately following the buyout, the company adopted a new compensation system that included an employee profit-sharing plan and an employee equity ownership plan. Both plans had the potential to contribute significantly to the compensation of hourly employees. The company had a highly unionized workforce with a long history of strained relations with management. Most of the hourly employees had a high-school education or less.

Cain Chemical's profit-sharing plan paid everyone in the company a bonus based on companywide EBDIT: earnings before depreciation, interest, and taxes. Part of the challenge management faced was educating hourly employees about what EBDIT was and how their actions affected it. The company undertook this effort in an interesting way—each quarter, top management held a meeting with hourly employees in which they reviewed performance, beginning with safety and moving on to EBDIT, and showing how pricing, volume, and cost had contributed to or detracted from that quarter's performance. At the end of the meeting, profit-sharing checks were distributed.

Cain's CEO explained how the compensation and educational programs worked together:

> The special meetings were a critical factor in our success—you have to keep the employees fully informed about what's going on. All seven plants got the report and checks within one week after the quarter closed, not three months later. We did this by visiting one or two plants a day. Because they received their profit-sharing checks immediately after discussing the quarterly results, employees understood where the money was coming from.

Shortly after the implementation of the new compensation system, one manager joked with hourly employees that "he didn't know what EBDIT meant either," but that they could assume it meant "everybody doing it together." After that, employees had T-shirts made with EBDIT on one side and "everybody doing it together" on the other. Surprisingly, given the historical recalcitrance of the unionized workforce, "everybody doing it together" became a rallying cry.

Despite the jokes, plant managers reported that their employees came to understand both the new performance measure and the new compensation system extremely well and very quickly—to the point of understanding quite precisely how their actions affected performance outcomes:

> [EBDIT] was a very simple goal. People knew what to do. If they didn't, then they went and found out. Keeping the plant running smoothly at high rates had a big effect on EBDIT, so employees would anticipate things that led to downtime. They were quicker to step in and take charge when things went wrong.

We eliminated a lot of waste, we were getting things done more quickly, and people were having a lot of fun. The night shift would go off duty and people would stick around to see how things were going.

Employees could relate the pounds we produced per hour to the margins we were getting on our products. It was almost as if we had a taxi meter that tracked our output in dollars and pounds. The employees knew what EBDIT would be for the quarter and they knew what their share was. If they found a way to get another one million pounds out of the plant, they knew that was $10 in their pockets; if they could shave one tenth of a cent off our unit costs, they knew that was another $20.

The ability of Cain Chemical's employees to understand the new compensation system and respond to it in short order illustrates how a well-designed and well-implemented compensation system can quickly mobilize specific knowledge. It also illustrates the importance of education regarding an organization's new objective. It is hard to imagine that these employees would have changed their behavior so dramatically if they had been educated about EBDIT without an accompanying change in the reward system that paid them for their efforts. It is also hard to imagine that they would have changed their behavior if managers had not spent time helping them understand the new performance measure.

Compensation Systems, Organizational Inertia, and Resistance to Change

From the vast literature on organizational change, several themes emerge.[34] One is that many organizations suffer from inertia or become rigid and unable to adapt to new economic circumstances.[35] The fourth role of compensation systems is to address this problem. Specifically, well-designed compensation systems motivate individuals to overcome their resistance to change and to begin working productively toward a new objective. In emphasizing this function of compensation systems, I depart from the standard analysis of incentive alignment. I am calling attention to the way compensation systems help motivate individuals to overcome strong, and sometimes irrational, resistance to change. Such resistance arises, at least in part, from individuals' perception that change is extremely costly. Compensation systems are one way to provide individuals with benefits sufficient to outweigh their perceived cost of change.

Research verifies that the demise of organizations can often be attributed to their inability to adapt efficiently—even when adaptation would make the organization and its employees better off.[36] In contrast, efficient adaptation takes place when an analysis of long-run costs and benefits dictates that change is optimal, and in response the firm undertakes change. Notice that my definition of efficient adaptation encompasses both incremental and discontinuous change. Discontinuous change will occur when, for example, there is an unanticipated major change in the economic environment.

Why does strong, inefficient resistance to change occur? One way to look for the answer is to draw on what we know about examining how individuals behave under challenging circumstances. Here, the theory and evidence on defensive and nonlearning behavior tells us a great deal. This work indicates that individuals are often poor processors of negative feedback. So poor, in fact, that they are capable of systematically ignoring or avoiding it altogether. Clearly, such behavior inhibits productive learning and change.[37]

Organizations in which major change is required are often hit with a barrage of negative feedback. In fact, strong, persistent negative feedback—from customers, suppliers, employees, and/or financial markets—is an important signal that change is necessary. In spite of the feedback, individuals in an organization will often ignore, or fail to acknowledge and confront, valuable information that dictates the necessity of change.[38] When the avoidance of negative feedback by individuals is widespread and systematic enough to influence outcomes, it renders an organization incapable of efficient adaptation.[39] This inability results in a persistence of the status quo long after it is apparent to many, both inside and outside the firm, that continuing the status quo is counterproductive.

There is evidence that, prior to the spin-offs, both Cooper Industries and American Cyanamid avoided incorporating negative feedback into their decision making. This avoidance hampered managers' ability to turn around the performance of the business units they eventually spun off. Cooper Cameron began to perform poorly three years before its spin-off, during a slump in the oil industry. This performance significantly reduced the earnings of the parent company as a whole. Top management hired outside consultants to determine whether the Cameron business unit's performance was attributable entirely to the slump or whether poor management played a role. The consultants' report identified management as a problem. The divisional president challenged the report, insisting that performance was driven by factors outside his control. Top management accepted his view for several years before opting for a spin-off.

One of Cooper Cameron's top managers, who worked for Cooper Industries at the time the consulting study was conducted, described how that process played out:

> Booz Allen was hired to do a market analysis of [Cooper] Cameron. In their report, Booz Allen concluded that we were losing market share. The president of Cameron was able to discredit the Booz Allen report and convince . . . other top managers [incorrectly] that we hadn't lost market share. There was no management or organizational response to the data from Booz Allen. But their data shouldn't have been necessary. Our own financial statements provided us with data that there was a problem.

At American Cyanamid, negative feedback was avoided in another way. It was made undiscussable; the fact that the Chemicals division (which would become Cytec) was a poor performer was understood but was not discussed openly with employees. The fact that the subject was avoided left employees with an uneasy feeling regarding their future, but with no way to take productive action.

After the spin-off CEO took over management of the business unit, one of his first actions was to hold a cafeteria meeting for Chemicals employees—an uncommon event at American Cyanamid. The new business unit head described the weak state of the chemicals businesses. He made a point of emphasizing his criteria for good performance: "We will not be judged based on any fancy plans or who we know. . . . We will be judged on our results." Another top manager described the impact of this meeting:

> It was the first time anyone had said out loud that we had a problem, described what the problem was and how big it was. People knew there were a lot of things wrong at Chemicals. They knew there were too many managers, that there was inefficiency and waste. But they didn't know the overall financial picture. Fry [the new CEO] made a point of being open about performance and educating people on what we meant by it. It was a watershed event.

The inability to discuss poor performance openly also plagued other parts of the parent company. A former director reported that American Cyanamid's top managers insisted that the company's failures in research and development were attributable to "insufficient resources and attention to pharmaceuticals." In taking this view they avoided discussing whether the firm was wasting resources and continued to approve ever increasing, but equally unproductive, outlays on additional R&D.[40]

A well-designed compensation system is a valuable tool for managers tackling the problem of resistance to change. To overcome such resistance, a compensation system must increase the cost to individuals of maintaining the status quo and/or increase the benefits of change. The goal is for individuals to view the benefits of change as greater than the cost, and thus create an environment in which people are willing to let go of attachments to old behaviors and to open up to new ways of working. To accomplish this, the shift in costs and benefits precipitated by a new compensation system must be abrupt, large, clear, and understandable to the individuals affected. This was certainly the case at both Cooper Cameron and Cytec. In both firms, managers report, radical changes in compensation motivated individuals to overcome their resistance to change, to accept negative feedback more productively, and to make better decisions.

It is worth considering that the substantial cost of change to individuals is one reason that compensation packages is turnaround situations, particularly for executives, are often lucrative and are strongly tied to the firm's performance, particularly stock value. A very high payoff for success is required to attract talented managers to the challenge of restructuring. In highly visible and contentious situations, such as when massive layoffs are required, the personal and professional costs are extremely high; they can include, for example, negative publicity and threats of physical violence to an executive and his or her family. For perhaps this reason, we observe compensation packages where the payoff for success is large enough to endow the families of top management.[41]

The Case for Changing Compensation Systems Sooner

Thus far, I have discussed each of the four ways in which compensation systems facilitate (or hinder) productive organizational change. The remaining issue is one of timing: If it is necessary to change compensation systems, when is the right time? This question raises, in turn, the difficult issue of how most effectively to sequence specific steps in a process of organizational change. There is a great deal of controversy over how the steps of change should be properly sequenced. Models of change put forward in the academic literature often overlook this issue. When the sequencing issue is addressed, it often is based on life-cycle or evolutionary models that broadly describe inevitable stages in a firm's life occurring independently of management action.[42] In the applied literature, models of change tend to be normative and prescriptive. They often set forward a sequence of steps managers *should* follow to ensure productive change, rather than documenting and statistically assessing what managers actually do.[43]

While both are useful and interesting, the gap between the academic and applied literature is substantial. For example, there is no academic model that generates a definitive, optimal sequence of steps to organizational change. Neither is there applied work that provides a definitive, structural model of the change process. My approach follows a middle path. Based both on theory and study of practice, I take the position that firms should, at a minimum, revamp compensation systems very early in the change process.

Treating the question of *when* to introduce changes in compensation systems as an empirical one, I report what I have observed in organizations undertaking major and highly successful restructuring efforts.[44] Managers of these firms implement compensation systems *after* they identify and adopt a new overarching objective for the firm, but *before* they completely specify how that objective translates into a new strategy and/or structure. The identification and adoption of the new objective manifests itself in a new set of aggregate performance measures, such as shareholder value creation or earnings before depreciation, interest, and taxes (EBDIT). These measures are then tied to compensation through, for example, management or employee share ownership plans, profit-sharing plans, and/or gain-sharing plans.

It is useful to juxtapose my observations regarding the timing of changes in compensation systems with more conventional approaches to managing change. It is not uncommon for scholars and practitioners to specify a sequence of steps that should be taken in a specified order to bring about productive change. Perhaps the most common change paradigm draws the sequence of its steps for productive organizational change from the three Ss—(1) strategy, (2) structure, and (3) systems. The recommendation is that a firm begin by identifying and implementing the appropriate strategy, then create a structure consistent with that new strategy, and finally deal with the organization's systems, including its compensation systems.[45]

Why do my conclusions stand in contrast to the conventional wisdom? The answer lies in the choice of performance measures. It is important to note that in my examples, the performance measures on which compensation is based are quite general—general enough to allow for substantial redesign in strategy and structure while retaining their relevance. Performance measures of this kind avoid a potential problem often used to justify the position that changes in compensation should be made late in the change process.[46] Specifically, it is often argued that premature adoption of a new compensation system exerts a counter productive influence on strategy. But there is a flaw in this logic. What is overlooked is the fact that specifying a new objective and tying that objective to compensation does not define a firm's strategy. Rather, it establishes a goal against which alternative strategies can be productively evaluated and, in addition, energizes individuals in the organization to strive toward that goal.

In the organizations I studied, the problem of premature strategy setting did not surface. It was avoided, in part, because initial changes in compensation utilized highly aggregate performance measures such as stock return or a measure of the firm's cash flow. Compensation plans based on more refined and disaggregate performance measures were not introduced until after the firm's new strategy and structure were more fully developed. In addition, some firms made changes to compensation systems only at the top levels of the firm. Changes in compensation for lower-level employees came later in the process, if at all. If motivating top managers to identify and implement an effective new strategy is a top priority in the early stages of a change process, which is likely, this approach makes a great deal of sense. Tying top management compensation to critical new aggregate performance measures motivates these key decision makers to identify an effective new strategy. Having top managers develop a new strategy under the old compensation system is likely to result in a weaker strategy—one that optimizes old, outdated performance measures rather than new, more appropriate ones.

In summary, it is my position that potential benefits of effective compensation systems are so great that it makes little sense to wait to change them. The argument for tackling compensation systems—especially top management compensation—is particularly compelling once the overarching performance measures for the firm are chosen.

Crisis, Change, and the Power of Misalignment

A second reason to change compensation systems early is that they can help generate a "crisis" or a "sense of urgency" that facilitates productive change. Researchers have documented that the process of organizational change is often discontinuous and abrupt.[47] Some go so far as to recommend that managers create a "crisis" of some kind as a way of building internal momentum for change.[48] Even if we agree, which many of us would, that a crisis can serve as a catalyst for productive change, we must acknowledge that not all crises serve this function. In addition, managers who do create a crisis (or manage themselves into one) often have difficulty sustaining the change once the immediate problems are past. This raises an important issue: When are crises followed by productive organizational change, and when aren't they?

It is my observation a crisis serves as a catalyst for productive change when it is part of a set of changes that create misalignment among a firm's incumbent strategy, structure, and systems. The persistence of the status quo draws its strength from alignment. When a firm's strategy, structure, and systems are aligned, its components are consistent, self-perpetuating, and self-reinforcing. This alignment is a source of strength for a firm operating in a stable economic environment. Unfortunately, however, such alignment becomes a major impediment to change when a firm must adapt to a new economic environment. As a result of alignment, individuals making efforts to change will feel pressured to revert to business as usual. Indeed, the ability of alignment to undermine change explains why incremental approaches are often ineffective; a small step toward change is quickly stomped out by a well-entrenched, highly aligned design. Part of the challenge of "breaking the code of change," therefore, is figuring out how to break the self-perpetuating, self-reinforcing set of characteristics that in many cases have brought great success in the past.

The power of crisis to bring about organizational change emanates from its ability to break the hold of alignment on an organization. Specifically, creating a jarring *misalignment* among elements of the organization's strategy, structure, and systems is a powerful first step in beginning a process of value-creating organizational change. Initially, the misalignment facilitates change by throwing the system into disequilibrium. This disequilibrium is productive when it throws the organization sufficiently off balance to create a sense of urgency around regaining alignment *and* creates enough discontinuity with the past that the process of realignment does not result in a regeneration of the status quo.

A new compensation system, by generating a massive shift in the costs and benefits of perpetuating the status quo, can serve both as part of a crisis and as a way of ensuring that a crisis is followed by permanent, and not temporary, change. Implemented early in the change process, a well-designed compensation system generates productive misalignment by creating a gap between performance expectations and the incumbent way of doing business. Ideally, it leads to the establishment of a new set of performance measures and standards that are too challenging for the company to meet them by continuing the status quo. In other words, individuals in the organization realize that they "can't get there from here" unless they make dramatic changes in their behavior.

In Conclusion

We know that incumbent compensation systems are contributors to poor performance in underperforming organizations. Why wait until later to change them? Doing so only prolongs an organization's problems and inhibits efforts to promote organizational change. It makes little sense to postpone reaping the benefits of effective compensation once they become available, and they become available sooner than is widely recognized. In addition, lack of complete information and/or analysis regarding the firm's future direction is not a strong reason to postpone the implementation of a new compensation system. When compensation is based on aggregate performance measures, it not only allows sufficient flexibility to accommodate major changes in strategy but productively influences the analysis conducted to determine strategic direction. A new, effective compensation system will increase the quality and effectiveness of other aspects of the change process as well.

The risks of changing compensation, especially top management compensation, early in the process are relatively low, and the potential payoff is high. The information necessary to make the change effectively is minimal, whereas the cost of not taking action or of implementing an unsuccessful change program is great.

For readers still attached to the notion that changes in compensation systems cannot or should not be made until late in the process, it is useful to revisit the characteristics of human behavior that underlie the power of compensation systems as extrinsic motivators. Compensation systems are powerful motivators not because individuals blindly and automatically chase monetary rewards. In fact, most of us would agree that individuals are more thoughtful than that and value many things more highly than monetary rewards. Rather, compensation systems are powerful motivators because organizations are populated by individuals who want to "do the right thing" but often have difficulty accepting negative feedback, do not understand clearly what the right thing is, and/or get little feedback on how their actions affect performance. Worse yet, they sometimes get negative feedback for positive performance. Well-designed compensation systems help communicate the definition of outstanding performance and tie an individual's success to progress toward that goal. In doing so, they help align individuals' goals with those of the organization, and help individuals learn how they can best contribute to performance. These are the ways that well-designed and effectively implemented compensation systems can serve as a powerful force for productive organizational change.

Notes

1. Markets do not have to be complete or frictionless to be well-functioning. This is too high a standard to impose, even in highly developed market economies. There are strong incentives to develop ways to resolve market incompleteness and to reduce market frictions. Nonetheless, when the costs of resolving problems are greater than the benefits, the problems will persist and this is optimal. To paraphrase Jensen and Meckling, who make the same point in a different context, observing market incompleteness or frictions and concluding that [market outcomes] are "non-optimal, wasteful or inefficient is equivalent in every sense to comparing a world in which iron ore is a scarce commodity to one in which it is freely available at zero resource cost, and concluding that the first world is 'non-optimal'" (p. 328). Michael C. Jensen and William H. Meckling, "Agency Costs and the Theory of the Firm," *Journal of Financial Economics* 3 (1976): 305–360.
2. See, for example, Karen Hopper Wruck, "What Really Went Wrong at Revco?," *Journal of Applied Corporate Finance* (summer 1991): 79–92.
3. Steven N. Kaplan, Mark L. Mitchell, and Karen H. Wruck, "A Clinical Exploration of Value Creation and Destruction in Acquisitions: Organization Design, Incentives and Internal Capital Markets," *Productivity of Mergers and Acquisitions*, ed. Steven Kaplan (Cambridge, MA: National Bureau of Economic Research, 1997).
4. Karen H. Wruck and Sherry P. Roper, "Cytec Industries' Spin-Off Case Series, Cytec Industries' Spin-Off (A): Sink or Swim?," Case 9-897-053 (Boston: Harvard Business School, 1997); "Cytec Industries' Spin-Off (B): Managing the Challenges of Success," Case 9-897-054 (Boston: Harvard Business School, 1998); Teaching Note, Cytec Industries' Spin-Off (A) and (B), Case 5-897-195; and Karen H. Wruck and Sherry P. Roper, "American Cyanamid Case Series, American Cyanamid (A): Board Response to a Hostile Takeover Offer," Case 9-897-048 (Boston: Harvard Business School, 1997); "American Cyanamid (B): Management's Response to the (A) Case," Case 9-897-064 (Boston: Harvard Business School, 1997); "American Cyanamid (C): Epilogue," Case 9-897-178 (Boston: Harvard Business School, 1997); Teaching Note, American Cyanamid (A, B, and C), Case 5-897-161; "American Cyanamid (A) and (B) Combined," Case 9-898-120 (Boston: Harvard Business School, 1997).
5. Stock price performance for Cytec is equally impressive, but Cooper Cameron's stock price performance is mixed. Cooper Cameron experienced strong stock price performance through 1997. Then in 1998 the stock price was severely impacted by softening oil and gas markets and the economic crisis in

Southeast Asia. One dollar invested in Cooper Cameron's stock and held through 1997 returned $3.44, while a dollar invested in the S&P 500 over the same period returned $1.64. By the end of 1998, $3.44 had fallen to $1.38 (the analogous S&P investment returned $2.11). Nonetheless, the company's OPBD hit its highest level of $323 million in 1998. In its 1998 letter to share-holders, management stated that "our challenge is to react quickly and manage our structure in the downside market as successfully as we did in the upside ones, and ensure that we will be prepared to take advantage of the recoveries in our business when they arrive." In contrast, one dollar invested in Cytec and held through 1997 returned $10.63, while a dollar invested in the S&P 500 over the same period returned $2.28. Cytec's stock was also negatively impacted in 1998 by the Asian economic crisis. The company's past performance, however, was strong enough to offset its 1998 stock price decline. One dollar invested in Cytec at the time of its spin-off and held through the end of 1998 returned $4.81. The same dollar investment in the S&P 500 returned only $2.94.

6. A 1996 study examined a large sample of spin-off firms that went public be-tween 1985 and 1995 and found that on average these firms experienced modest improvements in operating profits relative to the industry, but nothing like the dramatic performance of the two firms examined here. Eric G. Wruck and Karen H. Wruck, "Codependent No More: How Spin-Offs Affect Parent and Spin-Off Firm Performance" (unpublished manuscript, Ohio State University, 1996).

7. Edward E. Lawler, *From the Ground Up: Six Principles for Building the New Logic Corporation* (San Francisco: Jossey-Bass, 1996), 195. See also Edward E. Lawler, *Strategic Pay: Aligning Organizational Strategies and Pay Systems* (San Francisco: Jossey-Bass, 1990).

8. Kidder, Peabody accused Joseph Jett of recording false profits of $350 million on which he earned bonuses of $8 million. Jett was not convicted of criminal fraud, but he was found guilty by a Securities and Exchange Commission ad-ministrative law judge of "books and records violations and intent to commit fraud." He was ordered to return his $8 million bonus and pay a $200,000 fine. He is currently working in the money management business and has published a book, *Black and White on Wall Street*, in which he presents his view of events. Juliette Fairley, "Wrongly Accused Trader Tells His Story of Racism, Sex, Poli-tics," *USA Today*, 21 June 1999. Nick Leeson's trading practices resulted in a 650 million–pound loss for Barings and forced the investment bank into liqui-dation. Leeson was convicted of criminal wrongdoing and served three and a half years of a six-and-a-half-year sentence before being released from prison in 1999. Upon his release from prison his assets, consisting largely of 100,000 pounds paid to him by a tabloid to tell his story, were frozen by Baring's liqui-dators. He receives a monthly living allowance. Both a book and a movie had been made based on his story. Sarah Sands, "Comment: Leeson's Lesson: The Market Is the Star," *Daily Telegraph*, 16 July 1999; Andrew Garfield, "Leeson Faces Fresh Threat to Assets," *The Independent*, 19 July 1999.

9. Kenneth E. Goodpaster and Richard J. Post, "H. J. Heinz: The Administration of Policy (A)," Case 5-382-063 (Boston: Harvard Business School, 1984); Ken-neth E. Goodpaster, Thomas R. Piper, and Charles A. Nigel, "Teaching Note

for H. J. Heinz: The Administration of Policy (A)," Case 5-390-045 (Boston: Harvard Business School, 1984).

10. Donald Roy, "Goldbricking in a Machine Shop," *American Journal of Sociology* 57 (1952): 427–442.

11. The views of Crosby and Deming on compensation systems reflect this view. See, for example, Philip B. Crosby, *Let's Talk Quality* (New York: McGraw-Hill, 1989); Philip B. Crosby, *Quality Is Free* (New York: McGraw-Hill, 1979); W. Edwards Deming, *Elementary Principles of the Statistical Control of Quality*, revised 2d ed. (Tokyo: JUSE, 1952); W. Edwards Deming, *Quality, Productivity and Competitive Position* (Cambridge, MA: MIT Center for Advanced Engineering Study, 1982).

12. J. M. Juran and Shigeru Mizuno are two quality gurus who take the position that it is important to link rewards to good performance as it is defined in the context of an effective quality management program. J. M. Juran, *Juran on Leadership for Quality* (New York: Free Press, 1989), 211; Shigeru Mizuno, *Company-Wide Total Quality Control* (Hong Kong: Nordica International, 1988). I discuss compensation systems and the important role they play in quality management systems in Karen Hopper Wruck and Michael C. Jensen, "Science, Specific Knowledge and Total Quality Management," *Journal of Accounting and Economics* 18 (1994): 247–287, especially 270–281.

13. George P. Baker, Michael C. Jensen, and Kevin J. Murphy, "Compensation and Incentives: Practice vs. Theory," *Journal of Finance* 43 (1988), no. 3: 593–616, especially 597.

14. Much of this section on Cooper Industries draws liberally on Steven N. Kaplan, Mark L. Mitchell, and Karen H. Wruck, "A Clinical Exploration of Value Creation and Destruction in Acquisitions: Organization Design, Incentives and Internal Capital Markets," *Productivity of Mergers and Acquisitions*, ed. Steven Kaplan (Cambridge, MA: National Bureau of Economic Research, 1999). Our study draws information on Cooper Industries' incumbent compensation system from David Collis and Toby Stuart, "Cooper Industries' Corporate Strategy (A)," Case 9-391-095 (Boston: Harvard Business School, 1991), and David Collis, "Teaching Note for Cooper Industries' Corporate Strategy," Case 5-391-281 (Boston: Harvard Business School, 1991).

15. Quoted from David Collis and Toby Stuart, "Cooper Industries' Corporate Strategy (A)" and teaching note, note 14 above.

16. Much of what follows on Cytec Industries is drawn or quoted from Karen H. Wruck and Sherry P. Roper, "Cytec Industries' Spin-Off (A): Sink or Swim?," note 4 above.

17. Elton Mayo, *The Human Problems of an Industrial Civilization* (New York: Macmillan, 1933); Fritz Roethlisberger and William Dickson, *Management and the Worker* (Cambridge, MA: Harvard University Press, 1939).

18. For example, in the second relay assembly group experiment, the experimental group was paid based on the output of 5 persons rather than the output of 100 persons, which was the standard in the nonexperimental setting. This reduction in group size reduced what economists call the "free rider problem," and productivity increased quickly by 12.6 percent. "But the experiment caused so much discontent among the rest of the girls in the department who wanted the same payment conditions, that it was discontinued after only nine weeks. The

output of the five girls promptly dropped by 16 percent." Alex Carey, "The Hawthorne Studies: A Radical Criticism," *American Sociological Review* 32 (1967): 403–416, 406.

In Parsons, H. M., 1974, "What Happened at Hawthorne?," *Science*, 183: 922–930, he reports that the Hawthorne experiments show that the "combination of information feedback and financial reward" generated the improved productivity observed in the experiments. He concluded that "it is an example of the control of behavior by its consequences." Based on his analysis, Alex Carey reports that "the results of [the Hawthorne experiments], far from supporting the various components of the 'human relations approach,' are surprisingly consistent with the rather old-world view about the value of monetary incentives, driving leadership and discipline." He goes on to state that "questions are raised regarding how it was possible for studies so nearly devoid of scientific merit, and conclusions so little supported by evidence to gain so influential a place within scientific disciplines and to hold this place for so long" (p. 403).

19. For a readable summary of Deci's research findings, see Edward L. Deci, "Work—Who Does Not Like It and Why," *Psychology Today* 6 (1972), no. 3. Kohn has published a book on this aspect of compensation and a related article in the *Harvard Business Review*: Alfie Kohn, *Punished by Rewards: The Trouble with Gold Stars, Incentive Plans, A's, Praise and Other Bribes* (Boston: Houghton Mifflin, 1993); Alfie Kohn, "Why Incentive Plans Cannot Work," *Harvard Business Review*, September/October 1993. Also important for our purposes here is the fact that Deci's experiments are not conducted in a business setting, and are constructed in a way that measures productivity only during uncompensated periods. For example, one of Deci's experiments had students work four puzzles for a fixed period of time. He paid one group of students $1 for each puzzle they worked correctly; students in the other group were unpaid. Deci then measured how many puzzles students from each of the groups completed during "breaks" from the experiment—a time during which they could do whatever they liked. He found that students who were paid for completing puzzles during the experiment period completed fewer puzzles during breaks than those who were not paid. He concluded that extrinsic motivation drove out intrinsic rewards. Notice that his experiment contains no measure of the effect of compensation on total productivity, but rather measures productivity during artificially constructed "breaks" from tasks. Clearly, in a business setting total productivity is of major import.

20. Edward E. Lawler, *From the Ground Up*, note 7 above, p. 195.

21. Teresa M. Amabile, "A Model of Creativity and Innovation in Organizations," *Research in Organizational Behavior* 10 (1988): 123–167.

22. See, for example, Edward E. Lawler, "The New Pay: A Strategic Approach," *Compensation and Benefits Review* 27 (1995), no. 4.

23. My examples hold the net present value of the payoffs to various compensation alternatives constant and assume individuals select the highest expected net present value compensation scheme based on their knowledge of their own abilities. These examples are, of course, highly stylized and oversimplified. Thus, there are some restrictive assumptions being made to allow for the outcomes I describe in terms of self-selection. Most importantly, I am neglecting the role risk aversion, independent of ability and skill, plays in self-selection

processes. In fact, a risk-averse individual might prefer a more certain payoff profile independent of ability and skill. My examples assume that while risk aversion is present, the role it plays in the process of self-selection is a second-order effect at best.

24. At the time of the spin-off, Cooper's directors and executive officers as a group owned directly or through options approximately 0.76 percent of the company's stock. In contrast, Cooper Cameron directors and executive officers as a group owned almost 6.5 times more stock and options. Their percentage ownership totaled 4.87 percent of Cooper Cameron's equity—1.89 percent directly or through vested options, and an additional 2.98 percent in options that would vest by the year 2000.

25. As it turned out, this was not the case. American Cyanamid was acquired by American Home Products in 1996 for $9.6 billion. Following the acquisition many employees, including managers, lost their jobs.

26. Findings as reported in "Work Force Reductions Will Continue Throughout Corporate America," *Business Wire*, 13 July 1993.

27. Rick Haglund, "GM Tries Costly Way to Trim White-Collar Force," *Newark Star-Ledger*, 1 March 1993.

28. See, for example, Karen Hopper Wruck and Michael C. Jensen, "Science, Specific Knowledge and Total Quality Management," note 12 above.

29. Valuable specific knowledge exists at all levels of the organization. For example, specific knowledge about corporate strategy or interdependencies across departments or divisions is likely to reside with upper management; specific knowledge regarding particular machines or production processes resides with employees on the factory floor; and specific knowledge of customers' idiosyncrasies resides with sales personnel. Michael C. Jensen and William H. Meckling, "Specific and General Knowledge and Organization Structure," in *Contract Economics*, ed. Lars Werin and Hans Wijkander, (Boston: Harvard University Press, 1992), 251–274.

30. Jensen and Meckling label the cost of conflicts of interest between individuals and the organizations for which they work "agency costs." Michael C. Jensen and William H. Meckling, "Agency Costs and the Theory of the Firm," *Journal of Financial Economics* 3 (1976): 305–360.

31. See, for example, George P. Baker and Karen H. Wruck, "Organizational Changes and Value Creation in Leveraged Buyouts: The Case of O. M. Scott & Sons Company," *Journal of Financial Economics* 25 (1989): 163–190; Karen Hopper Wruck and Michael C. Jensen, "Science, Specific Knowledge and Total Quality Management," note 12 above; Karen Hopper Wruck, "Financial Policy as a Catalyst for Organizational Change: Sealed Air Corporation's Leveraged Special Dividend," *Journal of Applied Corporate Finance* 7 (1995), no. 4: 20–37; and Karen H. Wruck, "Ownership, Governance and Control of Organizations: Course Module Overview Note" (unpublished manuscript, Harvard Business School, 1997).

32. Organizational economics has a technical term for characteristics or sets of characteristics that reinforce one another—*complementarities*. Introduced by Paul Milgrom and John Roberts, both of Stanford University, this concept defines two internal activities as mutually complementary if "doing more of any one activity increases (or at least does not decrease) the marginal profitability of

each other activity in the group." See Paul R. Milgrom and John Roberts, *Economics, Organization, and Management* (Englewood Cliffs, NJ: Prentice-Hall, 1992), 108. So in organizational economic terms, managers of the firms I have studied find that effective compensation systems and firmwide educational efforts are complements.

33. This example from practice draws heavily on Michael C. Jensen and Brian K. Barry, "Gordon Cain and the Sterling Group (A)," Case 9-492-021 (Boston: Harvard Business School, 1992).

34. The vastness of the literature is attested to by the fact that Van de Ven and Poole identified more than 1 million published articles in the field. Of the 1 million articles, they review 200,000 titles, screen 2,000 abstracts, and critically review 200 articles. Andrew H. Van de Ven and Marshall Scott Poole, "Explaining Development and Change in Organizations," *Academy of Management Review* (July 1995): 510. Another review of the literature is provided in William P. Barnett and Glenn R. Carroll, "Modeling Internal Organizational Change," *Annual Review of Sociology* 21 (1995): 217–236.

35. Age is typically identified as the primary source of inertia. For example, in Hannan and Freeman's model of structural inertia, procedures, rules, and practices become well established and therefore more difficult to change as the firm ages. Michael T. Hannan and John Freeman, "Structural Inertia and Organizational Change," *American Sociological Review* 49 (1984): 149–164. Abernathy and Utterback focus on the age of the product, rather than the age of the firm. Their work describes how, as a product matures, firms naturally turn their attention to efficiency in production (or process innovation) as opposed to new-product innovation. The drive for efficiency in production shifts the firm's focus to smaller and smaller innovations, ultimately creating an organization incapable of change. William J. Abernathy and James M. Utterback, "Patterns of Industrial Innovation," *Technology Review* 80 (1978): 2–9.

36. See, for example, William J. Abernathy and James M. Utterback, "Patterns of Industrial Innovation," note 35 above; Rebecca M. Henderson and Kim B. Clark, "Architectural Innovation: The Reconfiguration of Existing Product Technologies and the Failure of Established Firms," *Administrative Science Quarterly* 35 (1990): 9–30; and Clayton M. Christensen, *The Innovator's Dilemma: When New Technologies Cause Great Firms to Fail* (Boston: Harvard Business School Press, 1997).

37. Chris Argyris and others argue that this behavior stems from basic characteristics of human nature: the desires to avoid being wrong, to remain in control, and to avoid conflict and emotional pain. The causes and effects of defensive behavior are analyzed extensively by the prolific Argyris. Perhaps his most accessible piece is Chris Argyris, "Teaching Smart People How to Learn," *Harvard Business Review*, May–June 1991, 6–12.

38. Indeed, scholars studying change management, such as Michael Beer and John Kotter, identify and address this issue and outline alternative approaches for creating enough pressure or dissatisfaction to motivate individuals to participate effectively in the change process. See, e.g., Michael Beer, "Leading Change," Case 488037 (Boston: Harvard Business School, 1991), and John P. Kotter, *Leading Change* (Boston: Harvard Business School Press, 1996), 35–46.

39. It is difficult to specify the circumstances under which counterproductive be-

havior on the part of individuals aggregates to characterize organizational behavior. I hypothesize that strong alignment of a well-established organizational
paradigm (e.g., strategy, structure, and systems) fosters such aggregation. Under this hypothesis, widespread defensive behavior on the part of individuals,
reinforced by a well-established organizational paradigm, generates inertia.
Note that this hypothesis contrasts with previous academic research. Although
widespread defensive behavior and a strong organizational paradigm are likely
to be positively correlated with firm and/or product age, two factors that researchers find are correlated with inertia, age is not the underlying causal factor.

40. Karen H. Wruck and Sherry P. Roper, "American Cyanamid (A)," p. 5, and related teaching note, note 4 above.

41. This was the case, for example, in the compensation package created to provide
Bill Anders with the incentives to restructure General Dynamics. General Dynamics' restructuring is analyzed in detail in Jay Dial and Kevin J. Murphy, "Incentives, Downsizing, and Value Creation at General Dynamics," *Journal of Financial Economics* 37 (1995), no. 3. This is also the case in the controversial
compensation payouts received by Al Dunlap, for example for his restructuring
of Scott Paper. See Stuart C. Gilson, "Scott Paper Company," Case 9-296-048,
and associated teaching note, 5-298-088 (Boston: Harvard Business School,
1997).

42. Van de Ven and Poole, note 34 above, identify four classes of change models.
Of the four, only two classes of models, life-cycle and evolutionary, have prescribed modes or steps of change; and these are dictated by a fixed sequence of
events that have little, if anything, to do with management decision making. In
the other two classes of models, teleological and dialectical, the steps of change
are constructive and emerge as the change process takes place.

43. Two examples of work along these lines are John P. Kotter, *Leading Change*, and
Michael Beer, "Leading Change," both note 38 above.

44. See, for example, George P. Baker and Karen H. Wruck, "Organizational
Changes and Value Creation in Leveraged Buyouts," note 31 above; Karen
Hopper Wruck and Michael C. Jensen, "Science, Specific Knowledge and To-
tal Quality Management," note 12 above; Karen Hopper Wruck, "Financial
Policy as a Catalyst for Organizational Change," note 31 above; and Karen H.
Wruck, "Ownership, Governance and Control of Organizations," note 31
above.

45. For example, Beer and Eisenstat identify "six steps to effective change." In their
model, changes in structure and systems, including compensation systems, take
place in step five. Making changes in structure and systems earlier, they argue, is
"likely to backfire." Given that step six is to "monitor and adjust strategies in response to problems in the revitalization process," structure and systems are in
fact the last things that change before the fine-tuning begins. Michael Beer,
Russell A. Eisenstat, and Bert Spector, "Why Change Programs Don't Produce
Change," *Harvard Business Review* (1990), reprint 900601. John Kotter, note 38
above, proposes an eight-stage process for creating major change in organizations. Changing structures and systems is also the fifth step in his program and,
as in the three-S approach, follows the development of vision and strategy (his
step three).

46. See, for example, John P. Kotter, 1996, *Leading Change*, and Michael Beer,

"Leading Change," both note 38 above; and Michael Beer, Russell A. Eisenstat, and Bert Spector, 1990, "Why Change Programs Don't Produce Change," note 45 above.

47. Much of the theory and evidence on discontinuous change is developed in the context of the adoption of new technologies. Articles by Tushman and Romanelli and by Tushman and Andersen utilize a punctuated equilibrium model of evolutionary change: "Technology evolves through periods of incremental change punctuated by technological breakthroughs that either enhance or destroy the competence of firms in an industry." Michael L. Tushman and Elaine Romanelli, "Organizational Evolution: A Metamorphosis Model of Convergence and Reorientation," *Research in Organizational Behavior* 7 (1985): 171–222; Michael L. Tushman and Philip Andersen, "Technological Discontinuities and Organizational Environments," *Administrative Science Quarterly* 31 (1986): 439–465. Rebecca Hendersen and Kim Clark, note 36 above, identify the difficulty firms have in incorporating "small" technological breakthroughs that "change the architecture of a product without changing its components." Clayton Christensen, note 36 above, explores the difficulties large, successful firms have in adopting new technologies, and how this can lead them to fail.

48. For example, John Kotter, note 38 above, emphasizes the need to create "a sense of urgency"; see especially pages 35–49. Kotter goes on to recommend courses of action managers can take to achieve this, including allowing financial losses or major strategic errors to occur, eliminating excessive executive perquisites, providing more data and information to employees and managers, and encouraging more honest discussion. As another example, Michael Beer, note 38 above, describes the importance of creating "dissatisfaction with the status quo" in order to create momentum for change. He goes on to describe ways in which firms can generate this kind of dissatisfaction.

14

COMPENSATION

A Troublesome Lead System in Organizational Change

Gerald E. Ledford Jr. and Robert L. Heneman

WHILE PREPARING this chapter, we heard the following story from a consultant. The CEO of a Fortune 500 firm was a turn-around specialist, and he had plenty of work to do in his new company. The firm he now headed was losing money and market share while its peer companies were not. The firm's strategy was ill defined, tentative, and ineffective. The previous chief executive had badly overpaid for a major acquisition, causing financial problems, then compounded the difficulty by overhyping the deal, which gave the firm a bad reputation in the business press. The organizational culture was toxic: highly po-litical, bureaucratic, full of meaningless turf battles. There was no shortage of organizational and human resource problems. After sur-veying this landscape, the new CEO decided that the place to start in changing the organization was the compensation system. He decided that his first change had to be big enough to capture the attention of managers and employees—to shake things up in a rigid, political, un-creative organization. Was the pay system a wise place to begin in changing the company? The story is still unfolding, so the case does not yet give us a definitive answer to our question. This paper explores the question and takes the position that the CEO was mistaken to be-gin organizational change with pay.

Issues of change sequencing and timing are basic to change strategy. No one undertaking a major organizational change effort can avoid these issues. Yet the question of whether the pay system should lead or lag other types of change is unresolved and largely ignored in the organizational change and compensation literatures. This is clearly a blind spot in our thinking about change. It is not difficult to see why there is little research on the topic. Large-scale survey studies based on samples large enough to be used for statistical analysis are very difficult to conduct, and data collected at one point in time about dynamic long-term patterns of organizational change is often suspect. On the other hand, solid case studies of major, complex organizational change efforts are relatively rare. Understanding even one case requires a long-term, relatively intensive, and privileged relationship with the organization that is the subject of the research. The database of cases good enough to allow us to draw strong research-based inferences about the most effective timing and sequencing of changes simply does not exist.

What is more surprising is that there is so little commentary and speculation in the practitioner and academic literatures about the timing and sequencing of changes in compensation systems. In a scan of major recent trade books and academic works on organizational change, we found almost no discussion of these issues. The compensation literature is equally silent. There have been a number of books about compensation strategy, design, and innovation in recent years, but we know of none that have given the lead–lag issue serious consideration. The only observer we have found who explicitly discusses in some detail the advantages and disadvantages of compensation as a lead system and as a lag system is Edward Lawler (e.g., Lawler 1981). We draw upon his arguments later in this chapter.

The possible role of compensation as a lead system is becoming an increasingly important consideration. For decades the issue was relatively unimportant because there was so little change in compensation systems, whether as lead incentives or as lag rewards. Until about 1990 compensation systems simply changed less than technology, operations, and human resource systems such as training, selection, or labor relations. During the 1990s, however, base pay, pay for performance, benefits, and virtually all other aspects of compensation changed dramatically (Heneman et al., in press; Lawler et al. 1998). An important strategic issue becomes whether such changes should precede or follow other organizational changes.

We both confess to being conflicted about the answer to our question. In this paper, however, we will take a strong stance for purposes of the debate that this paper joins. Our hope is that a sharp dialectic discussion can advance our thinking about an important but neglected issue.

Can Pay Systems Change Employee Behavior and Performance?

Before we consider the arguments against pay as a lead system, it is important to deal with one argument in opposition that is becoming popular in some quarters but is, in our view, flatly wrong. Some would argue that pay system changes should not lead organizational change because pay system changes are usually ineffective, counterproductive, or both. It is altogether fitting that we address this argument in a book published by the Harvard Business School, because the Harvard Business School has been more responsible for the propagation of this argument that any other academic institution.

The argument that pay changes are ineffective or counterproductive has been made at least since the beginning of the human relations movement the better part of a century ago, and it regains currency every decade or so. Human relations theory, an outgrowth of the famous Hawthorne experiments, argued that social relationships—especially work group relationships—are primary in determining employee motivation, satisfaction, and productivity, whereas objective conditions such as pay are much less important (Mayo 1933; Roethlisberger and Dickson 1939). We may note for the record that Mayo, Roethlisberger, and Dickson, who conducted the Hawthorne research, were faculty members from the Harvard Business School.

Herzberg (1966) added a different argument in the 1960s, claiming that intrinsic sources of motivation arising from the design of work are much more important than extrinsic sources in determining the level of employee motivation. Extrinsic motivation is the result of rewards that are external to the individual, such as pay, recognition from

peers, or praise from a supervisor. Intrinsic rewards are internally rewarding experiences, such as a feeling of accomplishment, that derive
from behavior such as performing the job. Herzberg's most famous
and influential statement appeared in the *Harvard Business Review*
(1968). In Herzberg's view, extrinsic sources are "hygiene" factors that
can have a negative effect but not a positive effect on motivation,
whereas intrinsic sources are true "motivators."

The distinction between extrinsic and intrinsic rewards has great
practical importance. The major approaches to increasing and directing employee motivation tend to be oriented primarily toward one of
these types. Compensation systems, for example, offer extrinsic rewards for performance; job design approaches are designed to increase
intrinsic motivation. Contrary to Herzberg's argument (although not
contrary to his data), contemporary scholars overwhelmingly concur
that extrinsic rewards are motivating. In a metanalysis of thirty-nine
studies of financial incentives, Jenkins and colleagues (1998) found a
.34 correlation between the use of financial rewards and job performance. Moreover, the vast majority of authorities on motivation conclude that motivation from extrinsic sources is complementary and additive to motivation from intrinsic sources. That is, total motivation is
greater if both extrinsic and intrinsic motivation are high (Scott et al.
1988). Also, low extrinsic motivation reduces total motivation even if
intrinsic motivation is high, and vice versa. In practical terms, this
means that managers should create both extrinsic rewards (such as pay)
and intrinsic rewards (for example, through job design) that are con-
gruent and consistent.

A more recent point of view has achieved considerable prominence
in the practitioner literature through the work of journalist Alfie Kohn
(1993). His polemic received a flood of attention after an article summarizing Kohn's book was published in the *Harvard Business Review*.
Based on a highly selective review of the research literature, Kohn argues that extrinsic rewards cannot work for several reasons. For example, he maintains that extrinsic rewards such as pay must be provided
continually to be effective, whereas sources of intrinsic rewards, such
as work design, by their nature continue to be available to employees
without continuous management action. Of course, no serious observer would disagree with the point that pay and recognition need to
be available continually for them to be effective. In addition, Kohn re-

hashes Herzberg's arguments about motivators and hygiene factors. Although Kohn's work aspires to be a serious review of the literature, it somehow misses the many criticisms of Herzberg's theory over the years—not the least of which is that Herzberg's own data did not support it. Researchers appreciate Herzberg's work because he helped draw attention to the importance of intrinsic motivation and job design, but the hygiene–motivator distinction is no longer considered credible by scholars in the field. As Dipboye and colleagues (1994) noted, Herzberg's theory is only "of historical interest" today.

Kohn also makes an argument based on work of Deci and his colleagues (Deci 1975; Deci and Ryan 1985). Deci contends that extrinsic and intrinsic motivation are not additive, and that in fact extrinsic rewards (including pay, praise, and recognition) undermine intrinsic motivation. Deci's theory is based primarily on laboratory research, in which he typically measures intrinsic motivation by the amount of time subjects voluntarily spend working on artificial tasks. It is important to note that Deci's work is not well accepted by motivation researchers. For example, Locke and Henne (1986) point to flaws in studies of Deci's theory and research. They conclude that studies in this tradition do not meaningfully test the theory, and that Deci's conclusions are misleading interpretations of the available results. In a comprehensive review of ninety-six studies, Eisenberger and Cameron (1996) found that "detrimental effects of reward occur under highly restricted, easily avoidable conditions" (p. 1154). The only consistent negative effect occurred when an expected reward was presented only once, regardless of the quality of performance. Indeed, the reviewers found that extrinsic rewards are more likely to have a positive than a negative effect on both intrinsic motivation and creativity. To repeat, then, extrinsic and intrinsic rewards should be considered as complementary, and managers need to make use of both types of rewards to motivate employees.

In summary, we can find no compelling arguments or data to support the argument that compensation systems should not be used as lead systems because compensation systems in themselves are ineffective or counterproductive as motivators. Hence, contrary to some who oppose compensation as a lead system, we will not oppose compensation as a lead system on these grounds.

We will argue, however, both from the perspective of human resource strategy and from the perspective of emotions typically attached to compensation, that compensation as a lag system is superior to compensation as a lead system.

Strategic Compensation Design

If compensation systems can have powerful, positive effects, should they lead or lag other organizational changes? We argue first that pay should be a lag system on strategic grounds: Compensation must be aligned with other organizational systems that must be designed first in order for it to be effective.

In reviewing the compensation design literature, we are struck by the degree to which the alignment perspective has become almost universal among authors in both academic and trade media. This perspective argues that no particular pay system design is effective or ineffective in the abstract. Rather, a given compensation design is effective to the extent that it is aligned with business needs and with other organizational systems. This perspective makes several assumptions. It suggests that different pay systems may be effective in different contexts. It argues that compensation system changes must be part of a web of mutually reinforcing systems, all pulling employee behavior in the same direction. Finally, and most important for our purposes here, it indicates that no pay system is effective unless it meets business needs. Figure 14-1 is our version of an alignment model.

The alignment perspective explains why compensation cannot truly by a lead system. The question we might ask is, "Leading what?" The compensation system cannot provide its own direction. It must follow at least some organizational changes if it is to be designed effectively. Using compensation as a lead system is like launching an unguided missile. It may hit the target, but it also may circle back and do damage to the place from which it was launched. For a compensation system to impact its intended targets, it must be given direction. Figure 14-1 suggests that the direction for compensation systems is derived from the business strategy of the organization, the manner in which the organization is structured, the culture of the organization, and other human resource systems. We consider these in turn.

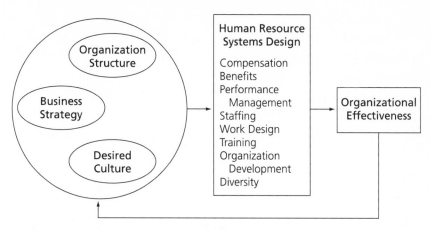

Figure 14-1 A Compensation Alignment Model

Business Strategy

An organization's business strategy provides considerable guidance about the types of reward systems that will be most appropriate for that organization. The strategy indicates how the organization will gain competitive advantage in the marketplace. Will the organization emphasize lower prices than those of competitors, higher quality, better customer service, or faster new-product innovation? A strategy helps give direction to the compensation system by indicating the types of employee behaviors and abilities that the company needs to be successful in the marketplace. For example, 3M famously rewards product innovation through significant rewards and penalties for managers; this system supports the 3M goal stating that each business must derive 30 percent of its sales from products introduced within the previous four years. Similarly, in high-technology startups the heavy use of broad-based stock options and companywide performance bonuses helps reinforce entrepreneurial behavior by rewarding risk taking and extraordinary effort.

True lead pay systems can be based only on generic business strategies that do not offer competitive advantage. Lead pay systems also tend to be stand-alone programs unrelated to the strategy of the organization, because designers of the systems do not know where to start. For example, generic job evaluation systems that emphasize general factors like skill, effectiveness, responsibility, and working conditions may have little relationship to the core capabilities the organization wishes to develop in order to support the business strategy. For business strategies to lead to sustained competitive advantage, decision makers must identify the core competencies of the organization that will be difficult for competitors to imitate (Barney 1996). Compensation systems need to support and reinforce these core competencies, but a generic compensation system is unlikely to do so.

Organizational Structure

The compensation system, intentionally or unintentionally, sends strong messages to employees about what organizational units and levels are most important. Unless management has first defined what units and levels it wishes to emphasize, the pay system is likely to send the wrong messages to employees. For example, does management wish to stress the team, plant or unit, division, or sector level of performance in the organization? Incentives can be designed that reinforce any level of performance, but they cannot be designed effectively to reinforce all levels simultaneously. Unless management has defined the levels of performance that have the highest priority, compensation systems are likely to follow fashion or whim but not organizational needs. For example, team-based rewards are widely used today and have received considerable attention in the compensation community. We have witnessed organizations that have prematurely developed team incentive plans without carefully considering organizational structure issues. Many organizations with team incentives should be reinforcing the plant or unit level, both because there are no adequate metrics for managing performance at the team level and because employees do not work in discrete teams.

Organizational Culture

Organizational culture expresses the organization's most deeply held values, beliefs, and assumptions. The culture helps define for employees what is good, proper, and sensible. Once management has defined the kind of organizational culture that it wishes to encourage, virtually any desired organizational culture can be reinforced by means of compensation systems. For example, a cultural variable that has long been shown to be important in pay system design is the degree to which management wishes to emphasize employee involvement (Lawler 1981). Involvement-oriented cultures tend to look systematically different and to be accompanied by such pay innovations as skill-based pay, gain sharing, profit sharing, and open communication about pay. These pay plans tend to be more effective in involvement-oriented cultures, which are able to make use of the greater skills and sense of responsibility that these systems encourage.

But an existing organizational culture can be a key detriment of the effectiveness of compensation (Beer and Katz 1997). Lead pay systems are sometimes used to help bring about changes in culture. Stories abound, however, about the resistance created by such a strategy. This is especially true when a pay-for-performance plan is used as a lead system to promote a shift from an egalitarian culture to one of a meritocracy. Research clearly shows that people in blue-collar occupations, women, and labor union members prefer an egalitarian method of reward distribution over a performance-based system (see Heneman 1992 for a review). In the absence of other systems needed to support a pay-for-performance culture, a lead compensation system may create a culture of dissension rather than high performance. Compensation as a lag system, in contrast, allows time for people to adjust to the need for a new plan. Moreover, it allows employees the opportunity to be educated on how the system works and to upgrade their capabilities to take full advantage of the new compensation plan.

Ideally, organizational structure and culture follow from the business strategy. Together these three factors give business direction to the organization. Without such direction, designing compensation system changes that meet the organization's needs is simply a matter of luck. We cannot imagine how one could responsibly design the compensation system for a given organization without the kind of understanding of organizational needs that an analysis of strategy, structure, and culture provides.

Alignment with Human Resource Systems

Although we are firmly convinced, and we believe that most authorities would agree, that compensation system design should lag behind the definition of business needs, there remains the question of whether compensation design ought to lead or lag the design of other human resource systems. Here authorities are not unanimous. Some (e.g., Beer et al. 1990) argue that pay system change is most appropriately used as a lag system after other systems, such as training, communication, and appraisal have changed. Others (e.g., Galbraith 1995) argue that once business direction is set, other changes can be adopted in essentially any order, recognizing that eventually all will have to change to support the new business direction. The research to resolve these differences of opinion does not exist, so we must determine the answer as best we can.

We argue that compensation should be a lag system even among human resource systems, because communication, training, and other changes are needed to make any reward system change effective. Compensation systems usually are complex and require extensive communication to help employees understand them and understand the differences between the old and new systems. Training is also required, to give employees an understanding of how the system works and to provide them with new skills that may be needed. Installing the pay system first and hoping to create the supporting infrastructure later is a recipe for disaster. Employee confusion and resistance are highly likely, and changes in the pay system are unlikely to produce changes in behavior.

For example, a well-developed method of performance assessment is critical for the effective functioning of a compensation system. We may look at the experience of the federal government with the implementation of merit pay as a lead system aimed at changing the culture from one based on seniority to one based on performance. This change was made prior to, rather than after, the creation of a sound method of performance management. According to all documented accounts, the change had disastrous results. Another example concerns labor relations. Petty and colleagues (1992) reported on an electric utility where a very well developed and effective incentive plan was abandoned because of a conflict between labor and management officials. Both of these illustrations show the need to lag compensation behind the development and integration of complementary human resource systems.

Emotions and Pay Systems

Another major reason to view compensation as a troublesome lead system for organizational change is that compensation changes tend to provoke intense and counterproductive emotional responses from employees and managers. Although any organizational change has the potential to provoke negative emotional reactions, compensation changes tend to be particularly loaded with affect.

Researchers have rediscovered emotions as an important effect and cause of behavior in organizations (George and Brief 1996). One of the most important reasons to be concerned about intense emotional responses among employees is that managers, like other human beings, tend to deal with such reactions poorly. When possible, they avoid making changes that may provoke emotional outbursts. Managers' defensiveness and fear can lead to inappropriate choices during an organizational change. On the other hand, employees who react with a high level of emotion to an organizational change may react defensively as well, failing to deal constructively and effectively with problems surrounding the change.

Several factors increase the emotional reactions of employees to organizational changes. Emotional responses increase to the extent that a change has a direct and tangible impact on perceived employee well-being. Changes in business strategy, for example, often provoke little emotional response from employees, because the effects of the changes seem remote and difficult to interpret. Conversely, changes in seemingly inconsequential personnel policies often lead to extreme emotional reactions. Emotional responses also increase to the extent that more employees are affected by the change. Shutting down an entire business unit has a greater emotional impact than scattered layoffs, and layoffs carry more emotional impact than the firing of a single poor performer.

Pay systems in organizations are emotionally loaded relative to other human resource systems, as indicated by figure 14-2. Please note initially that this figure does not attempt to suggest the objective importance or organizational impact of different human resource systems, only the degree of emotion invested in each system by employees.

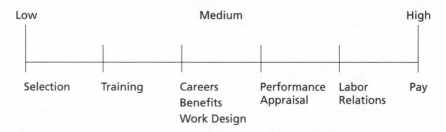

Figure 14-2 Emotion Attached to HR Systems

External selection tends to be low in the emotionality that employees attach to it, because this system affects people who are not yet in the organization. Indeed, selection matters most to people who *do not* become members of the organization, rather than to current employees.

Employees and managers alike almost universally value *training*. However, the value of training compared to that of pressing daily activities usually is ambiguous. The payoffs of training to the organization and the individual are usually long-term and less concrete than the opportunity cost of trainees' inability to complete day-to-day tasks while enrolled in a training program. This explains why an activity that is so universally appreciated is so routinely deferred without incident. Thus, the emotions attached to training are positive but not strong.

Changes in *careers, benefits,* and *work design* tend to create a moderate emotional response. Career issues, including promotion, can affect the self-interests of many employees. However, not all employees expect or want career advancement; and changes in career patterns are often ambiguous and remote, because they are long-term. Benefits have a direct impact on employee well-being, and sometimes (as in the case of changes in health care benefits in recent years) changes can provoke an intense employee reaction. However, employees usually have a limited understanding of the pros and cons of different benefits and benefit options. In addition, changes in many benefits have remote consequences. For example, few employees need to make use of life insurance benefits, and retirement benefits tend to be so long-term that they are of limited concern to many workers. Work design changes can have a direct effect on employee emotions, but changes in work design rarely affect a large number of employees at one time. Thus, all of these changes tend to have a moderate emotional content, either because the changes tend to affect few employees or because the changes have limited or ambiguous effects on employees interests.

Performance appraisal tends to be a relatively emotion-laden human resource subsystem. Appraisals have a direct impact on employee pay for many employees, and the appraisal event itself can be a highly emotional event. Yet not all employees receive performance appraisals. In many organizations, moreover, the performance appraisal event typically is handled in a perfunctory and ineffective way. In such organizations managers and employees conspire to keep the emotional content to a minimum. Finally, changes in performance appraisal systems often have little emotional effect, because changes often are relatively trivial (such as changes in the appraisal form).

Labor relations can have high emotional content. Labor relations often are extremely contentious in unionized settings. However, a relatively small percentage of people in the U.S. workforce are members of unions, so relatively few employees are directly affected by this system.

Compensation, on the other hand, has the highest emotional content of any human resource system. It directly affects all employees, all the time; and almost all employees greatly value their compensation. Employees value compensation for many reasons: as a means of meeting basic needs, as a source of status, as a signal of success, and so on (Lawler 1981). Employees closely monitor the pay system and tend to show a level of awareness and concern about pay system changes that is absent for other types of changes.

The research literature shows that as emotion increases, attention focused on the source of that emotion increases as well (George and Brief 1996). Consequently, employees become very focused on changes in pay systems. Not only do people have global reactions to the pay system; they also form reactions to components of the pay system (Heneman and Schwab 1985). Because of this attention, a high level of scrutiny is given to outcomes from the compensation system as well as to the design, implementation, and administration of the system (Greenberg 1987).

The intense scrutiny that pay system changes receive is a double-edged sword for organizational change. Changes in pay systems emphasize for employees that management is serious about organizational change. However, concerns about changes in pay may drown out interest in other changes. The organization's expectation of getting to other organizational changes sometime later may never be realized if problems with the pay system are too severe. We know of several instances in which pay changes were intended to be the first in a series of organizational changes but led to the failure of the entire organizational change effort—because the pay system changes failed and poisoned the atmosphere for related changes.

It takes time to carefully craft a pay system that is likely to be acceptable to employees. When a company designs and implements a pay plan as a lead system, often the time needed to develop a successful plan is not available. Moreover, the event is extremely salient to employees, as it is placed in the forefront of change and it concerns their income. Expectations regarding the plan may therefore be inflated and errors in the plan magnified. By contrast, a compensation plan that is a lag system can be more carefully crafted and can be kept out of the limelight until it has been fully scrutinized.

Summary

We began this chapter by reviewing the possible argument that compensation should not be a lead system in organization change because it is ineffective at changing employee behavior. We dismissed that argument based on considerable research evidence: Compensation system changes can indeed be powerful. But the question of whether compensation changes should be a lead or a lag system remains. We have offered two arguments for making compensation a lag system. First, the alignment perspective, now the dominant theoretical perspective on compensation design, requires that business direction be set first. Compensation cannot lag business strategy, structure, and culture, and probably should not lag the adoption of other human resource systems either. Second, we have argued that compensation is a highly emotional topic. It makes a poor candidate for leading organizational change, because it is more likely than other kinds of changes to generate employee resistance and thus to cause management to abandon the entire change effort rather than developing necessary supporting systems.

References

Barney, J. B. 1996. *Gaining and Sustaining Competitive Advantage*. Reading, MA: Addison-Wesley.

Beer, M., R. Eisenstat, and B. Spector. 1990. *The Critical Path to Corporate Renewal*. Boston: Harvard Business School Press.

Beer, M., and N. Katz. 1997. Do Incentives Work? The Perceptions of Senior Executives from Thirty Countries. Unpublished manuscript, Harvard Business School.

Deci, E. L. 1975. *Intrinsic Motivation*. New York: Plenum.

Deci, E. L., and R. M. Ryan. 1985. *Intrinsic Motivation and Self-Determination in Human Behavior*. New York: Plenum.

Dipboye, R. L., C. S. Smith, and W. C. Howell. 1994. *Understanding Industrial and Organizational Psychology: An Integrated Approach*. Fort Worth, TX: Harcourt Brace College.

Eisenberger, J., and R. Cameron. 1996. Detrimental Effects of Rewards: Reality or Myth? *American Psychologist* 51: 1153–1166.

Galbraith, J. R. 1995. *Designing Organizations: An Executive Briefing on Strategy, Structure, and Process*. San Francisco: Jossey-Bass.

George, J. M., and A. P. Brief. 1996. Motivational Agendas in the Workplace: The Effects of Feelings on Focus of Attention and Work Motivation. In *Research in Organizational Behavior*, ed. B. M. Staw and L. L. Cummings, vol. 18, 75–110. Greenwich, CT: JAI Press.

Greenberg, J. 1987. Reactions to Procedural Justice in Payment Distributions: Do the Ends Justify the Means? *Journal of Applied Psychology* 72: 55–61.

Heneman, H. G. III, and D. P. Schwab. 1985. Pay Satisfaction: Its Multidimensional Nature and Assessment. *International Journal of Psychology* 20: 129–141.

Heneman, R. L. 1992. *Merit Pay: Linking Pay Increases to Performance Ratings*. Reading, MA: Addison-Wesley.

Heneman, R. L., G. E. Ledford Jr., and M. Gresham. In press. Compensation and the Changing Nature of Work. In *Compensation in Organizations: Progress and Prospects* (Society for Industrial and Organizational Psychology Frontiers of Industrial and Organizational Psychology Series), ed. S. Rynes and B. Gerhart. San Francisco: New Lexington Press.

Herzberg, F. 1966. *Work and the Nature of Man*. New York: World.

———. 1968. One More Time: How Do You Motivate Employees? *Harvard Business Review*, January–February.

Jenkins, G. D. Jr., A. Mitra, N. Gupta, and J. D. Shaw. 1998. Are Financial Incentives Related to Performance? A Meta-analytic Review of Empirical Research. *Journal of Applied Psychology* 83: 777–787.

Kohn, A. 1993. *Punished by Rewards*. Boston: Houghton Mifflin.

Lawler, E. E. III. 1981. *Pay and Organizational Development*. Reading, MA: Addison-Wesley.

Lawler, E. E. III, S. A. Mohrman, and G. E. Ledford Jr. 1998. *Strategies for High Performance Organizations: The CEO Report.* San Francisco: Jossey-Bass.

Locke, E. A., and D. Henne. 1986. Work Motivation Theories. In *International Review of Industrial and Organizational Psychology,* ed. C. L. Cooper and I. Robertson, 1–35. Chichester, UK: Wiley.

Mayo, E. 1933. *The Human Problems of an Industrial Civilization.* New York: Macmillan.

Petty, M. M., B. Singleton, and D. W. Campbell. 1992. An Experimental Evaluation of an Organizational Incentive Plan in the Electric Utility Industry. *Journal of Applied Psychology* 77: 427–436.

Rothlisberger, F. L., and W. Dixon. 1939. *Management and the Worker.* New York: Wiley.

Scott, W. E., J. L. Farh, and P. M. Podsakoff. 1988. The Effects of "Intrinsic" and "Extrinsic" Reinforcement Contingencies on Task Behavior. *Organizational Behavior and Human Decision Processes* 41: 405–425.

15

PAY SYSTEM CHANGE: LAG, LEAD, OR BOTH?

A Commentary on Wruck, Ledford, and Heneman

Edward E. Lawler III

CHANGES IN an organization's pay system are usually high in visibility, high in impact, and difficult to execute. As a result they are often considered "hot" change levers that potentially can derail as well as support an organizational change effort. It is precisely because of their impact that it is appropriate to ask when and how compensation changes are best deployed as part of an overall change effort. The Wruck and Ledford papers make important points about the advantages and disadvantages of making reward systems changes at different points during a change effort. I find the arguments of both Karen Wruck and Gerald Ledford convincing—but not necessarily as conflicting as the authors' strong advocacy of their positions suggests. The discussion of pay and organizational change that follows will, I hope, make it clear why I have reached this conclusion.

Pay and Organizational Change

Before presenting an overall way of thinking about reward system change in organizational change efforts, I would like to establish some basic points about pay, organizational effectiveness, and organizational change.

Types of Organizational Change

There are a wide variety of different types of organizational change efforts. Pay system change does not necessarily need to be managed in the same way in all different types of organizational change; indeed, it probably should not be handled in the same way. Similarly, when different change objectives are targeted, it is important to use reward system changes selectively and to fit them to the outcome or outcomes that the change effort is focused on.

In order to focus and simplify this discussion of change efforts, I would like to concentrate on a particular type of organizational change: efforts in which a major discontinuous or transformational performance change is the objective. The discontinuous performance change may be either a dramatic rise in an organization's performance level or the creation of whole new performance areas, such as those created when a company enters new businesses or establishes very different products.

Changes in multiple organizational systems are almost always needed in order to produce discontinuous change in an organization's performance. By this I mean changes not just in one organization system, such as the reward system, but in the organization's structure, information and decision processes, and business strategy. This is the type of change situation that raises the most interesting questions about when and how to change the pay system, and it is the type of change I believe Wruck and Ledford have in mind in their papers.

Performance Impacts of Reward Systems

There are many different features of an organization's pay and reward system. Elsewhere I have described these in considerable detail (Lawler 2000). Rather than discussing all of them here, I will only consider the two features that have been identified as the most powerful features of a pay system. The first involves the degree to which rewards are based on performance, and the second involves how the salary or base pay of an individual is determined. These two dimensions of a reward system seem to be particularly important in determining individual and organizational behavior.

Pay for performance and base pay constitute a significant piece of the employment contract that individuals have with their organizations. Other parts of this contract include the amount of job security individuals have; the type of work they do; the opportunities they have for learning; and, of course, how they are treated by the organization in the areas of due process and supervision. Virtually any major change in the reward system requires altering the fundamental characteristics of the employment contract. Thus, reward system changes are often hot issues.

It is beyond the scope of this discussion to go into great detail about the many impacts that reward systems have on individual and organizational behavior, but it is important to point out that they do have multiple impacts (Lawler 1990). The most important impacts involve their effect on motivation and on the attraction, retention, and development of employees. A great deal of evidence demonstrates how reward systems impact these behaviors (Lawler 2000). In essence, rewards affect motivation when they are effectively tied to performance and significant amounts of reward are given. Attraction and retention, on the other hand, are a function of how well individuals are rewarded relative to their opportunities in the labor market.

In addition to affecting motivation, attraction, and retention, pay systems can strongly effect skill development. When learning skills can increase an individual's reward level, the reward system can motivate skill development. Pay systems can also reinforce organizational structures and in many ways drive the culture of an organization. They affect structure by either uniting or dividing individuals, groups, and business units. Thus, I view reward systems not as an inconsequential organizational system but as a potential key driver of individual and organizational performance.

Reward Systems and Change Strategy

It is precisely because reward systems affect behavior that change in the pay system and other reward systems is almost always needed when major organizational change is attempted. This point is made by those organizational effectiveness theories that emphasize the concept of fit. For example, the classic star model of organizational effectiveness argues that organizations are effective to the degree that their strategies, structures, processes, rewards, and people strategies fit one another (Galbraith 1973). It goes on to argue that if a change in organizational performance is needed, it is rarely adequate simply to change one of these, because this only creates a misfit and a possible decrease in organizational effectiveness. To enable the company to move to a new and more effective level of performance, all of the elements of the star model need to be changed. This, of course, is what makes change so difficult and why organizations often do not change even when their performance is no longer effective.

I have argued that in order to move to a high-involvement approach to organizing, a company needs to change the distribution of four elements—information, knowledge, power, and rewards (Lawler 1996). Any employee involvement change effort that does not shift all four of these to the lower levels of an organization inevitably creates an imbalanced situation that is potentially ineffective and dysfunctional from an organizational design point of view. For example, failure to move rewards to the lower levels of an organization runs the risk of creating behavior without responsibility or consequences. This can be particularly problematic if considerable decision-making power is given to individuals at lower levels of the organization. On the other hand, simply moving rewards down is unlikely to increase organizational effectiveness if individuals do not have the information, knowledge, and power they need to act in ways that will influence performance and help them understand the reward system.

The literature on organizational change suggests that most organizational change efforts go through three phases. Each needs to be effectively executed in order for the overall change effort to be successful. The first phase involves the unfreezing of the organization. During this period the organization needs to recognize the need for change, explore change alternatives, and develop a willingness to change. The second phase involves the implementation of changes targeted at improving or changing the performance of the organization. The third phase involves making the new ways of performing standard operating procedure, not something new to be learned and experimented with. Increasingly, because of the dynamic nature of the business environment and the need for continuous change, theorists argue that the final phase should be thought of as part of the beginning of the next change sequence. For the purposes of this discussion, I would like to look at each of these three phases separately and consider what role pay system changes can and should play in making each of them successful.

Unfreezing

The key task in the first phase of change efforts is to create a willingness to abandon the old and to search for new, more effective organization designs and management practices. Much of the literature on organizational change emphasizes the problem of resistance to change and argues that almost inevitably people resist major organizational changes. There are many reasons why individuals resist change. Some of these include perceptions that the change will have significant negative consequences for them. The negative consequences can range from layoffs to jobs' being made smaller so that individuals lose job evaluation points and therefore fall into a lower pay grade.

Just as the pay system can contribute to resistance to change, it can potentially foster a willingness to consider change. What kind of reward practices are likely to do this? The paper by Wruck does a good job of pointing out the answer to this question. Compensation systems that reward people for organizational performance as a whole can be a powerful motivator of change, because they can create dissatisfaction with the existing performance of the organization and can offer the prospect of increased rewards.

Particularly if the organizational changes that are proposed can be clearly tied to improvements in organizational performance, profit-sharing plans, stock ownership plans, stock option programs, and other programs that reward individuals for organizational performance can help motivate the search for and the acceptance of change. In some organizational change situations, these types of plans may already be in place and therefore need only to be highlighted and related to the need for organizational change in order to motivate behavior change.

Installing pay-for-performance plans before a change program is implemented can have a second advantage. It can avert the negative effects of executives' gaining tremendously from an organizational change effort while the employees lose or gain nothing. This is not a trivial point; large outcome differences among organizational members can threaten the long-term effectiveness of a change effort.

One other sequencing possibility exists with respect to the use of organizationwide reward systems such as stock plans and profit-sharing plans. Some organizations have promised their employees that these plans will be installed once an organizational change has been put into place. In essence, the installation of these plans has been offered as a reward for not resisting the change. This is a potential way to use pay as a kind of lead system, but probably is not as effective as actually putting the plans in first and using the rewards that these plans may generate as an incentive for exploring and accepting change. In most cases putting in the plans is likely to be more effective simply because it makes more tangible the rewards that individuals will get if the right changes are identified and effectively implemented. Motivation to change is only marginally enhanced by a rather vague promise that at some point in the future an undeveloped plan will be installed that will give an undetermined amount of reward to individuals if the change effort is undertaken and is successful.

There is one final way to use the reward system as a way of unfreezing the organization. This approach is probably appropriate only in organizations that have severe financial problems and need to introduce rapid major change. It involves reducing the rewards of individuals but offering them the opportunity to return to their previous reward level if they implement successful change. For example, some organizations have reduced the base pay of individuals but told them that if the organization develops and implements changes that produce an improved company performance level, the employees will be able to recapture their lost money, either through pay increases or through the payment of a bonus.

Change Implementation

The motivation to implement change is a key requirement for successful change that the reward system can help meet. Several variable payment approaches can be used to facilitate implementation. I have already mentioned some of them in my discussion of unfreezing; for example, organizationwide profit sharing, stock option plans, or other stock plans that reward individuals for improved organizational performance. Gain sharing has not been mentioned yet, but it is frequently installed early in the change implementation process (Lawler 2000).

Rewarding performance can encourage implementation, just as it can encourage readiness to change; but pay-for-performance plans have a critical weakness with respect to change implementation. They are not specifically targeted to the implementation process. Thus, the so-called line of sight between implementation and the reception of financial rewards may be weak. This suggests the need for a short-term bonus plan specifically targeted at implementation.

It is possible and often desirable to identify implementation milestones and goals and to tie variable payments to the achievement of these goals. This type of goal-sharing plan is becoming increasingly popular (Lawler et al. 1998). It is usually structured to reward the ongoing performance of an organization, but it can also be used to highlight particular performance areas and implementation activities that are part of an organization's strategic agenda. For example, General Electric used this type of plan when it installed its Six Sigma quality program. Specific implementation targets for the quality effort were set, and reaching them was an objective in the bonus plans of most senior managers. At the plant level, goal-sharing plans covered all employees, not just the management population.

Giving an important reward for implementing a change is potentially a quite powerful way to be sure that change actually happens in an organization. This kind of reward plan can be difficult to manage, however, because it requires establishing clear implementation goals and the ability to estimate the implementation time of specific parts of the change process. Thus, it is a reward system approach to change that does not fit every change situation; but when it does fit, it is likely to be effective, because it creates a clear line of sight.

Given that change often requires individuals to learn new skills and to change the kind of work they do, change implementation can be aided by pay systems that reward individuals for acquiring new skills, knowledge, and competencies. The growing popularity of knowledge/skill-based pay systems is a testimony to the potential effectiveness of these plans in changing the skills of individuals (Lawler et al. 1998).

In some cases knowledge/skill-based pay plans involve an increase in the base pay of individuals, but in others they simply consist of a one-time payment to individuals who learn new skills. Where it is being used to support the implementation of a major change, a knowledge/skill-based pay plan that pays a bonus amount for learning new skills is often the most appropriate. Base pay changes increase the fixed pay costs of an organization, and this may be a significant negative particularly if the organization's employees are already reasonably paid. Thus, it often makes sense to keep base pay the same and to encourage change by giving a one-time bonus to individuals who master the new skills they need in order to operate effectively in the changed organization.

Effectively designing a knowledge/skill-based pay system to support a change process requires that the organization understand the changes well enough to be able to identify the specific skills and knowledge that individuals need. But this is not always possible when a major organizational change process is first undertaken. Thus, it may not make sense to make this kind of intervention when the change implementation begins. Instead, it may be better to keep it for later in the change process and to use it more as a lag system.

So far, I have been discussing approaches that will motivate individuals to implement change, not approaches intended to reduce the resistance to change. As mentioned earlier, resistance to change often comes about precisely because individuals feel that they will lose out on financial and career opportunities as a result of the change. One way to prevent this concern from being a resistance factor is to guarantee individuals at the beginning of the change implementation that they will not lose either pay or other rewards as a result of the change process. This assurance is often combined with an employment security guarantee protecting individuals from negative consequences as a result of the change process. In essence, what organizations can do is to create an employment contract that is based on loyalty and essentially says that the organization will be loyal to individuals if they go along with the change process.

Despite the appeal of the loyalty contract approach, there is little evidence to suggest that that it leads to effective change. In a recent study of change in Fortune 1000 corporations, we found that this approach is not associated with the effective implementation of the changes required in employee involvement, reengineering, and total quality management efforts (Lawler et al. 1998). However, we did find that stating an employment contract that emphasizes the importance of performance and learning new skills is associated with successful implementation of these change efforts. Apparently it works better to tell individuals that supporting change is necessary if they are to keep their job and current pay rate than to tell them that they will not be harmed by the change regardless of how they respond to it.

A more extreme change management practice than stating a performance/learning employment contract is to tell individuals that they no longer have jobs but that they are free to apply for jobs in the "new" organization. They are then offered the opportunity to interview for jobs in the new organization when it is created. When they are selected for new jobs, they get a new and different pay rate depending upon the job that they acquire. This approach clearly is a way to unfreeze the organization and eliminate old ways of doing things. It also creates a strong interest in the rapid creation of the new organization. However, it runs a great risk of driving away a significant number of employees, and it always causes a major disruption in an organization's performance. Thus, this tactic fits only situations of extreme crisis in which an organization needs to motivate individuals to rapidly identify and accept a new approach to operating.

Refreezing: Creating an Operating Approach

My focus so far has been primarily on reward system practices that can be used to reward and encourage the development and implementation of change. Now it is time to consider reward system changes that are expected to be part of the ongoing operating systems of an organization. In many respects this is the most difficult issue to address. As indicated earlier, there are a wide variety of reward system features and practices that need to be aligned to support the way an organization operates. Pay system changes usually are needed with respect to performance-based pay, the market position of pay, and job evaluation, not to mention changes in other features of the reward system, such as promotions and perquisites. What is clear is that all features of the reward system need to be assessed so that all features will fit with the new operating approach that the organization wants to establish after the change process is complete.

It is important to put in place a reward system that does not just encourage the adoption of a new way of operating but supports the organization's ongoing effective operation. In most cases this means tying rewards to the key learnings, behaviors, and performance focuses that are necessary for the organization to operate effectively. Thus, the design of the reward system needs to take into account issues such as the types of capabilities the organization needs; the strategic focus of the organization; the key organizational design features; and the need for cooperation, teamwork, and interdependent action.

Often some of the pay system changes that are needed cannot be identified and developed until the new operating approach is actually in place. For example, often a relatively permanent knowledge/skill-based pay system can be developed only after individuals have done their new work for a while. Time is needed to allow the development and specification of the skills and knowledge that individuals must have. Often, the nuances of a very targeted bonus plan can be developed only after an organization has operated in a particular manner for a while. It is also clear that work teams can make pay decisions about their members only after they have matured and developed. Thus, in a change to a team-based organization, it does not make sense to start with a team-based performance management system that involves pay (Lawler 2000).

There is considerable evidence that many pay practices (e.g., gain sharing, skill-based pay) work best when they are developed by the employees who will be affected by them (Lawler 1990). In order to participate in the design of the reward system, individuals need knowledge of how the organization should operate. Delaying the design process can help individuals gain an understanding of what the reward system needs to do to help the organization be effective. Thus, there are some clear arguments for waiting until the new operating mode has been achieved before starting to develop many of the pieces of the reward system that must fit with it. In essence, the learning that takes place during the early operating period can be an invaluable input to the process of establishing the final form of the reward system.

Before we conclude that operating or steady state pay changes should always lag other operating state changes, it is important to note how gain-sharing plans that generate organization-wide bonuses that are based on improvements in operating results have been used. They are a good example of how a permanent feature of the pay system can lead change. The research clearly shows that putting in gain sharing as a permanent reward system feature can stimulate other change activity. But it is also clear that when an organization is not ready to follow the implementation of the gain-sharing plan with other changes, gain sharing is a poor and ineffective way to create a new operating approach.

The lesson from gain sharing is clear: For a new reward system to operate effectively, its implementation needs to be carefully positioned in the sequence of the new operating systems that are put in place. In some instances gain-sharing processes and other reward system changes should be among the first of the permanent operating practices of an organization to be put in place; in other cases, they should not be. It is hard to generalize about when reward system practices such as pay for performance, bonus plans, knowledge/skill-based pay, employment contracts, and so forth should be put in place. This question can be answered only when specifics are known about what other changes are planned. The changes that are likely to be effective and to create support for other planned changes are the ones that should be implemented first.

A Strategic Approach to Pay System Change

It is clear that there is no simple answer to the question of whether pay system change should lag or lead other key changes. It is also clear that pay system change must occur in order for organizational change efforts to be successful. Table 15-1 presents an approach to thinking about the different periods of a change process and the reward system changes that can support each stage of the process.

The first stage of the change process, unfreezing or opening up the organization to change, is perhaps the simplest to consider from a reward systems point of view. It clearly calls for pay-for-performance approaches that encourage individuals in the organization to think about improvement and increased organizational effectiveness. The best vehicles for doing this typically are profit sharing, stock options, and other forms of variable pay that reward company performance. In situations in which organizations need to develop and change on a continuous, ongoing basis, it makes sense to keep these plans in effect.

Table 15-1
Phases of Change

	Unfreezing	*Implementation*	*Operating*
KEY ISSUES	Motivation for developing change effort	Motivation for skill learning and adoption of change	Motivation and capability to perform effectively
REWARD ACTIONS	Profit sharing and stock ownership	Bonuses for change implementation Knowledge/skill-based pay for new skills New employment contract Possible bonuses for achieving new performance targets	Pay-for-performance systems focusing on strategic performance and on the attraction, retention, and development of high performers Strategic practices that support systems that are or soon can be put in place

Things get more complicated in the implementation phase. One alternative is to put in place transition pay-for-performance plans that specifically reward implementation of the change effort. This makes particular sense when the implementation process can clearly be measured and a time line specified. It also can make sense to reward individuals for developing the skills they need in order to operate the new organizational systems and do their jobs.

In some cases it may make sense simply to skip the use of implementation bonuses and to move directly to bonuses and variable pay plans that reward successful operation in the new system—that is, to identify the key performance indicators that should improve as a result of the change process and to begin rewarding individuals based on their performance in these areas. The risk in doing this is that it may take a while for performance to improve and trigger bonuses; as a result, individuals may not be as highly motivated to work on the implementation process as they would be if they were directly rewarded for it.

Most difficult to specify is how reward system changes should be sequenced and designed to support the ongoing operations of the organization. In this area it is particularly important to state that it all depends on the nature of the organizational change and on how and when the new reward system practices can be developed.

In general, it probably makes sense to wait on many of the major reward system design decisions if there are sufficient incentives to unfreeze an organization and to motivate its members to implement the other changes that are part of the organizational change effort. This is a big if, however. In many cases new pay practices do need to become a permanent part of the organization's operating system and are required for implementation of other changes. The challenge, therefore, is to combine and sequentially introduce temporary reward system changes that will encourage the implementation of change as well as permanent ones that are intended to become part of the ongoing operation of the organization.

Conclusion

My answer to the question of whether pay system changes should be a lag or lead factor in large-scale organizational change is now clear: They should be both. They should be used as a lead variable in most cases to stimulate the development of the change process and to encourage its implementation. They should be used as both a lag and a lead variable in supporting the ongoing operations of the organization once the change process has been completed. In short, there is no single answer to how pay system change should be managed in a change process. We can say, however, that it is always important to recognize what reward system options there are and what impacts the reward system can have on behavior, and to use this knowledge in determining when and how to introduce pay system change. Finally, it is important to remember that ignoring reward systems is not an option. Change efforts that make this mistake are sure to fail.

References

Galbraith, J. R. 1973. *Designing Complex Organizations*. Reading, MA: Addison-Wesley.

Lawler, E. E. *Strategic Pay*. 1990. San Francisco: Jossey-Bass.

———. 1996. *From the Ground Up: Six Principles for Creating the New Logic Corporation*. San Francisco: Jossey-Bass.

————. 2000. *Rewarding Excellence: Pay Strategies for the New Economy*. San Francisco: Jossey-Bass.

Lawler, E. E., S. A. Mohrman, and G. E. Ledford Jr. 1998. *Strategies for High Performance Organizations: The CEO Report*. San Francisco: Jossey-Bass.

SECTION VI

CONSULTANTS' ROLE IN CHANGE

Large and Knowledge-Driven or Small and Process-Driven?

THOUGH IT IS OFTEN undiscussed, especially in the academic literature on organizational change, outside consultants typically play a very important role in most change efforts. Since the early 1980s management consulting has been one of the fastest-growing industries in the world. The extensive use of consultants, and the enormous differences among them in terms of their practice, raises the question the papers in this section tackle: What is the consultant's proper role in change?

In the first paper in this section, Terry Neill argues that consultants can help bridge the knowledge gap between the world of ideas and the world of practice. He suggests that there is a huge gap between what a typical firm knows and the knowledge resources that exist. One reason for this gap is that the knowledge developed by academics is often locked up in the ivory towers of universities and is not translated into practical usable knowledge. Another reason is that the experiments conducted by firms are not monitored, and therefore the lessons of best practice are often lost. Neill believes that one of the ways consulting firms can add value to clients is to bridge this knowledge gap. Consulting firms may be in a unique position to serve this bridging function because they can test what works and what does not. Neill further argues that for change to be effective, it must also be systemic.

Firms cannot afford to have a partial view of the human system. They must recognize that the human system is a nested complex of many layers and that a firm can bring about lasting change only by changing all these elements simultaneously. Neill's perspective suggests the consultant's role in change is to be the expert advisor who can deploy a large team of experts to help an organization implement changes that reflect best practice along multiple fronts—all at once.

Robert Schaffer, in the second paper in this section, provides a very different perspective on the role of consultants. If the ultimate objective is to create a learning organization, he argues, then large consulting firms staffed by smart people delivering elegant packaged solutions will not work. Such engagements are rarely successful in getting results. Their failure lies not in the quality of the solution but in the organization's capacity to enact it. Schaffer argues for much smaller projects aimed at obtaining measurable results. Consultants do not bring in the solution; they lead relevant organizational members through a process of analysis, redesign, and change. In this process the organization develops the commitment and capability needed to enact the solution.

Robert Miles reconciles these two perspectives on the role of consultants in the final paper of this section. He argues that as long as there is an abiding focus on delivering measurable results, consultants of various kinds can be successful. What can be problematic is focusing on a process or technique as an end in itself. He further suggests that the type of consultant that is best suited to a change effort may depend on the type of change initiative. Some initiatives may require large-scale interventions, others a smaller process intervention. The mistake would be to assume that one size fits all.

16

HUMAN PERFORMANCE THAT INCREASES BUSINESS PERFORMANCE

The Growth of Change Management and Its Role in Creating New Forms of Business Value

Terry Neill and Craig Mindrum

ODAY THE PROFESSIONAL services field known as "change management" is undergoing major transformation. From the beginning, the field has focused on the human dimension of organizations,
although for some years that focus was somewhat limited in its scope—
restricted primarily to human resources and training. In subsequent
years the field broadened its scope to include the study and practical
application of ways to support organizations and their people as they
move through large-scale change initiatives. Throughout this most recent period, however, there has been a growing feeling that a stronger
link needs to be made between optimum performance of people and
the overall performance of the business. That is, how can we track our
investments in optimizing human performance and definitively link
those investments to increases in shareholder value and other kinds of
measurements?

This chapter proposes a framework that allows us to make this
critical link. We will first identify the most important strands of work
within change management today. Following a short historical perspective, we will turn to current leading-edge work we have conducted
at Andersen Consulting. Our objective is to develop a dynamic framework—informed by the science of systems thinking—by which to design and implement business performance solutions for organizations

from a combined human and organization performance perspective. In the final section we will suggest some ways in which this perspective alters the manner in which consulting interventions are designed and delivered.

Research That Matters

For several decades a large body of academic material from various fields has promised to help organizations focus on optimizing the human dimension of their business. Work done not only in fields such as education but also in the social sciences—psychology, sociology, contemporary anthropology, organizational behavior—has had wide practical application in many endeavors, including management consulting, which in turn incorporated these fields of study into one particular competency of consulting, change management.

And change management has become an important proving ground of this academic research. Many of these fields are relatively young in comparison to most disciplines in natural sciences, and for this reason many research findings are fragmented and sometimes contradictory. Additionally, the social sciences are forced to address very challenging issues that pertain to complex systems—human interactions—which further complicates their efforts to replicate findings consistently. As large management consulting firms such as Andersen Consulting have incorporated academic theories into the manner in which we help our clients, we have learned firsthand what works and what doesn't; what sounds good in theory and what works in practice; and what the challenges are as organizations attempt to move hundreds or thousands of people through large-scale strategic and technological change, and as they attempt to optimize the performance of their workforce.

The field of change management has now moved to a new level of sophistication. One of the strengths of a management consulting firm is its ability to devise frameworks—logical orderings of the various components of organizational solutions—and then use these frameworks to more quickly develop subsequent solutions. At Andersen Consulting, for example, we have used this approach for many years to design and implement information systems. Today, this same approach can be used in the design of human performance solutions within organizations. People are not things, nor are they as generally predictable as a database or a server connection. Yet they are not totally unpredictable, either. We know a great deal about how people work, what they need in order to perform optimally, how they react under stress, what forms of leadership and performance support are necessary for them to do their jobs, and so forth. This knowledge can now give us a basis for designing a "human performance system" within an organization, one that is in harmony with the strategies, processes, and technologies of the whole company.

This holistic understanding of human performance has three distinct, though related, applications. First, it identifies all of the areas, from a human performance perspective, where we need to focus our attention as organizations embark on particular change journeys. Second, it allows us more easily to identify how interventions designed to maximize human performance translate directly into increases in business performance. Third, it allows us to create new kinds of value for organizations through those human performance interventions. It's this last point that takes change management to a new level. Rather than being an adjunct or an afterthought to other forms of work (strategic thinking, technological innovation), change management consultants can now address company executives and say, "We have a way to increase your share price by optimizing the performance of one of your overlooked resources: your people." We've known for years that companies' strategic change initiatives can fail if they neglect the human dimensions of change. This approach is the converse to that point of view: "Let's begin with the people, and find ways that maximizing their performance can lead to strategic advantage." Consulting solutions here will touch all aspects of the business—but they will look at the business through a human performance lens, as it were.

In the end, this work also represents a way to bridge the worlds of academe and management. For too many years, academics have done excellent work in organizational theory and human performance that has not fully penetrated into the everyday lives of executives. This cannot be good for either side of the equation. Imagine how it would be if computer scientists in the academy were talking among themselves about the benefits of universal networking and communication . . . but that information was not reaching into the ways companies were organizing themselves and conducting business. It is time to open the everyday lives of companies to cutting-edge research about human performance within organizations—and it is time to subject that research to the fires of real business experience.

Stages of Change Management's Growth

Change management as a branch of management consulting has been through several stages in its development over the past three decades or so. As knowledge and experience increased, the next stage did not necessarily make the older ones obsolete; more often, each stage built upon its predecessor to expand the work and extend its impact. Figure 16-1 summarizes how these different strands of thought have evolved over time, in each case resulting in greater impact on the business as they evolved to the next stage.

Stage 1: HR and Training

Change management began as a professional field with two primary emphases: one having to do with traditional human resources work, and another with educational and training endeavors. Both emphases were fairly straightforward, because companies generally had both a human resources department and a training department. Management consultancies like our own developed specialized tools, techniques, and strategies in these areas, and worked with clients to innovate and streamline within fairly traditional boundaries.

Stage 2: Support for Strategic and Technological Change

The second stage of change management growth began roughly in the early 1980s, when both HR and training consulting began to have an impact beyond the specialized departments and moved closer to the boardroom on the one hand, and to the IT shop on the other.

First, the work that came to be known as "strategic human resources management" began to address in a consistent way the challenges of dealing with increasing competition, scarcity of resources, and the highly educated professional employees who soon came to be known as "knowledge workers." As Charles Fombrun has written,

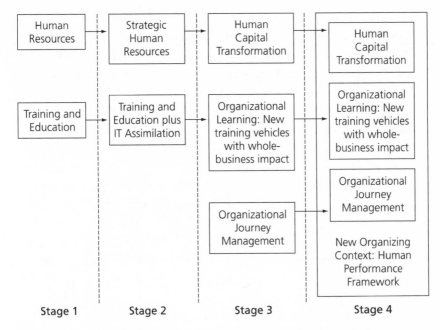

Figure 16-1   Each Stage of Change Management Results in Greater Impact
on the Business

strategic human resources management was born under the assumption that "the untapped contributions of the human resources in organizations could make the difference between efficiency and ineffi-
ciency, death and survival in the marketplace."[1]

Second, training and education consulting began to support other
kinds of initiatives, most often related to the implementation of new
technology. The transition from mainframe-based to client/server
computing solutions especially made this work important. Technology
was driving new ways of working. People needed help assimilating the
technology and learning to work with it, and the systems themselves
had to be designed with usability in mind. Change management developed new methods for ensuring that corporate investment in technology paid off with a workforce that could perform better.

Stage 3: Organizational Journey Management

The years since about 1990 have been marked by a recognition that
the pace of marketplace change and the intensity of competition de-

mand new ways to move an entire organization through major change. Corporate executives have been growing increasingly frustrated at the failures of strategic initiatives—failures that occurred in large part because the corporate culture could not or would not embrace the change.

Greg Brenneman's experience turning around Continental Airlines is a case in point. When Brenneman took over the ailing airline, he reports in his case study,[2] he "had never seen a company as dysfunctional as Continental." Interestingly, he puts the problem in very human terms. Because the company had been through so many changes in top leadership, the workforce had adopted the tactic of doing nothing while awaiting new management. "Managers were paralyzed by anxiety," Brenneman writes. The turnaround plan for Continental is a classic story of organizational journey management. It's a combination of some fairly simple and straightforward corporate and operational strategies, coupled with some very sensitive and powerful leadership actions. Strategy had to be clear, and its implementation had to be decisive, so that people would feel they were being led somewhere. People had to be let go, yes; and some operations had to be shut down. Yet Brenneman carried out these moves while treating people humanely and with dignity, lest he destroy the trust of those who remained. And he devotes the largest portion of his case study to his efforts to turn around the corporate culture of Continental. The workplace "needn't be repressive," he writes. "In fact, if employees aren't having fun at work—that is, if they aren't engaged in the process and treated with respect—your turnaround will not succeed."

A great many models, tools, and techniques have arisen in recent years to organize and manage the many different components of major organizational change. An example: our firm's journey framework (figure 16-2), which gives us a simple yet powerful way to communicate to our clients the most important categories of work that must be done to ensure that a workforce both can and will perform over the course of a change journey. The journey framework divides organizational change issues into four categories, along two important axes. The first axis is supply versus demand. That is, organizations must attend not only to programs that "push" the change initiatives, but also to programs that create a "pull" for the change from within the workforce itself. The second axis is macro versus micro. That is, major

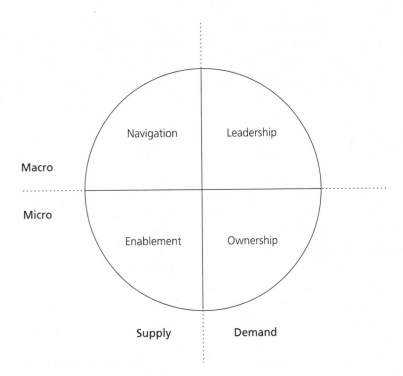

Figure 16-2 Journey Framework
Copyright © 1999 Andersen Consulting

change requires both high-level programs that affect the entire organization and programs that touch each individual person.

The journey framework axes result in four major factors that produce major organizational change:

- *Leadership.* Activities that develop and nurture executives who will support and sponsor the change initiative.

- *Ownership.* Actions designed to ensure that the entire corporate culture accepts the changes and will continue to be motivated to high levels of performance during the change.

- *Enablement.* Training, education, knowledge management, and other related activities that provide the workforce with the capability to perform at high levels.

- *Navigation.* Management activities dedicated to managing the many different strands of a change program.

The organizational journey management stage in the development of change management has also been marked by the development of new and more sophisticated approaches to HR and training work. "Human capital transformation" initiatives, as we call them, integrate a suite of interventions that continuously align the workforce with a company's evolving business strategy and work environment. These initiatives today also focus on aligning the HR processes, organization, and technologies to support management of human assets to deliver against that strategy.

In organizational learning, our work in recent years has focused on new techniques for ensuring that an organization's workforce can reach optimal performance levels quickly, and that new learning can be assimilated quickly without excessive risk to the company. Here, a learn-by-doing approach—which goes back at least to the educator John Dewey—results in retention rates that are far superior to traditional methods of teaching. (Some research indicates that percentage effectiveness of a learn-by-doing approach is as high as 75 percent, compared to rates as low as 5 percent for lecture-oriented approaches.)

Learning by doing has always been favored by those who train airline pilots. When it comes to learning the skills needed in business, however, individuals' first real practice of decision making within the context of their business very often occurs in a live business environment. Andersen Consulting has been pioneering the development of "flight simulators for business": virtual environments that match the realities of a business and in which employees can practice at their own pace, free to make the mistakes they need to make in order to become truly effective. We believe this is a far better alternative than either allowing those employees to make their mistakes in a real business environment—with potentially disastrous results—or disregarding the necessity for the mistakes to be made.

Stage 4: A Comprehensive Framework for Human Performance

We are now linking various techniques and research findings into a comprehensive understanding of human performance within organizations. Here we have something to learn from other fields that are farther up the maturity curve. After a certain amount of experience and knowledge have been gained in real-life applications over a period of years, a field of endeavor begins to arrange that experience, codify it, and attain a degree of rigor, consistency, and predictability. We can call this step the development of an architecture or a framework. This framework cannot only optimize the performance of an organization's workforce, but also identify where new forms of value can be created within the human dimension of the company.

To understand this framework, we first must understand what human performance really means in an organization setting.

The Human Performance System

Any business entity can be thought of as multiple systems working together to produce an economic result. Among the many systems that make up a business, the system of entities, influences, and adaptive relationships relating to workforce performance is perhaps the most complex of all. This system—the system of human performance—is also likely to be the one that receives the least attention and is the least well understood. But the consequences of failing to understand the human performance system of an organization are steep. As Geary Rummler and Alan Brache write in their book *Improving Performance*, "An organization behaves as a system, regardless of whether it is being managed as a system. If an organization is not being managed as a system, it is not being effectively managed."[3]

A systems understanding of organizations is one of the hottest approaches in organizational theory today. Such books as Peter Senge's *The Fifth Discipline*, Margaret J. Wheatley's *Leadership and the New Science*, and Gareth Morgan's *Images of Organization* have asked us to think in more organic ways about organizational life. This approach leads naturally to thinking of change management work not as a simple, programmatic approach with direct cause-and-effect relationships but as a series of complex influences—as one might think about influencing an ecosystem, for example.

Michael Porter's concept of "complementary activity systems" is a way of helping companies overcome the error of trying to locate competitive advantage in operational improvement measures—single and unrelated efforts. Even when these isolated measures are successful, says Porter, they are too easily imitated by others and so are never a source of sustained competitive advantage. Sustainable advantage comes only from *systems* of activities that are *complementary;* that is, in which an activity that provides an advantage in one area will also provide advantages in other areas. This is how we think of organic entities: One cannot isolate effects in one part of an organism but must consider the influences of any part on the whole. "Companies with sustainable competitive advantage," says Porter, "integrate lots of activities within the business: their marketing, service, designs, customer support. All those things are consistent, interconnected, and mutually reinforcing."[4]

But the insights of systems thinking can be frustrating for companies, as well. Management may mistakenly come to believe that it is too difficult to influence a complex system. The right kind of mindset is no good if one has only the old tools. Systemic understanding must be accompanied by systemic tools with which to influence the system.

What exactly does it mean to say that human performance in organizations is a "complex adaptive system"? The quickest way to answer this question is by analogy. An ecosystem, for example, or the human body, is made up of many components at many different levels. If we wish to change or influence such a system, we have to be aware that there are different levels, and that any actions taken will have multiple consequences of which we have to be aware.

As Rummler and Brache write, "The anatomy of the human body includes a skeletal system, a muscular system, and a central nervous system. Since all of these systems are critical and interdependent, a failure in one subsystem affects the ability of the body to perform effectively." Thus, just as an understanding of human anatomy is required for a physician to diagnose and treat ailments, so an understanding of the entire system of human performance is necessary for an executive to diagnose a company and make it fully healthy.[5]

We can understand human performance, then, as a system involving several related layers (see figure 16-3):[6]

- The *environment,* a set of influences over which the company generally does not have direct control, but which affect the company and, ultimately, its people. These influences may be economic, regulatory, social, technological, or physical.

- The *strategy* of the company, including the corporate and business unit strategy as well as the organizational strategy.

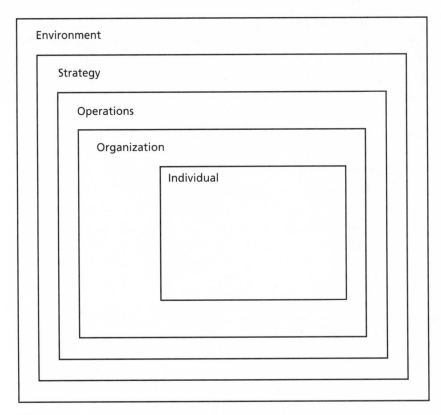

Figure 16-3 The Layers of the Human Performance System

- The *operations* of the company—essentially, the "layer" where the real work performance takes place: performance of processes, enabled by technology, in a particular physical setting.

- The *organization*, meaning the structure of the organization and the programs and interventions designed to influence people and their performance of work.

- The *individual* himself or herself, acting either alone or as a member of a team, driven by his or her distinctive abilities and motivations.

Influencing the Human Performance System: A Framework

But how does one influence a system and optimize its performance? It is one thing to be *aware* of the importance of human performance

. . . and quite another thing to know how to *do* something practical about it. Here we must be careful about how we use metaphors. The metaphor of an ecosystem, for example, is extremely powerful for helping people understand the fullness of what human performance means. At the same time, however, by promoting the ecosystem analogy we may unwittingly be contributing to a sense of futility among business executives. "If it's all that complex," they may well think, "then how can we ever hope to influence it in any way that is not almost accidental, or a nonrepeatable success? How can we predict in any way the multiple loops of cause and effect that make up a complex adaptive system?"

In the face of the complexity at the heart of human performance, organizations and their leaders may make critical mistakes.

- Executives may view human performance solutions as a sort of "art" and thus take actions that are subjective, with no way to measure or even to detect the effects of these actions. Executives in this category may be in danger of simply falling prey to the latest management fad—like the executive several years ago who announced that he hadn't gotten any results from "process reengineering" and was now moving to a "learning organization" approach.

- With the best of intentions, executives may take actions that are only point solutions and lack the power to penetrate throughout the entire human performance system. One government manager, for example, became quite enamored with the idea of employee empowerment. He announced major initiatives and set his organization on a course to ensure that this empowerment took place. There was only one problem: His employees simply weren't the type of people who were motivated to be empowered. They were people who were quite content to be told what to do, do it, collect their paycheck, and go home.

- Executives may take actions that have a positive effect at one place in the system but have unintended negative consequences elsewhere. Incentive programs and reward/recognition systems are sometimes notorious in this regard. If an organization is not careful, it can motivate 5 percent of the workforce at the expense of the other 95 percent. Failing to account for prime motivators may be another problem. In one case, for example, we were able to prevent a client from encountering major workforce problems when its management sought to eliminate the firm's long-standing overtime policy. As it turned out, our diagnosis of the workforce system revealed, overtime was among people's strongest motivators. Had the company simply announced a new overtime policy with no input from the workforce, major problems would have occurred.

In short, because human performance appears "soft," organizations may fail to construct solutions that are "hard"—that is, solutions built on solid knowledge of human performance and on methods that are rigorous, repeatable, and measurable. It's not enough just to say that we can see something the right way. Again, the right kind of vision or mindset is not enough if one has only the old tools. *Systemic understanding must be accompanied by systemic tools with which to influence the system.*

Such a tool is the Andersen Consulting Human Performance Framework. In any field there comes a time when we have gained enough experience to abstract knowledge from that experience and organize that knowledge into components of a generic solution. In the field of information systems delivery, for example, there came a time when the IT world had delivered enough of these systems that it could find common aspects of solutions, identify these aspects, and reuse them in building other systems. Solutions, then, can be analyzed; repeatable components of those solutions, found across many different environments, can be identified and abstracted into a framework. One of the benefits of a framework or architecture—whether for technology or for human performance—is that complexity is hidden behind a depiction that is simple and easy to communicate. A framework is an aid to understanding and structuring a problem. As a generic grouping of reusable components, it can serve as a basis for a detailed solution for a particular organization.

The Human Performance Framework (figure 16-4), developed through Andersen Consulting research and validated and enhanced through our work with companies around the world, is based on the layered depiction of the human performance system shown earlier in figure 16-3. Each of the layers of the framework should be familiar to most people. And as one goes deeper into each of the components or

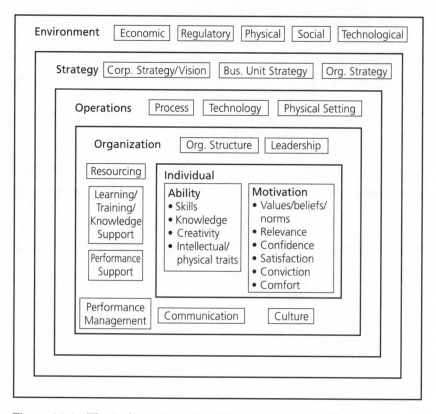

Figure 16-4 The Andersen Consulting Human Performance Framework
Copyright © 1999 Andersen Consulting. Patent pending.

"influence systems" within each layer, these too will sound familiar to most. In fact, there is little that is new in any single part of the framework. What *is* new is the holistic point of view it provides, along with the confirmation of the fact that there is no "silver bullet" for optimizing human performance. No one piece by itself will accomplish the goal. Just as a physician requires an understanding of the whole human anatomy to diagnose and treat ailments, so an executive needs an understanding of the entire system of human and business performance in order to diagnose a company's condition and make it fully healthy.

How does the framework help enhance the performance of organizations? One way is by helping companies see more clearly how their actions ripple through the whole system of performance. By understanding the complex cause-and-effect relationships, an organization can ensure that investments in interventions pay off—and can weigh various kinds of actions based on how much bang for the buck will result. For example, one large government agency strengthened the odds that recently redesigned processes would succeed by using the Human Performance Framework. With the framework as a guide, they could document where the effects of the process change were going to be felt most strongly. They could then determine—based upon the organization layer of the framework—which management interventions would offer the most benefits for the investment.

The ability to predict and then track financial benefit through organization and human performance interventions is one of the key advantages provided by the Human Performance Framework. Working with a major North American auto manufacturer, we used the framework as a basis for diagnosing the current level of performance by employees of the company's customer assistance center, or call center. Financially, the center had been losing money. And a series of projects over the past few years, intended to enhance the performance of the center, had only made matters worse, because the projects had been limited point solutions that sometimes had had negative unintended consequences.

Through a series of interviews with management, supervisors, and employees, we were able to assess the health of the human performance system at the call center. Our systemic approach revealed the primary problems related to both the abilities and the motivation of the workforce. Everyone knew intuitively before the diagnostic that the attrition rate was far too high, causing too much expense to train new representatives and poor service as a result of an inexperienced workforce. Everyone also knew that it was taking too long to bring new employees up to a satisfactory level of proficient performance. But what was *behind* those problems? By analyzing each of the components of the framework, particularly within the organization layer, we were able to delve deeper into the problems with customer service representatives' abilities and motivation. For example, in terms of the abilities of the workforce, we found that

- The prerequisite skill set among new customer service representatives was inconsistent.

- The maturity and professionalism of new representatives had been far too variable.

- The distribution of skills and performance was far too uneven.

In terms of motivation, we found that

- Employees were not getting the sense of consistently being treated as valued individuals.

- Staying motivated in a tough environment had been too difficult.

- Limited career diversification opportunities were causing frustration and reduced commitment.

Now the financial payoff became somewhat easier to predict. We knew what the operation of the center was costing per year given the current level of performance. We could put a number on the cost of the interventions we wished to recommend in order to address the linked problems of attrition and proficiency. And we were able to predict, based on projected changes in attrition and proficiency, what the financial performance of a more effective call center would be over a five-year period. Putting all that information together resulted in a number that was guaranteed to turn any executive's head: Over a three-and-a-half-year period, the benefits would be $2.5 million.

We predicted other benefits from this work, as well, in addition to the formal business case:

- reduction in call time (roughly $1,000,000 for each minute of call time saved);

- additional savings from increased retention (e.g., availability of team leaders, support for new service representatives);

- realistic job previews for new representatives, which would identify borderline performers sooner; and

- easier scheduling because of a more experienced workforce.

Implications for Change Management Consulting Interventions

No consulting intervention can be successful unless it addresses all aspects of a company—its strategy, processes, technology, and people. The amount of effort necessary at each level will vary with each company and each business need. But some things can never change if we are to initiate real and lasting change:

- The perspective must be systemic: It must attempt to look at the whole company, focusing not just on random interventions here and there in the company's ecosystem but on the complex cause-and-effect relationships throughout the system.

- Expertise must be found to assist with the interventions at each level. It's not enough to bring in just a strategy expert, or a technology expert, or a human resources expert. Expertise provided by multiple teams must be coordinated and managed, much as a general contractor manages the experts required to construct a new building or house.

- The entire intervention must be managed as a journey. The company is moving from its present state to some desired future state. This will take time, and effort must be focused directly on planning and managing the journey.

Andersen Consulting plans and executes its consulting interventions according to a comprehensive methodology in four phases: planning, delivering, managing, and operating. Teams of consultants, working most of the time in partnership with employees of the company, specialize in the change management, strategy, process, and technology aspects of the work.

The *planning* phase begins with a business diagnosis, through which we gain a holistic understanding of the problems and opportunities by assessing the client company's internal and external context. We then align the corporate or business unit strategy with the marketplace and work to understand the implications of those strategies, including the impact on organization performance. Finally, we establish a business architecture by defining the organization performance requirements for fulfilling the value proposition.

As noted, the role of the Human Performance Framework is critical in the business diagnosis phase; the framework provides a comprehensive picture of the company's influences, particularly in the vital area of human performance.

The *delivering* phase begins with capability analysis and design: We design the business capabilities and validate them against the value

realization plan. Here we also design the organization and the competencies required in the new performance environment. We then implement the business capabilities, taking into consideration all components of the solution, including transitioning the workforce to new
kinds and levels of performance. Along the way, we measure results to
ensure that the business case levels of performance are being achieved.

It is within the delivering phase that we find initiatives that most
strongly support the development of optimal human performance:

- developing and refining the human performance infrastructure

- defining and deploying the appropriate physical environment

- designing and applying performance support tools

- transitioning the workforce

- implementing new policies and procedures

The *managing* phase is perhaps the most demanding aspect of
change journeys. In journey management we focus on delivering the
desired business results by ensuring that the right programs and projects are defined and that the organization is able and motivated to take
advantage of the resulting capabilities as they are delivered. Program
management, another critical aspect of comprehensive change journey
management, provides continuous direction. Through program management we help the company plan and manage projects in an efficient
and cost-effective manner, using appropriate disciplines, tools, and
techniques to organize the work required to deliver the business
capability.

In the *operating* phase we not only monitor the performance of the
existing solution, but ensure that it can evolve over time to meet new
business challenges.

Conclusion

The Human Performance Framework is, first of all, a way of seeing; it
is a way of looking at human performance and of communicating its
fullness in an integrated manner. As noted, however, this new way of
seeing must be accompanied by practical tools and techniques: Only

by linking theory to practice would we even dare to bring this framework to the attention of the CEOs of our clients. As the framework is used, it becomes a tool by which to guide the development of human performance solutions for companies of all sizes, in all industries, and in all places around the world.

In summary, the framework is

- a distillation of our experience in developing solutions and of our research into human performance within organizations;

- a tool that can be used by our professionals to analyze, diagnose, document, and communicate the shape of a solution; *and*

- a communication medium, including shared and commonly understood terminology.

We can identify a basic set of key statements about the Human Performance Framework:

1. The framework shows that human performance, and the means by which to influence and optimize it, are complex matters. However, neither human performance nor the actions that can be taken to influence it are a mystery.

2. There is little that is "new" within the framework. What is new is the holistic manner in which performance is described and communicated; also new is the holistic manner in which a suite of solutions is designed and implemented.

3. Unlike some gurus in the marketplace, Andersen Consulting shows through this framework that there is no silver bullet solution—no single approach or technique applicable to all environments.

4. Human performance involves some dimensions that are influenceable or "architectable" by our professionals; it also involves some dimensions that are not. Even factors outside our control, however, must be accounted for in our design for a solution. Natural disasters, for example, cannot be controlled; but we can build disaster recovery into a solution. Death of a spouse or family member cannot be controlled; but we can design jobs and roles, and deploy our people, in such a manner that the temporary absence of any individual does not ripple through to decreased business performance.

5. The individual layer of the framework is the foundation of human performance and is where our interventions are felt most strongly. All intentional interventions to influence human performance apply either directly to individuals and groups of individuals, or indirectly through the operations layer (process, technology, physical setting).

6. The organization layer identifies the elements that are directly architectable by the human performance architect.

7. The operations layer and the strategy layer identify things that influence human performance, but they may not be designed by a human performance architect. In those layers, a human performance architect provides input to the design of other architectures.

8. The impacts of our interventions on human performance are predictable at a macro level, and they can be measured.

This last statement brings us to a major challenge for consulting professionals today: the need to develop a comprehensive set of measures to demonstrate the added business value of investments made to optimize human performance. We now know with certainty that human performance is critical to successful implementation of business strategy. As Jeffrey Pfeffer has written in his book *The Human Equation*, "Success comes from implementing strategy, not just from having one. This implementation capability derives, in large measure, from the organization's people, how they are treated, their skills and competencies, and their efforts on behalf of the organization."[7]

Pfeffer's book nicely assembles the findings of research conducted over recent years to demonstrate the value of human performance interventions. The Human Performance Framework shows promise of helping us to demonstrate this value comprehensively and predictably. Only this capability will enable human performance theory and methodology to move beyond the management fad level and into the mainstream.

Recent research conducted by our firm suggests the difficulties faced by those of us who wish to link optimized human performance in organizations to overall business performance. Although the human dimension of organizations is frequently given lip service, it is not at the forefront of many executives' thinking. More often than not, executives have to be prompted to see their people as a potential source of increased business value. This is not just the fault of these executives. In the face of sometimes contradictory theory about human psychology and performance, and feeling an understandable distrust of some theories as "only the latest fad," executives want something rigorous, proven, and measurable.

All of the change management–related work described here is part of a larger picture of delivering greater business value through human performance. (Indeed, so convinced has the Andersen Consulting global organization become about this new route to creating business value, that we have changed the name of one of our major competency groups from "Change Management" to "Organization and Human Performance.") The Human Performance Framework represents the vital step in convincing executives—and ourselves, in some instances— that we can deliver solutions that are not just one-offs but can be codified, structured, and repeated in many different environments. This is exciting work, and there is much more excitement ahead.

Notes

1. Charles Fombrun, Noel M. Tichy, and Mary Anne Devanna, *Strategic Human Resources Management* (New York: Wiley, 1984), ix.
2. See Greg Brenneman, "Right Away and All at Once: How We Saved Continental," *Harvard Business Review*, September–October 1998.
3. Geary A. Rummler and Alan P. Brache, *Improving Performance: How to Manage the White Space on the Organization Chart*, 2d ed. (San Francisco: Jossey-Bass, 1995), 13.
4. Richard Pastore, "Competing Interests" [interview with Michael Porter], *CIO*, 1 October 1995, 66.
5. Rummler and Brache, note 3 above, p. 18.
6. Others have worked with a layered understanding of human performance. See, in particular, Rummler and Brache, note 3 above, and Hackman's orienting framework for understanding work teams, *Groups That Work (and Those That Don't)* (San Francisco: Jossey-Bass, 1990).
7. Jeffrey Pfeffer, *The Human Equation: Building Profits by Putting People First* (Boston: Harvard Business School Press, 1998), 17.

17

RAPID-CYCLE SUCCESSES VERSUS THE TITANICS

Ensuring That Consulting Produces Benefits

Robert H. Schaffer

MANAGEMENT CONSULTING activity has been expanding explosively around the world. A key dimension of this trend is the expansion of the scope of individual projects. Consulting assignments encompass increasingly larger parts of the organization. They take more time to carry out. They use ever larger troupes of consultants. And they ask the client to pay ever more astronomical fees.

While much good undoubtedly results from these tens of billions of dollars of effort, the evidence suggests that as projects grow in scope and duration, the risks of failure increase commensurately. I believe these failures are much more prevalent than most would expect, and much more costly.

> Example: A well-known financial services company with offices throughout North America decided to totally revamp its business in order to assure competitive strength. The heart of the "new company" was a major information system to be installed by two consulting firms. After three years and close to $150 million of investment, the company realized it could never achieve its intended goals and abandoned the project.

Example: A company with a very large number of sales offices throughout the United States decided it might be much more profitable to distribute products and services directly to customers. A consulting firm sent in a team of about eight consultants who conducted a fifteen-month, multimillion-dollar study. When the findings were presented, senior management suddenly confronted the risks that the move might entail and put off any action indefinitely.

Example: A corporation that had acquired a group of smaller manufacturing companies undertook to make them more competitive by rapidly introducing highly sophisticated manufacturing methods and equipment. The company spent about $75 million on help from several "big six" consulting firms. The consultants pursued this mission willy-nilly, while mismanagement sunk the company into ever larger losses and to the edge of bankruptcy.

Example: A large equipment manufacturing company undertook a major study to speed up new-product development time (which was generally about three or four years). A team of internal and external consultants undertook a major reengineering project. After two years of work, the team was still doing studies, reviewing possibilities with senior management, and fighting on a variety of political battlefields.

The main reason these failures occur is that the larger the project, the greater the likelihood that the client organization lacks the requisite implementation skills, the managerial consensus, and the motivations necessary to exploit the consultant's ideas successfully.

A much better alternative to these high-risk behemoth consulting undertakings is a model based on a continuous series of rapid-cycle projects. Each of these rapid-cycle projects yields some measurable returns while also expanding the client organization's capacity to carry on subsequent change. This paper will argue that the logic of shifting to such a mode seems clear and compelling. It will also highlight the numerous psychological and economic forces that obstruct such a positive shift and suggest how to overcome them.

Illustrative Case: A "Simple" Consulting Project

Updyke Supply, an automotive parts supplier with one center of operations near New York City and another near Cleveland, was suffering from an increasing number of logistical problems. Many orders had to be shipped in several installments for lack of the needed parts in inventory. Yet at the same time the overall levels of inventory were well beyond budget, resulting in increased warehouse costs and excessive cash tied up in unneeded inventory. After attempting for many months to alleviate these difficulties, Updyke's management invited a consulting firm to help.

After some initial exploration, the consultant proposed a study of the company's sales forecasting and inventory management procedures. It was a focused study, modest in scope, and was carried out in about three months. At the end of the study, the consultant developed a set of recommendations that focused on two primary shifts: (1) an improved sales forecasting system that would make for more accurate predictions of future order requirements; and (2) a modified inventory and purchasing system to impose a more orderly process for maintaining certain standard levels of inventory and for ordering parts to replenish inventory.

Compared to many consulting projects, this one was rather sharply focused. But focused as the project may have been, Updyke Supply would nevertheless have to make many changes in many parts of its business in order to benefit from the consulting input. The way reordering decisions were made would have to change. The responsibilities of the people involved in these decisions would change. And as these decision-making processes changed, many other individual job responsibilities would also have to change. New methods for tracking inventory and reporting on inventory status would have to be developed and implemented. The communication patterns among individuals, and the organizational relationships among units, would have to change as new work methods and decision rules were introduced. In fact, if a full accounting of all the kinds of changes required by the Updyke management were to be created, it would be extensive. A partial list is presented in table 17-1.

In identifying where these changes would have to take place, we

Table 17-1
Kinds of Changes That Might Be Required

- Work flows
- Design of individual jobs (skills, routines)
- Information gathering and processing
- Decision points
- Decision criteria
- Accountabilities
- How new work procedures created; how introduced
- Communication patterns (formal, informal)
- How to solve problems; diagnose and overcome weaknesses
- Record keeping
- Performance measures and criteria

would discover that our "simple" project involved complex changes in many functions. The sales and marketing would be responsible for the new sales forecasting process. But they would have to coordinate these changes with manufacturing, finance, information systems, and various other groups. Then changes would have to be made in production scheduling and order processing. Purchasing systems would be modified significantly. Human resources would have to revise job evaluations, compensation, and various related metrics. As the loci for required change were identified, it would gradually become evident that in order for the company to benefit from the consultant's recommendations, many kinds of changes (table 17-1) would have to take place and would involve many different functions—as illustrated in table 17-2.

Thus, to implement this very focused, modest project, aimed at ensuring that the right levels of parts and products would be in the warehouse when an order was received, dozens and dozens of interrelated changes would have to be made in the way work was done at Updyke. These would include changes in decision-making processes, in the relationships among jobs and functions, in work flows and measurements—and they all would have to be made in some kind of coordinated way. While the consulting team might help make some of the technical changes, chances are they would assist with only a small

Table 17-2
Where?

- In sales department
- In order processing
- In plant production and scheduling
- In inventory control and logistics
- In purchasing
- In final assembly
- In shipping
- In accounting and control functions
- In human resources
- In product design
- In customer service

number of the changes outlined in tables 17-1 and 17-2. The rest would have to be figured out and carried out by the organization itself.

Is it a certainty that Updyke Supply, or any business organization for that matter, could and would successfully carry out such an array of changes well enough to yield the desired results? By no means! In most organizations there are many barriers and hazards to making such changes successfully.

First, senior management would have to coordinate the various implementation steps so that they were carried out in ways that support one another. But if senior management had not had much experience in orchestrating changes of this type, they may not know how to manage such a process. In fact, if they do not feel confident playing the leadership role, they may well avoid trying to do so, and simply rationalize that others need to take the lead.

Further, if the organization had not carried out changes like this before, managers at lower levels may not have the knowledge or skills to manage their parts of the job. They may not know how to assemble transition working groups and coordinate their work. They may not know how to create change work plans, conduct review meetings, involve the right people, and see to it that superior managers do what they must do to support the process.

Beyond the lack of skill in managing change and the absence of mechanisms to discipline it, there may be a variety of psychological barriers that obstruct progress. Key managers and employees may not understand or approve of specific changes and may resist them. Managers may be comfortable with the way they do their jobs now and argue that the new methods would not be as effective. Functional blinders that have permitted each unit to act in its own individual way may prevent people from coordinating their change plans with those in different units. Implementation of the consultants' recommendations may require additional work, at least for a brief period. Many of the people who have to make changes will insist that they are unable to shoulder the additional burden unless additional resources are provided to help them keep their daily jobs going while they carry out the changes.

These are just a few of the barriers that can impede the successful implementation of a consultant's recommendations. Such barriers exist to a greater or lesser extent in every client organization, and can—and do—sabotage success.

The Updyke Supply case demonstrates that to successfully implement even a simple, focused consulting assignment requires that dozens of interrelated changes be carried out in an interrelated fashion, a process calling for skills and capabilities and motivation that may be missing. Thus, even modest and sharply focused projects run the risk of failure—not because the consultants' recommendations or the methods they introduce are not sound, but because not all of the associated changes may be carried out properly. If that is true, consider what happens when the complexity is multiplied many times over.

Can Projects of Titanic Proportion Succeed?

If a great many changes are required in a modest project such as Updyke Supply's then the number of changes that have to be implemented and coordinated in a far-reaching, comprehensive consulting project such as a total reengineering effort, a major systems redesign, or a "culture change" project are incalculable. Certainly many thousands of changes would be required. Consider the following example. It describes a fairly large-scale project carried out by a well-known and respected consulting firm with a health insurance provider.

Because of the drastic changes in the health care management field and the rapid rise in costs, this insurance company had not been profitable for several years. It had launched several programs to increase sales and reduce losses, but senior management decided that they also needed to reduce overall expenses by about 20 percent. They engaged a consulting firm to help with this cost-reduction effort. The head of the consulting firm, who had some familiarity with the company from previous engagements, assured its president that a comprehensive reengineering project would make the 20 percent cost reduction attainable.

Once the project was approved, the consulting firm launched a large-scale study staffed by about twenty-five consultants, most of whom were relatively new M.B.A.s. The team was subdivided into individual process redesign teams. Groups of company people were periodically taken off their jobs and asked to serve with the teams.

The assessment and redesign planning activity by these various teams required about a year to complete. There were periodic progress reports to senior management. Management were not encouraged to become active in the project, however, and that was fine with them. They were under so much day-to-day pressure that they were content to attend the occasional review sessions. There they would hear about the enormous opportunities for process improvement and cost reduction that the teams were identifying.

At the end of the year, several huge volumes of recommendations and support documents were presented to the company's senior managers. The consultants' plan called for all sorts of major work process redesign and related changes. The changes were to be carried out more or less simultaneously both at headquarters and in the field. Certain offices were declared redundant and were to be consolidated. Others were to be redesigned. The company's products and services were to undergo fundamental shifts. Staff reductions were also to occur.

Unfortunately, all this had to be carried out in a company whose managers had very little experience in implementing this kind of complex change, and it had to be led by a senior management team that had almost no experience in leading it.

The company began acting on the consultants' recommendations, but the effort soon bogged down. People lacked the time, skills, and confidence to make it happen. The net effect of this project was that a year was lost, huge expenses were needlessly incurred, and the business was worse off than it had been.

Here, as in most projects of this kind, the consultant had conducted a thorough study and produced a comprehensive and creative set of recommendations for accomplishing what the client company said it wanted to accomplish. But, as often happens, the client was not even close to being able to implement and coordinate successfully the many thousands of necessary changes.

Am I asserting that these titanic projects cannot succeed? Not at all. Many do succeed, and when they do the gains for the company can be enormous. But the risks of failure are very great. Failures are very frequent, and I argue that they are very costly. Moreover, they are unnecessary—because, as this paper will show, a much less risky strategy can help companies achieve the goals the behemoths are aimed at. I believe that a fundamental paradigm change is required in order to lower the risks and increase the benefits of consulting.

Frequency of Failure: Enough to Worry About?

How can I say that consulting failures are too frequent and too costly, when the consulting business has been growing explosively and organizations are apparently willing to invest tens of billions of dollars in consulting services? Here is some of the evidence for this assertion.

What We've Observed

In the last twenty years, while consulting has been on its rapid ascent, my colleagues and I have done considerable research on consulting. We have talked to many people who have observed consulting projects under way. In gathering data for my book, *High-Impact Consulting: How Clients and Consultants Can Leverage Rapid Results into Long-Term Gains*, I interviewed many company executives, journalists, academics, and consultants. Our observations and virtually all of the data gathered for the book support my conclusions.

Published Research

The consulting profession is more immune from accountability than any other profession comparable in scope and importance. There is very little published research on the topic, but the findings that have been published support my conclusions.

For example, in the late 1980s and early 1990s, the popularity of the total quality management approach made it a major focus for consulting firms. A great number of consulting projects during those years were focused on improving quality. Several investigations during this period, however, indicated very modest or poor results. For example, the American Electronics Association conducted a survey of TQM efforts in more than 300 high-technology companies. The study revealed that although most of the companies had an active TQM program under way, 63 percent of those surveyed had been unable to improve quality defects by even 10 percent.[1]

Similarly, in 1992 *The Economist* reported on a survey by Arthur D. Little of 500 manufacturing and service companies. Of these, only a third felt that their total quality programs were having a "significant impact." The article also quoted a study by A. T. Kearney of more than 100 British firms. Only a fifth of those had achieved tangible improvements.[2]

In the 1990s reengineering replaced TQM as a hot consulting product. But a study of more than 100 corporations published in the *Harvard Business Review* revealed that in most of the companies, reengineering efforts had produced some process improvements but had yielded little if any improvement in overall business results.[3] James Champy, one of the reengineering movement's founders, reports that "even substantial reengineering payoffs appear to have fallen well short of potential."[4]

The futility of expecting expert-driven organizationwide change programs to yield performance improvement was highlighted in a study conducted by a Harvard Business School team headed by Michael Beer. In a comprehensive study, the team analyzed numerous large-scale corporate change attempts, both successes and failures. They found that companywide change programs installed by staff groups did not lead to successful transformation. As the authors colorfully put it, "wave after wave of programs rolled across the landscape with little positive effect."[5]

In their book *Dangerous Company*,[6] journalists James O'Shea and Charles Madigan of the Chicago *Tribune* documented a series of consulting disasters involving high-profile client companies and some of the world's most respected consulting firms. O'Shea and Madigan concluded that projects run into trouble when

- goals, time frames, and costs are not clearly defined and measured;
- clients hand the project over to consultants, giving up participation and control;
- engagements are not tailored to the specific realities of the client business; and
- client employees are not fully utilized and respected.

Interestingly, these factors are the very ones that my colleagues and I argue are inherent in large projects carried out under the conventional consulting paradigm.

Disguised Failures: The Definition of Success Loads the Dice

Support for our conclusions also comes from the fact that many consulting projects that masquerade as successes are essentially failures. These failures typically disguise themselves as successes in two ways: (1) The consultants define success in terms of the consulting products they will deliver, with no sense that actual client performance improvement is necessary for a project to be successful; and (2) projects become so large, so long-term, and so amorphous that the impact of the consulting is impossible to assess.

Success as the Delivery of a Deliverable

One of the great mysteries of the consulting field is how hard-nosed business managers accept contracts that permit consultants to call a project successful if the consulting product has been delivered, whether or not it can be demonstrated actually to have yielded better results. And yet, no matter what clients want consultants to help them achieve, the contract will almost always be written in terms of the products the consultant will produce or the activities the consultant will carry out. While it is implied that client benefits will ensue, consultants almost never agree that the achievement of measurable performance improvements will be the criterion of success.

Thus, once the new system is installed or the consultants' recommendations have been delivered, the project is considered to have been successfully completed. The consulting firm in the health insurance case cited above might well have argued that its work should be viewed as a success—after all, the consultant showed the management of the company how it could save the 20 percent in costs it wanted to save. We argue, however, that without actual measurable improvement, a consulting project is a failure, albeit a disguised one.

The Endless, Amorphous Project

The other way disguised failures occur is this: In many projects, the roles and tasks of the consultant team(s) are so amorphous, affect so many aspects of the client organization, extend over such long periods of time, and shift so much in scope and definition that it is impossible to link the consultant's inputs to any specific outcomes in the client organization.

Here is one typical example. A financial services company decided to effect a major change in how it worked with clients. Instead of having different representatives independently calling on clients, the company would form a multidisciplinary team to serve each client. This meant a major reorientation of its marketing and client services functions. A prestigious consulting firm was engaged to help with the transformation. The firm sent a large team to participate. They set up an office in the client organization. Two or three or four consultants attended virtually every meeting of the marketing function and of many other functions. The consultants took on a wide variety of assignments. They wrote all sorts of papers. They organized various seminars and training sessions. They made many erudite presentations to senior management. Periodically individual members of the consulting team were transferred to different assignments and replaced by others.

At the end of about eighteen months, unrelated to any particular event, the client began to cut back the use of the consultants, and the consultants shortly left the scene. No one in the client organization chose to assess how much had been invested in the consulting help or what it had contributed. It was assumed that because the consultants were around, were knowledgeable and eager to please, and charged so much money, they had to have been useful.

The evidence convinces us that a great many consulting projects are like this one. They are so large, so complex, so long-term, and so amorphous that it is impossible to tell what is a success and what is a failure. But I would say once again that where there is no direct link between consulting input and measurable client results, the project cannot be counted a success.

In both kinds of disguised failures—producing the consulting product and the big amorphous job—there is nothing to prevent the consultant from claiming credit if the client company's results improve. On the other hand, if the client company's results deteriorate, the consultants can assert that their input was successful but that "despite the extensive help provided by us and the many new programs and systems we installed, the client was unable to benefit sufficiently."

Clients often accept this explanation. The consulting profession has been more successful than any other in convincing clients that when the desired outcomes are not attained, it is the clients themselves who are responsible, given that the consultants have done what they said they'd do.

The Fatal Flaws: The Right Answer versus the Workable Answer

The ways in which conventional consulting arrangements can undermine project success are illustrated in the Updyke Supply and the health care insurance cases I described earlier. A company must be capable of managing complex interrelated changes in order to achieve positive outcomes based on consulting assistance. This is especially true in large-scale projects. Nevertheless, consultants, in designing their projects, generally fail to assess what a client may actually be able to carry out. Instead, they tend to focus on the subject matter of the study (marketing, information technology, inventory management, cost reduction, etc.). They typically design their projects so that they gather the information needed to develop the "best" ideas, solutions, or systems. "Best" is often equated with most comprehensive; and thus do projects grow in scope, time, and number of consultants utilized.

Very often—as with the health insurance company—project scope grows way past the capacity of the client organization to absorb and respond to the recommendations. The reason for this is that it rarely occurs to consultants to match the project design with what a client is likely to be able (and motivated) to successfully carry out. For many consultants, in fact, the idea of scaling a project to match what the client might realistically be expected to carry out is taboo. After all, adjusting project design to client readiness is viewed by these consultants as a form of cheating. Taking such considerations into account would erode the "objectivity" of the study.

A final consequence of the dimensions of large-scale projects is that there is little opportunity to help the client people expand their capability to implement change. So much labor is involved in the large-scale project that it requires large teams of consultants to do the work. When the work is completed, the consultants hand over their recommendations. Meanwhile, clients keep on with their regular work and fail to develop new skills in implementing change. They also fail to develop the enthusiasm and personal commitment to the project that direct, meaningful involvement could provide.

All of this evidence convinces us that consulting failures are not only very frequent but very costly. We also assert that the great preponderance of them are not due to client incompetence or lack of motivation. They are, in fact, built into the very nature of the conventional working arrangements between clients and consultants, especially in large-scale undertakings.

High-Impact Consulting: Rapid-Cycle Successes

The alternative to the conventional large-scale consulting model is the well-tested approach that I call high-impact consulting. Its paradigm is quite different from that of conventional consultant project designs.

High-impact consulting takes into account the fact that no matter how brilliant the consultant's contribution, the client's implementation capability is the key to success. Thus, instead of trying to eat the entire whale in one sitting, the consultant devises an approach based on carving off bite-size, rapid-cycle subprojects. Each subproject is selected so that it represents a step toward the overall solution and also so that it offers the client an opportunity to benefit quickly from a successful experience in orchestrating and carrying out change.

Here is one illustration. The senior management of a New England aluminum-processing company decided that they wanted to radically accelerate the firm's growth and market penetration. Because they had never before attempted such a shift, they realized they would have to develop the capabilities to make it happen. One goal in the planned expansion was to multiply the output of the company's rolling mills. To achieve this goal, the company, over a period of about five years, invested heavily in outside consulting help and in the purchase of an automated rolling mill control system the consultant recommended. Still, productivity gains were only a few percentage points a year.

A consultant practicing in the high-impact mode was asked to collaborate with an internal consultant to address the need for greater productivity. The consultants invited a group of mill operators and supervisors to a series of brainstorming sessions on how to get greater benefits from the automated system. At these sessions, resistance and hidden agendas surfaced, along with some good ideas. The consultants encouraged senior management to address the people's concerns before going any farther. After management had met with the team of mill personnel and answered their questions, the group agreed to shoot for a 15 percent productivity gain in six weeks—an aggressive performance target, given results to date.

It was made clear that the mill group was responsible for the project, and that the consultants would be available to provide methodological help. All members of the team were encouraged to contribute ideas. By the end of the six weeks, productivity had risen by 17 percent. This level was not only sustained in subsequent years but actually increased, and without further capital investment.

In contrast to the health insurance company case, the aluminum-processing company underwent a high-impact consulting experience: A rapid-cycle project, understood to be only the first step in a process, was designed to be completed in less than two months. Some valuable results were attained and began yielding dividends at once. Moreover, the project enabled management to increase its own capacity to lead and manage change. And management also learned something about how best to work with their new consultant.

In high-impact consulting, no matter how large or complex the ultimate change objective may be, it is divided into a series of rapid-cycle subprojects. The aims of each project, as in the aluminum company example, are

1. to produce some measurable results and thus to provide some confidence that the new methods will work;

2. to develop management's capability to carry out increasingly ambitious aspects of the change; and

3. to introduce and test new methods and ways of working.

In order to ensure that tangible success happens fairly quickly, the high-impact consultant designs each rapid-cycle project to match what a client is ready, willing, and able to achieve. Instead of the high risk inherent in large-scale projects, rapid-cycle interventions offer dice that are loaded for success. Each rapid-cycle project also provides experience for client employees and management in taking responsibility for and executing change. Each project provides opportunity for client management and internal consultants to use and practice specific change management tools and disciplines. And each project highlights areas of commitment, of creativity, and of resistance—information that the consultant and client managers can use to design later projects. Thus, at the end of a rapid-cycle success, not only are dividends flowing back to the client, but both the client and the consultant are better equipped to move on to the next projects.

For example, the confidence and experience that the aluminum company gained through its first, highly successful rapid-cycle project (to increase rolling mill throughput) was then applied to the next challenge. The company had decided it needed to improve its on-time shipment record, which was only about 80 percent. Management was about to engage a consultant to install an order-tracking system at a cost of several millions of dollars. But the success of the rolling mill productivity project caused them to think again. Rather than go for a purely technical solution, the company decided to ask the same consultant to help them achieve some rapid-cycle results on the on-time shipment problem. Again in collaboration with internals, and without making any changes in the information system, the consultant proposed and helped carry out the following pilot project.

First, the managers agreed to try, with some consulting assistance, to ship 100 percent of orders on time for one "test week"—simply by doing everything right. They were not asked to commit to any particular level beyond the test week.

Next, a month of preparation time was scheduled before the test. During that period virtually all of the employees of the company were asked to help and to volunteer their ideas.

During the test week, and the next week also, every single order was shipped on time. After that, delivery performance never fell below 95 percent. In addition, the pilot project clarified what kinds of improvements in the company's order-processing information system were actually needed. Those improvements were made, at a fraction of the several millions called for in the tracking system proposal.

These two rapid-cycle consulting projects both yielded significant immediate results that significantly enhanced business results. At the same time, the projects provided senior management with developmental experiences in the orchestration of increasingly complex change and performance improvement projects. Thus, the work on these two projects provided considerable new data and insight into what the company would need to do in order to confront and deal with its most pressing strategic objective—growing its market share in the face of rapidly increasing competition. And in due course the company tackled this major strategic issue with confidence and eventual success.

"Low-Hanging Fruit"?

Other consultants often disparage this rapid-cycle, high-impact learning mode as merely "picking the low-hanging fruit." The implication is that the selection of easy targets ensures success but does not help the client to deal with critical strategic challenges. This, however, is as valid as saying that the use of small bricks limits the size of the building. The fact is that rapid-cycle successes create the foundation upon which ever larger ventures can be constructed.

In the year or more that most titanic projects require just to do their initial research, several rapid-cycle improvement efforts can be carried out. The results start flowing at once, and the organization's capacity to manage change grows. Instead of the major challenge being tackled as one big Herculean task, many small projects, each loaded for success, are pieced together in an "architecture for success."

This approach has been built into many far-reaching corporate change efforts. The GE Workout process, aimed at major performance improvement throughout the corporation, spawned hundreds of rapid-cycle improvement efforts as the vehicles for the overall goal. At Motorola the Organization Effectiveness Process that began in the mid-1980s required business units to implement a never ending stream of rapid-cycle improvement projects. Dun & Bradstreet's Information Services Division used rapid-cycle "breakthrough projects" to achieve bottom-line gains of more than $75 million per year with a modicum of outside consulting help. Small steps do not limit the organization to a modest journey or to a slow pace.

The Fur-Lined Mousetrap

Although this high-impact approach is sound, entails very low risks, and has proved itself over and over again, it presents both managers and consultants with some anxiety-provoking challenges. These challenges cause many of them to stick with the more familiar high-risk, costly large-scale approach.

From the client's point of view, for example, the traditional large-scale consulting approach permits management to breathe a sigh of relief once a consultant is hired. At that moment the problem has been turned over to the consultant, who will eventually return to management with the "answer." What a relief for management, who are now free to carry on with their other work. In contrast, the high-impact consulting approach demands that the client managers take personal responsibility for collaborating with the consultants in actually achieving the result.

This and the other sources of anxiety in rapid-cycle success consulting are summarized in tables 17-3 and 17-4. In these tables I refer to the pull of traditional consulting as the fur-lined mousetrap—comfy at the moment but painful in the long run.

In the traditional mode, when a name-brand consultant has been hired and the fees are sufficiently astronomical, the client manager is in a no-lose situation. If real performance results ensue, of course the client manager is a winner. If the project fails to yield results, the client

Table 17-3
The Fur-Lined Mousetrap for the Client

In Traditional Consulting	*In High-Impact Consulting*
• The burden shifts to the consultant.	• I take personal responsibility for results.
• Definition of success vague—consultant's report? New system?	• Success or failure is clear, measurable.
• I keep doing what I am doing while consultant gets to work.	• I must become involved from the beginning.

Table 17-4
The Fur-Lined Mousetrap for the Consultant

In Traditional Consulting	*In High-Impact Consulting*
• I contract to deliver what I know I can deliver.	• I'll be judged on actual client results.
• I can lay out the work, schedule my people, and do our thing.	• I have to figure out how to collaborate with various client people.
• Once project is authorized, we can get going.	• We need to define the key client—the internal person accountable for producing results with our help.
• Economically rewarding because much of the work is done by the least experienced consultants.	• Fewer, more senior consultants are needed.

manager can blame it on the consultant. Or the client can say that despite the best that a world-renowned consulting firm could do, the problem could not be solved. So who can hold the client manager responsible for not solving it?

In the high-impact consulting paradigm, there are no such escape hatches. Success or failure is measurable and unambiguous, and the client has made a public commitment to achieve success with the consultant's help.

Thus, while the traditional large-scale project carries major risks, the risks are offset by the variety of anxiety-easing psychological escape routes and rationalizations this paradigm provides to the client manager under pressure. And similar dynamics occur with consultants.

From the consultants' point of view, the traditional paradigm allows them to do the work that comes most easily to them—studying a situation and devising solutions. It allows them to maintain their aloof and respected position as "experts." And it allows them to be judged on what they can completely control—their own output—not on what they have much less control over—client results. The high-impact approach, on the other hand, requires consultants to collaborate closely with various client people and treat them as if they actually know something. This having to work in a shared control situation is a source of anxiety for many consultants.

Finally, under the traditional approach, the behemoth projects earn the most money for consultants and permit the engagement of hordes of neophytes just out of school. This is attractive, given the income requirements of large consulting firms. The high-impact approach, by contrast, uses far fewer consultants, even on a large project, and each consultant needs to be much more experienced.

Nevertheless, despite the many comforts of the fur-lined mousetrap of traditional consulting designs—both for consultants and their clients—I argue that adopting the high-impact approach to consulting will produce far greater benefits for clients, and with far fewer risks.

A Big Opportunity That Is Easy to Exploit

The contrast between the pragmatic, results-focused approach of the rapid-cycle mode and the unrealistic expectations that underlie traditional large-scale projects was highlighted in Nitin Nohria and James Berkley's 1994 article, "Whatever Happened to the Take-Charge Manager?"[7] The authors give many examples of how managers avoid the tough work of producing tangible results in favor of pursuing the latest popular management fads. They urge the importance of empirical testing: "Managers will often profit most by resisting new ideas entirely and making do with the materials at hand. However unfashionable this may seem, it is precisely as it should be. The manager's job is not to seek out novelty; it is to make sure the company gets results. Pragmatism is the place to start" (pp. 129–130). This admonition is directly applicable to the use of consultants.

In many aspects of life, people will often stick to certain patterns of behavior even when other patterns have been demonstrated to be superior. The reasons are usually psychological rather than logical. I believe that tendency is at the root of the willingness of clients to go along with the traditional, high-risk large-scale consulting approach. For years I have been hearing various versions of the statement, "At last, more and more clients are wising up to what is going on. You are going to see some changes soon." But the changes don't come. Managers seem to be stuck with the old mode and are not sure how to escape.

My advice to client managers: Don't wait for your consultants to take the lead. You are the one with the stakes in this game. You can take a low-risk approach in trying the low-risk mode of using consulting help that I advocate. Focus on one area where you feel you have to make some major changes, then get a consultant who is willing to work with you on a pilot effort on the basis I have described here. Make sure that the project is designed to achieve rapid results and that it is carried out so that you and your people develop your own abilities to run such projects.

Achieving some tangible success in a short period of time and sharpening your own sense of how to maintain the momentum will be truly liberating. Most experienced consultants will be capable of learning to practice in this mode once their clients insist that they do so.

Notes

1. Pittiglio, Rabin, Todd, and McGrath, *Productivity Survey* (Mountain View, CA: American Electronics Association, 1991).
2. "The Cracks in Quality," *The Economist*, 18 April 1992, 67–68.
3. Gene Hall, Jim Rosenthal, and Judy Wade, "How to Make Reengineering Really Work," *Harvard Business Review*, November–December 1993, 119–131.
4. James Champy, *Reengineering Management* (New York: Harper Business, 1995).
5. Michael Beer, Russell A. Eisenstat, and Bert Spector, "Why Change Programs Don't Produce Change," *Harvard Business Review*, November–December 1990, 158.
6. James O'Shea and Charles Madigan, *Dangerous Company* (New York: Random House, 1997).
7. Nitin Nohria and James Berkley, "Whatever Happened to the Take-Charge Manager?," *Harvard Business Review*, January–February 1994.

18

ACCELERATED ORGANIZATIONAL TRANSFORMATION

Balancing Scope and Involvement

A Commentary on Neill, Mindrum, and Schaffer

Robert H. Miles

How should a business leader select an organizational change consultant? What are the most important elements of practice to consider? How may they be optimized within a partnership between a client system and a consulting firm? These are the questions raised in the chapters that summarize the practices of Andersen Consulting and Schaffer & Associates.

The two chapters offer, on the one hand, sharply contrasting approaches, and on the other, two essential and complementary aspects of all successful organizational transformations. Some of the differences alleged by the authors are valid and important. Others appear to be somewhat overstated, perhaps to make a point. And a few are simply red herrings that get in the way of our understanding and assessing the two approaches to organizational change.

A careful reading of the chapters suggests a couple of areas of at least partial agreement. Both consultants are concerned about the assessment and development of employee competencies and motivation to achieve the desired level of performance. For instance, Terry Neill, who heads Andersen's global organizational change practice, poses two critical questions for effective change management: "Can the workforce perform at the desired level of competence?" and "Will the workforce perform at the desired level of competence?" Both chapters also emphasize the need to focus on business results, although they differ dramatically on the scale of results that should be targeted for achievement. As Robert Schaffer said in concluding his panel presentation at the Harvard Business School conference, "Good management consulting has to focus on results and simultaneously be organization development and management development."

Beyond these important similarities, however, the differences between the two authors' views on change management practices are striking. For example, Robert Schaffer implies that process approaches to organizational change are more efficacious than content approaches. One gets the impression that he sees the Andersen consulting approach as more of a strategy intervention. When pressed on this point during the panel discussion of his paper, Schaffer referred to Andersen Consulting as follows: "They want to do the big study, which usually takes a long time and a lot of money. And it comes up with recommendations well beyond what the clients are able to do." His references to "studies" implies that Andersen-like approaches are geared primarily toward creation of expert content and recommendations without a responsibility to help implement the findings. This may be the case for a strictly strategy boutique, but the Andersen methodology does outline various phases of implementation and makes extensive use of project management methodologies. Indeed, one wonders what drives the selection of projects the Schaffer outfit works on in client organizations if not some sort of strategy work up front.

Terry Neill provides an exhaustive, panoramic view of Andersen Consulting's change management elephant, but not much about its internal anatomy. His chapter leaves us with an overwhelming feeling of all the elements that ought to be accounted for and articulated if large-scale change is to be achieved. But it offers few insights into how the Andersen architecture of change is put into practice or how the many elements it sets in motion are orchestrated from start to finish. Little is said about the respective roles of managers and consultants and how they need to evolve over the duration of a large-scale corporate transformation project. Presumably, Andersen implements its holistic approach by breaking down the whole into a more simultaneous, less sequential set of initiatives or projects that then may be performed with varying degrees of involvement by consultants versus employees.

Schaffer also asserts that more organization change comes out of a series of small projects from which learning accumulates and diffuses across the organization over time than from big bang consulting interventions. To Schaffer, getting something that you can wrap your arms around so as to produce a rapid result is the ultimate criterion for shaping a change intervention.

What curiously is absent in Schaffer's framework are the external business realities confronting the organization. Consultants and their clients must trade off such competitive realities, which are increasingly dictating a more rapid pace of change, against the internal assessment of capabilities in order to gauge the scope, pace, and intensity of the client–consultant partnership and the practice intervention required. First, the competitive world does not stand still for work in the sandbox to be completed and diffused throughout the enterprise. Second, successful change in an isolated part of an organization in no way guarantees that the change will be rapidly adopted with high verisimilitude in all the other parts of the organization. As the pace of change in the competitive environment continues to increase, the likelihood of keeping up, much less getting ahead, seems remote with the Schaffer method. In the words of Terry Neill, "the pace of marketplace change and the intensity of competition demand new ways to move an organization through major change."

Attempting to draw a line in the sand, Schaffer has chosen a title that emphasizes what he believes is the essential difference between large-scale and small-scale change consulting projects: "Rapid-Cycle Successes versus the Titanics." The message appears to be that small change projects deliver results, whereas large change projects end up on the ocean floor! The title signals a preference for small, continuous improvement projects as opposed to large transformation efforts. My initial reaction was to search for a less pejorative title upon which to base this comparative analysis, and I generated a list of candidates: "PT Boats versus Battleships." "Project Management versus Corporate Transformation," "Small Steps versus Bold Leaps" or even "Sequential versus Simultaneous Changes." But even though these titles may be less one-sided than Schaffer's, the dichotomy implied by all of them is false.

How it is possible that two such different practices of change management consulting could flourish in the same business milieu?

An underlying sociology of consulting may be inferred from the two chapters. Schaffer's penchant for delimited scope probably comes from the psychological and organizational development traditions in his firm, with its predilection toward well-defined tasks and learning agendas, as well as from the small scale (only sixteen consultants) of the firm. Such traditions also reinforce a preference for in-close, high-involvement, process-driven engagements. In addition, what has always been a refreshing extension of the Schaffer methodology is its focus on performance results. This I can explain only on the basis of the founder's deep-rooted belief that consulting begins and ends with results in mind. But the narrowness of scope that Schaffer recommends is probably better termed "rapid-cycle" than "high-impact" consulting.

Andersen Consulting grew up with a different set of intellectual traditions and predispositions. As an offspring of a major professional accounting firm, it was born in the new information technology era. Its marrow is full of accounting, systems integration, and information technology infrastructure. Its vast organization, which employs more than 53,000 consultants worldwide, offers enormous scale of coverage and trains all its consultants in project management, which helps them subaggregate vast organizational change efforts into manageable and achievable projects. Little wonder that its scope is organizationwide and that its preference is for total systems interventions involving a heavy dose of content expertise.

Instead of offering a deep understanding of human behavior and social process on the part of senior consultants in close-in engagements, Andersen Consulting substitutes project management skills and systems integration expertise to deal with large measures of scope and complexity. Given the lower aggregate consulting experience base at Andersen, this firm probably falls short of the Schaffer ideal in its ability to foster a high grade of involvement of employees engaged at the project level. Indeed, during the panel discussion, Neill admitted that for Andersen Consulting, "the richest, least-explored territory is to create and develop an architecture and delivery mechanism for building human and organizational capability and performance. . . ."

To some extent, then, the Andersen and Schaffer approaches outlined in the two chapters serve almost as archetypes or caricatures at the extremes of available approaches to organizational transformation.

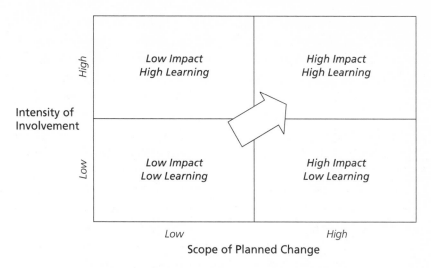

Figure 18-1   Scope and Intensity in Organizational Transformation

Although many alleged differences between the consulting practices may be found in the chapters, two dimensions appear to capture most of the fuss. As shown in figure 18-1, the dichotomy created by the Andersen and Schaffer approaches really comes down to the scope of planned change and the intensity of employee involvement. As the model suggests, the greater the scope of planned change, the higher the impact will be on overall organizational performance. And the more intensive the degree of employees' involvement, the greater will be their learning about and mastery of change leadership.

On the scope of change continuum, Schaffer's practice anchors the end of the continuum where small, limited-scope change projects reside. The practice at Andersen Consulting could not be more different on this dimension, with everything being geared toward large-scale, sometimes massive interventions whose scope often is organization-wide in nature.

The other dimension in the dichotomy is the degree to which managers and employees in the client system are involved in defining, planning, and implementing the change process. Intensity of involvement is directly related not only to executive and employee understanding and commitment but also to the development of their change management capability. However, intensity of involvement need not covary directly with the scope of the effort. The degree of involvement is an implicit or explicit choice of the consulting and client systems. It reflects the extent to which both parties view such things as employee motivation and skill development as priorities alongside rivals such as the degree of urgency imposed by the business environment, the style of the particular transformational leader, or the brand of practice of the consultant.

In leading fundamental change—organizational transformation— executives need to draw upon both ends of the consulting continuum. The challenge sweeping over almost all industries today is the need to achieve rapid-cycle organizational transformation. Not rapid-cycle, project-based incremental change or slow, lumbering, organization-wide transformation.

Large, complex organizations do not rapidly change by sequentially pursuing a series of short-cycle projects. The learning cycle involved in such an approach is simply too protracted and the anticipated diffusion of learnings throughout the enterprise too unpredictable to keep up with the increasing pace of change imposed on the organization by the external environment. As management expert Peter Drucker has observed, "Theories of business won't last long. Every few years you'll have to sit down and think through the theory of the business, very critically." Similarly, feeling the press of the increasing pace of industry change, Microsoft founder and chairman Bill Gates has said, "We're always two years away from failure."

So how do we speed up the process of corporate transformation and at the same time increase the capacity of leaders/managers and employees at all levels? Together the Andersen and Schaffer archetypes suggest a hybrid; an approach that integrates large scope with intense involvement, one that I have used over the past decade to combine the need for speed with the need for mastery. I call this approach *accelerated organizational transformation*.

In accelerated organizational transformation, change leaders achieve *high impact* by setting an aspiration for organizationwide transformation, disaggregating it into a limited set of transformation initiatives, and then holding all parts and levels of the organization accountable for initiating quantum change projects in pursuit of those initiatives. Project or program teams are largely led by client system personnel, with appropriate levels of content and process consulting support within a structure of well-defined stretch goals and milestones.

In short, I have concluded that when change is needed in large, complex organizations, it needs to be large and complex in scope. But such change, to be effective, must be broken down into an orchestrated set of actionable projects that can be led to conclusion by employees. This is simultaneous, not sequential, change—which is what the increasing pace of change demands.

The trick is to narrow the focus of transformation down to a few organizationwide initiatives, no more than four or five, that are targeted for quantum, not incremental, change in a short period of time, say two to three years. Such initiatives usually are made up of a mixture of business goals (performance outcomes) and cultural elements (organizational values and people enablers). For example, after succeeding Lee Iacocca as chairman and CEO of Chrysler Corporation, Robert Eaton targeted the following five transformation initiatives for quantum change: Customer Focus, Inspired People, Continuous Improvement, Financial Success, and Company Reputation. Similarly, Southern Company, the largest utility in the United States, embarking on a transformation so as to compete in a deregulated marketplace, placed its bets on the following business and cultural initiatives: Business Focus, Adaptive Culture, Low-Cost Producer, Empowered People, and "Fence Management."[1]

Organizations achieve *high involvement* in such large-scale interventions by intensively involving all employees in high-engagement cascades that create understanding, dialogue, feedback, and accountability and that empower people to simultaneously launch dozens, sometimes hundreds of rapid-cycle improvement projects aligned with one or more of the organization's transformation initiatives.

What goes on inside a high-engagement, all-employee cascade?[2]

The stage is set by the executive leader, who explains the business realities, strategic vision, and business success model. Then members of the leadership team introduce all managers and subsequently all employees to each transformation initiative, using a high-engagement methodology. Peer groups organized into tablework teams, all assembled in a large room that can accommodate all members of a subunit, hear about the vision, stretch goals, and metrics for each initiative before spending time in dialogue to translate these constructs for meaning and action in their immediate units and jobs. At the conclusion of each dialogue module, the tablework teams report their preliminary translations and job-level objectives and learn about those of other teams. Then the tablework teams reconvene to discuss what they have learned. They conclude by drafting a near-final set of job-level objectives to enable them to align their job behaviors with the initiative. The process is repeated over and over until all four or five transformation initiatives have been translated for job-level action. To complete the cascade process, all subunits, managers, and individual contributors delineate job-level objectives that have a clear line of sight back to the handful of organizationwide transformation initiatives. Employees finalize such job-level objectives with their supervisors during the next two weeks.

At this juncture the executive and business leaders have set the transformation template, and managers and employees at all levels have gone through a compressed cycle of understanding, dialogue, feedback, and goal alignment—a process that enables people to use their creativity and job knowledge to take prudent risks at their own job levels to drive the transformation challenge in their spheres of influence. This part of the accelerated transformation process is consistent with the conclusion drawn from more than two decades of field research by J. Richard Hackman, a Harvard organizational behaviorist: "Team effectiveness is enhanced when managers are unapologetic and insistent about exercising authority about direction, the end state the team is to pursue. Authority about the means by which those ends are accomplished, however, should rest squarely with the team itself."

Upon reflection, I came to the realization that the high-engagement goal-alignment cascade process also serves as a compressed leadership development intervention. In it, all managers at different levels have to (*a*) confront business realities, (*b*) develop a compelling vision and business success model, (*c*) focus on quantum improvement initiatives, (*d*) construct clear performance expectations, (*e*) engage all employees in dialogue, (*f*) quickly encourage and respond to feedback, (*g*) establish accountability, and (*h*) follow through for execution.

Once the organizational table is set with a clear understanding of competitive realities, a compelling vision and business model, and a clear line of sight connecting organization-level transformation initiatives with the job-level objectives of all managers and employees, the whole effort is knitted together by the creation of a learning organization in which early failures and successes at the subunit and project levels may be quickly analyzed and shared with all parts of the organization. Skill or competency deficiencies can now be engaged more fully in the context of a focused, accountable, and truly motivated system. Employees now seek out training and other competency-enhancing opportunities. The organization can refresh the entire accelerated transformation process on a quarterly, semiannual, or yearly basis by maintaining a process architecture, which consists of the business leader and his or her executive team, the normal line and staff management structure, transformation initiative champions, a quarterly cycle of leadership follow-through meetings, and occasional focus groups that tap various parts and levels of the enterprise.

The aim here is not to lay out all the details of my alternative model of change as a counterpoint to the models already provided by Schaffer and Neill. I wish merely to demonstrate that the lines drawn between their change management practices are unnecessary.

The fundamental challenges confronting organizations across all industries today require competency in accelerated transformation, and these challenges will only increase in the future. It is not necessary to settle for either limited-scope incremental improvements or consultant-led master plans offering few opportunities for client involvement or employee mastery. A hybrid approach, which combines high-impact scope with high-involvement development to meet the accelerated transformation challenge, has been offered here. Together with the approaches developed by Schaffer Associates and Andersen Consulting, I hope these insights will help others as they rise to the increasingly pervasive challenge of accelerated organizational transformation.

Notes

1. Robert H. Miles, *Leading Corporate Transformation: A Blueprint for Business Renewal* (San Francisco: Jossey-Bass, 1997) 38–45.
2. ———. "Leading Corporate Transformation: Are You Up to the Task?" In Jay A. Conger, Gretchen M. Spreitzer, and Edward E. Lawler III, eds., *The Leader's Change Handbook* (San Francisco: Jossey-Bass, 1999) 221–267.

SECTION VII

RESEARCH ON CHANGE
Normal Science or Action Science?

T HE PRACTICE OF CHANGE is at least in part embedded in research on change. Though many managers act on their own intuitive theories of change, they also live in a world where they are being constantly bombarded and influenced by more research-based theories of change. Some of this research is done by consultants, some by journalists, and some by academics. In short, there is a growing industry of people involved in producing knowledge for the consumption of managers and one another. The question is: What is the best way to do research on change?

Andy Van de Ven answers this question for scholars who work in professional schools, such as business schools. In the first chapter in this section, Van de Ven argues that scholars must embrace a system of inquiry that can be called professional science—an approach that is distinct from basic or applied research, theoretical or empirical research, or other such distinctions. The professional science model starts with the formulation of a research problem grounded in management practice, proceeds through theory-building and research design phases, and ends with a solution that enables problem solving in practice. Van de Ven maintains that the professional science model has several virtues. It advances theory and practice; it is teachable; and it is tolerant of a wide variety of intellectual tastes, and can thus transcend the various polarities that plague management research today.

Chris Argyris is less sanguine about the merits of professional science. He contends that the problem with most management research is that it is not usable. Scientists tend to draw generalizations that obscure the specific actions a practitioner would take. For instance, suppose we argue that increased participation and involvement increases the likelihood of successful implementation of change. Argyris suggests that we need to specify more precisely exactly how managers should go about involving others, whom they should involve, when they will know if they have achieved the desired level of involvement, and what specific behaviors will enable them to verify this general claim. Argyris thus makes a claim for what he calls action science, in which the emphasis is on the usability of knowledge. According to him, what we need is not high-level generalizations. Instead, we need theories in use that specify the intended consequences, the action sequences to produce the consequences, the causal relationships between the actions and the consequences, and the relevant governing values from which the action designs are derived.

In the final paper in this section, Michael Beer reflects on the relative merits of these two views. He concludes that Van de Ven and Argyris employ totally different logics in the research methods they advocate. Both agree that research and advice by academics and consultants must be relevant. However, while Van de Ven acknowledges that implementing relevant research findings is important, it is difficult to do and unexplored by researchers. Argyris' criticism of advice given by academics and consultants is exactly that. Beer contends that research and advice that emerges from it must meet the criteria of relevance and implementability.

19

PROFESSIONAL SCIENCE FOR A PROFESSIONAL SCHOOL

Action Science and Normal Science

Andrew H. Van de Ven

L ET'S DISCUSS the kinds of research we do in a professional school of business or management. A central mission of scholars in a professional school is to conduct research that contributes knowledge to a scientific discipline, on the one hand, and to apply that knowledge to advance the practice of management as a profession, on the other. I will argue that this mission represents a collective challenge of achieving tolerance and balance among scholars in a professional school, and a challenge for each scholar to undertake professional research that transcends the polarities between "normal" and "action" science. I hope that this argument will provide a platform for constructive discussion and possible debate.

The Collective Challenge of a Professional School

The mission of professional schools—such as schools of agriculture, engineering, medicine, law, education, business, public administration, architecture, journalism, and social work—is to educate individuals in the practice of a profession requiring some specialized body of knowledge, and to conduct research that advances knowledge applicable to the practice of the profession. The information and skills relevant to

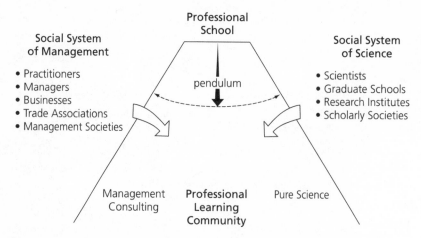

Figure 19-1   Pendulum Swing to and from a Professional Learning
Community

this mission come from the social system of practitioners and the social
system of scientists in the relevant disciplines. These social systems
themselves have elaborate institutions and procedures for storing,
transmitting, developing, and applying knowledge. In business, the
institutions are business firms, trade associations, and professional
management societies. In the sciences, the institutions are graduate
schools, research institutes, and scholarly societies. Generally speaking, the main way in which an organization can get access to the information and skills of a social system is to participate in it. A never ending challenge of faculty in a professional school is to achieve active and
balanced participation in these social systems of management and science. Figure 19-1 illustrates this never ending challenge with a pendulum swinging to and from a balanced ideal—a professional learning
community.

Herbert Simon (1976) offers an excellent discussion of the purpose
and organization of professional schools. Simon points out that a business school, if left to itself, gravitates toward a bimodal separation of
the faculty on the opposite ends of the pendulum in figure 19-1. One
segment gets absorbed in the applied culture of managers and businesses. It is dependent on the world of business as its sole source of
knowledge inputs. Instead of creating new knowledge that can advance
the profession, this segment becomes a slightly out-of-date purveyor

of almost-current business practice. The other segment, often trained intensively in a basic discipline, gets absorbed in the culture of that discipline and largely dependent on it for goals, values, and approval. Largely sealed off from the practitioner's environment, these discipline-oriented researchers begin to view the management profession as an irrelevant source for generating, developing, or applying new knowledge. If left unchecked, this evolutionary drift also breeds intolerance and polarized conflicts between faculty members espousing either the basic or the applied research extreme. This polarization among scholarly groups can produce a void in the middle of the pendulum, where it is most needed for professional learning.

Building an internal organizational culture that respects and tolerates diversity among basic and applied researchers, Simon (1976) argues, is very much like mixing oil with water. "It is easy to describe the intended product, less easy to produce it. And the task is not finished when the goal has been achieved. Left to themselves, the oil and water will separate again" (p. 338). This natural separation occurs not only between practitioner-oriented and discipline-oriented scholars, but also between scholars from different disciplines. Such separations prevent the professional school from achieving its mission. According to Simon, if these natural separations are permitted to drift, the consequence is death for the school.

> On the one hand, the members of each discipline in the professional school demand increasing autonomy so that they can pursue the goals defined by their discipline without regard to the "irrelevant" professional school's goals. On the other hand, the professional school environment loses any special attraction it might have as a locus for research and teaching, and the group becomes less and less able to attract and retain first-class members. . . . [The end result for the school] means mediocrity and inability to fulfill its special functions. (Simon 1976, p. 351)

Achieving an internal culture that values integration across boundaries requires schoolwide programs and forums that encourage ongoing dialogue among faculty, students, and practitioners across departments, disciplines, and organizations. These programs can be especially effective when they have an agenda that attracts attention and pulls (rather than pushes) individuals across boundaries. Important questions or research themes relevant to the management profession can serve as lightning rods to pull multidisciplinary scholars together, because adequate treatment of such questions often transcends disciplinary boundaries.

Research questions can emerge in a variety of ways. They do *not* require that every individual faculty member be equally balanced between pure and applied research at a point in time. A professional learning community requires that the faculty as a *whole* achieve a reasonable balance, undertaking fundamental research that addresses questions or problems of the management profession and advances knowledge in a basic discipline. It also requires *respect, tolerance,* and *ongoing interaction* among basic and applied researchers from different disciplines. Such a culture among scholars in a professional school is highly conducive to the creation of new knowledge. Significant invention calls on two quite different kinds of knowledge: applied knowledge about the practical issues or needs of a profession, and scientific knowledge about new ideas and processes that are potentially possible.

Invention is easiest, and likely to be incremental, when it operates at one extreme along the range from end-user requirements to basic scientific disciplines. For example, scholars who lean toward applied research tend to immerse themselves in information about problems of the end users and then apply known knowledge and technology to provide solutions to their clients. When an obvious solution is not available, the scholar turns to more basic scientific knowledge that may not have had practical application before. When it comes off, this kind of solution invention is likely to have far larger impact than routine consulting. But more important, the professional school is not simply an environment in which faculty with strongly applied interests can take known scientific principles or techniques and use them to solve practical business problems. If this were the only kind of "research" that went on, the school would abrogate its mission of creating new knowledge that advances the discipline *and* the profession. At the other end of the range, pure scientists immerse themselves in knowledge from their disciplines to discover what questions have not been answered and then apply known research techniques or develop new techniques to answer these questions. If scientists cannot answer their initial questions, they can modify or simplify them until they show promise of being answerable. If this process repeats itself, as is customary, the research questions and answers become increasingly trivial contributions to science, and even more irrelevant to practice.

But if scholars are equally exposed to both the social system of management practitioners and the social system of science, they are likely to be confronted with real-life applied questions and at the forefront of knowledge creation. This setting increases the chance of significant invention and research. As Louis Pasteur stated, "Chance favors the prepared mind." Research in this context is also more demanding, because scholars do not have the option of substituting more simple answerable questions if they cannot solve the real-life problems. But if research becomes more challenging when it is undertaken to answer questions posed from outside science, it also acquires the potential to become more significant and fruitful. The history of science and technology demonstrates that many of the extraordinary developments in pure science have been sparked by problems or questions from outside. Necessity is indeed the mother of important inventions. Thus, as Simon (1976, p. 341) concludes, the business school *can* be an exceedingly productive and challenging environment for scholars who understand and can exploit the advantages of having access to the "real world" as a generator of basic research problems and a source of data.

The Individual Challenge of Professional Science

How might individual scholars exploit these research opportunities and challenges in a professional school? I have argued that the likelihood of making significant research contributions increases when scholars in a professional school (1) confront questions and anomalies arising from the management profession; (2) develop alternative theories and undertake research to examine these questions; and (3) translate their findings not only to contribute knowledge to a scientific discipline, but also to advance the practice of management. How might individual scholars in a professional school implement these steps? What methodological training should we provide to individuals who aspire to conduct the kind of research advocated here in a professional school?

I have struggled often with these questions over the past twenty-five years while periodically teaching a course on theory building and research design for Ph.D. students at the Wharton and Carlson schools of management. This course has changed dramatically over the years as my understanding of these questions has evolved, from an initial focus on methods and techniques for data collection and analysis to a greater appreciation of philosophy of science and the variety of skills a complete research project requires. Along the way I concluded that if one is to exploit the research opportunities and challenges in a professional school, a broader perspective on the research process is needed than is commonly discussed or covered in research methodology texts.

In recent versions of the course, I have been adopting a general systems approach to inquiry (as discussed by Segasti and Mitroff 1973) in order to develop a broader perspective on science in a professional school. This perspective provides a metatheory (a theory of theories) for linking and transcending polarities often construed to exist between basic and applied research and between "normal" and "action" forms of science. Specifically, this general systems approach suggests that when professional school scholars undertake a research study, they should carry out four core activities: (1) diagnose the problem or situation as it exists in the real world, (2) select a conceptual model and a research question to deal with this problem or situation, (3) build a theory and design research to examine the research question, and (4) conduct the research and analyze the findings to produce a solution that addresses the real-world problem or situation. I refer to this general systems view of inquiry as *professional science*, in order to distinguish it from other typical classifications of normal or action research that may vary in relative emphasis on basic or applied; deductive or inductive; theory building or theory testing; variance or process theory; cross-sectional or longitudinal; quantitative or qualitative data; and on laboratory, simulation, survey, archival, or other observation methods. Depending on the problem or question being investigated, professional science may involve any of these different kinds of research. The critical task is to adopt and execute the right research methods for the research problem.

Adapting a baseball analogy, I use a *diamond model*, illustrated in figure 19-2, to capture the major processes entailed in a *professional research* project or study. The model focuses on running four bases—

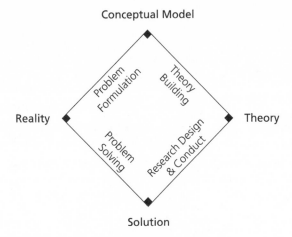

Figure 19-2 Professional Research Diamond Model

problem formulation, theory building, research design, and problem solving. Unlike baseball, the diamond model allows one to begin a research project on any base. This permits investigators to begin from different starting conditions and preferences and to apply different methods and styles of inquiry. However, as in baseball, I argue that an investigator must cover all the bases to "hit a run" and thereby complete a research project. And as in baseball, although a particular investigator may prefer or be more skilled at playing a particular base, the investigator must learn to play and run all the bases if he or she wants to play professional research.

The course has an outcome-based educational objective: to have each student develop a good research proposal. A good research proposal is defined as one that covers all the bases of the diamond model, and proposals are evaluated in terms of the criteria presented in table 19-1. Students submit different parts of the proposal about every week of the term. As instructor, I review and provide feedback on students' in-progress proposals, and each student revises his or her proposal several times until it is judged to be of sound conceptual quality and operational clarity. Thus, through several revise-and-resubmit iterations, students develop a research proposal that they will submit for funding and implement either as a research project or as an initial draft of their dissertation proposal.

Table 19-1

Criteria for Evaluating Research Proposal

A "good" research proposal is one that accomplishes the following outcomes, using this evaluation scale:

1 = Not addressed or evident in the proposal.
2 = Attempt made, but the result needs more work, elaboration, or revision.
3 = Attempt made with good result; issue accomplished; no further work needed.
4 = Attempt made with excellent result; issue accomplished with distinction.

1. The problem or phenomenon examined in this research proposal
   a. is clearly defined and grounded or mapped in reality. _____
   b. a manageable part of the problem has been chosen for study. _____

2. The research question
   a. is stated in analytical and researchable terms. _____
   b. permits more than one plausible answer. _____

3. The research proposition
   a. clearly states and explains expected relationships among concepts. _____
   b. directly addresses the research question and problem. _____
   c. is "crucial"—it compares plausible alternative answers. _____
   d. is interesting or classic (as defined by Murray Davis). _____

4. The assumptions
   a. specify the boundary conditions within which the proposition holds. _____
   b. are not confused with definitions, propositions, research design. _____

5. The definitions of concepts, constructs, and variables
   a. are clearly stated in the affirmative and by negation. _____
   b. travel (do not stretch) across levels of abstraction. _____

6. The research hypotheses are clearly stated as
   a. operational relationships or comparisons between variables/events. _____
   b. being logical and consistent deductions from proposition. _____

7. The research design clearly spells out
   a. unit of analysis. _____
   b. case/experimental design for variance or process theory. _____
   c. sample or replication logic and sample selection. _____
   d. definitions and measurement procedures for variables or events. _____
   e. threats to internal, statistical, external, and construct validities. _____

8. Research implementation and problem solving:
   a. Schedule and budget for conducting the research are reasonable. _____
   b. A responsible plan is proposed to implement the findings. _____
   c. Statement of how research findings will be used/applied is prudent. _____

Comments:

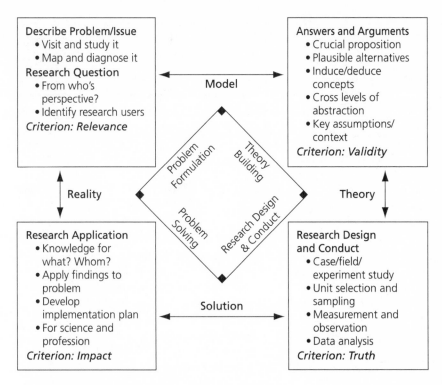

Figure 19-3   Running the Bases of Diamond Model

Let's look more closely at the four bases of the professional research process and at the basic activities entailed in "running the baselines" of the diamond model (see figure 19-3).

The *problem formulation baseline* consists of developing a concrete description of symptoms, conditions, or anomalies as they exist in the real world on a topic or issue. All the unorganized perceptions or facts pertaining to a topic or issue in the management profession belong here. Students acquire recognition of these perceptions or facts through experience, observation, or judgments of a problem, opportunity, or issue existing in a realistic situation. "Reality" provides all the data, value judgments, and initial inputs to the investigator and often constitutes the starting point for the professional science process. However, it is obvious that different observers may see different "realities," and that the very concept of reality itself is a social construction; it does not exist independently of the observer's schemata or conceptual frame of reference (Weick 1989). As a consequence, the formulation of a research problem involves a complex sensemaking process; we must apply various conceptual templates or models to determine what to look for in the real world and how to unscramble raw data into a recognizable and meaningful research problem.

In the course students experiment with a variety of methods to learn how to ground their research problem in "reality," including the following activities:

- Map the problem/subject space as fifth graders are trained to do.

- Answer the journalist's questions of who, what, where, when, why, and how the problem exists.

- Conduct interviews or nominal group meetings with people who know the problem, as discussed by Delbecq, Van de Ven, and Gustafson (1975).

- Clarify the problem: Give a concrete example, an anecdote, or an experience with a problem.

- Apply the medical diagnosis process: Identify how the symptoms existing in reality add up to a problem or disease.

- Review the literature to understand and situate the problem.

- Focus on the part of the problem or issue that merits study and research.

- Bring the problem statement full circle by stating the consequences of studying the problem for theory and practice.

- Ask yourself: Will study of the problem, as you have formulated it, amount to a contribution?

The *conceptual model and theory-building baseline* of the diamond model involves selecting or developing the research question and the body of knowledge that is relevant to the research problem. A conceptual model is the mental image or framework that an investigator brings to bear on the research problem. Conceptual models exist at various levels of abstraction from reality. Scientific knowledge is packaged and indexed in a nested hierarchy—by discipline, paradigm, school of thought, and theories on various subjects. Conceptual models not only index bodies of knowledge, they also structure our views of reality by specifying what problems and what aspects of problems are relevant and not relevant. The choice of conceptual model is perhaps the most strategic choice that an investigator makes, for it significantly influences the research questions the investigator will ask, the concepts and constructs he or she will look for, and the kinds of propositions and hypotheses that will be set forth to answer these questions.

For example, if confronted with a real-world problem of declining innovativeness among U.S. compared to Japanese semiconductor manufacturers, an economist might view it as a resource allocation problem and propose that U.S. firms increase their investments in research and development (Nelson 1982). A professional researcher, on the other hand, would apply several disciplinary templates in order to consider the social, political, and economic dimensions of the problem, and would probably bring a broader set of considerations to bear on the problem (e.g., Lenway 1994). Such considerations might include, for example, the lower cost of capital for Japanese versus U.S. semiconductor firms due to stable bank debt and equity shareholders that are forbidden by U.S. laws; unfair dumping practices by Japanese firms in U.S. markets; and cooperation among competing Japanese firms through MITI to create a commercial infrastructure for new semiconductors, at a time when U.S. firms are sitting on the fence waiting for someone else to create this infrastructure.

Because a conceptual model is so influential in directing (or tunneling) an investigator's mode of inquiry, I encourage students to undertake several different thought trials in selecting plausible alternative conceptual models, research questions, propositions and concepts to address their research problem. For example, in specifying the research questions, I emphasize the following:

- State the question in analytical terms by relating or comparing key dimensions of the problem.

- A research question ends with a question mark; it is open to several possible solutions.

- Permit and entertain at least two plausible answers to the question. Alternative answers increase independent thought trials (Weick 1989).

- Use metaphors or analogies to conceptualize alternatives (Tsoukas 1991).

- Use different methods to deal with paradox: Juxtapose opposites, levels, or times, or introduce new concepts (Poole and Van de Ven 1989).

- Is your question interesting? Is it classic? (as discussed by Davis 1971, 1986).

Conceptualization involves disciplined logic. After a primer in logical analysis, students are shown how to specify the following kinds of definitions for the concepts in their research questions and propositions.

- Semantic definitions—a concept is defined in terms of other concepts:

  Positive definitions: Concept A is similar to concepts B, C, and D.
  By negation: Concept A is not concept E, F, or G.
  Concepts defined by negation are determinate, those without negation are indeterminate (Osigweh 1989)

- Constitutive definitions—a concept is defined in terms of its component constructs:

  Concept A consists of a1, a2, and a3 dimensions.

- Operational definitions—a construct becomes a variable when you specify the activities or operations necessary to measure it.

- Measurement definitions and experimental definitions.

The above definitions entail climbing the ladder of abstraction:

  Ascend in ways that retain precision by decreasing the number of attributes or properties of the concept.
  Descend by adding to the number of attributes and properties that characterize the concept.
  Make your concepts travel, don't stretch them (see Osigweh 1989).

As students work on developing propositions, I encourage them to develop "crucial" propositions that "carve at the joints" by juxtaposing or comparing two plausible answers (as discussed by Stinchcombe 1968). Plausible alternatives promote a critical research attitude and leverage knowledge. Social science knowledge of many topics has advanced beyond the stage of hypothesizing that a relationship between two variables or events is different from zero. Such a finding may add little new knowledge if previous research has already shown this to be the case. More significant knowledge is produced when tests of *rival plausible* hypotheses are undertaken. Such tests are likely to add significant value to theory and practice. Testing rival plausible hypotheses also provides insurance of a win–win outcome for the investigator: No matter what test results are obtained, the research, if properly executed, will make an important contribution.

As Strauss (1987) discusses, all scientific theories require that they be conceived, then elaborated, then checked. *Induction* consists of actions that lead to discovery of a proposition or hypothesis from observations of particulars. *Deduction* consists of drawing implications from propositions or hypotheses for the purpose of verification. *Verification*, in turn, is total or partial negation of a hypothesis. A common concern of students is that deductive theory-testing does not allow for a more inductive grounded theory–building approach to research. It is important to note that the difference between induction and deduction has to do with an investigator's timing and sequence in running the theory-building and research design baselines of the diamond model. When undertaking an inductive or exploratory study, the investigator typically develops propositions after data collection and analysis. In this case, students apply the methods discussed above to develop propositions and hypotheses after or while the data are being collected and analyzed. However, any observations presuppose a selective frame of reference—a chosen object and concepts. Before students go into the "field" to collect data, I therefore ask them to explain and justify the concepts they have chosen for observation. These recommendations are in complete agreement with the iterative cycle of induction, deduction, and verification in grounded theory building.

Running the *theory and research design baseline* of the diamond model involves developing a solution to the research question along with operational procedures for bringing valid scientific evidence to bear on this solution. A theory is an operational statement of relationships between two or more constructs that are hypothesized to hold within a set of assumptions or boundary conditions. A hypothesis spells out the operational meaning of a proposition by descending the ladder of abstraction and by following deductive or inductive norms of correspondence (discussed by Kaplan 1964). Given the fact that there can be an infinite number of hypotheses for each proposition, parsimony dictates that investigators focus on only the most important ones.

The formulation of hypotheses sets the stage for selecting the following other well-known components of a research design, as discussed in Cook and Campbell (1979):

- unit of analysis

- mode of inquiry: variance or process, static or longitudinal, idiographic or nomothetic

- type of design: case study, quasi-experimental, or true experiment

- measurement and psychometric procedures for evaluating measures

- data collection instruments and experimental procedures

- sampling strategy and sample size

- factors threatening internal, external, statistical, and construct validities

- data coding and analysis procedures

- resource restrictions, budget, and proposals for grants and funding

The *solution and problem-solving baseline* of the diamond model can be considered as the set of activities that link the outputs of the research process back with reality in the management profession and the scientific community. Generally, running this baseline involves executing the research design to produce scientifically valid evidence for a solution to the research problem and question that initially motivated the research. At a minimum, a research solution entails a report of empirical research findings and a discussion of their implications for theory and practice. Because professional research is undertaken with at least two user communities in mind, two reports are typically necessary: (1) a scientific paper that draws out the contributions of the research for advancing knowledge in an academic discipline, and (2) a professional paper that draws out the contributions of the research for advancing the practice of management. Crafting such papers requires intimate knowledge of the different frames of reference, cultures, and languages of the two audiences. Researchers are seldom equally conversant in the cultures of both audiences and typically need professional editorial assistance in drafting and disseminating these research reports.

Of course, it is one thing to document research evidence, and quite another to suggest how to implement a solution. The latter requires developing an action plan for implementing a change process designed to intervene in or solve the problem addressed in the research. The development of a realistic implementation plan typically requires that potential users become actively involved to identify promising ways to interpret and apply the research findings. Argyris (1993) discusses a variety of ways to create actionable knowledge. They emphasize the importance of repeated consultation and feedback sessions among practitioners and academics while running each base of the diamond model. Such ongoing interactions promote learning among co-investigators (researchers and practitioners) and decreases the unintended consequences that result from the way research is traditionally conducted (Argyris 1968).

One reason why gaining organizational access has been problematic for many researchers is that in their studies they have seldom put themselves into the manager's frame of reference or involved managers and co-investigators. As Van de Ven and Poole (1989) discuss, without observing a change process from a manager's perspective, it becomes difficult (if not impossible) for an investigator to understand the dynamics confronting managers who are involved in a strategic change effort, and thereby to generate new knowledge that advances the theory and practice of the subject being investigated.

If organizational participants do not understand the relevance of a study, there is little to motivate their providing access and information to an investigator. At issue here is *not* the question of whether management research should incorporate elements of consulting practice. The issue is one of formulating and addressing important research questions that capture the attention and interest of scholars and practitioners alike. Clearly, the outcomes of research on an important question may not provide an immediate payoff to practitioners or academics. Often, by definition, truly important research questions do not have clear solutions until after the research has been conducted. Researchers and practitioners must often co-produce the solutions. Thus, while running all bases of the diamond model, prospective solutions to applied problems are secondary in comparison with the importance of the research question. A good indicator of such a research question is its self-evident capability (when properly articulated) to motivate attention and enthusiasm among both scholars and practitioners.

In launching our Minnesota Innovation Research Program, my colleagues and I found that a useful way to begin this kind of professional research was to conduct periodic meetings with small groups of managers or representatives (eight to twelve people) from various organizations that were engaged in comparable strategic change efforts or ventures in their organizations. In these meetings we repeatedly discussed the meanings and implications of the research question (e.g., "How and why do innovations develop over time?"), explored how the question was important to advancing theory and practice, and developed a longitudinal real-time research strategy for studying the research question in comparable field settings over time. Participants then shared their opinions of the research question, discussed why it was important or useful to study, and suggested how the research design might be modified to be more workable in their organizational settings. These meetings produced many useful ideas that guided the longitudinal research and led to the dynamic insights about the innovation journey discussed in Van de Ven et al. (1999).

Discussion

The reader may have detected an apparent contradiction in my argument. At the collective level I called for respect, tolerance, and balance among faculty in the professional school to support a variety of normal and action research studies undertaken from different disciplinary perspectives. But at the individual level I encouraged each investigator to undertake professional research by covering all the bases of the diamond model. This apparent contradiction vanishes, however, if we recognize that the professional science perspective proposed here represents an overarching process. By incorporating a variety of research methods, it can simultaneously contribute knowledge to scientific disciplines and advance the practice of management. Each of the four core activities—problem formulation, theory building, research design, and problem solving—of the professional research process admits to any of a wide variety of research approaches, as appropriate for the problem or question being investigated.

Although professional science entertains a wide variety of research methods, it directs the research process by specifying the core set of activities that need to be performed from start to finish of a research project. Because the core activities of problem formulation, theory building, research design, and problem solving are highly interdependent, so also will be the methods that are selected for doing these activities in a given project. Thus, the critical task is to adopt and execute the right research methods for the research problem.

For any given research study, the differences in methods employed by various scholars may also arise because of different disciplinary backgrounds and the different epistemologies (theories of the nature and grounds of knowledge) underlying these disciplines. This point has been developed more fully by Churchman (1971) and Mitroff (1973). According to Mitroff, to conceptualize a problem is to conduct an inquiry into its nature by gathering some information about it. In this sense, information is not separable from inquiry (or epistemology), because what we know about a problem is not independent of how we obtained that knowledge—that is, of the particular system of inquiry we used. Because knowledge is so closely tied to inquiry, it is important to consider alternative systems of inquiry in the philosophy of science.

Churchman locates four fundamentally different systems of inquiry in the philosophies of Leibniz, Locke, Kant, and Hegel (see table 19-2). Very briefly, Leibnizian inquiry systems are the archetype of abstract, formal, mathematical, or logical inquiring processes. In a Leibnizian inquiry system, these processes provide a means to finding "truth," which is seen as an objective, obdurate, absolute, and concrete reality. This inquiry system represents the dominant base of science, as reflected in the hypothetico-deductive method of theorizing, verification, and refutation. Lockean inquiry systems view truth as a social construction and emphasize subjective, experiential, inductive, and consensual data-gathering methods. With the rise of a cognitive and phenomenological paradigm in the social sciences since the 1980s, the Lockean mode of inquiry has gained increasing attention and credibility. It appears most useful for ethnographic, exploratory, and grounded theory development. Kantian systems are the archetype of multidisci-

Table 19-2
Alternative Inquiring Systems

	Leibniz	*Locke*	*Kant*	*Hegel*
WHAT IS TRUTH?	Objective Obdurate Absolute Concrete	Subjective Phenomenological Relativistic Social construction	Integrative Complementary Partial views Cumulative	Pluralistic Dialectical Multiple truths Synthesis
METHODS TO TRUTH	Abstract Formal logic Deductive Mathematical Axiomatic	Experiential Consensual Inductive Authoritative Credible judges	Multidisciplinary Multimodels Crucial experiments Plausible alternatives Convergent	Paradoxical Juxtapose opposites Debate pros/cons Power of arguments Divergent
SITUATIONS	Testing theory Verification Refutation	Grounded theory Discovery Description	Broadened theory Holistic knowledge Comprehensive	Critical theory Conflict reconciliation Radical change
STATUS	Dominant base of science	Exploratory research	Renaissance scholarship	Ideological discourse neo-modernism

Source: Abstracted from C. W. Churchman, *The Design of Inquiring Systems*, New York, 1971.

plinary, integrative processes of inquiry; they attempt to use both formal theory and data matched to the theory in order to build holistic metatheories of complex phenomena. The professional science perspective of research presented here exemplifies a Kantian mode of inquiry. Hegel's dialectical mode of inquiry seeks truth in the synthesis produced by the strongest possible debate between opposite and strongly conflicting models. This mode of inquiry underlies critical theory as well as the rise of deconstructionism and neomodernism in many social sciences today. Each of these systems of inquiry represents a fundamentally different yet legitimate philosophy of science. One should expect that the system of inquiry adopted implicitly or explicitly by a researcher will significantly influence the way he or she runs the bases of the diamond model.

Summary

To repeat: A central mission of scholars in a professional school of business or management is to conduct research that contributes knowledge to a scientific discipline, on the one hand, and to apply that knowledge to advance the practice of management as a profession, on the other. However, there has been little discussion or debate on the implications of this research mission. This paper has endeavored to provide a platform for initiating such a discussion and possible debate. In particular, two planks in this platform merit constructive discussion and debate:

- Collectively, professional school scholars should respect, tolerate, and achieve balance between basic research that advances knowledge in scientific disciplines and applied research that advances the practice of management as a profession.

- Individually, each one of us could make a greater contribution if we adopted a professional science process in our research. This process can link and transcend the unproductive polarities between normal and action sciences. Indeed, a leading proponent of action science, Professor Chris Argyris stated (in private correspondence) his agreement with the value of the diamond model, and sees little difference between his kind of research and the professional science process discussed here. Adopting a professional science process means undertaking four interrelated core activities in any research project:

1. diagnosing the research problem or situation as it exists in the real world,
2. electing a conceptual model and a research question to deal with this problem or situation,
3. building a theory and designing research to examine the research question, and
4. conducting the research and analyzing the findings to produce a practicable solution that addresses the real-world problem or situation.

References

Argyris, C. 1993. *Knowledge for Action.* San Francisco: Jossey-Bass.
———. 1975. Dangers in Applying Results from Experimental Social Psychology. *American Psychologist* (April): 469–485.
Churchman, C. W. 1971. *The Design of Inquiring Systems.* New York.
Cooke, T., and D. Campbell. 1979. Validity. Chapter 2 in *Quasi-Experimentation: Design and Analysis Issues for Field Settings.* Chicago: Rand McNally.
Davis, M. 1971. That's Interesting. *Philosophy of Social Science* 1.
———. 1986. That's Classic! *Philosophy of Social Science* 16: 285–301.
Delbecq, A. L., A. H. Van de Ven, and D. H. Gustafson. 1975. *Group Techniques for Program Planning.* Glenview, IL: Scott-Foresman.
Kaplan, A. 1964. *The Conduct of Inquiry: Methodology for Behavior Science,* Chapter 8. New York: Chandler.
Lenway, S. 1994. The Institutionalization of Innovation: A Longitudinal Analysis of the U.S. Flat Panel Display Industry. The University of Minnesota, Minneapolis, Strategic Management Research Center working paper.
Mitroff, I. I. 1973. On the Methodology of the Holistic Experiment. *Journal of Technological Forecasting and Change* 21: 269–281.
Nelson, R. 1982. Government and Technical Progress: A Cross-Industry Analysis. New York: Pergamon.
Osigweh, C. 1989. Concept Fallibility in Organizational Science. *Academy of Management Review* 14, no. 4 (October): 579–594.
Poole, M. S., and A. Van de Ven. 1989. Using Paradox to Build Management and Organization Theories. *Academy of Management Review* 14, no. 4 (October): 562–578.
Segasti, F., and I. Mitroff. 1973. Operations Research from the Viewpoint of General Systems Theory. *International Journal of Management Science* 16.

Simon, H. 1976. The Business School: A Problem in Organizational Design. Chapter 17 in *Administrative Behavior*, 3d ed. New York: Free Press.

Stinchcombe, A. 1968. The Logic of Scientific Inference. Chapter 2 in *Constructing Social Theories*. New York: Harcourt Brace and World.

Strauss, A. L. 1987. Chapter I in *Qualitative Analysis for Social Scientists*. Cambridge, UK: Cambridge University Press.

Tsoukas, H. 1989. The Validity of Ideographic Research Explanations. *Academy of Management Review* 14, no. 4 (October): 551–561.

———. 1991. The Missing Link: A Transformational View of Metaphors in Organizational Science. *Academy of Management Review* 16, no. 3: 566–585.

Van de Ven, A. H., and M. S. Poole. 1990. Methods for Studying Innovation Development in the Minnesota Innovation Research Program. *Organizational Science* 1, no. 3 (1990): 313–335.

Van de Ven, A. H., D. E. Polley, R. Garud, and S. Ven Kataraman. 1999. *The Innovation Journey*. New York: Oxford University Press.

Weick, K. 1989. The Process of Building Good Theory. *Academy of Management Review* 14, no. 4 (October): 516–531.

20

THE RELEVANCE OF ACTIONABLE KNOWLEDGE FOR BREAKING THE CODE

Chris Argyris

IT IS INTERESTING to analyze the writings of world-renowned line executives and change professionals on the subjects of leadership, learning, change, and commitment. All writers agree that the next challenge is to produce knowledge that transforms the status quo (Argyris 1999). But their advice is full of gaps and inconsistencies. Indeed, if the advice were followed correctly, it would lead to consequences that the advisors themselves condemn. The good news is that the advice is crafted in ways that make it impossible to act upon. The bad news is that the givers of the advice do not appear to be aware that they are contributing to reducing the credibility of change management practice (Argyris 2000).

I will begin this chapter with a few cases illustrating the problems with much advice on managing change. Then I will propose a solution: a theory of effective action.

Illustrations of Gaps and Inconsistencies

Two published works and one workplace anecdote exemplify the gaps and inconsistencies in the experts' wisdom.

Communication

Stephen Covey (1989) advises readers that they should deal with poor performers in ways that are straightforward and trusting. They should focus on personal responsibility, an approach that generates positive energy. Covey provides a lengthy example in which he includes what he would say in an actual conversation. Actual conversations are crucial, in that they reveal the extent to which Covey (or anyone else) walks his talk. Although the case involves his son, Covey claims, and I agree, that the lessons apply to most superior–subordinate relationships.

Covey and his son agreed that the son would clean up the yard. The son did not perform as promised. After several days of private frustration and bewilderment, Covey said, "Son, let's walk around the yard together and you can show me how it's going in your stewardship" (pp. 175–179). The son responded, in effect, It's hard. Covey wondered privately, "What's so hard? . . . You haven't done a single thing." The son told him that he could not pick up some trash because it made him sick.

Both Covey and his son were covering up their real feelings, presumably in the name of creating positive energy. Covey covered up his disappointment and annoyance. The son covered up his own frustrations about his performance and acted as if he had not been lazy and irresponsible.

Covey praised his son for being honest, and they jointly solved the performance problem. But let us dig a bit farther. Covey and his son never examined the reasons for their cover-ups. Perhaps Covey felt that he was in a double bind. If he expressed his honest feelings, he would be seen as negative and uncaring. If he suppressed his feelings and views, he would violate his own advice to be open, forthright, authentic, and self-responsible.

If this double bind occurred, why was it not discussed? As I read the example, Covey was not aware of the double bind. But if this is so, what caused him to be unaware?

How Leadership Works

In *Real Change Leaders* (Katzenback and RCL Team 1995) the authors describe RCLs as exhibiting limitless energy for hard work and a deep

Table 20-1
RCL Effectiveness?

Claims	Questions
1. I talked for an hour and a half.	1. What did she say? How did she craft it? If RCLs are concerned about employees' taking initiative and empowering themselves, how does an hour-and-a-half-long speech cause that?
2. It caused everyone to realize the potential if they pulled it together.	2. What did Mary and others say that caused the realization? What does "pulling it together" mean? How was it caused?
3. It caused final products that were excellent.	3. What actually caused these products? Was it Mary? Was it the way Mary dealt with her people? What contributions did her people make?

commitment to meeting challenges and producing high performance. RCLs challenge the status quo, but they do so in ways that show care and concern for other people. They are committed to genuine democratic participation. They especially encourage open dialogue.

The descriptions that Katzenback and his coauthors provide do not, in my opinion, illustrate their claims. For example, Mary, an RCL, describes her actions as follows:

> I brought them in, and just started talking—for about an hour and a half—about all the things I had been thinking about. We all began to realize that the potential of this was phenomenal if we could just pull it together. All I can tell you is that when they came back with their final work, it knocked my socks off. (p. 95)

Embedded in Mary's brief description are several claims, about which I would raise a series of questions (table 20-1). When we look closely, we can see that in effect Mary is saying, "I know what happened; the inferences that I made are valid; and my conclusions are correct." In other words, Mary crafts her claim as "Trust me, I am right." This is the equivalent of telling others that if they think the way she does, then they will see the light. Her logic—and that of most of the RCLs cited—is self-sealing.

The authors' claim is that what causes RCLs to be effective is that they are appropriately tough, that they emphasize both accountability and open dialogue. But it is possible to reach a different set of conclusions. The RCLs portrayed in the book were unilaterally controlling of the goals. For example, in most of the cases they pointed out clearly that if the business problems were not solved, people could lose their jobs and their security. In one case the RCL was rebuffed by top management when he tried to surface the "real" causes of problems; namely, the defensive routines at the top. The RCL bypassed the top management actions, covered up the fact that he did so, and covered up the cover-up. This particular RCL turned out to be correct, and a hero. I would add that he became a hero by acting unilateral, secretive, and not open. I am not questioning the RCL's success. I am claiming that the causes of his leadership were not what the authors claim they were.

Business versus Human Factors

Tom, a senior change consultant in a very large and forward-looking company, was engaged in a transformational change program. The objective was to integrate the business issues with the human factors so that the numbers were met at the same time that trust and internal commitment were generated. Tom had vowed to implement this objective. The activity began with the line managers.

After a while, Tom noticed that the line managers were working hard to meet the numbers but were distancing themselves from the human factors. Tom asked the line managers why. They responded, in his judgment, defensively. As time went by, the line managers separated the business issues from the human issues. They told Tom that he could hold whatever meetings he wished on the human issues, but it would have to be done separately from meetings that engaged the business issues. This bewildered Tom. He called a meeting to discuss what he considered to be a violation of the basic goal of integrating the business and human issues.

An analysis of Tom's own description of what happened at the meeting shows that he produced a dialogue that violated such goals as openness, learning, and internal commitment.

The line managers denied that they were separating the business and human issues. If it seemed that way, they said, it was because Tom was not helping them gain the knowledge and the skills required to implement integration. Tom agreed, but said that he was confident that the answers could be developed if they all genuinely participated to identify ideas and practices that would promote successful integration. The line managers expressed doubt that such meetings would be productive. The meeting ended with Tom and the line managers feeling frustrated.

I have used Tom's case in workshops for senior change professionals. At each workshop I asked the participants to act as consultants to Tom. We taped the sessions, and the tapes showed that the change professionals acted toward Tom the way they told Tom not to act toward the line managers. Moreover, they were unaware that they were doing so. These results were replicated in three different workshops, all attended primarily by senior change professionals.

In the end, the professionals in all three workshops realized that they did not have an adequate theory of how to achieve integration. Nor did they have the requisite skills. Indeed, given these gaps and given the skills they did have, the line managers were correct to be doubtful if further workshops on integration would work.

How Come?

When I ask audiences what is going on here, I get answers that are easily recognizable as springing from current ideas about leadership, learning, and change. For example, "The problem is that they are not walking their talk!"

That is true. But what is also true is that this explanation is simply another way to state that gaps and inconsistencies exist. It does not explain what causes them. If this reasoning is correct, how come both the advice givers and the users seem to accept advice that does not explain the gaps?

In order to answer these questions we need a theory of effective action.

A Theory of Action Perspective

One such theory is a theory of action perspective (Argyris 1982, 1990, 1993, 1999a, 2000; Argyris and Schön 1974, 1996; Argyris, Putnam, and Smith 1985). The basic premises of this perspective are:

- At the core of human and organizational life is effective action.

- Actions are produced by individuals using their mind/brain.

- The way the mind/brain produces actions is to use designs that are stored in and retrievable from the human mind/brain.

- The designs are causal. They specify the intentions to be achieved, the actual behavior required to achieve them, and the values that govern the actions.

- The designs that are actionable must also be testable, or else we can never assess our effectiveness.

- Individuals hold designs that they espouse and designs that they actually use. The key to change and learning is to get at the designs in use or theories in use.

Let us apply these ideas to the cases. The gaps and inconsistencies in each case were actions or behaviors produced by change professionals. According to our theory the only way these gaps and inconsistencies could have been produced was if the professionals activated designs that produced gaps and inconsistencies.

Does it make sense to claim that these world-renowned executives design their actions to be inconsistent? Yes and no. Yes, because actions are designed. Indeed, it is not possible for individuals to knowingly design to produce inconsistencies; because if their actions are designed, and if they produce what they designed (recall that that is the only choice they have), then they must be producing actions that are consistent with their designs in use. If so, that is a match; it is not an error.

Then how do we explain the gaps and inconsistencies? One explanation might be that the change professionals were unaware that they were producing gaps and inconsistencies.

But unaware is also action. Hence, unawareness must be designed.

How can unawareness be designed? One answer is that unawareness can be caused by the fact that a person's actions are skillful. What Covey said, how the RCLs acted, how Tom dealt with the managers, and how the senior change professional dealt with Tom: All these are skillful actions. Skillful actions are spontaneous, taken for granted, and automatic. The skilled individual pays little conscious attention to producing such actions. Indeed, to reflect might even make the actions self-conscious. As odd as it may sound, the ability to produce skillful actions is based on designed ignorance.

Back to the theory. We have found that indeed human beings do hold designs. We call them theories of action. One type are espoused theories. The other type are theories in use. Espoused theories vary widely (for example, those of Covey, RCLs, and Tom). Theories in use, however, do not. They do not vary by age, sex, race, education, wealth, organization, or culture.

The dominant theory in use (called Model I) specifies values, actual behavior, and consequences. The governing values include Be in unilateral control; Win, do not lose; and Suppress negative feelings. The three dominant action strategies are Advocate views, Evaluate performance, and Attribute causes or explanations. When these are produced consistently with Model I values, they will result in defensive consequences such as escalating errors, self-fulfilling prophecies, and self-sealing processes. Moreover, Model I encourages, at best, routine learning, and it discourages nonroutine learning intended to change the status quo. Yet this is the kind of learning that is recommended by all the authors and all the line and human resources professionals in the books and articles that I received.

Defensive reasoning is the core thinking process of Model I. It drives human beings to use premises that are tacit, to make inferences that are also tacit, and to reach conclusions that are self-sealing and whose validity is not independently testable.

Defensive reasoning also produces organizational defensive routines. The bottom-line features of organizational defensive routines are that they protect players from experiencing embarrassment or threat, and they prevent others from identifying the causes of failures. Organizational defensive routines are antilearning and overprotective. These self-reinforcing antilearning routines are so powerful that they flourish even though they violate the basis of managerial stewardship

and even though management education and human resources practices demand that they be reduced, if not eliminated.

Mixed messages are classic examples of organizational defensive
routines. The theory in use is:

- State a message that is mixed (inconsistent).

- Act as if this is not so.

- Make the above undiscussable.

- Make the undiscussability also undiscussable.

Covey, the "real change leaders," Tom, and the senior change professionals in my workshops produced defensive routines. Either they
would deny that they were producing them, or they would reflect and
say they were unaware of them. Or say they were aware but had no
choice because of the organizational defensive routines. The results of
defensiveness are self-reinforcing and self-sealing processes that produce ultrastable states that are difficult to change. Indeed, the examples illustrate how these attempts reinforce defensive routines.

Is it necessary to introduce this complexity? Yes. For example, if
Covey had understood this complexity, he would have realized that
much of his theory is composed of espoused generalizations that are
not actionable. He would have also been able to reflect on the case
with his son and see the gaps and inconsistencies that he produced.
Finally, he would have been able to ask himself why was he unaware of
the gaps and inconsistencies. The answers to these questions would
have provided him with guideposts for designing different educational
experiences.

Similarly, Tom would have realized that he lacked a valid and actionable theory for integrating the business and human issues. The
same is true for the senior change professionals, who, in advising Tom,
acted in ways that were counterproductive in relation to their own intentions. By the same token, with an appreciation of this complexity,
the RCLs would have realized that their advice was abstract and not
actionable. They would also have been able to reflect on their descriptions and see that their explanations were abstract and incorrect.
The authors of the book about RCLs would have been able to
analyze their material in ways that would highlight the RCLs' gaps and
inconsistencies.

By the way, if the above theory is correct, it is simply inaccurate and wrong to label human actions as soft. Designs in use are as "hard wired" as are the more objective and quantitative disciplines. It is the reasoning of line management and change professionals that is soft. It is time that we educate ourselves not to use this defensive logic. If we do not, I predict that genuine changes in leadership, learning, change, and commitment will be limited to routine ones, even though they will be sold as producing double-loop change. At best the advice will have a short life; it will exist as a fad only.

Examples from Scholarly Research

In an analysis of rigorous empirical research (Argyris 1980), I found that the advice scholars gave for action contained the same problems as I have just described. For example, in chapter 19, Andrew Van de Ven proposes a fourfold classification of the theoretical and research perspectives now in good currency among scholars conducting research on organizations. The ideas described by Van de Ven are consistent with normal science rules about developing theory and research. The four perspectives are teleological theory, life-cycle theory, dialectic theory, and evolutionary theory. (The classification deservedly received an award.) Van de Ven then specifies some core features of the theories:

- Each of these theories specifies a generating mechanism or "motor" that triggers and guides the sequence of events in which change unfolds in any organization.

- These theories are process theories that specify what subjects or motors create change and how the change cycle unfolds.

- These theories are not causal. They specify only the necessary conditions for change to occur. The theories are probabilistic and not deterministic. They lack the Galelean perspective where one exception can disconfirm a claim (Lewin 1935, 1936).

May I return to what I said above about the human mind. The features that Van de Ven identifies may be valid for those mind activities that are used to understand and explain. They are not valid for those activities where the understanding and explanation are in the service of action. For example: How can the human mind produce action that is intended to produce intended consequences when it does not have the theories-in-use or action-designs that specify the actual behavior? Action-designs are deterministic. They may result in consequences that are not fully intended (hence the feature of being probabilistic). But, they produce these consequences deterministically.

To put this another way, in order for the human mind to produce actions that are observed to be unclear, it must use a clear, ruthlessly programmed action-design. Imprecision is produced through precision.

How can knowledge be actionable if the causal mechanisms are not specified? For example, what are "motors" to the human mind? What actions do such "motors" produce in order to "trigger" or to "guide"? How do these actions produce "unfolding" processes?

I should now like to turn to a second aspect of scholarly research. It is related to the time-honored rule held by many social scientists that their fundamental task is to describe the universe. Such descriptions, they suggest, will eventually add up to knowledge that can be used to educate human beings to produce effective actions or to create organizations that are more effective at, let us say, learning. Elsewhere, I have tried to show that this claim is probably more of a myth than an empirically demonstrable consequence (Argyris 1980, 1993). Description is a necessary first step. But the description should be in the service of action, especially in the domains of leadership, learning, change, and commitment.

Van de Ven's description of how the present universe resists double-loop transformation is a valid description of the universe as it is. Hence, researchers who aspire to be descriptive limit the validity of their generalizations. If this is true, and if they are unaware of the dysfunctionality, then the sources of their actions are defensive routines. Also, if researchers are concerned only with describing the universe as it is, their fundamental strategy is, in effect, a normative strategy of remaining in the status quo.

For example, researchers who use the behavior theory of the firm specify that their relational variables are key to understanding and explaining. They conduct research that illustrates empirically that these relational variables (e.g., limited learning, quasi-resolution of conflict, coalition group warfare) are indeed crucial. To my knowledge, these researchers have shown little interest in creating a universe where these conditions might be significantly reduced (Argyris 1996). I suggest that the reason is that their generalizations depend on the universe's not changing. Hence, they become servants of the status quo.

On Actionable Knowledge

I should like to conclude by addressing a few observations to those who conduct empirical research.

1. I believe that the most powerful knowledge that we can produce is valid *and* actionable. We can use such knowledge to generalize *and* to act in a concrete situation. To adopt one set of propositions for the "many" and another for the individual case is neither user friendly nor scientifically rigorous. Knowledge must be crafted in ways that allow its predicted consequences to be tested by practitioners *and* scholars under conditions of everyday life.

2. In order for knowledge about effective action to be valid and actionable, it must be descriptive in the service of normative conditions and actions. Propositions about effective action (at any level) are normative because they are based on values and goals chosen by human beings. They are not based upon some objective truths. Research that separates description from normative features violates the core of what people require in order to act effectively.

3. In order for propositions to be actionable by the human mind, they have to be crafted in the form of theories in use or designs in use. They should specify

   • the intended consequences;

   • the behavioral or action sequences to produce the consequences;

   • the causal relationship between the actions and the consequences; and

   • the relevant governing values from which the action designs are derived.

   Empirical generalizations that describe observed variance are not likely to be actionable. Such generalizations cannot be actionable, because they do not contain the properties of action designs described above.

For example, consider a rigorous description based upon the study of variance. Let us say that the description specifies a monotonic relationship between trust and some other variables (e.g., risk taking, loyalty to others, etc.). Such a description does not specify the action design that the mind must have in order for human beings to create trust or risk taking (or whatever) or the causal connection between the design and the behavior. It does not state how actors can produce or create these connections in everyday life in the first place.

4. If normal science research methodology is consistent with Model I theory in use, then its propositions will contain similar ethical issues, as found in everyday relationships. For example, Barker, Dembo, Lewin (1943) identified a curvilinear relationship between creativity and frustration (Argyris 1993).

Let us assume that a leader of a group wishes to produce mild degrees of frustration in order to mobilize a desired degree of creativity. How will she do it? The research studies suggest only that she should block the group's action.

How will she block action? How will she know when the frustration is mild? How will she know when frustration becomes counterproductive? The researchers can specify how she could find out, because the researchers faced the same challenge. They developed several different types of measuring instruments. But how will the group leader introduce the use of these instruments? Should she tell the group members about her intentions and about the measuring instruments? How would she interrupt the flow without confounding her problem? Could not the very mention of her plans increase the frustration?

If there were a way to cover up her strategy, then she would have to cover up the cover-up. What are the ethical issues of researchers' producing knowledge that requires creating such undiscussable tactics? What would happen to the sense of trust between the leader and her group if they ever found out? Indeed, what would happen to the credibility of the researchers in the eyes of society?

The next step to break the code is to *create* knowledge that can be used to create transformational, nonroutine, double-loop changes in individuals, groups, intergroups, and organizations. This requires the specification of a theory of action with theories in use that apply to many cases and to the individual case.

References

Argyris, C. 1980. *Inner Contradictions of Rigorous Research*. San Diego, CA: Academic Press.

———. 1982. *Reasoning Learning and Action*. San Francisco: Jossey-Bass.

———. 1990. *Overcoming Organizational Defenses*. Needham, MA: Allyn and Bacon.

———. 1993. *Knowledge for Action*. San Francisco: Jossey-Bass.

———. 1996. Unrecognized Defenses of Scholars: Impact on Theory and Research. *Organization Science* 7, no. 1: 79–87.

———. 1997. Field Theory as a Basis for Scholarly Research–Consulting (Kurt Lewin Award, Society for the Psychological Study of Social Sciences). *Journal of Social Issues* 53, no. 4: 809–824.

———. 2000. *Flawed Advice*. New York: Oxford University Press.

Argyris, C., R. Putnam, and D. Smith. 1985. *Action Science*. San Francisco: Jossey-Bass.

Argyris, C., and D. Schön. 1996. *Organizational Learning II*. Reading, MA: Addison-Wesley.

———. 1974. *Theory in Practice*. San Francisco: Jossey-Bass.

Barker, R. G., T. Dembo, and K. Lewin. 1943. *Frustration and Regression*. In Child Behavior and Development, ed. H. Wright. New York: McGraw–Hill.

Covey, S. R. 1989. *The Seven Habits of Highly Effective People*. New York: Simon and Schuster.

Katzenback, J. R., and the RCL Team. 1995. *Real Change Leaders*. New York: Random House.

Lewin, K. 1935. *A Dynamic Theory of Personality*. New York: McGraw–Hill.

———. 1936. *Principles of Topological Psychology*. New York: McGraw–Hill.

2 1

RESEARCH THAT WILL BREAK THE CODE OF CHANGE

The Role of Useful Normal Science and Usable Action Science

A Commentary on Van de Ven and Argyris

Michael Beer

A GAP EXISTS regarding our knowledge about effective organizational change and the needs of managers. With the exception of a few widely heralded change efforts such as those at General Electric and Asda (a U.K. grocery chain whose case was discussed at the conference), the failures are many.

A substantial proportion of the Fortune 500 companies of 1980 have disappeared. Others still exist but have lost their once dominant position in their industry. For example Apple Computer's relative position in terms of size, market share, and return to shareholders has declined significantly since the early 1980s. This occurred despite the fact that its board of directors had the foresight to hire John Scully, chief operating officer at PepsiCo, as Apple's new CEO in 1983. Without the knowledge and skill he needed, Scully did not succeed in his attempts to change the company, and he was forced to resign in 1992.

That CEOs lack specific knowledge and skills in leading change is also evident from statistics about CEO turnover. Average CEO tenure in the United States is half of what it was in 1990—5.5 years versus 10.5. Once a pattern of organizational behavior has been established, organizations appear to have significant rigidities that make change difficult. It is unlikely that Scully's failure, and that of other CEOs who lost their jobs, can be attributed to lack of motivation to manage change. Scully launched many initiatives to change Apple, including four organizational changes in five years.

The knowledge-and-skills explanation is bolstered by research into the effectiveness of various change initiatives undertaken by companies in the 1980s and 1990s. Approximately 70 percent of all total quality management programs are perceived by top management to have fallen far short of their aspirations for these programs when they were launched.[1] Approximately the same percentage of reengineering programs fail to achieve their objectives.[2] Efforts to install a new strategy, structure, and incentive system or to develop collaborative and team-based cultures also fail to achieve the ends envisioned by their creators. Several researchers have documented what has been labeled the fallacy of programmatic change.[3] Perfectly valid best practices adopted by managers at the advice of academics and consultants fail to be institutionalized. A study of consulting effectiveness showed that virtually 50 percent of all consulting engagements end in failure because of ineffective implementation, not because of the quality of consultants' ideas.[4]

It seems clear that knowledge about best practice does not equal successful adoption. That is because a comprehensive, widely accepted theory of organizational change does not exist today. Knowledge is fragmented and piecemeal. Academics and consultants of different persuasions give dramatically different advice about how organizational change can be brought about. All this can be traced to the paucity of good research.

In this chapter I will distill the essential differences between Chris Argyris's and Andrew Van de Ven's views about good research in organizational change. I argue that relevance of research, Van de Ven's point of view, is only one test of good research, particularly research on change. How actionable research findings are, Argyris's point of view is equally if not more important. I then discuss why we have been unable to make more progress in breaking the code of change. The chapter ends with my views on what type of research is needed to increase our understanding of why and how organizations change.

The Van de Ven and Argyris Arguments

Chris Argyris and Andrew Van de Ven are equally committed to scholarly research in organizational change. Both have dedicated considerable parts of their professional careers to this enterprise. Each of their papers is excellent in its own right—but the two papers reflect very different views about what constitutes good change research and theory. These views are based on wholly different assumptions about what knowledge needs to be developed and how it should be developed. They also appear to be based on different values and objectives for the research enterprise. Argyris and Van de Ven operate in different worlds.

Van de Ven is concerned about the relevance of research, the extent to which it helps managers identify what management practices are effective and under what circumstances. He makes an excellent argument for why research in professional schools of business should both contribute to a scientific discipline and advance the practice of management. This can be done, he argues, only if business schools create an environment that integrates and pulls together discipline- and practice-oriented scholars. His argument is that a dialogue among researchers and practitioners from different departments, disciplines, and organizations will help produce knowledge that will be scientifically rigorous as well as relevant to practitioners. Van de Ven goes on to describe a comprehensive process designed to ensure that research problems are defined in relevant and theoretically meaningful terms. He is catholic with regard to research methods that might be used to investigate these problems.

There can be little argument that professional schools must produce relevant knowledge and that to do so requires an environment that prevents discipline- and practice-oriented scholars from separating like "oil and water." There is also little doubt that developing such an environment is extremely challenging. I have seen this problem emerge at the Harvard Business School, which historically has had a strong practice orientation, as more scholars from the disciplines are recruited to the faculty. Van de Ven's views aroused little controversy at a conference of academics, consultants, and CEOs committed to developing relevant knowledge about organizational change.

Argyris's argument goes well beyond the need for relevant research. He takes it for granted that academics should ground their research questions and solutions in the real world of practice. Argyris is, however, concerned that even relevant academic research and the advice to which it leads are typically unimplementable. He illustrates this through three case examples of management expert or professional consultant advice full of gaps and inconsistencies. If followed by managers, he argues, the advice would lead to unintended consequences that the academics and consultants themselves would condemn. He argues that this occurs because advice givers do not specify how their ideas/solutions are to be implemented in a way that will avoid inconsistencies and unintended consequences. In two of the cases he illustrates how the advice givers themselves behave in a way inconsistent with their own advice. He implies that if experts cannot act in a way consistent with their own advice, managers themselves will certainly be unable to implement the advice without unintended consequences.

Unintended consequences, Argyris reasons, are likely to destroy the very new and improved management practices managers are trying to adopt. Why is consistency important? Inconsistencies and the human tendency not to discuss them, Argyris would argue, lead to lowered trust. Lowered trust makes it still more difficult to confront management about gaps between what they say they intend to change (what Argyris calls espoused theory) and the reality of what is happening as the change unfolds (what Argyris calls theory in use). Many of the gaps between the intentions of managers (derived from the advice of academics and consultants) and what actually unfolds occur because of the change leaders' own incompetent, self-serving, or political behavior or that of others in the organization.

If these behaviors cannot be confronted, the changes being implemented will not work. Why? The inability to confront gaps leads to a further reduction in trust, increased cynicism, and reduced commitment. It also makes it impossible for leaders and lower-level managers to learn how their behavior is undermining the very changes they want to make. In a study of change that crossed many organizational units in six companies, I and my colleagues found a very high correlation between support for the change and the perception at lower levels that the leadership team was struggling to change its own effectiveness and behavior.[5] Without commitment and learning the mutual adaptation that must take place between the intended change and existing skills and values cannot occur. Lower levels will not or cannot adapt their behavior and values to fit the new management practice being introduced by top management. The new practice being introduced cannot be modified by top management to fit the skills, values, and experience of implementers at lower levels. And without an environment of trust, commitment, and learning, top management is unable to learn about those who cannot change or to take action to replace them in a way that does not erode trust and commitment. The new organization or management practice atrophies, and change does not take.

The essence of Argyris's argument is that academic theories and recommendations derived from them cannot be implemented effectively unless academics take into account the human tendency to behave inconsistently and to defend against learning about these inconsistencies. He argues that researchers who recommend a new managerial solution (Van de Ven's relevant what) must also specify the how in great detail. The how is the process by which change will be managed. It must include the means by which management will learn about the efficacy of the change they are enacting—and about the role their own inconsistent behavior may be playing in degrading the intended outcomes of the changes in practice, the what they are undertaking.

Van de Ven and Argyris do not differ about the importance of implementation. Van de Ven's recommended research model includes explicit attention to implementation. He says:

> Of course, it is one thing to document research evidence, and quite another to suggest how to implement the solution. The latter requires developing an action plan for implementing a change process designed to intervene in or solve the problem addressed in the research. The development of a realistic implementation plan typically requires that potential users become actively involved to identify promising ways to interpret and apply the research findings.

But Van de Ven does not provide the detail and specificity Argyris demands. Indeed, Van de Ven admits that "the most appropriate ways to involve users are unknown (because it is done too infrequently)." He goes on to say that he and his associates "have relied upon a series of consultations and feedback sessions with practitioners and academics in which progress reports and preliminary research findings are presented and discussed."

This process hardly seems sufficient, considering the difficult and tortuous process of learning about gaps and inconsistencies that must be undertaken for real change to occur. Some years ago Russell Eisenstat and I fed back data to a CEO and a group of top executives in which we raised questions about the success of the changes in practice we had been part of designing and implementing. The feedback raised questions about the company's culture and the CEO's assumptions regarding leadership. Though not confronted directly, the CEO responded defensively. There was no time, nor had the groundwork been laid, for exploring the inconsistencies among the new management practice the CEO had endorsed, the company's culture, and the CEO's own assumptions about leadership. Something had to give. He and the company culture had to struggle to adapt to the new research-based management practice they had decided to adopt, or the new practice would have to be abandoned. Feedback sessions such as this one, Argyris would argue, could work only if they were continued over time. In these sessions academics and consultants working with management would have to help management confront inconsistencies between their espoused behavior and behavior in action. Of course, management would have to agree that they were willing to engage in such a learning process so as to make change a reality. And, academic researchers interested in making their findings and recommendations usable will have to specify through implementation research the process by which managers can learn successfully.

The need to design a process of implementation that enables organization members to learn is critically important in the field of organizational change. Indeed, it is what organizational change is about. One of the confusions in the debate is between the what of change, the management practice relevant research has identified as effective, and the how of change, the means by which the practice can successfully be embedded in the organization. Change research must be concerned with both. The difficulty of bridging these two worlds was evident at the conference in the discussion of the Argyris and Van de Ven papers. Van de Ven's views on scientific research that contributes to both theory and practice were accepted without question. In contrast, Argyris's view that the academics and consultants in the room were not producing knowledge that was actionable was greeted with a great deal of skepticism, defensiveness, and even hostility. This reaction may have been due in part to Argyris's proactive style. But it also reflects genuinely different assumptions about what constitutes practical advice, about the objectives of scholarly research, and about the roles of academics and consultants in the research enterprise. The two sides were talking past each other—and this despite the fact that before the conference Argyris and Van de Ven had had several discussions that were aimed at ensuring engagement. The inability of the two sides to engage these issues underlies in part our failure to break the code of change.

Why the Code of Change Has Not Been Broken

Three groups of actors are essential to an effective inquiry into organizational change: the managers, who lead change through choices of change means and ends; the academics, whose principal role is to conduct research leading to better theory and practice; and the consultants, who advise management about the changes to make and how to make them. The paucity of knowledge about change can be traced to differences in goals and values and to an unconscious collusion among these actors to leave unexamined the how of organization change: the processes, values, skills, and context that underlie success and failure.

Academics

Academics in professional schools of business have deep roots in the disciplines. Even though they may be working in a professional school, their identity is tied to the disciplines from which they come. They gain legitimacy and achieve recognition and ultimately promotion by employing the language, intellectual paradigms, and methods of their disciplines and by publishing in academic journals that embrace these. Training in the scientific method leads academics to adopt the stance of objective observers. Their work is to describe phenomena accurately and rigorously. The research tools they bring to the task enable them to measure phenomena and make probabilistic statements about them.

If the environment of the professional business school encourages relevance in defining problems, as Van de Ven urges, the result can be important and useful insight about what practices tend to work on the average. Most research colloquia I attend focus on the definition and measurement of variables and the statistical evidence that allows the researcher to reach his or her conclusion. This is where most colloquia end, however. Occasionally the researcher will spend five minutes on the implications for practice. Almost never do researchers discuss how managers might take their ideas about best practice in a particular situation and act on them in a way that will produce change. The assumption is that education and communication (Van de Ven's consultation and feedback sessions) will lead to implementation.

Consider the following example of a company's efforts to act on excellent applied and relevant research. In 1985 Becton Dickinson (BD), a global medical technology company, found itself in need of new organizational arrangements to implement its global strategy. Dissatisfied with the recommendations of a consulting firm, they turned to a highly regarded business school academic who was just completing research on how global companies organized and managed their enterprises. This academic's research utilized the clinical case method and therefore was grounded in what the companies studied actually do.[6] It was not abstract but focused on a real management problem. Moreover, the researcher was involved in helping management implement the "transnational" form of organization he was advocating based on his research. He designed and taught an extremely well conceived workshop in all parts of the corporation's worldwide operations. The workshop engaged BD's managers in applying to each worldwide business an analytic framework for deciding on alternative organizational designs. Top management was enthusiastic about launching the new organization, as was shown by their attendance at the workshop sessions.

Despite these efforts, the corporation's vice president of strategic management reported, at an academic conference on designing global organizations, that though the framework for "transnational management" was useful, it was not usable.[7] The research had provided little or no guidance on how to implement the change to the new organization. Indeed, BD went back to the researcher on several occasions and reported these difficulties. The researcher renewed his efforts to educate management. Finally, growing tired of the project, he told management to "just do it." Encountering further difficulties, management once again approached the researcher for help. This time he referred the executives to an expert in organization development and change. Implicit in this referral was the recognition that implementation of best practice depends on organizational and human factors the academic's research and theory did not incorporate.

It took Becton Dickinson a full decade to make significant progress in its efforts to implement transnational management. The opportunity costs of this long delay are incalculable but undoubtedly were large. Fortunately for the company, its competitors were not more agile. That will not, however, be true for BD or for other companies as competitive pressures increase the cost and risks of slow implementation.

This is not an isolated incident. Few management scholars specify the process managers should use to implement their theories, concepts, and methods without incurring unintended consequences. Fewer still take issues of implementation and change into account in choosing their research method. Nor can it be said that inadequate theory or lack of rigorous relevant research is the cause of implementation failures. Richard Hackman and Gregory Oldham, widely recognized for their research on job design, were unsuccessful in seeing their ideas effectively implemented in the 1980s.[8] Robert Kaplan reports significant implementation difficulties in introducing the Balanced Scorecard, an innovation in management control rooted in academic research and theory.[9] The gap between social science research and the formulation and implementation of public policy illustrates the same problem in another field.[10]

In short, excellent relevant research that defines the what of change does not automatically lead to knowledge about how to implement the change. Discovering an effective practice from a statistically significant relationship (often one accounting for a relatively small percentage of the variance) between practice A and result B does not ensure successful adoption of practice A in a specific company. Other factors, such as management's purpose in making the change, the company's competitive context, and its culture and leadership, for example, may not be aligned. Successful implementation of the transnational organization in the Becton Dickinson case depended on a good deal of learning and change in the behavior of many groups and individuals, including top management. This is what Argyris is concerned with and why he stresses that advice without specification of an implementation process from which managers can learn rarely leads to change without unintended consequences. Without such a process change occurs only when all the stars happen to be aligned. Organizations are systems, and the elements in the system have to be mutually adaptive to make something work. That is why successful organizational transformations involve changes in multiple policies and practices adopted in concert.[11]

To develop implementation processes on the basis of their research, academics would have to go beyond the "normal science" research process discussed by Van de Ven. They would have to become consultants to management or partner with consultants to help management implement the changes they recommend. Only this approach would reveal to them what processes might be needed to implement their relevant research findings. But academics are clearly ambivalent about taking on this "action science" role. Their orientation and training, their skills, and the reward systems of the academy do not align well with the role of scholar–consultant.[12] Moreover, this role would confront academics with value issues they believe are not the domain of science. Yet a science in service of practice cannot be value free. Finally, the test of implementation would quite often lead them to find that the practice their research recommended did not take. As someone who has done this type of work and found that my ideas did not work—or at least, did not work as I had hoped—I can testify to feelings of self-doubt. Are all my previous writings about this subject wrong? Can I get what I just learned published? What do I really know, and what can I claim?

All of these issues may be responsible for the skeptical and even hostile response of academics to Argyris's point of view. They are also responsible for the paucity of change research. As will be clear below, I do not claim that relevant descriptive research cannot help us map the conditions associated with successful organizational change. I do claim that developing a comprehensive map is probably impossible. Even if it were possible, such a map would have no practical value. In the end change is a complex real-time process of mutual adaptation between managerial intention; the strategy and organizational design management choose to achieve their intentions; and human motivation and skill, both management's and that of employees. Actionable theories of change will have to specify how this process of learning is to occur without the unintended consequences that often derail organizational change.

Managers

The success of a change effort must be judged at least in part against the purpose and goals the CEO or general manager had in initiating change. By an objective measure of shareholder value, Al Dunlap, CEO at Scott Paper, was extremely successful, and Andy Sigler, CEO at Champion International, was not.[13] When judged against their purpose and goals, however, both can be judged to have been effective. Sigler's primary goal was to change corporate culture and improve organizational capability. He achieved this. Unfortunately we often don't know the leader's goals. Did Scully at Apple intend to change the culture of the company from individualism to teamwork? Did he intend to compete with PCs and take market share away from PC companies? We can guess that he did, but Scully would have had to be revealing about his intentions in order for us to understand what he was trying to do.

CEOs are reluctant to reveal their real, often implicit goals. They are frequently just as reluctant to allow evaluation of the extent to which their objectives were met. CEOs are even more reluctant to allow close observation of the process of change as it is occurring, particularly if this is likely to reveal something unflattering about their leadership. If the change initiative is high-profile, they may allow documentation only if performance improvements have occurred. This leads to several problems. Researchers are not able to observe the change in real time. Retrospective sensemaking by managers may make it impossible for a researcher to understand what choices were made, why they were made, how they were made, and what responses they met. Moreover, a bias in favor of studying successful companies emerges.

One of the barriers to organizational change research, then, is the reluctance of CEOs and general managers to allow open inquiry into what really happened and to reveal their own struggle as leaders of change. Without deep case studies it is hard to link outcome to process, process to choices made by leaders, and choices made by leaders to their own inner assumptions and values (see Andrew Pettigrew's paper in this volume, chapter 12). Understanding these linkages is the first step in developing an understanding of organizational change. Like academics, however, leaders do not really want to find out about whether they are being successful in managing change or what role they may have played in failure.

Consultants

Consultants, too, are reluctant to allow inquiry into the success or failure of their engagements. Clearly, they have a business interest in purveying the impression that their interventions have been successful. Yet consultants play a crucial role in the change drama. Their advice about what practices to adopt is of course important. Far more important is what they say and do as the change process unfolds. Do they discuss with their clients potential threatening issues regarding behavior and values that are blocking change? Do they work with CEOs to help them learn about inconsistencies between change goals and their values and skills?

To be effective in helping managers implement the advice they offer, consultants will have to develop skills in dialogue and process many don't have. A senior consultant in a well-known management consulting firm recounted to me how colleagues often called him complaining that their good advice was not being implemented because of the incompetence of the CEO. They apparently did not have the skills to help the CEO learn or the inclination to examine if their consulting model was part of the problem. An examination of why advice is not being implemented—a step needed if we are to understand the role of consultants in change—could call into question the expert model of consulting on which the economic success of many firms is based. Employing legions of M.B.A.s to do the analysis and develop the recommendations is a source of profits but may actually hurt implementation. (See chapter 17 of this book by Robert Schaffer.)

To understand the forces that govern success or failure, we will need to understand what consultants do and the skills with which they do it. But there is a disincentive for consultants to participate in such an inquiry.

Requisite Characteristics of a Change Research Enterprise

It appears, then, that our inability to break the code of change can be traced to the ambivalence of all three actors—academics, leaders, and consultants—to inquire into the effectiveness of their practice. This inquiry is essential.

Deep longitudinal inquiry will reveal crucial details about the process of change and its success. As Andrew Pettigrew has pointed out elsewhere as well as in this volume, linking process to outcomes and understanding outcomes in the context of managerial purpose and intention is important if we are to develop a theory of change with predictive power.[14] This can only be done through paired longitudinal case studies of success and failure. And if these rich case studies can be gathered in different contexts (industries, nations, organizational history, and different levels of urgency to change) we can begin to map the conditions for success and failure.

In chapter 3 of this volume, Joe Bower suggests the following approaches to conducting good process research:

- Seek out natural experiments that control variety so that the relationships among a few of [the many variables in the system] can be studied;

- Conduct longitudinal studies of process using a shared model of strategy activity so that the work of different researchers can cumulate;

- Where possible, conduct longitudinal studies.

As Bower points out, this type of approach is very similar to the way medicine has made progress in understanding the effects of various interventions on the complex human system. The approach requires academics to adopt a more clinical and systems orientation to their work. It requires that they accept a common language and framework for describing organizations as systems, and that they see the evaluation of interventions as legitimate and important work—a stretch, given the reward system that exists in academic institutions. Moreover, this approach will require that academics, consultants, and CEOs cooperate in the inquiry process. Without their cooperation in the research, crucial detail about the interaction between best practice academic research and the implementation process led by managers with the advice of consultants will not be revealed.

Mapping the conditions for success and failure will produce a relevant and richly textured descriptive theory of organizational change. Van de Ven's perspective and research model can help us develop this descriptive probabilistic theory. As important as such a theory is to our understanding of change, however, it will not be actionable in any given situation or for any given manager for reasons outlined by Argyris and discussed above. We can educate managers about the theory of change. But this does not ensure that mismatches between their values and skills on the one hand and the practice they want their company to adopt on the other will be revealed to them. The knowledge we will have produced will be useful for understanding but not usable.

To make knowledge usable, an action science approach is needed. Change researchers will have to take understanding derived from descriptive research and theory and craft processes of change that specify exactly what organizational leaders and members must do to achieve desired outcomes. These processes will have to include a means for revealing to leaders mismatches between their own values and skills and those they espoused implicitly or explicitly when they adopted the change goals and process. Descriptive theory will, in effect, have to be translated into a social technology that itself will have to be researched for its efficacy, the extent to which it achieves its goals, in a procedure similar to clinical tests for new medical interventions.

What would such an approach look like? Russell Eisenstat and I, in collaboration with the top management of a large corporation, have developed an intervention a top team can use to assess the capability of an organization to implement strategy and then to make needed changes.[15] We crafted a detailed process, incorporating existing research-based knowledge about organization effectiveness and change as well as our own experience. The process requires the top team to develop a compelling business direction as a team. Management then commission an inquiry process into the capabilities of the organization, conducted by a task force of their own employees, and receive feedback from the task force. Management must then craft an action plan dealing with organizational and behavioral issues identified by the task force, including their own efficacy as a top team. Finally, the process requires the employee task force to review and critique the plan and to provide feedback to management over time about progress and management's leadership of the change. This process is a joint inquiry by managers and scholar consultants from which both management and we, as scholar consultants, have learned.

By embedding the same intervention into different organizations and different situations, we are beginning to learn what conditions are needed for the intervention to work and what modifications in the intervention will increase the probability of success. This type of action science contributes to the development of an action *and* descriptive theory of change. And it produces the social technology managers can use to deliver the theory.

Because research such as this has the potential to yield benefits for managers, academics, and consultants, it offers a possible framework for cooperative inquiry. Academics who engage in this research will have to adopt a new role, that of scholar consultant. This role requires that academics combine knowledge of the literature in organizational change, research skills, and the interpersonal and process skills needed in effective consultation. It requires them to be open to an implementation test of their theories—or else to state clearly on the cover of their books that their theories may not be implementable. This is clearly a greater stretch for academics than are the more distanced clinical and longitudinal studies that I argue are needed to develop a good descriptive theory of change.

If independent consultants have participated in crafting the intervention, they too have to be open to honest inquiry into its effectiveness. This may actually be good for business in the long run and will contribute to their clients' effectiveness. Nevertheless, many may see the stakes as too high, reinforcing the need for a scholar–consultant role.

Finally, the action science research model requires managers who have the intellectual honesty and personal integrity to disconfirm their assumptions about management and themselves in the interests of a successful business enterprise and good research. Such a stance, I have found, actually enhances the credibility and influence of leaders. As pointed out earlier, my own research shows that employee support for change is highly correlated with the perception that management is struggling with its own assumptions and behavior.[16]

Conclusions

In order for progress to be made in breaking the code of change, two parallel, but equally important, research streams need to be undertaken. The first stream, consistent with Van de Ven's views and research model, will produce relevant descriptive theories of organizational change; the territory of organizational change can then be mapped. We will learn what processes tend to succeed in producing specified outcomes in many different situations. The purpose of the second stream will be to make descriptive knowledge actionable by generating valid theories of the change process itself.

These action theories must specify the exact processes managers should use to achieve defined outcomes as well as the governing values that underlie those processes. The theories must incorporate propositions regarding how managers can learn about gaps between the practices and the change processes they espouse and their own values and skills.

Action theories will close the gap in knowledge Van de Ven admits exists—the gap between academics' and consultants' desire to help managers implement research findings and the difficulty of doing so. The ambivalence of academics, managers, and consultants about inquiring into their own practice is a big barrier to progress in change research. This ambivalence has many roots: business interests and lack of skills among consultants; rewards, legitimacy, and lack of skills among academics; and potential exposure of failure and incompetent leadership on the part of managers. On the other hand, managers' cooperation in an inquiry into their own practice will improve and enhance that practice. Academics will have to take the lead in developing these cooperative efforts. It will take substantial changes in scholars' role and skills to break the code of change. They must come to see the implementation as a legitimate field of inquiry. They must come to see consulting with management and inquiry into that consultation and its consequences—as relevant and important scholarly work.

To enable scholars to change their roles and skills, the norms of professional schools of business must change regarding standards of research and promotion. This in turn, will, of course, require academic institutions to confront the efficacy of their own practice and the governing values that block an examination of that practice.

Notes

1. Bert Spector and Michael Beer, "Beyond TQM Programs," *Journal of Organization Change Management*, 1994.
2. Gene Hall, Jim Rosenthal, and Judy Wade, "How to Make Reengineering Really Work," *Harvard Business Review*, Nov.–Dec. 1993.
3. See Michael Beer, Russell A. Eisenstat, and Bert Spector, *The Critical Path to Corporate Renewal* (Boston: Harvard Business School Press, 1990), and Robert H. Schaffer, *The Breakthrough Strategy: Using Short-Term Success to Build the High-Performance Organization* (Cambridge, MA: Ballinger, 1988).
4. Andrew Skoler, Report on "Consulting Effectiveness to Fortune 500 Companies," Harvard Business School Independent Field Study, 1995.
5. Beer, Eisenstat, and Spector, note 3 above.
6. Christopher A. Bartlett and Sumantra Ghoshal, *Managing across Borders: The Transnational Solution* (Boston: Harvard Business School Press, 1989).
7. Ralph Biggadike, "Research in Managing the Multinational Company: A Practitioner's Experiences," in *Managing the Global Firm*, ed. Christopher A. Bartlett, Yves Doz, and Gunnar Hedlund (London: Routledge, 1990).
8. Richard Hackman and Gregory Oldham, *Work Redesign* (Reading, MA: Addison-Wesley, 1980).
9. Robert Kaplan, "Companies as Laboratories," in *The Relevance of a Decade*; ed. Pavla Duffy (Boston: Harvard Business School Press, 1994).
10. See Charles Lindbloom and David Cohen, *Useable Knowledge: Social Science and Social Problem Solving* (New Haven, CT: Yale University Press, 1979).
11. There is a rich literature on the systemic nature of organizations and the need for alignment among various facets of the organization. For recent research evidence of the importance of these factors in organizational change, see Casey Ichiowski, Kathryn Shaw, and Giovanna Prenushi, "The Effects of Human Resource Management Practices on Productivity: A Study of Steel Finishing Lines," *American Economic Review*, June 1997, 291–314, and Richard Whittington, Andrew M. Pettigrew, Simon Peck, Evelyn Fenton, and Martin Conyon, "Change and Complementarities in the New Competitive Landscape: A European Panel Study, 1992–1996," *Organization Science*, 10 October 1999, 4.
12. This term was coined by Chris Argyris.
13. The Scott Paper and Champion International cases were discussed at the conference. They are examples of change efforts with diametrically different goals. The cases can be obtained through Harvard Business School.

14. Andrew M. Pettigrew, *The Awakening Giant: Continuity and Change at ACI* (Oxford: Blackwell, 1985).

15. See Michael Beer, Russell A. Eisenstat, and Ralph Biggadike, "Developing an Organization Capable of Strategy Implementation and Reformulation: A Preliminary Test," in *Competitive Advantage and Organizational Learning,* ed. Bertrand Moingeon and Amy Edmondson (London: Sage, 1996) and Michael Beer and Russell A. Eisenstat, "Developing an Organization Capable of Implementing Strategy and Learning," *Human Relations* (UK), 1996.

16. See Beer, Eisenstat, and Spector, note 3 above. See also Michael Beer and Gregory Rogers, "Hewlett-Packard's Santa Rosa Systems Division," Case (Boston: Harvard Business School, 1997). The latter shows how the leadership effectiveness of a general manager increased as a result of an open inquiry that revealed leadership problems and made him feel vulnerable.

ENDING AND BEGINNING

Participating in the "Breaking the Code of Change" conference was an exhilarating experience. When the dust settled, however, we were confronted with some important questions. Did the conference break the code of change? What did we learn that was distinctive? How should the field of organizational change evolve if the code of change is to be broken?

These were the questions we were pondering in the weeks following the conference when we received a letter from Roger Martin. The letter was so well written and the points made were so challenging that we decided to ask Martin to write a concluding chapter to this volume.

Martin's view, identical to the one we express in the Epilogue, is that despite the ferment of ideas at the conference, the code of change was not broken. For that to have happened, he argues, a causal theory was needed. We did not have one. Martin argues that such a theory is one that can be falsified, which can only be done by specifying exactly what leaders and their organizations must do in given situations to make change happen and then observing if their intentions are fulfilled. Like Argyris in Chapter 20, he argues that a change can only be judged a success if the leaders' espoused intention is reflected consistently in their actions. Unintended results do not count. While Archie Norman at Asda, who, we argued in the Introduction, was more successful than Al Dunlap at Scott Paper in building economic value *and* organizational capability, may have espoused a different purpose than Dunlap, his behavior, Martin argues, was no different. Indeed, he argues that Dunlap may have been more successful in that he did exactly what he espoused. Is consistency between intention and action the right measure of success in organizational change? Do intentions, even if carried out inconsistently, matter? These are questions future researchers of change will have to answer.

To understand change we must understand the status quo, Martin argues. This is essential if leaders are to overcome it. Choices made at various levels of the organization are what creates that status quo. Though he does not propose a causal theory, Martin posits several factors that influence choices, one being the aspirations of the managers making them. These can blind leaders to alternative choices. Managers' level of insight at their disposal also influence choice. Further, they often don't know what they don't know. Finally, incentives also affect choices made.

The capacity of leaders to manage change, Martin argues, is a function of their ability to change these factors and their relationship to each other. For that, another factor must be considered—learning. By learning, Martin means the capacity of organizational members to detect and correct errors *and* to seek new insights that will enable them to make better choices, ones that result in outcomes they intend to produce. Martin believes that a causal theory has to take these factors into account and that it can only be developed through collaboration of managers, academics, and consultants. That is precisely what everyone at the conference also concluded.

In the Epilogue we identify several barriers to collaboration. First, deeply held assumptions and values cannot be resolved by fact alone. To understand them they must be made discussible, something that is alien to academics who believe that values have no place in science. This concept of science will have to be rejected, we argue. A second barrier is the lack of cooperative learning models among academics, consultants, and managers. Last, rapid change alters the phenomena studied by scholars of organizational change; the cooperative process of developing usable knowledge will have to be speeded up.

The good news is that a similar group of academics, consultants, and mangers will assemble in Toronto for "Breaking the Code of Change II." This conference will focus on an examination of several causal theories of change. Ending has led to a new beginning.

22

Breaking the Code of Change

Observations and Critique

Roger Martin

"Breaking the Code of Change" was a great conference. It brought together a terrific mix of academics, consultants, and business leaders to tackle one of the most important business issues of our time. I enjoyed the conference throughout. However, for me the conference ended on a down note. When the final list of "to dos" went up on the board, I had, in the words of that great philosopher Yogi Berra, that "déjà vu all over again."

The Case Team Leader's Dilemma

After eighteen years of strategy consulting, I feel like I keep seeing the same movie over and over. The movie typically stars an earnest, brilliant Case Team leader who comes to me with a "workplan" several weeks into a consulting project. Not unlike the conference to-do list, the workplan has many items, each of which involves substantial work, some of it quite difficult, all of it time-consuming. Do an industry analysis. Do a literature search. Talk to industry experts. And so on.

It is hard to argue against any of these steps, just as it would be hard to argue against any of the items on the conference to-do list. They all have some utility. However, they distract from the real problem, the hard problem: cracking the case. By this I mean coming up with a testable causal hypothesis as to why the current problem exists and what might be a solution. Whenever I let the Case Team leader and his/her team race off and tackle the long list of items on the workplan, I get the same result: lots of *stuff*—some of it even interesting—but little advance in solving the true problem at hand. The data on this outcome is frighteningly consistent.

If, instead, I refuse to let the team do any work without first developing a testable causal hypothesis, I typically get two things. The first is enormous whining and complaining. The Case Team leader doesn't want to engage in the exceedingly difficult task of coming up with a causal hypothesis; he or she would prefer to start on the workplan items and hope something good pops up. The second is remarkable progress on solving the case—because all the brilliant minds (which we have in abundance at the consulting firm) are working directly on the hardest part of the real problem *before* doing a bunch of relatively aimless *stuff*.

Hence the reason for my letdown at the end of the conference. That room was full of people who are as smart as the consultants with whom I have worked for the better part of two decades *and* who have enormously greater experience and knowledge bases. Like the Case Team leader, we faced a terrifically difficult problem: breaking the code of change. At the end, instead of putting our minds directly to the tough task, we put up a long list of stuff that will keep us busy. Like the time of our wonderfully hardworking consultants, I fear our time may be largely wasted on that long list.

What, you may ask, would be better? The answer, I believe, is to put these great minds to the task of creating a testable causal model for why change doesn't happen now and how to make positive change actually happen. This is hard work. I believe it will require some level of collaboration among the people in that room; because, to my knowledge, no single individual has come up with an integrative model of change.

To get this particular ball rolling, let me take a step back and define *testable causal model* by way of illustration. Consider this proposition:

> **Because winter in Canada is very cold and the sources of food are covered with snow, Canada geese gather in large flocks in the fall and migrate to the southern United States for the winter.**

This is a causal model because it specifies a cause (coldness and inaccessibility of food) and an effect (migrating south). It is a testable causal model in that it can be falsified. We can find a flock of Canada geese and observe whether they indeed gather in the fall and fly south. We could even get more sophisticated in the testing: To make sure they don't migrate because of, say, lunar cycles, we could provide them with a heated environment and lots of food in the winter to see if they stop migrating south. Sure enough, as some city dwellers are finding to their dismay, these garbage-eating birds are finding the winters somewhat hospitable around Canada's big cities with their abundant garbage and waste heat.

In contrast, the following is not a testable causal model:

Good managers are more successful than bad managers are.

It is causal, in that it does contain a cause–effect relationship (between goodness and success); but it is not testable, because it is so general as to be not falsifiable (at least in any way I know). Hence, it is an untestable causal model, which is of limited value because we never can be sure that its prediction of effect is valid.

The model Andrew Van de Ven described in his conference presentation typifies still another type of model: the testable descriptive model. Van de Ven defined and described four types of organizational change models. I believe that this description is testable, in that it appears to provide sufficient detail on each of the models that several observers could independently watch an organizational change effort and consistently classify it into one of the four types. However, this model does not specify a cause-and-effect relationship. For example, Van de Ven did not say (largely because it was not his intention): "There are four observable models, and the most successful is the life-cycle theory, and the least successful is the teleological theory." This would specify a cause and an effect and could be made subject to falsification (if "success" were defined).

Michael Beer and Nitin Nohria take a valuable first step toward creating a testable causal model with their Theory E and Theory O concepts. These are models for change. At this point, however, Theories E and O are mainly descriptive theories; they describe differential ways in which Scott Paper Company, Champion International, and Asda Group PLC appeared to have engineered changes. Beer and

Nohria start down the path toward a testable causal model with their attempt to integrate Theories E and O into a combined causal model. This is an important step, because we need a causal theory that predicts that if we take these steps, we will produce those changes. If we have a causal theory, we can test it and refute or refine it. With sufficient testing and refining of a causal model, we can actually hope to succeed in breaking the code of change.

I don't have a fully refined causal theory to offer at this point, but I can offer some framing comments to get the ball rolling. My intent is to start from first principles to lay a foundation for causal theories. I will use the Scott, Champion, and Asda cases to illustrate where feasible, and the reference citations that follow are to those Harvard Business School cases.

What Is Change?

If we are to build a robust causal model of change, we need a robust definition of change in order to provide testability. To change is to take different actions than previously. To take different actions than previously means to make different choices. Different choices produce change. The same choices produce sameness, a reinforcement of the status quo.

To define change robustly, we must take heed of Chris Argyris's distinction between espoused theories and theories in use. To espouse a different operating principle (e.g., we have decided to become customer focused) from the past does not represent change. Only if different choices lead to action on the different operating principle will change be produced. As Argyris observes, there is often a substantial gap between espoused theory and theory in use.

A case in point is Asda, which Beer and Nohria assess as representing a productive combination of Theories E and O. That is, the Asda story represents a combination of the economic value–oriented, top-down, incentive-driven, consultant-intensive Theory E model of change, and the learning-oriented, high-involvement, commitment-driven, internally driven Theory O model of change. This is in contrast to Scott, which is assessed to be pure Theory E.

However, Asda's level of Theory O is primarily, if not entirely a function of espoused theories, not theories in use. In his first address to senior management, Archie Norman espouses a dramatically changed CEO operating model:

> Finally, a few words of warning about me and my management style. First, I am forthright and I like to argue. Secondly, I want to discuss issues as colleagues. I am looking for your advice and your disagreement. I want an organization that is transparent. That means sharing knowledge, plans, and intentions. (Asda (A1), p. 2)

However, across the Asda cases (A, A1, B, C) there is no concrete evidence to corroborate anything espoused by Norman in the statement above, and there is a huge weight of clear evidence to the contrary. For example, one of Norman's first actions was to bring in a consultant/psychologist friend from his Kingfisher days to interview and assess the top thirty or forty managers, because *"a number of them, Norman believed, were clearly burned out"* (Asda (A1), p. 3). He did not want to perform the interviews directly, however, because *"he felt that it might be a little less intimidating if he did not do it himself"* (Asda (A1), p. 3). Intimidating indeed, to be interviewed with a secret rationale, a hidden hypothesis about burnout, and opaque evaluation criteria. Hardly forthright or transparent! Or consider Norman's treatment of Richard Harker, the head of marketing and buying: *"Norman recalled, 'I knew that it was very unlikely that there would be a role for Harker in 12 months' time, but I needed him for that 12 months'"* (Asda (A1), p. 3). There is no hint that Harker was informed in a spirit of forthrightness and transparency of his impending fate.

To me, the Asda model in use features centralization, top-down control, intimidation, and hard-edged incentives, while espousing the opposite. From forced soccer games (*Leighton: "I think the other directors felt they had to play or we would think they were too old and fire them"* [Asda (B), p. 5]) to forced behavioral change (*Styles: "Managers would have to support the changes we were making and be capable of implementing them or be replaced"* [Asda (B), p. 9]) to firing on the basis of performance on tests (*There was a perception [among managers] that the test results alone decided the fate of some GSMs who had good store performance* [Asda (B), p. 11]), the command-and-control operating style stands out.

My point is not to accuse Norman of consciously duplicitous behavior. I suspect that he believed his espoused theory and simply was not sufficiently skilled to produce a theory in use that matched the high ideals of his espoused theory. In fairness, the challenge of living up to his espoused operating philosophy was enormous. If anything, his error was to espouse a set of ideals that he was incapable of enacting.

Rather, my point is that action—real choice—not espoused intention must be the measuring stick. In many respects, if we were forced to ignore all the rhetoric in both cases and look only at the actions, it would be very difficult to distinguish the change model of Asda from the change model of Scott. In both cases, hordes of consultants engaged in unilateral testing and analysis, the result of which was widespread firing of managers. We can credit Norman with having a heavy heart as he fired, whereas Al Dunlap appeared to be somewhat gleeful; to this case reader, however, the results and key aspects of the procedures appear eerily similar. So I would argue that the Asda case provides an excellent illustration of the need for us to focus on changes in actions, which are produced by changed choices, rather than on changes in espoused intentions as we build a causal model for change.

The Asda case also illustrates the need to develop a clear definition of successful change. We are not interested in any change, but rather in change that produces results superior to those from the status quo. Although Asda is portrayed as a great change success, both in Asda C and in Allan Leighton's presentation at the conference, the data is more ambiguous. At the time of the cases, the U.K. grocery retailing market has four key players (Tesco, Sainsbury, Safeway, and Asda) occupying a market in which most commentators thought only three could prosper. If we compare Asda's results in 1996, the fifth year of Norman's tenure, to 1991, the last year before Norman's takeover, the key numbers are no better. For example, in the grocery business, firm-level sales are important because of economies of scale in buying and advertising. In 1991 Asda was third among the four players at 65 percent of the size of the leading Tesco. In 1996 Asda was still third and was 52 percent the size of Tesco. Profit margin on sales illustrates the strength of a chain's economic model and its ability to produce profit on sales. For Asda, 1991 profit margin was in third place at 72 percent of first-place Sainsbury. By 1996 it had dropped to fourth place at 66 percent of Sainsbury. Finally, sales-per-square-foot figures demonstrate the strength of the store concept and location to produce traffic.

On this dimension Asda showed modest improvement between 1991 and 1996, from fourth place at 56 percent of Sainsbury to third place and 72 percent of Sainsbury.

There is no question that Norman and his team arrested a decline. That is a significant and commendable achievement. Perhaps arresting a long-term decline in competitiveness is enough to qualify a change effort as successful. However, I would be inclined to utilize a higher standard of tangible success. In the case of Asda under Norman, by far the greatest tangible successes were in increasing sales, increasing customer visits, and increasing the stock price. In all three of these areas, the turnaround statistics benefited from extremely low bases at the time of Norman's arrival. For example, in the two years before Norman's arrival, the stock price had dropped to one sixth of its prior value. Interestingly, it rose six times in the six years following Norman's arrival, to return to its level of eight years earlier. Sales per square foot were lowest among the four key competitors, 11 percent lower than those of the firm that was next worst when Norman arrived.

So at best, Norman could be credited with bringing about changes that moved Asda from last place among four players in a three-man game into a tie for third (and nowhere close to second) over the five-plus years of the case study. This should be seen as success in the sense of turning negative momentum into positive momentum, but only as modest success in the sense of taking a highly untenable competitive position and converting it into a not-quite-tenable competitive position.

To overcome the ambiguities of the Asda case as we build a causal model of change, we therefore must be clear about how we define success in producing change in choices and actions.

Why Are Things the Way They Are and Not Some Other Way?

Having defined change as an alteration in actions that is produced by changes in choices made, not intentions espoused, I will assert a first principle about change that helps me consider a causal model for change:

To understand change, we must first understand the status quo.

The tragic error of many change agents is that they fail to under-stand the status quo well enough to overcome it, and their failure to understand the status quo undermines their change effort. The reason for this phenomenon is that individuals take up the mantle of change agent precisely because they despise the status quo. Because they hate the status quo, they don't respect it enough to understand it. A great recent example is the case of Hillary Clinton and the U.S. health care system. I would argue that Mrs. Clinton hated the status quo so much that she didn't bother to understand why it was the way it was—that is, why the U.S. public loved a system that was expensive and bureaucratic in many respects and left a significant fraction of the population with-out coverage. While she was busy creating a new health system, the health insurance industry was running the wildly successful "Harry and Louise" television commercials portraying a middle-American couple fretting about losing the patient–doctor relationship they so coveted. The health insurance industry understood the status quo, in which the patient–doctor relationship was extremely important; Mrs. Clinton did not understand it, and meddled with the patient–doctor relationship. And the health insurance industry succeeded, whereas Mrs. Clinton most assuredly did not.

How, then, can we conceptualize and understand the status quo? I find it useful to conceptualize the status quo as *a set of cascading choices*, which cascade from the top of the organization right to the bottom as diagrammed in figure 22-1. In this conception of the organization, ev-erybody in the organization makes choices and, on the basis of those choices, takes the actions that define the status quo. A CEO may make a typical higher-order choice, such as in what business the firm should compete. A frontline employee may make a lower-order choice, such as how to serve the customer standing at the counter.

There are a few key aspects to note about this conceptualization of the status quo.

The Imaginary Dichotomy

First, in this conceptualization, there is no dichotomy between strat-egy formulation and implementation. The traditional definition holds

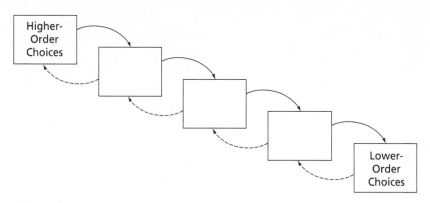

Figure 22-1   The Status Quo: A Cascade of Choices

that leaders at the top of organizations think deeply and carefully about the broad choices facing the corporation and make choices in order to *formulate* strategy. Often they collect data broadly and even consult down through the corporation on the choices. But they make the choices; and once made, the choices are given to the organization to *implement*, to carry out, to do. In this world, the choosers choose and the doers do. However, this traditional definition prompts the question: How would I know implementation if I saw it, and how would I distinguish it from strategy choice?

Conventional wisdom suggests that strategy entails choosing among mutually exclusive options. So if I see an individual considering options—for example, *Should we win on the basis of customer service or on the basis of product-line breadth?*—I can safely assume I am observing a strategy activity. But if I see the individual, for example, providing customer service, then I know that I am looking at implementation. The dilemma for me, however, is that when I observe people providing customer service, I typically see them making choices; for example, as to what combination of activities would define good service for the particular customers standing in front of them. Yet if I ask these individuals if they are setting strategy, they tend to reply with shock that no, they are just doing their job.

The imaginary dichotomy between choosers and doers is highly counterproductive, because it denies the reality that there are no simple executors, no choiceless doers. Every employee, right down to the frontline customer-facing employee, faces and makes choices every day regardless of how detailed the "strategy" handed down may be. Each time that a frontline employee responds to a customer request or question, he or she is making a choice about how to represent the corporation, a choice on the fundamental value proposition the corporation is offering. However, in a world in which the employee's job is categorized as one of *execution*, not *choice*, he or she makes the choice based on an interpretation of what management would regard as faithful execution, not based on what would be best for the customer within the broad bounds of the "strategy" of the corporation. This limits the employee's options and choices and makes the employee appear to the customer as a bureaucrat. In fact, he or she has little choice but to be a bureaucrat.

Upstream versus Downstream Choices

Second, though every employee makes choices that define the status quo, not every employee makes every choice, nor are the choices unconnected to one another. The choices tend to cascade from the top of the corporation to the bottom, with each upstream choice setting a context in which the choice immediately downstream is made. Within this cascade of choices, executives at the top of the corporation make the more broad, abstract choices involving large, long-term investments, while the employees toward the bottom make more concrete day-to-day choices that impact on customer service and satisfaction.

Where in the hierarchy of the corporation choices get made is a function of a tension between choice-making skills and access to data (in particular, what Michael Jensen refers to as "specific knowledge"). Typically, the higher one moves in the organization, the greater one's decision-making skills—that is, the greater one's ability to process more complicated data in more difficult contexts and to make difficult decisions. However, as one moves higher, one typically becomes more and more distant from the data that are critical to making strategic choices—for example, how customers think and react in the moment, what competitors are actually doing in the marketplace, how the product actually gets produced on the shop floor. Many of these data literally must be seen to be understood fully.

So ironically, those with the greatest skills and experience in decision making are most distant from the data on which to make those decisions, especially in today's large corporations. This creates a natural tension in how to structure the cascade of choices. *Access to data* drives the choices downstream, whereas *choice-making skill* drives the choices upstream. Typically this tension is decided in favor of the upstream, with choices made disproportionately by skilled but data-starved senior executives. This resolution in favor of the upstream both results from the separation of strategy choice from implementation and reinforces its continuance.

The Two-Way Cascade

Third, the choice cascade should work both ways. Managers making upstream choices set the context for and constrain downstream choices. However, sometimes these upstream choices inadvertently make the downstream choices impossible or suboptimal. In such cases, for the optimal set of choices to be made downstream, the chooser must flow the dilemma back upstream to encourage the upstream chooser to reconsider and modify the upstream choice. In the most efficient choice cascade, downstream managers feel comfortable asking upstream managers to revisit their choices, and upstream managers respond productively to such requests.

Under the strategy-versus-implementation dichotomy, however, the upward flow of insight tends to be curtailed, because the frontline employees, who are considered simple executors of strategy despite the reality that they must make difficult choices daily, feel disconnected from senior managers. This overall sense of disconnectedness tends to cause them not to collect or deliver customer data to more senior managers. As a result, senior managers are starved for the best source of customer data: their own frontline employees. Consequently, they are required to work around their own organization to get the data they need in order to make decisions. Because these data come from outside the organization, typically from consultants, senior managers often produce choices that are inexplicable to frontline employees, who are then reinforced in their views that they are disconnected from their own corporation (and, as Dilbert would tell us, are working for idiots).

Overall, then, the status quo is a result of the myriad of real choices made by members of the organization across the choice cascade. The quality and success of the status quo will be determined by the functioning of the choice cascade. So, to understand change and produce change, I argue that we need to understand first why the current set of choices is made the way it is made now. That is, we need a causal model for the choice cascade of the status quo.

What Maintains the Status Quo?

I don't claim yet to have a robust causal model for the status quo, but I will posit several factors that influence the myriad choices made across the choice cascade that produces the status quo. I will posit three factors that I consider more direct and one factor that is more indirect, in that it influences the status quo primarily through influencing the three direct factors. I will illustrate these influencing factors using data from the prechange period in the three case studies (i.e., Champion prior to the retirement of Andrew Sigler, Scott prior to the arrival of Al Dunlap, and Asda prior to the arrival of Archie Norman).

Aspirations

Aspirations influence choices made throughout the choice cascade. Managers' choices will be influenced by what they and their organization hope to accomplish. For example, the aspiration of Champion was to be an organizationally innovative firm. Hence, choices were made in support of that aspiration. Choices were not made in support of other aspirations, such as having a distinctive and productive competitive strategy. The result was a set of choices throughout Champion that produced an organizationally innovative firm that struggled competitively.

Similarly, in the case of Scott, being an upstanding, stable Philadelphia firm seemed critical, and the choices were consistent with that aspiration. Like Champion, Scott did not make choices consistent with gaining competitive advantage. In the case of Asda, the original aspiration appeared to be to change grocery retailing in the United Kingdom by creating a new format and a new positioning (big store, low price). However, the original aspiration appeared to migrate and get muddled as Asda diversified into a broadly based retailing conglomerate.

Aspirations alone do not determine choices, however; they influence choices in conjunction with other factors.

Insight

A second factor influencing the status quo is insight. Managers don't know what they don't know; they will make decisions based on the level of insight they have at their disposal. The insight in question may concern something more micro, such as the theory of warehouse location/sizing, or something more macro, such as the dynamic evolution of industries.

For example, in the case of Champion, its managers seemed to have very little insight into theories of competitive strategy, or customer needs, or changing competitive dynamics. However, in part because of their aspirations and in part because of interaction with outside consultants, they had insight into organizational dynamics, the function of teams, and so on. So Champion managers made what appear to have been intelligent decisions about the inner workings of Champion while ignoring vast tracts of territory that a manager with competitive strategy insights would have found salient. At Champion, aspirations and insights lined up quite nicely: The company had aspirations for things about which it had insights. But Champion was hurt by the fact that it had few insights in the territory in which it lacked aspirations; and when its aspirations changed in 1996–97, the company had little in the way of insight to power changes in the choice cascade.

In the pre-Norman era, Asda also appeared to possess few insights into the competitive dynamics of U.K. grocery retailing. It appeared not to understand the scale dynamics of the industry at the firm level or the competitive dynamics of the southern England market. It appeared to think that by virtue of its success in the grocery business, it could succeed in various other businesses. These gaps in insight helped produce a troubled but stable choice cascade by the late 1980s.

As seen in the case of Champion, aspirations and insight go together. Aspirations help define what insights are valuable, and such insights are pursued to the exclusion of other insights. In the case of Champion, management appeared to spend enormous time and money on organizational development consultants who helped them achieve a refined level of insight on organizational dynamics, because such organizational dynamics were central to the aspirations of the firm. Thus, insight on organizational development was heightened, but insights elsewhere did not take shape.

Incentives

The third factor influencing the choice cascade of the status quo is incentives. Even with an unambiguous aspiration and clear insights, employees at whatever level will make choices that are consistent with the aspirations and within the capabilities of the insights only if the prevailing incentives encourage rather than discourage such choices. The incentives in question are both monetary and nonmonetary. As Michael Jensen suggests, the level, composition, and shape of the rewards for behavior will influence choices made.

At Champion, choices consistent with the Champion Way were encouraged, and choices not appearing to be consistent were severely punished: *"Over time, those managers who did not change their style left the business. Some left on their own or retired; many were asked to leave. Between roughly 1987 and 1989, the top manager at each of Champion's 14 major mills was replaced, along with many other managers within the mills"* (Champion International, p. 7). This represented a very hard-edged incentive, with an unclear performance measurement system. The Champion Way statement contains no reference to competitiveness and only one passing reference to customers (*"and strengthening customer service"* [Champion International, Exhibit 4]). In this context, it is not surprising that there was no hint of pursuit of competitiveness in the entire case and, in contrast, much indication of Champion Way behavior (though whether espoused behavior or real behavior is somewhat of a question).

Scott and Asda provide little explicit data on the incentives under the status quo. Reading between the lines, however, the incentives appear highly supportive of choices that reinforce the continuation of the status quo.

The Three Direct Factors in Combination

The three direct factors—aspirations, insight, and incentives—influence choices made by everybody throughout the choice cascade. And the three factors influence one another. New insights can produce new aspirations, as in the case of Dennis Didier at Champion. Didier, a newly appointed plant manager, attended a training program, which provided him new insights on the market that he was serving. This insight raised his aspirations concerning customer service (Champion International, p. 9).

Similarly, incentives influence insight. At Champion incentives to pursue the Champion Way influenced the hiring and involvement of organizational development consultants, which in turn raised the insight of managers on organizational issues throughout Champion.

The three factors can best be thought of as a mutually reinforcing system that produces and reinforces the status quo cascade of choices.

Learning Capacity

A fourth factor, learning capacity, influences each of the three factors and thereby also influences the choice cascade. By *learning capacity* I mean the capacity of members of the organization to detect and correct errors and to seek new insights that would enable them to make choices that better produce outcomes that they seek. If learning capacity is high, members of the organization have a better chance of adjusting to changes in their marketplace. If learning capacity is low, they will find themselves making choices that are less capable of matching the aspirations they hold, and having difficulty adjusting to changes that present themselves.

Learning influences the setting of aspirations, as in the case of Dennis Didier at Champion, who learned new insights about customers at a training program and raised his aspirations as a result. Had Didier been closed to learning, he would not have raised his aspirations. Learning capacity also influences the level of insight. As Asda experimented with superstores, its managers developed new and proprietary insights into the operation of large-format stores in the U.K. market. Finally, learning capacity influences the incentive system. As

Champion learned about shareholder value in response to investor complaints about the languishing share price, Champion management altered the incentive system to encourage choices consistent with shareholder value maximization.

In the context of the choice cascade, learning capacity is enhanced when the choice maker above promotes a learning dialogue with the choice maker below by

1. specifying a choice and the rationale for that decision;

2. describing the nature of the next-level decision that the choice begets;

3. offering to assist the choice maker below in making the resultant choice, to the extent that the next choice maker desires assistance; and

4. offering to revisit the choice if the choice maker below finds the choice above to be counterproductively constraining of his or her resultant choice.

Learning capacity is further enhanced when the choice maker below promotes a learning dialogue with the choice maker above by

1. specifying a choice and the rationale for that choice;

2. if necessary, describing the way in which the choice above constrained the choice below in ways that are counterproductive for the overall organization; and

3. encouraging the choice maker above to revisit his or her choice to improve the overall choice cascade.

In pre-Norman Asda, there is incomplete information, but indications are that the organizational learning capacity was quite low. The Asda case stresses the formal hierarchy, the separateness of management, the lack of questioning of authority, the intimidation, the imperious buyers, and the lack of feedback from the store level (Asda (A), pp. 6–7). Not surprisingly, there appears to have been modest learning about the changing environment in which Asda operated. This is no surprise, because as managers within Asda made choices, the dialogue and the data sharing appear to have been highly limited. Certainly, the corporate environment would not have produced a flow of market insights up the choice cascade. As a result, the status quo embodied modest aspirations, narrow insight, incentives consistent with the modest aspirations, and little learning capacity. Such a configuration resulted in a sticky status quo in which all the individual microchoices along the choice cascade served to maintain the status quo, even in the face of substantial environmental changes and declining performance.

The Scott case data is more sparse on this point, but the pattern seems similar to that in Asda. There appears to have been little fundamental learning even when things started to go bad. There were successive waves of layoffs and write-downs, but no fundamental rethink of the base business, no change in aspirations, insights, or incentives. Rather, the status quo choice cascade continued to remain entrenched until the arrival of Dunlap.

The Champion case is quite different with respect to learning. There is evidence of considerable learning, but in a narrow range. There is learning about how to work in teams, learning about one another, learning about the Champion Way. But there is little or no learning about the outside world. To quote new CEO Richard Olson in 1997:

> It is amazing how little we knew about the business. To some extent, Andy (Sigler) sheltered us all from the outside world. We were internally focused—we seemed to think we could make what we wanted, that we had good quality and service, and good facilities. What we discovered is that the external world has changed a lot. My greatest learnings have come through interfacing with the outside world. (Champion International, p. 16)

The narrowness of learning inadvertently constrained development of important insights, left aspirations too low, and provided incentives only in a narrow range of choices. In the end, Champion was shown to have a choice cascade powered by narrow insight and narrow learning.

To sum up, the status quo is a product of the choices and actions of members of the organization from top to bottom. The choices people make take the form of a cascade in which the choices above set the context for and constrain the choices below. I posit that four factors influence the choices made along the choice cascade. Three factors are direct; the fourth influence the other three, which in turn influences the choice cascade. I suggest that to change the choice cascade, we have to first understand the current set of choices and what made those choices what they are today. In each of the cases—Scott's as of April 1994, Champion as of October 1997, and ASDA as of December 1991—the status quo can be understood in terms of the influencers of the choice cascade. In each case the company's troubles could have been predicted and are not surprising.

What Can We Learn from Changing the Choice Cascade at Scott, Champion, and Asda?

Change then requires alteration of the choice cascade throughout the organization. The tools are the one indirect and the three direct influencers of choice. We can predict that if we alter these factors, we can influence the choice cascade and produce real change. Further, if we develop dexterity at adjusting these factors, we can produce change in a direction we desire. That is the assertion. Let's look at the three case studies through the lens of the four influencers to see whether the changes are predictable based on the manipulation of the factors.

Scott

Al Dunlap entered the picture and quickly changed aspirations to focus on shareholder value maximization. He changed insight by replacing the old management team with a new team and by making intensive use of consultants throughout the operation. Finally, he changed the incentives of the senior management team to be totally aligned with share price appreciation. In particular, the incentives rewarded a short-term share appreciation and the sale of the company, because of the provision for immediate vesting under change of control.

However, Dunlap did not change or improve learning capacity at all. Trusted colleagues were brought in as senior managers to make predetermined changes. Consultants were employed to identify and bring about cost savings with little participation by managers. New senior executives and consultants, both in possession of absolute authority, were not about to learn through dialogue with managers or to impart their insights to managers.

I suggest that the overall choice cascade didn't change much. The change model employed required centralized control by powerful and non-learning-oriented executives and consultants. It also required centralized stock market incentives, limited to the key decision makers.

The results are what we would expect. There was centrally driven cost cutting designed to improve profitability, followed by a decision to sell, which triggered the change-of-control provisions and locked in huge gains for the senior management team (dramatically accentuated by an upward turn in the pulp and paper price cycle).

Kimberly-Clark, a formidable global competitor in sanitary tissues, bought Scott for purposes of total assimilation rather than for any managerial or choice-making capabilities. It is widely reported that Kimberly-Clark found Scott to be a disappointingly stripped-down shadow of the former great firm and experienced substantially higher integration costs than anticipated.

So in many respects the change model at Scott avoided the competitive test through capital market exit. I would have predicted a great crash at Scott, had Kimberly-Clark not rescued it, because of the lack of development of learning capacity and the absence of incentive changes for the vast majority of the choice cascade. However, that is not a fair criticism of Dunlap, because the Scott board created an incentive environment for him that made his strategy optimal for himself and for the shareholders—though only because he executed the sale before the pulp and paper price crash of 1996.

Champion

In 1997 Olson changed aspirations at Champion to focus on shareholder value and changed the incentives throughout the organization to align with the creation of shareholder value. However, there was no change to insight; in particular, insight with respect to competitive strategy, the historical blind spot of Champion. The three-pronged "strategy" announced by Olson in October 1997 is simply not a strategy: *"One—Focus on businesses where it can create shareholder value. Two—Improve the profit potential of ongoing business. Three—Exercise strong financial discipline in all areas of spending."* This is a statement of the generic tenets of any modern corporation, not a specific strategy designed to help Champion *"become the best paper company in the world,"* the aspiration stated by outgoing chairman Sigler. With respect to capacity for learning, the case is unclear. There may have been a greater level of discussion and dialogue that may have advanced learning, but that is unclear at the moment (Champion International, pp. 15–17).

I predict that Champion will change, based on the changes in aspirations and incentives, but that it will not come close to achieving Sigler's parting aspiration without dramatically increasing insight into competitive strategy. Otherwise, Champion will continue to perform at the level of the average North American large pulp and paper company, which will yield disappointing returns for the shareholders and for Richard Olson.

Asda

Asda represents the trickiest diagnosis. It is the subtlest of the three cases. The components are there, but the overall picture is unclear, and the Asda story has been truncated by the Wal-Mart acquisition.

Aspirations changed with the arrival of Norman. Insight, too, was dramatically changed and enhanced with the arrival of Norman, an experienced strategy consultant and retailing executive, as well as numerous new executives and a veritable phalanx of consultants. Incentives were changed with a compensation system heavily weighted toward share appreciation.

However, the impact on learning capacity was less clear. A number of formal mechanisms were introduced, suggesting a focus on greater learning (e.g., saunas, PAGs, and SHITMs; see Asda (B), pp. 12–13). But it is unclear whether these formal mechanisms represented real dialogue and learning or pro forma rituals, given the centralized control and intimidation I discussed earlier. It was clear that managers had to be seen to be participating and seen to be following the Asda Way of Working (AWW) or face dismissal. As a result, it is hard to determine from the case whether actual exchanges of ideas and learning dialogue that changed managers' insights took place.

Despite the espoused theory that *"The heart of the Asda Way of Working is very good communication between everyone—up, down, and sideways!*" (Asda (B), p. 10), there is significantly more evidence of senior management not listening than listening:

1. The first meeting with the senior management team at Asda: *"The meeting took 30 minutes. After Norman finished there was no discussion or questions"* (Asda (A1), p. 2).

2. Norman replacing the CFO: *"Having decided to replace the CFO, Norman saw no sense in delay. The meeting consisted of Norman informing the CFO and managing his departure"* (Asda (A1), p. 2).

3. Observation of Norman by a manager in the field: *"Usually Archie said he wanted something to happen, and it did"* (Asda (B), p. 10).

These are not bad management practices per se and may have been appropriate in each case, but they do not form a pattern of dialogue aimed at increasing the learning capacity of members of the organization.

Even listening alone is not particularly conducive to building learning capacity. It can be a highly unilateral activity. For example: *"A store manager explained that Norman was known to show up unannounced at a store with a blank pad of paper, just start talking with colleagues on the floor, and leave a few hours later with pages of notes"* (Asda (B), p. 10). This is a positive example of Norman's showing learning capacity by listening to a store manager so as to build his own insight and thereby make better decisions as a CEO. However, this is a far cry from building the learning capacity of the organization, beginning with that of the store manager who provided the thinking captured in the notes. Norman could have engaged in joint decision making and mutual learning with the manager in question, rather than asking enough questions to fill a notepad and retreating to the executive suite with the insights garnered. Had he done so, he would have enhanced the learning and learning capacity down the choice cascade rather than simply enhancing the learning at the top.

There may be a great deal of evidence not included in the case study that would suggest genuine dialogue and learning across the organization. In that case, Asda would represent a constructive pulling of all four influencing levers. But if the case study represents a reasonably random sample, then the behaviors of senior management, in particular those of Norman and Leighton, are inconsistent with building the learning capacity of the organization. As such, I see the Asda case as a story not of producing profound change in the overall choice cascade, but rather of muscling the top end of the cascade with superior senior management insight and power.

As I mentioned above, Asda's sale to Wal-Mart truncates the experiment to a great extent. At this point it is unclear whether Asda attained or was even on the path to attaining a sustainable competitive position in the U.K. grocery-retailing environment. Now we will never know, because Wal-Mart will undoubtedly engage in total assimilation and conversion of the Asda chain, as it has done with acquisitions in countries such as Canada. Wal-Mart wants the store locations, the initial market share, the distribution apparatus, and about nothing else.

Where Do We Go from Here?

So where are we now? My crude causal model posits the following things:

1. The status quo is manifest in and maintained by a choice cascade that pervades the organization, ranging from the highest-order to the lowest-order choices.

2. Employees throughout the organization from top to bottom who make real choices and take action define the status quo.

3. Their choices are influenced directly by aspirations, insight, and incentives.

4. Aspirations, insight, and incentives are influenced by learning capacity, which thereby influences the choice cascade indirectly.

5. To bring about change, one must change the choice cascade.

6. Espoused theories and intentions do not produce change.

7. Changes in the choice cascade at all levels of the organization are important.

8. Changes at the top of the choice cascade can be undermined by lack of change lower down in the cascade.

9. Change agents have four levers to pull: aspirations, insight, incentives, and learning capacity.

10. A robust model of change utilizes all four levers in coordination.

I have been working in earnest on this causal model for the past two years, using a methodology suggested at the conference; that is, combining the efforts of academics, consultants, and practitioners. I have been working collaboratively on the model with two firms, a very large bank and a very large consumer products firm. As part of the effort, I have assembled a team consisting of three academics, a handful of strategy consultants from Monitor Company (most of whom are involved in the work with the two clients), an organizational development consultant, and two members of the client firms. The team has met over the course of the work to reflect on the consulting work and did the model in real time. Working with two members of the clients as partners rather than clients has been a wonderful aspect of the experiment. These individuals are actively involved in the model building, not just passive recipients of the output. The fact that their organizations are paying substantial amounts for the work encourages them to enforce on the work a rigorous and objective measure of success. The inclusion of academics ensures that we are maintaining academic rigor in the process.

So where do we go from here? As a learning community, we need to develop and refine alternative causal models of change. They require scrutiny, testing, and refinement by academics, consultants, and business executives. In this chapter I have put forward a crude causal model, which I have developed in conjunction with the team above. I am continuing to refine the model and pilot it in the two firms. I would call for other conference participants to provide a critique of this model and to introduce other models to the group.

EPILOGUE

I N ORGANIZING the conference on which this book is based, we started with a high ambition. We wanted to break the code of change—to untangle and lay bare the mysteries of the change process. By doing so we hoped to help practitioners improve the odds of successfully transforming their organizations—a responsibility of great social consequence. A success ratio of 1:3 is simply too wasteful from a social and economic standpoint. We can and must do better.

As we come to the end of this book, we need to assess how much progress we have made. Let's start by first admitting that we have not broken the code of change. We don't yet have consensus on a workable set of principles that a practitioner could follow and reliably increase the odds of succeeding in implementing a change initiative. Having admitted that the goal has not yet been fully achieved, we do believe we have made considerable progress. We have more sharply identified the divergent perspectives that we call Theories E and O of change, and we have begun the process of searching for a synthesis. Though several authors, including us, have proposed ways to synthesize the divergent perspectives we observe in both the theory and the practice of change, we believe this task remains unfinished. We have provided a start, but much more work needs to be done to bring us to a broadly shared synthesis that will meet the demanding criteria of being theoretically sound and practically useful.

In order to advance in our continuing quest to break the code of change, we will need to overcome three challenges. (1) We will need to find ways to make explicit and discussable the values that underlie our different approaches to change. (2) We will need to create better learning partnerships among the various actors involved in producing and using knowledge on change. (3) We will need to speed up the process of producing and disseminating knowledge, because the context of change keeps changing. Below we discuss each of these challenges in more detail and offer some ideas on how to meet them.

One of the greatest revelations of our conference was the extent to which both theories and practice of change are rooted in deeply held assumptions and values. Even though most of the participants were uncomfortable about the debate format, preferring the comfort of a polite middle ground, their conversations revealed genuine ideological differences. There were those who hated Al Dunlap with a startling degree of emotion. It was hard to get them even to acknowledge the increase in shareholder wealth he had created. Others applauded his actions as if he were a white knight—an upholder of shareholder rights in a sea of managers who were simply interested in their own jobs or were too weak-kneed to stand up to their employees. It was hard to get these participants to see that Dunlap had not built any lasting organizational capabilities. We have tried to capture these ideological differences under the labels Theory E and Theory O, in parallel with Douglas McGregor's famous distinction between Theory X and Theory Y.

The problem with ideological differences is that they cannot be fully resolved by facts alone. Facts can certainly help, but different people attach different values or significance to the same facts. Take the case of Al Dunlap again. The facts are that he dramatically increased Scott Paper's value from the perspective of the shareholder. The fact is also that the company ceased to exist as an independent entity. Is this a success story or a failure story? The facts themselves will not provide an answer. They certainly did not at our conference. How you assess this case depends on your values.

Therefore, we must make values discussable. As scientists (of one stripe or another) we espouse the belief that ideology and values have no place in scientific matters. But this value-free ideal is something we will have to reject, because it simply prevents us from having the discussion we really need to have. We must accept that part of what guides our views on organizational change is our values. A more open and honest discussion of these underlying values is the only way to achieve broader understanding instead of continuing misunderstanding. Greater understanding should, in some instances, also lead to a higher-order synthesis.

The second challenge that must be overcome is the lack of good cooperative learning models across academics, consultants, and practitioners. The topic of organizational change is of considerable interest to all three groups. Indeed, one of the highlights of our conference, which most of the participants remarked upon, was how unusual it was for members of these three groups to come together to share their perspectives. Though this certainly made us happy as conference organizers, it reveals a deeper problem that we must overcome if we are to make further progress on breaking the code of change. Despite some common interests, practitioners, academics, and consultants rarely work together to pool their resources and capabilities. This is not to say that such collaboration never happens. There were several individuals at the conference, notably Peter Senge, who had devised models of learning partnerships that combined the talents of these three groups. But these examples were the exception and not the rule.

Perhaps we can learn from the model of the medical community, where doctors, pharmaceutical companies, and academics are tightly intertwined in advancing the frontiers of medicine. Each group has discovered the complementary abilities of the others, and they have established norms of interaction and guidelines for the distribution of benefits that appear to work for everyone involved.

The challenges in our field of managing change are, of course, somewhat different. It is hard to imagine conducting double-blind trials. Which companies would volunteer to join the "placebo group"? But that is not the point. All we are proposing is that there exist greater opportunities for working together. We will need to try different approaches to collaboration to see what works and what does not. The incentives and interests of academics, consultants, and managers may overlap, but they also diverge. Academics need to publish articles and books that will be respected by their colleagues. Consultants need to create proprietary consulting tools that can be applied across different companies and that can be taught to entry-level consultants. Managers must solve unique problems in their own companies and then move on to solve the next set of problems. In addition, managers are interested in seizing competitive advantage, not in sharing knowledge with competitors. Despite these differences in interests, we believe there is room for collaboration. We hope that in the near future there will be greater efforts to forge better learning partnerships.

The final challenge we need to confront is endemic to the phenomenon we are studying. As Heraclitus noted 2,500 years ago: "All is flux, nothing stays still." Sadly, this is as true today as it was then. We confronted a vivid example of this dilemma at our conference. One of the strongest criticisms we hard was that the cases we had selected were passé—that they dealt with the change problems of the past, not the change problems of the future. The challenge of reversing organizational decline for large, mature companies like Scott Paper, Champion International, and Asda was deemed by many to be no longer at the forefront of management attention. What we should have been studying, these critics argued, was the challenge of change in emerging companies such as Microsoft, America Online, and e-Bay, or the challenge facing traditional companies in responding to the Internet revolution and the brave new world it is creating.

Even though we believe that some of the ideas we have developed are applicable to these new challenges, this criticism cannot be easily dismissed. There is no doubt that the focus of management attention has shifted. When Jack Welch, the CEO of General Electric, was asked recently what his top three concerns were in his remaining years, he said: "First, the Internet, second, the Internet, and third, the Internet."

The problem we confront in developing valid and usable knowledge is that the Internet phenomenon is still so fluid that it is hard to draw any generalizations with confidence. It is much easier to develop theories and prescriptions of change when there is a large body of evidence to sift through and the patterns of failure and success are relatively clear. How does one theorize in a world where what appears to be a success, such as Amazon.com, suddenly declines in market value by 50 percent in the span of three months? Yet managers can't wait until the evidence is in. They have to act, now! The situation is comparable to the state of affairs in the early 1980s, when large companies were just beginning to restructure. At that time the road to recovery was uncertain. What advice could we have given that would have been valid and useful when it was needed most? Today our advice may be useful, but it does not have the same currency.

We don't have any clear answers to this dilemma, except to suggest that we need to speed up the process of producing usable knowledge. The product development cycles in our field are simply too long. Ironically, this book is a good example. It will be published about two years after we held our conference. But our experience is typical.

Perhaps the Internet revolution will also usher in a revolution in the production and dissemination of management knowledge. Until that happens, we need to rely more on such techniques as cases on best practice (knowing full well that today's success can be tomorrow's failure). Again, a more active collaboration among managers, academics, and consultants can help, because we can pool knowledge more quickly. But we must find a way of remaining closer to the change frontier as it evolves.

In conclusion, we want to reiterate that, these challenges notwithstanding, we believe that the code of change can and should be broken. We hope this book will encourage others to join in this quest.

INDEX

About the Contributors

Chris Argyris is James Bryant Conant Professor of Education and Organizational Behavior at Harvard University. He has served as special consultant to the governments of England, France, Germany, Italy, and Sweden on problems of executive development and productivity. Professor Argyris is the author of three hundred articles and thirty books, including *Flawed Advice and the Management Trap*, *Knowledge for Action*, *On Organizational Learning*, and *Overcoming Organizational Defenses*. Professor Argyris has received numerous awards, including the Academy of Management's Irwin Award for Lifetime Contributions to the Discipline of Management.

Christopher Bartlett is Daewoo Professor of Business Administration and Chair of the Program for Global Leadership at Harvard Business School where he teaches courses on Strategic Management, International Management, and Management Ethics. Prior to joining the faculty of Harvard Business School, he was a Marketing Manager with Alcoa in Australia, a Management Consultant in McKinsey and Company's London office, and General Manager at Baxter Laboratories' subsidiary company in France. Professor Bartlett's primary research interests focus on the strategic and organizational challenges confronting managers in multinational corporations, the organizational and managerial impact of transformational change, and the strategic application of human resource management. He is the author, co-author, or editor of seven books, including *Managing Across Borders: The Transnational Solution* (with Sumantra Ghoshal) and *The Individualized Corporation*, winner of the Igor Ansoff Award for the best new work in strategic management. He has also authored or co-authored over forty chapters or articles for journals such as *Harvard Business Review*, *Sloan Management Review*, and *Strategic Management Journal*, and has written over one hundred case studies and teaching notes.

Michael Beer is Cahners-Rabb Professor of Business Administration at the Harvard Business School, where he teaches in the areas of organization effectiveness, human resource management, and organization change. Prior to joining the Harvard faculty, he was Director of Organization Research and Development at Corning, Inc., where he was responsible for stimulating a number of innovations in management. He has authored or co-authored several books and articles. *The Critical Path to Corporate Renewal*, which deals with the problem of large-scale corporate change, won the Johnson, Smith and Knisely Award for the best book in executive leadership in 1991 and was a finalist for the Academy of Management Terry Book Award that year. In the last several years, Mike Beer has developed and researched a process by which top teams can assess and develop their organization's capability to implement their strategy. Professor Beer has served on the editorial board of several journals and the board of governors of the Academy of Management, is Chairman of the Center for Organizational Fitness, and has consulted with many Fortune 500 companies.

Warren Bennis is University Professor and Founding Chairman of The Leadership Institute at the University of Southern California. He also serves as Visiting Professor of Leadership at the University of Exeter and Fellow of the Royal Society of the Arts (UK). He is the author or editor of over 26 books on such topics as leadership, change management and creative collaboration. Bennis has not only studied and reflected on leadership, he has also done it, first as the youngest infantry commander fighting in Germany at age 20, decorated with the Bronze Star and Purple Heart and then as President of the University of Cincinnati from 1971 to 1997. He consults with a number of global corporations as well as political leaders. His book, *Leaders*, was recently designated as one of the top 50 business books of all times by the *Financial Times*. *Forbes* magazine refers to him as the "Dean of Leadership Gurus." His latest books, *Organizing Genius* and *Co-Leaders* bring together Bennis's main interests: leadership, change, great groups, and powerful partnerships.

Joseph L. Bower, Donald Kirk David Professor of Business Administration at Harvard Business School, is a leader in the field of corporate strategy and organization, and serves as faculty chair of TGMP. For more than three decades, he has taught and developed courses in the fields of business policy, strategic management, business, and government. His research has focused on problems facing today's top management as they deal with the tumultuous environment of today's global markets. Author of a dozen books and numerous articles, his *Disruptive Technologies: Catching the Wave* won the McKinsey Award for the best *Harvard Business Review* article in 1995. Professor Bower serves on the board of directors and as an advisor to a number of companies in the United States and abroad.

Allan R. Cohen is Edward A. Madden Distinguished Professor of Global Leadership at Babson College where he has recently completed seven years as Chief Academic Officer. He has returned to the faculty to teach leadership, change, and negotiations. He is the author of several books including, *Managing Excellence, Influence Without Authority*, and most recently *Power Up: Transforming Organizations through Shared Leadership* (co-authored with David Bradford). His textbook, *Effective Behavior in Organization*, (with Richard D. Irwin) has been adopted by over 300 colleges with much impact on the teaching of organizational behavior. Dr. Cohen also consults for many major corporations.

Jay Conger is Senior Research Scientist at the Center for Effective Organizations at the University of Southern California, Los Angele, as well as the former executive director of the Leadership Institute at University of Southern California. In addition, he is Professor of Organizational Behavior at the London Business School, a visiting professor at Harvard Business School, and is involved in executive education at INSEAD. While at McGill University, his teaching skills rewarded him with McGill's Distinguished Teaching Award on two occasions. He is the author of over sixty articles and eight books, including his most recent, *Building Leaders*. He is currently working on a volume examining the governance issues facing corporate board of directors. Outside of his work with Universities, he consults with a worldwide list of private and nonprofit organizations and is Associate Editor of the *Leadership Quarterly*.

Dexter Dunphy is Distinguished Professor, University of Technology, Sydney. He has also held positions at Harvard University, University of New South Wales, Sydney, and the Australian Graduate School of Management. Dr. Dunphy has consulted to over 150 private- and public-sector organizations. His main research and consulting interests are in corporate sustainability, the management of organizational change, and human resource management. He has published over sixty articles and fifteen books, including, *Beyond the Boundaries* and *The Sustainable Corporation* (with Andrew Griffiths). Dr. Dunphy currently directs a research project on corporate sustainability at University of Technology, Sydney, and is working on the University's strategic planning and change implementation process.

Jay R. Galbraith is an internationally recognized expert on organizational design. He is Professor of Management and Organization and a Senior Research Scientist at the Center for Effective Organizations at the University of Southern California. He is also affiliated with the International Institute for Management Development (IMD) in Lausanne, Switzerland, where he was on the faculty from 1995 to 2000. Prior to joining the faculty at USC, he directed his own management consulting firm and served on the faculties of the Wharton School and the Sloan School of Management. Dr. Galbraith has written numerous articles and is the author or co-author of nine books. His current research focuses on organizational units that are rapidly reconfigurable to suit quickly changing demands of customers and markets across multinational boundaries.

Sumantra Ghoshal holds the Robert P. Bauman Chair in Strategic Leadership at the London Business School where he also serves as the Director of the Aditya V. Birla Indian Center. His research focuses on strategic, organizational, and managerial issues confronting large, global economies. He has published eight books, over forty-five articles, and several award-winning case studies. He serves as the Chairman of the Supervisory Board of Duncan-Goenka, a large, diversified business group in India, and as a non-executive Director of Allied Deals Plc. in the UK. He also maintains teaching and consulting relationships with several companies worldwide.

Robert Heneman is Professor of Management and Human Resources and Director of Graduate Programs in Labor and Human Resources in the Max M. Fisher College of Business at the Ohio State University. Prior to joining the Ohio State University, he worked as a Human Resource Specialist for Pacific Gas and Electric Company. Professor Heneman's primary areas of research, teaching, and consulting are in performance management, compensation, staffing, and work design. He has written over fifty publications and his work has been cited in numerous publications such as the *Wall Street Journal, USA Today, Money Magazine,* and ABCNEWS.COM. He is the founder and editor of the *International Journal of Human Resource Management Education,* and is on the editorial boards of several other publications. The author of five previous books, Professor Heneman is currently working on two new book projects: *Human Resource Strategies for High Growth Entrepreneurial Firms,* and an edited collection entitled, *Human Resource Management in Virtual Organizations.* He has consulted with over sixty public- and private-sector organizations throughout the world including IBM, Time Warner, American Electric Power, AFL-CIO, U.S. Government Office of Personnel Management, and the states of Ohio and Michigan.

Larry Hirschhorn is Principal with the Center for Applied Research, Inc., a management consulting firm in Philadelphia. He is also an adjunct associate professor at The Wharton School, University of Pennsylvania. He is the past president and founding member of the International Society for Psychoanalytic Study of Organizations. He has published five book and numerous articles, including *The Workplace Within, Reworking Authority,* and *Managing in the New Team Environment.* He consults widely to senior executives in health care, higher education, pharmaceutical companies, and professional service firms. His research interests are in the strategy formulation of process, the campaign approach to organizational change, and the links between thinking and feeling in the executive decision-making process.

Michael C. Jensen is Jesse Isidor Straus Professor of Business Administration at Harvard Business School. He has also held faculty appointments at the William E. Simon Graduate School of Business Administration, University of Rochester, where he founded the Managerial Economics Research Center and served as its Director for over ten years. Professor Jensen is the author of more than fifty papers, comments, and articles on a wide range of economic, finance, and business-related topics. He is author or editor of numerous books, including *Foundations of Organizational Strategy, Theory of the Firm, The Modern Theory of Corporate Finance* (with Clifford W. Smith, Jr.), and *Studies in the Theory of Capital Markets.* Dr. Jensen has received numerous awards and accolades, including "Scholar of the Year" by the Eastern Finance Association, one of the "Year's 25 Most Fascinating Business People" by *Fortune* magazine, a McKinsey Award, the Joseph Coolidge Shaw, S.J. Medal from Boston College, the Graham and Dodd Plaque given by the Financial Analysts Federation, and the first Leo Melamed Prize from the University of Chicago's Graduate School of Business. Dr. Jensen has served as consultant to various corporations, foundations, and governmental agencies and has given expert testimony before congressional and state committees and state and federal courts. He is Past President of the American Finance Association and the Western Economic Association International, and a member of the Boards of Directors of Analysis Group and Chatham Technologies, Inc.

Edward E. Lawler, III is Professor and Director of the Center for Effective Organizations at the University of Southern California Marshall School of Business. Prior to his time at University of Southern California, he served on the faculties of Yale and University of Michigan. He has been honored by many professional organizations in his field and is the author or co-author of over 200 articles and thirty books, including *From the Ground Up* and *Rewarding Excellence.*

Gerard Ledford is Practice Leader of Employee Performance and Rewards at Sibson & Company. Dr. Ledford is a nationally recognized

authority on a variety of approaches to improving employee effectiveness and employee well-being. He has consulted, researched, and
published on innovative rewards systems, employee involvement,
organization design, job design, and selection systems. Before arriving
at Sibson in 1998, he was Research Professor at the Center for Effective Organizations, Marshall School of Business, University of Southern California. Dr. Ledford is the author of over sixty articles and book
chapters and is the co-author of six books, including his most recent,
Strategies for High Performance Organizations. He is a frequent speaker
at professional and business events, and his research and opinions have
been cited in many national media outlets, including *The Wall Street
Journal, Business Week, The Washington Post, The Los Angeles Times,* and
PBS.

Roger L. Martin is Dean of the Joseph L. Rotman School of Management and Professor of Strategy at the University of Toronto. Prior to
joining the Rotman School, he was Director of a leading global strategy consulting firm. His practice focused on building the capabilities
of management teams to work productively together to resolve strategic challenges. Combining strategic analysis and organizational learning disciplines, he created a new process, *Strategic Choice Structuring,* to
help teams make challenging strategic choices and convert such
choices into action. He is currently working on his first book, *The Responsibility Virus,* which focuses on the challenge of productively ap-
portioning duties and tasks across managers in organizations. He
serves on the Boards of Thomson Corporation, Celestica Incorporated, and The Hospital for Sick Children.

Robert H. Miles, President of Boston-based Corporate Transformation Resources, is a thought and practice leader in the fields of corporate transformation and executive leadership. Over the past two decades, he has pioneered an *Accelerated Corporate Transformation*
methodology at many leading corporations. He is the author of many
books on corporate transformation and organizational effectiveness,
including most recently *Leading Corporate Transformation.* Dr. Miles
has been a member of the Yale School of Management and the Harvard Business School faculties. At Harvard he served as Faculty Chairman of the intensive Managing Organizational Effectiveness executive

program. Miles also was Dean of the Faculty and Isaacs Stiles Hopkins Professor at the Goizueta Business School of Emory University and has served on the Stanford Executive Institute faculty at Stanford University.

Craig Mindrum is an independent management consultant and Professor at DePaul University in Chicago where he teaches courses in organizational ethics and change. He is the author of several books on human performance, especially in technological environments. Working with several Andersen Consulting professionals on behalf of the firm, he directed the original development of the Human Performance Framework

Terry Neill has been responsible for shaping and leading the development of Andersen Consulting's global change and human performance practice, which he has grown to some 5000 professionals around the world. He works with client organizations to reach beyond strategy and theory to deliver measurable business benefits at scale. During his career, he has worked with a wide range of clients in financial services, utilities, telecommunications, manufacturing, and government. He has served four terms as chairman of Andersen Worldwide and is Chairman of the London Business School's European Advisory Board.

Nitin Nohria is Richard P. Chapman Professor of Business Administration and Chairman of the Organizational Behavior Unit at the Harvard Business School. His research interests center on leadership and organizational change. His latest book, *The Arc of Ambition*, co-authored with Jim Champy, examines the role of ambition in the making (and breaking) of great achievers. He is currently working on a book titled, *Changing Fortunes*, which examines how this vibrant economic sector came to be called the "old economy" and what are its future prospects. Professor Nohria has written several other critically acclaimed books including, *Fast Forward, Beyond the Hype, Building the Information Age Organization*, and *The Differentiated Network* which won the 1998 George R. Terry Award. Professor Nohria lectures to corporate audiences around the globe and serves on the advisory boards of several small and large firms. He has been interviewed by ABC, CNN, and NPR, and cited frequently in *Business Week*, *Economist*, *Financial Times*, *Fortune*, *New York Times*, and *The Wall Street Journal*.

Andrew Pettigrew is Professor of Strategy and Organization at Warwick Business School, where between 1985 and 1995 he founded and directed the internationally renowned Centre for Corporate Strategy and Change. He is a distinguished scholar of the US Academy of Management and a Founding Academician of the Academy of Social Sciences (UK). He is the author, co-author, or editor of fifteen books. His most recent are *The Innovating Organization* and *The Handbook of Strategy and Management*.

Robert H. Schaffer is Founder of Robert H. Schaffer & Associates (RHS&A), a management consulting firm devoted to helping managers exploit that "hidden potential," and not just provide expert advice. The RHS&A firm has worked with such clients as, Allied-Signal, Fidelity Investments, General Electric, IBM, as well as a number of government and social agencies. Dr. Schaffer is the originator of the firm's unique results-driven approach described in his book, *The Breakthrough Strategy*. RHS&A employs this strategy in helping organizations to achieve major performance improvement and to accelerate the pace of change. He has authored or co-authored several articles on performance improvement, change acceleration, management consulting, and other topics including "Demand Better Results—And Get Them" and "Successful Change Programs Begin with Results." Schaffer has played a leadership role in the consulting profession as a founding director of the Institute of Management Consultants and as chairman of its Professional Development Committee in the U.S. for four years. He also authored *High-Impact Consulting* that advocates for consultants to take responsibility for ensuring that their work yields sustainable results. He helped to launch the *Journal of Management Consulting* and has served as an editor for many years.

Peter M. Senge is Senior Lecturer at the Massachusetts Institute of Technology and has lectured extensively throughout the world. He is also Chairperson of the Society for Organizational Learning. He is the author of the widely acclaimed book, *The Fifth Discipline*, and coauthor of *The Fifth Discipline Fieldbook* and *The Dance of Change*. *The Journal of Business Strategy* names Dr. Senge as one of the 24 people who had the greatest influence on business strategy over the last 100 years

Andrew H. Van de Ven is Vernon H. Heath Professor of Organizational Innovation and Change in the Carlson School of Management of the University of Minnesota. Prior to this appointment, he taught at Kent State University and the Wharton School of the University of Pennsylvania. His current research focuses on processes of organizational innovation and change. He is coauthor of *The Innovation Journey*. Professor Van de Ven is Vice President of the Academy of Management, and Program Chair of the Chicago '99 conference. He was Consulting Editor for *Academy of Management Review*, Senior Editor of *Organization Science*, and on editorial boards of several other journals and book series.

Karl Weick is Rensis Likert Collegiate Professor of Organizational Behavior and Psychology and Professor of Psychology at the University of Michigan. He is a former editor of *Administrative Science Quarterly*. Weick studies processes of organizing and how people make sense of equivocal information when they are under pressure. His current work focuses on wildland firefighting, marine navigation, medical errors, and ways in which organizational learning and collective mind produce error-reduction in each of these settings.

Karen Hopper Wruck is Associate Professor of Finance at the Max M. Fisher College of Business at the Ohio State University. Prior to joining the OSU faculty, she served on the faculty of the Harvard Business School. Dr. Wruck conducts research and teaches in the fields of organizational economics and financial economics. Of particular interest to her is the question of how managers set corporate financial policy and its implications for the management of organizations. Her recent work focuses on the impact of major financial restructurings on performance and shareholder value. A recognized expert in her field, she has published numerous articles in leading academic journals and developed highly successful courses for delivery to MBAs and executives. In addition, her work and opinions have been highlighted in business periodicals, including *Economist*, *Fortune*, and *CFO Magazine*. She is the editor of the *FEN-Course Electronic Journal* and an associate editor of *The Journal of Financial Economics*, *The Journal of Financial Research*, and *European Financial Management*.